Re/collecting Early Asian America

In the series

Asian American History and Culture

edited by Sucheng Chan, David Palumbo-Liu,
and Michael Omi

Re/collecting Early Asian America

Essays in Cultural History

EDITED BY

Josephine Lee, Imogene L. Lim, and Yuko Matsukawa

TEMPLE UNIVERSITY PRESS

PHILADELPHIA

Temple University Press, Philadelphia 19122
Copyright © 2002 by Temple University
Published 2002
Printed in the United States of America

⊗ The paper used in this publication meets the requirements of the American
National Standard for Information Sciences—Permanence of Paper for Printed
Library Materials, ANSI Z39.48-1984.

Library of Congress Cataloging-in-Publication Data

Re/collecting early Asian America : essays in cultural history / edited by Josephine
Lee, Imogene L. Lim, and Yuko Matsukawa.
    p. cm.
Includes bibliographical references and index.
ISBN 1-56639-963-7 (cloth : alk. paper) — ISBN 1-56639-964-5 (pbk. : alk. paper)
   1. Asian Americans—Historiography. 2. Asian Americans—History.
3. Asian Americans—Ethnic identity. 4. Asian American arts. 5. Memory—
Social aspects—United States. I. Title: Recollecting early Asian America.
II. Lee, Josephine D. III. Lim, Imogene L., 1954– IV. Matsukawa, Yuko,
1962–

E184.06 R43   2002
973'.0495'001–dc21   2001050821

Contents

Part II: Crossings

Part III: Objects

List of Tables and Illustrations

Tables

Illustrations

Acknowledgments

We would like to express our gratitude to our contributors for their enthusiasm, dedication, and willingness to share their scholarly talent. Everyone's patience and good humor through the lengthy and challenging process of putting this book together was much appreciated. In addition, we are indebted to the careful readers who, at various stages of this process, contributed their thoughtful and detailed comments. David Palumbo-Liu's insights, in particular, helped us to focus and reshape both the individual and collective visions of "recollecting" that appear here. Our many thanks are extended to our editor, Janet Francendese, for her wise and patient counsel. We also thank Gelston Hinds Jr. for his assistance in editing Amy Ling's essay.

We thank our family and friends for their encouragement, devotion, patience, and sustenance. For the support of our colleagues and students at our respective institutions, we are grateful. This project was funded in part by grants from the University of Minnesota and SUNY Brockport.

One of our contributors, Amy Ling, passed away in 1999, before the final publication of this volume. The essay she wrote for us on Yan Phou Lee was part of her ongoing project of recollecting early Asian American writers. Indeed, it was through Amy's consistent efforts that early Asian American women writers such as Sui Sin Far and Onoto Watanna now receive critical attention, so it is no surprise that here she directed her scholar's eye to an even earlier writer to reconsider the origins of Asian American writing. Her tireless efforts in uncovering, teaching, researching, chronicling, and promoting the work of Asian American artists have resulted in the wider recognition of Asian Americans writers past and present. With her death, we have lost not only a courageous pioneer in Asian American studies but also a kind and generous mentor and colleague. Those of us who recollect early Asian America are deeply indebted to her scholarship and advocacy. We are honored to be able to include her essay in this collection and dedicate this volume to her.

Finally, here's to family, friends, and friends who have become family.

Re/collecting Early Asian America

*Yuko Matsukawa, Josephine Lee,
and Imogene L. Lim*

I   Introduction

collect (kə-lĕkt′) *v.* -lect·ed, lect·ing, lects.   —*tr.* 1. To bring together in
a group; gather; assemble. 2. To accumulate as a hobby or for study: *collect stamps.* 3. To call for and obtain payment of: *collect taxes.* 4. To
recover control of: *collect one's emotions.*   —*intr.* 1. To gather together;
congregate; accumulate. 2. To take in payments or donations: *collecting
for charity.*   —*adj.* With payment to be made by the receiver: *a collect
phone call.*   —*adv.* So that the receiver is charged: *send a telegram
collect.* [ME *collecten* from Lat. *colligere*: com-, together + *legere,*
to gather.]   —col·lect′i·ble, col·lect′a·ble *adj.*

recollect (rĕk′ə-lĕkt′) *v.* -lect·ed, lect·ing, -lects.   —*tr.* To recall to mind.
—*intr.* To have a recollection. [Med. Lat. *recolligere*, recollect, from
Lat., to gather up: *re-*, again + *colligere*, to collect.   —see COLLECT.]
—rec′ol·lec′tive *adj.*   —rec′ol·lec′tive·ly *adv.*
     —*American Heritage Dictionary,* 2d College Ed.

The deliberate slash in our title, *Re/collecting Early Asian America,* reminds us that
the word "recollect" has two related but somewhat discrete meanings: to remember
and to collect again. The derivation of "recollecting" carries the same kind of double
meaning as words such as "represent" and "remember." In each of these cases, the
prefix "re-" suggests a simple act of repetition, a return to a previous moment. However, in the case of Asian America, the "re" in "re/collecting" is particularly important. To recollect "early Asian America," for instance, implies a forestalling of forget-
fulness and a prevention of collective amnesia: a bringing back into focus that which
has deliberately or unconsciously been overlooked.

   The many meanings of "collecting" also suggest active and self-conscious practices
of gathering, accumulating, accounting, and recovering. Most importantly for us as editors of this volume, "collecting" has as one of its primary definitions "to bring together
in a group." If many instances of recollecting are profoundly private—poring over
objects acquired, conjuring up memories, pulling oneself together—others define themselves through their collaborations, relying on their active and present relationships with

others to exist and be viable. The essays included here join a growing body of scholarship that explores the manifold history and cultural practices of early Asian America. As our volume's title suggests, each essay concerns itself with a specific instance of collecting, remembering, interpreting, and writing the past; taken together, they become a cooperative exercise in recovery and discovery.

The sometimes-contested term "Asian American," used to describe the experiences, identities, and cultures of peoples of Asian descent in North America, suggests an act of correction. It replaces now-suspect terms such as "Oriental," "Asiatic," and "Mongolian." Any re/collecting of early Asian America, then, must be a revisionist project, addressing the conspicuous absence of Asian Americans in "official" histories and correcting stereotypes, myths, and false assumptions. This historical reconstruction necessarily carries with it political and social consequences that can substantively change the lives of individuals and communities.

Defining "Early Asian America"

Re/collecting early Asian America means not only uncovering, describing, and examining the cultures of the past, but also recognizing the political stakes of this undertaking. For our purposes in this anthology, "early Asian America" dates from the beginnings of Asian migration to the Americas in the 1800s to the eve of North American policy changes in the mid-1960s. We chose to consider many and diverse events and experiences under this rubric because they simultaneously establish and challenge what we have learned to articulate in the last four decades as Asian American.

The social, political, legal, and artistic changes set in motion in the 1960s redefined the experiences and identities of those of Asian descent in the United States and Canada. A key change in U.S. immigration law and policy occurred with the 1965 Hart-Cellar Act, although policy changes had begun with the 1943 repeal of the 1882 Chinese Exclusion Act and the 1952 McCarran-Walter Act, which allowed all immigrants to apply for citizenship. By abolishing the quota system, the Hart-Cellar Act accelerated immigration from Asia, which increased from 16,000 in 1965, to more than 100,000 by 1972, to more than a quarter million in 1989. According to recent data from the U.S. Census Bureau, in March 1999 the Asian and Pacific Islander population in the United States numbered 10.9 million, constituting 4 percent of the total population (Humes and McKinnon 2000, 1).

Canada also launched major immigration policy changes in this period. Before 1961, only 1.9 percent of Canadians were of Asian ancestry (Badets and Chui 1994, 20), identified primarily as Chinese, Japanese, and South Asians. After 1962, "country of origin" was no longer a criterion for admission, and in 1967 a point system, free of racial considerations, was established as a means of regulating entry. Since the liberalization of these policies, the face of Asian Canada has changed dramatically. By 1996, Asian Canadians represented 7.25 percent of the total population; Census Canada identified Filipinos, Southeast Asians, and Koreans among the major Asian ethnicities, in addition to the early pioneer groups (CSC 1998, 8).

Thus 1965 ushered in a period of new diversity in Asian American communities in terms of origin, generation, socioeconomic background, education, and experience. Beyond demographic change, this period also marks "Asian America" as a political and cultural entity: the emergence of Asian American activism, the flourishing of Asian American arts and culture, and the establishment of Asian American studies as a viable academic field.

In the forward momentum that has accompanied these social and political changes, the events that preceded the 1960s have not been forgotten. Asian American history has come to occupy significant space in the more recent cultural and political imagination. As David Palumbo-Liu notes, "Asian American subjectivities are not simply the effects of the contemporary; . . . the contemporary holds in it the effects of the historical past" (1995, 60). History has always held a privileged place in both the activism of the Asian American movement and the academic field of Asian American studies. Those engaged in constructing this history have often faced considerable scholarly challenges, as well as institutional pressures; Asian American histories register the marginality and disenfranchisement of individuals and communities through both what is recorded and what is not. Records show the denial of the right to enter the country, to own land, to become a citizen, to vote, to receive an education, to intermarry; the lack of records points to how Asian Americans and other racial minorities were often considered subjects not worthy of recording. Groups of people were reduced to nothing more than numbers—on plantations, workers wore "bangos . . . small brass disks with their identification numbers stamped on them. In the old country, they had names and their names told them who they were, connecting them to family and community" (Takaki 1989, 136). Rarely did anything more than a brief note in a diary or journal document their presence. Such was the case when Captain John Meares and his crew, including seventy Chinese laborers, landed in 1788 on the west coast of Vancouver Island, the first instance of Chinese in western North America documented in the English language (Wright 1988, 2, 15).

History has a constitutive relation to the symbolic formation of Asian America, a pan-ethnic racial category. As Lisa Lowe has suggested, Asian American culture "re-members" the past, not only embodying experiences of the past but also creating a present community of bodies (1996, 29). Despite great differences in the actual conditions of immigration and settlement, such a "racial" history strategically emphasizes the commonality of shared experience in patterns of legal and institutional exclusion and oppression, in acts of racism, and in stereotyping. The emphasis on a shared history, on common experiences, and on collective symbols countenances the necessary emphasis on political alliances and coalitions that extend beyond obvious divisions and differences of culture, generation, class, gender, and sexuality.

And yet there can be no single definition of "Asian American experience." Location, time, generation, citizenship, language, and relation necessarily change this designation. Scholars have rightly questioned the move to define "Asian America" in narrow ways. Sau-Ling Wong, for instance, has pointed out the problems inherent in authenticating the contemporary identities of Asian Americans as American by emphasizing a long-term presence in the United States, English as the language of expression, or the disavowal of what is "Asian" in favor of what is "Asian American" (1995, 3–4). On the one hand, the long-term presence of those of Asian origin in the Americas is of great significance in any retelling of American history. Asian Americans were at the forefront of broadening the civil liberties for all Americans; when Wong Kim Ark petitioned the U.S. Supreme Court on his eligibility for citizenship, the 1898 decision provided the guarantee of citizenship to all who are born within the United States. As Gary Okihiro suggests, by seeking inclusion and equality, Asian Americans "helped to preserve and advance the very privileges that were denied to them" (1994, 151). On the other hand, scholars also must work to present a more varied picture of history, to avoid the valorization or idealization of only certain working-class, native-born, and English-speaking communities.

As Patricia Limerick notes, the history of the American West is for many synonymous with European settlers' westward movement from the East Coast (1995, 89). However, it is insufficient to revise such a model with alternative paradigms that reimagine immigration and settlement simply by replacing Europe with Asia or westward expansion with eastward movement. The early history of Asian immigration was indeed tied to other points of emigration, many of them in the Pacific Islands, as well as other points along the North American continent. For example, as early as 1763, Filipino "Manilamen" settled in Louisiana; the names of their communities (Leon Rojas, Bayou Cholas, Bassa Bassa) resonate with the images of their former homeland. These men were members of the Spanish galleon trade between Manila and Acapulco. Their descendants occupy an "Asian American" space that is greatly different from, say, the Chinatowns of the West Coast (Okihiro 1994, 38).

Thus many concerns arise in trying to realize "early Asian America" anew. For instance, a continued emphasis on Chinese American and Japanese American history and a paucity of other ethnic histories—which unfortunately characterizes this as well as other volumes of research—becomes even more problematic given our contemporary awareness that new patterns of immigration, such as the increasing numbers of arrivals from Southeast Asia, will change the nature of Asian American communities. Representing a truly panethnic Asian American history is but one of many challenges for today's scholars. As the multitudinous and varied histories of Asian Americans confirm, such a past cannot be imagined only in terms of one kind of emblematic immigrant journey from "Asia" to "America" and the subsequent generations thus engendered; the path to Asian America was neither unilinear nor unidirectional.

Those who write Asian American histories are still inspired by the common ground of fighting Eurocentrism and drawing attention to racism. But many are also aware of the pressures that such charges place upon the method and manner of collecting and writing history. Many Asian American studies scholars have long been aware of the larger patterns of narrative action—and their accompanying political uses—that underlie the writing of history, through both the "constructive imagination" of the historian and the different modes of "emplotment" used in both "official" and unofficial histories (Collingwood 1946; White 1987). To understand something of the varied racial, ethnic, national, gender, and cultural identities and experiences of Asian Americans demands an ever more flexible framework. In *Asian Americans: An Interpretive His-*

tory, Sucheng Chan suggests that "no work of synthesis on the history of Asian Americans can be definitive" (1991, 188); her disclaimer presents both a warning and an opportunity to reflect upon the continuing challenge of resurrecting "Asian America" in its myriad incarnations.

Reading Cultural Histories

The essays in this book bear this heterogeneity in mind. All take part in the ongoing reassessment of how the past events of North American history might be exhumed, resurrected, and redressed in light of present formations of "Asian American" identity, politics, and scholarship. But that these essays work collaboratively here does not mean that they are uniform in argument, topic, or method. This volume draws upon a number of different disciplines, scholarly perspectives, approaches, and methodologies—from academic fields as different as history, anthropology, archaeology, sociology, geography, literary studies, women's studies, theater arts, film and visual studies, and ethnic studies. Its essays range from models of primary research to extended considerations of larger theoretical paradigms; they incorporate a diverse selection of written and printed documents, material objects, photographs, oral histories, films, and play scripts. While each displays a different way of unearthing, analyzing, and reframing past events, experiences, and artifacts, these essays all focus on particular aspects of early Asian America and reveal particular strategies for writing its cultural history. In bringing them together, we hope to provide both a range of perspectives and an opportunity for comparing and querying modes of analysis. We present these essays not as comprehensive overviews or as models of scholarship but rather as different templates or case studies that might be of interest not only to scholars of Asian American studies but also to other readers.

In selecting essays, we have tried to emphasize how one might rethink the "why" and "how" as well as the "what" of writing Asian American cultural histories. Many of our essays reference tropes that have already been used to conceptualize Asian American histories. These encompass the imagined, physical, and political formation of communities (both as "ethnic enclaves" and as places where American legal, juridical, and economic institutions and cultural roles are constantly in negotiation); narratives of movement (immigration, settlement, and/or relationship between North America and Asia); and the identification of both what is "Asian in America" (including stereotypical representations) and what is "Asian American" (including artistic expression). With these tropes in mind, our volume does not group its essays by chronology, ethnic group, or subject matter. Rather, it uses four headings: "Locations and Relocations," "Crossings," "Objects," and "Recollections."

These headings are intended not to limit or "package" the essays, but rather to suggest conceptual affinities and dissonances among their various areas of concern. These four rubrics might of course be read as exemplifying a well-known trajectory: the pattern of immigration, settlement, objectification, and self-expression that is frequently evoked in models of "minority" or "immigrant" culture in the Americas. However, as our essays illustrate, there is a danger in assuming that Asian American experience always follows this tidy model. Asian American experiences both diverge and converge around these terms. Each of the essays presents a unique instance of current scholarship in recollecting Asian American cultural history; collectively, they testify that there is no unifying vision of "early Asian America," that this is as dynamic, fluid, and highly contested a terrain as the Asian America of the present.

Locations and Relocations

James Clifford urges scholars to think in terms of locations rather than fixed places; according to Clifford, the term "locations" is more apt because it does not assume an inherently natural set of fixed geographies. After all, "everyone's on the move and has been for centuries" (1997, 2). His distinction suggests that "locations" are geographical, psychological, and political markers that indicate a tentative ongoing inquiry pertaining to a particular spot. Once such markers become more stable and significant, they lose their status as "locations" and become "sites" or "places." Because of its ephemeral nature, a location needs to be acknowledged and named before such a transformation can be effected; this naming is essential to how a location acquires the legitimacy of an identity and a readable history.

David Palumbo-Liu reminds us that "the history of Asian America is indeed legible in a history of spatialization and respatialization, of different deterritorializations and reterritorializations, disenfranchisements, reclamations, and (re)constructions" (1999, 7). Locating early Asian America is indeed a challenging task, one that involves not only unearthing evidence and drawing increasingly accurate maps, but also considering how such details are made legible and meaningful. In this spirit, each of the essays not only describes certain historic locations and relocations, but also discusses the particular challenges of recovering artifacts and narratives, draws attention to the often problematic nature of sources, and/or looks at the stakes of historical reconstruction.

This section of the book opens with "Pacific Entry, Pacific Century: Chinatowns and Chinese Canadian History," in which Imogene L. Lim describes her role during the summer of 1996 in the first archaeological investigation of Vancouver's Chinatown. Lim's essay conveys the immediacy and excitement of participating in a hands-on reconstruction involving archaeological excavation and oral history as well as written sources. It also makes a direct appeal for continuing to collect different forms of data from the past in order to counter myths, misunderstandings, and racist stereotypes. A concern with what is still missing in accounts of Asian American history—places as well as people who have been overlooked—carries over into Randall Rohe's "Chinese Camps and Chinatowns: Chinese Mining Settlements in the North American West," which focuses on mid-1800s Chinese camps and Chinatowns built during the boom of the mining frontier. These essays by Lim and Rohe demonstrate the immense importance of different modes of discovery, documentation, interpretation, and preservation of material objects, printed texts, and oral histories in providing a legible account of the past. Emma J. Teng's "Artifacts of a Lost City: Arnold Genthe's *Pictures of Old Chinatown* and Its Intertexts" comments on the more suspect modes of recording space, both written and visual. Using Arnold Genthe's photographs, an accompanying text by Will Irwin entitled "Old Chinatown," and Frank Norris's story "The Third Circle," Teng explores the imagining of San Francisco's Old Chinatown as a mysterious "architectural uncanny," the hellish subterranean, and an aestheticized, romanticized slum. While Rohe and Lim map out the details of what might be thought of as "real," albeit forgotten, communities and sites, Teng is more concerned with how ideology and fantasy dictate the terms of spatial perception.

Genthe's, Irwin's, and Norris's versions of Chinatown may seem ludicrously exaggerated today; however, as Teng's essay suggests, the documentation of a "location" is always mediated by particular desires, relationships, and conditions that make its presentation seem natural. Contemporary reclamations of Asian American history, despite their important differences in perspective, also bring specific agendas and assumptions to bear upon their views of the past. The next two essays, while still preoccupied with the historical reconstruction of events and communities, focus as well on how such "locations" are made meaningful in the present. Rajini Srikanth's "The Komagata Maru: Memory and Mobilization among the South Asian Diaspora in North America" focuses on the symbolic significance of the 1914 *Komagata Maru* incident, in which British subjects of Indian origin were denied entry to Canada (Vancouver, British Columbia). Srikanth places this event in the context of not only past discriminatory immigration regulations adopted by the Canadian government to stop the immigration of Indians, but also current political mobilization by South Asian Americans and South Asian Canadians. In "Community Destroyed? Assessing the Impact of the Loss of Community on Japanese Americans during World War II," Lane Ryo Hirabayashi presents case studies of urban and rural Japanese American communities, narrating how such scholarship was first undertaken to construct a compelling legal case for reparations for the destruction of Japanese American communities by internment and relocation. Indian exclusion and Japanese American internment serve as symbolic moments that fuel the fires of collective action; the recollecting of Asian American history urges public commemoration, social reform, and legal redress. Hirabayashi's survey of multiple communities, urban and rural, contrasts with Srikanth's focus on a specific historical incident; but both essays emphasize the modes of resurrecting the past in the present and the intense investments that accompany these processes—the highly personal and yet always public nature of relocating Asian America.

Crossings

The essays in "Locations and Relocations" complicate as well as represent Asian American locales, places, and sites of inquiry. "Crossings," the second section of the book, illustrates how different Asian American crossings—the passage and circulation of bodies, ideas, and racial identities across space and over time—are equally complex in nature. One type of crossing commonly pictured imagines the Asian American as an immigrant who voyages from the old world (Asia) to the new (North America).

Such a depiction assumes an originary point and a final destination, a linear and uni-directional trajectory, and a set of experiences defined by clear temporal and national boundaries. These essays complicate as well as expand upon this paradigm through chronicling multiple dimensions of immigration as well as crossings, exchanges, and returns.

In "From Colonial Subject to Undesirable Alien: Filipino Migration, Exclusion, and Repatriation, 1920–1940," Mae M. Ngai points out that the history of Filipino work-ers in the early twentieth century blurs the boundaries between the American colonial subject and the Asian immigrant. The experiences of these Filipinos in the United States demonstrated the contradictions between U.S. policies of manifest destiny and "benev-olent assimilation" in the Pacific and anti-Asian exclusion at home.

If Ngai problematizes the paradigm of the Asian American as "immigrant" through her consideration of U.S. colonialism and Filipino repatriation, Adam McKeown's "The Sojourner as Astronaut: Paul Siu in Global Perspective" also complicates uni-directional paradigms of immigration. Focusing on the work of Chinese American soci-ologist Paul Siu, McKeown's essay considers another aspect of crossing through recon-sidering the sojourner, the figure who travels between cultures who can be dismissed or expelled as a temporary presence. Asian American cultural nationalism has had a vested interest in establishing Asian Americans as a long-term but continually repressed presence throughout the history of the United States and Canada. This insistence strategically emphasizes the historical erasure of Asians as American and the system-atic racism that has affected law and policy, both domestic and international. Yet it also discounts the sojourner as a temporary (and therefore less valid) Asian American identity. McKeown's important analysis of the sojourner suggests that scholars of Asian American culture must reexamine different kinds of crossing, from North Amer-ica to Asia as well as the reverse.

Asian American concerns are too often defined only as they are manifested by and affect political practice, artistic production, and identity within the borders of North America. In "Between Fact and Fiction: Literary Portraits of Chinese Americans in the 1905 Anti-American Boycott," Guanhua Wang refutes the notion that Asian Ameri-can history begins and ends in the United States, or that only immigrants felt the impact of exclusion laws and racism. By examining several novels written about the Chinese boycott of U.S. products in the summer of 1905, Wang suggests the actively political, tangible, and strategic (rather than simply nostalgic) ties of Chinese Ameri-can immigrants to China. Wang highlights a different kind of crossing, in which emo-tional affinity, cultural identification, information, and activism are shared across national boundaries.

Catherine Ceniza Choy's "From Exchange Visitor to Permanent Resident: Recon-sidering Filipino Nurse Migration as a Post-1965 Phenomenon" also suggests ways in which "Asia imagines America," by documenting how early-twentieth-century U.S. colonial education in the Philippines and mid-twentieth-century exchange programs influenced the migration of Filipino nurses to the United States. Like McKeown, Choy provides an important perspective on another kind of sojourning. Her examination of

Filipino nurse migration not only counters the gender and class emphasis in many existing studies of Filipino American history, but also reveals a pattern of transnational migration by exchange students and temporary workers that continues to the present day.

This section ends with a personal account by fourth-generation Chinese Peruvian Fabiana Chiu-Rinaldi. "China Latina" pieces together family history through journals, letters, documents, and photograph albums. Chiu-Rinaldi's stories of Chino Latinos and Asian/Latino/Americans testify to the transnational and multidirectional history of Asian American crossings and demonstrate firsthand the intricacy of those movements that define Asian America.

Objects

Any historical recollection of early Asian America must address the prevalence of the racial stereotype in public representation. From the mid–nineteenth century onward, caricatures of "Orientals" as inferior, alien, deviant, subservient, and threatening have dominated popular representations of Asians in American culture.

The exotic Orientals, queued and rat-eating Chinamen, Fu Manchus, emasculated Asian men, and hyperfeminine Asian women described by these essays seem all too familiar in the present. Unfortunately, stereotypes—many of them variations on those generated more than a century ago—have tremendous force and significance still. Thus it is even more crucial that contemporary analyses make clear how they are produced, reproduced, disseminated, and read within the confines of specific racial discourses and tangible social conditions. The docile and submissive geisha girl or lotus blossom; the dangerous dragon lady; the mysterious, demonic Fu Manchu; the plump, Buddha-like Charlie Chan who spouts fortune cookie aphorisms, the bespectacled nerd who speaks in broken English, all have become embedded in the public imagination through very particular means. Although seemingly ubiquitous, inevitable, and at times even "natural," they are nonetheless products of time and place.

With this in mind, the essays in "Objects," the third section of the book, use the word "objects" in two ways. First, they comment on how stereotyping reduces Asians and Asian Americans to objects of curiosity and desire or hatred, fear, and abuse. Second, these essays object to this method of representation by exposing stereotypes as the constructed (rather than natural or self-evident) products of specific social ideologies and discourses, techniques of production and manufacturing, modes of dissemination, and terms of reception.

In "Exotic Explorations: Travels to Asia and the Pacific in Early Cinema," Jeanette Roan investigates the use of film images in the travel lectures of John L. Stoddard and E. Burton Holmes, and the way incorporation of these early cinema practices makes possible the American consumption of visions of Asia as a foreign locale. Roan's essay stresses the ever-present racial and national fantasy of the "Orient," a typology acknowledged by many of these essays. However, as Yuko Matsukawa's "Representing the Oriental in Nineteenth-Century Trade Cards" indicates, this exoticization exists in concert with another view of the "Oriental." Matsukawa's essay analyzes how images from nineteenth-century advertisements for food, soap, starch, clothing, and other household products reflect both the craze for the mysterious spectacle of the East and the violently anti-Chinese sentiments of late-nineteenth-century America. Matsukawa moves toward a discussion of what problems are engendered when the "foreign"—the object of fascination, curiosity, and desire—becomes the "alien," the imagined contaminant of the U.S. body politic (Lee 1999, 3).

While Roan and Matsukawa highlight how instances of both "foreign" and "alien" stereotypes are generated, reproduced, and disseminated by nineteenth- and early-twentieth-century technologies such as film and chromolithography, essays by Tina Chen, Meredith Wood, and Helena Grice focus more on how the stereotypical bodies exhibited by popular culture also have the potential for ambiguity, instability, and contradiction. Each of their essays finds a different source of tension within stereotypes that at first seems quite definitively marked by race, gender, and sexuality. Chen's "Dissecting the 'Devil Doctor': Stereotype and Sensationalism in Sax Rohmer's Fu Manchu" analyzes how Fu Manchu might be read as a racial hybrid, able to move between binary categories of East and West and therefore embodying the threat of new transnational coalitions. Wood's "Footprints from the Past: Passing Racial Stereotypes in the Hardy Boys" calls to our attention scenes of cross-gender and cross-racial passing that appear in one of the early Hardy Boys series books, *Footprints under the Window*; these moments complicate readings of the racialized, gendered, and sexualized stereotype of the effeminate Asian male. Finally, Grice's "Face-ing/De-Face-ing Racism: Physiognomy as Ethnic Marker in Eurasian/Amerasian Women's Texts" illustrates how literary texts by biracial women might be read in the context of long-standing anxieties about visible racial identity and difference, anti-miscegenation, and the pseudoscience of physiognomy. Each essay reveals some fundamental anxiety inherent in stereotypical representation and makes evident the fault lines in the seemingly impervious face of the "Oriental."

Recollections

Literature, theater, and other forms of artistic expression hold a place of privilege in Asian American culture. Invested in these forms is the recognition, preservation, and validation of hitherto marginalized experiences and identities, and the hope of individual and communal empowerment. Much of the critical analysis of this work begins, therefore, with celebration. Because works by pre-1960s Asian American artists often lacked adequate recognition in their own time, present "recollections" of such works strive both to restore them to their proper historical contexts and to create more appreciative audiences for them in the present.

Celebrations of early Asian American artists, however, must be tempered by an awareness of how our political and personal investments influence the process of recollection and reevaluation. Retrieving early Asian American artistic production raises vexed and complicated questions about what counts as art and what constitutes certain work as Asian American. Each essay in the fourth section of the book, "Recollections," wrestles with a different aspect of these issues: how we discover old works anew, how we enshrine them in literary and other artistic canons, and how we invest in them our longing for origin, authority, and voice.

The first two essays examine writers whose works reveal valuable insights into the diverse professional and personal situations of Asians living and writing in America in the nineteenth and early twentieth centuries. Both combine scholarly research and critical interpretation to emphasize not only the continued importance of looking for early Asian American authors, but also the complications of claiming them as Asian American. In "Yan Phou Lee on the Asian American Frontier," Amy Ling examines the life and literary work of Yan Phou Lee, author of the 1887 book *When I Was a Boy in China*. In "'A Different Mode of Speech': Yone Noguchi in Meiji America," Edward Marx looks at the poetry and prose of Yone Noguchi, written during his stay in the United States from 1893 to 1903. Ling makes a case for why Lee deserves a "place of distinction" as a "founding father" of Asian American literature. Marx's investigation of the "American" work of Noguchi, a writer already distinguished in Japan, takes on the somewhat more daunting question of how the term "Asian American" might be usefully applied to writers who are already claimed as "Asian."

Worries over the parameters of early Asian American literature and the question of who qualifies as Asian American also begin Josephine Lee's "Asian Americans in Progress: *College Plays 1937–1955*." Lee's essay highlights a selection of plays by student writers that are substantively different from the later mainland drama that usually defines Asian American theater. Lee's concern with how these works from pre-statehood Hawai'i might broaden the category of "Asian American theater" and her specific readings of the tensions of cultural identity, assimilation, and mobility in these plays link her essay to Robert Cooperman's "The Americanization of Americans: The Phenomenon of Nisei Internment Camp Theater." Cooperman examines the theatrical performances of "Western classics," light comedies, and traditional kabuki plays that took place within the confines of the camps. Although he stresses the history of productions rather than interpretations of plays, Cooperman also reads theatrical practice as a complex response to the competing pressures of accommodation, forbearance, and resistance felt by internees.

The heterogeneity of "Asian America" makes the interpretation of literary and theatrical work from early Asian America a challenging task. The constant reevaluation of critical and aesthetic terms, judgments, and values includes an ongoing reassessment of known writers. Guy Beauregard's "Reclaiming Sui Sin Far" brings us back around to the present moment, laying out the terms by which contemporary critics have "reclaimed" the writings of Sui Sin Far and assigned her status as a major figure in nineteenth-century Asian American women's writing. Beauregard's essay reminds us of the continued political engagement and vigilance demanded of scholars who engage in the work of textual and cultural interpretation. Motivated both by the pressures of contemporary claims on writers and the need to understand the past through its literary figures, those who would try to "recollect" the works of Asian American authors, dramatists, and other artists find that the stakes remain high.

Works Cited

Badets, Jane, and Tina W. L. Chui. 1994. *Canada's Changing Immigrant Population.* Focus on Canada Series. Ottawa: Statistics Canada.

Canada, Statistics Canada (CSC). 1998. "1996 Census: Ethnic Origin, Visible Minorities." *Daily,* 17 February. Online at <http://www.statcan.ca:80/daily/english/980217/d980217.htm> (3 July 2001).

Chan, Sucheng. 1991. *Asian Americans: An Interpretive History.* Boston: Twayne.

Clifford, James. 1997. *Routes: Travel and Translation in the Twentieth Century.* Cambridge: Harvard University Press.

Collingwood, R. G. 1946. *The Idea of History.* Oxford: Clarendon.

Humes, Karen, and Jesse McKinnon. 2000. "The Asian and Pacific Islander Population in the United States: Population Characteristics, March 1999." In "Current Population Reports," U.S. Census Bureau, September. Online at <http://www.census.gov/prod/2000pubs/p20-529.pdf> (3 July 2001).

Lee, Robert G. 1999. *Orientals: Asian Americans in Popular Culture.* Philadelphia: Temple University Press.

Limerick, Patricia Nelson. 1995. "Common Cause? Asian American History and Western American History." In *Privileging Positions: The Sites of Asian American Studies,* ed. Gary Y. Okihiro, Marilyn Alquizola, Dorothy Fujita Rony, and K. Scott Wong, 83–99. Pullman: Washington State University Press.

Lowe, Lisa. 1996. *Immigrant Acts: On Asian American Cultural Politics.* Durham, N.C.: Duke University Press.

Okihiro, Gary Y. 1994. *Margins and Mainstreams: Asians in American History and Culture.* Seattle: University of Washington Press.

Palumbo-Liu, David. 1995. "Theory and the Subject of Asian American Studies." *Amerasia Journal* 21, 1–2: 55–65.

———. 1999. *Asian/American: Historical Crossings of a Racial Frontier.* Stanford: Stanford University Press.

Takaki, Ronald. 1989. *Strangers from a Different Shore: A History of Asian Americans.* New York: Penguin.

White, Hayden. 1987. *The Content of the Form: Narrative Discourse and Historical Representation.* Baltimore: Johns Hopkins University Press.

Wong, Sau-Ling C. 1995. "Denationalization Reconsidered: Asian American Cultural Criticism at a Theoretical Crossroads." *Amerasia Journal* 21, 1–2: 1–28.

Wright, Richard Thomas. 1988. *In a Strange Land: A Pictorial Record of the Chinese in Canada, 1788–1923.* Saskatoon: Western Producer Prairie Books.

Part I

Locations and Relocations

Imogene L. Lim

2   Pacific Entry, Pacific Century: Chinatowns and Chinese Canadian History

In the latter half of the 1990s, Asian Americans were once more newsworthy in a negative sense.[1] In the United States, they were targeted in the Democratic campaign-finance abuses, and in Canada, identified with increasing crime (gangs and drugs). Although specific individuals were involved in these situations, their identity as Asian or Asian American recreated and restored a stereotyped image from the past, one that assumed nefarious behavior as a racial threat. Once more or, perhaps, as always, Asians and Asian Americans were viewed as an unassimilable mass of people ready to transform the "North American way of life," that is, one that was British- or north European–derived. Recalling the late-nineteenth-century specter of "the Yellow Peril," the contemporary response included white flight from urban areas, racist diatribes in the media, and xenophobic graffiti ("white power," "kill chinks," "go back to China") (Cernetig 1995).

Yet even in writing that actively challenges these popular misconceptions, scholars often homogenize Asian American experience by extrapolating exclusively from a U.S. perspective. For many, the "America" in "Asian America" is the United States of America, not the Americas (i.e., inclusive of all countries in North, Central, and South America). Yet early immigration and migration by Asians, beginning in the 1800s, was not limited to the United States.[2] During this first notable wave of Asian immigration, mainly Chinese, Gum Saan (Gold Mountain) was the destination—not a specific place called Canada or the United States. And these countries were not configured as we now know them.[3] How do we create memory or history when it is a tapestry of perspectives? The history of Asian Americans is not commonly acknowledged or told, especially in Canada. Canada has no equivalent of the ethnic-specific programs emphasizing Asians that have taken root in the United States.

If the past has something to teach us about our future, then the archaeology of Chinese Canadians provides an opportunity to bring past and present together—to educate ourselves about the path taken by those early pioneers and to learn from them. This was evident in the first urban archaeological excavation in Vancouver's Chinatown.[4] The project generated mainstream interest in Chinatown and in the Chinese Canadian community, as well as extensive media coverage. In speaking to the public and to the media, the project became a platform to extend the discussion beyond archaeology to issues of racism, immigration, and diversity in Canada and, more specifically, in Vancouver.

Chinese Canadian History

For the earliest period, the history of Chinese in Canada is the same as that of Chinese in British Columbia. Vancouver Island was the first extensively settled area of what was to become British Columbia; only in the year 1858 was the Colony of British Columbia established—not until 1871 would it become a part of Canada (see Morton 1977, 259–60). Also in 1858, the Fraser River gold rush brought the first conspicuous numbers of Chinese to "Canada." Although many came during this period, their impact was more on the building of the province than on this extractive activity. From this initial group began service occupations that continued into the present (laundries and restaurants). Throughout the latter half of the nineteenth century, Chinese migrants and immigrants contributed to the growth and development of the West when there was a need for large numbers of laborers: in coal mining; in the construction of the Cariboo Wagon Road; in public works (the digging of ditches and dikes in the cities of Victoria and New Westminster); in stringing telegraph wire for Western Union; and, of course, in building the Canadian Pacific Railway. In many cases, Chinese labor made the difference to the success of a project. The most obvious of these was the rail link between the East and the West that had induced British Columbia to join Confederation (see Morton 1977; Wickberg 1982).

In addition to physical labor, Chinese provided services to both members of their own community and those outside it. For example, in 1871 they came to work in Nanaimo's coalfields on Vancouver Island (Morton 1977, 27; Bowen 1982, 70). A decade later the 1881 census documented 290 in the subdistrict of "Nanaimo and Noonas Bay." Only 4 were female. Of the males, 242 were identified as holding the occupation of "general laborer"—in all likelihood, labor associated with coal mining. "Cook" and "launderer" were the primary service occupations (see Table 2.1) and although there were two categories of "cook," all but two were employed by non-Chinese, including private individuals, hotels (3), boardinghouses (2), and, in one case, a group of four miners (CDA 1882).

This Chinese contribution of labor to building the West was largely ignored in the late nineteenth century, while their gold-mining activity drew hostile attention. Chinatowns were indeed created in gold-mining towns (Barkerville and Quesnelle Forks most notably); they also existed in urban areas and coal-mining towns, primarily on Vancouver Island, with Nanaimo being but one example. In general these Chinatowns declined in the 1920s and 1930s, leaving the cities of Victoria and Vancouver as the

TABLE 2.1. Occupations of Chinese in
Nanaimo, 1881

Butcher	1
Clerk (retail)	1
Cook	10
Cook (private)	7
Farmer	1
Laborer (general)	242
Launderer	10
Medical doctor	1
Proprietor (retail)	10
Tailor	3

Source: CDA 1882.

major centers of Chinese occupation in British Columbia (Lai 1988, 70–80). Yet the image of thousands of Chinese seeking fortunes in the gold rush continues to dominate people's imaginations to this day. For this reason, Chinese were viewed as contributing little to the local economy while taking from the land. This justified, in the minds of many, the animosity toward the Chinese (see Roy 1989, 7–10).

In 1881, the Chinese in British Columbia (4,350) represented 99.2 percent of *all* Chinese in Canada (4,383). A decade later, Chinese remained primarily in British Columbia (97.6 percent), 8,910 of the 9,129 in all of Canada. The Chinese formed 8.79 percent of British Columbia's population in 1881, and 9.07 percent in 1891 (Roy 1989, 269). As the primary Pacific entry point and destination for most Chinese, British Columbia became the province most vocal in expressing its opinion about Chinese migration and immigration. This situation paralleled that in California, another Pacific entry point for Chinese (Sandmeyer 1991).

The response was overt and covert discriminatory policies. Anti-Chinese sentiment produced numerous provincial and federal legislative bills that limited and restricted Chinese immigration and employment opportunities, specifically, the Franchise Act of 1885; the head tax of 1885, 1901, and 1904 ($50, $100, and $500, respectively); and the Immigration Act of 1923 (Roy 1989, Chap. 5; Wickberg 1982, Chaps. 6, 10). In some cases, Chinese faced outright physical violence. One of the most notable examples was the Vancouver riot of 1907, which developed from an anti-Asiatic parade sponsored by the Asiatic Exclusion League. The crowd damaged both the Chinese and Japanese quarters, Carrall and Powell Streets respectively (Ward 1978, Chap. 4). Partly in response to earlier hostile actions, the Chinese settled among themselves, creating Chinatowns. These were generally on the periphery of larger communities in which they worked. The residents provided refuge for each other and in self-help organizations, such as the Consolidated Chinese Benevolent Association and clan societies. Due to restrictive immigration policies and the Chinese tradition that restricted women to the ancestral home, the Chinese population in Canada was predominantly male (see CCNC 1992, 17–18; Wickberg 1982, Table 10, 306–7). Chinese wives and children were a rarity, making these Chinese communities in British Columbia and other North American locales unlike traditional ones in China. No other immigrant group who came to these shores was so actively persecuted as to be unable to form communities that resembled their traditional ones.

During that early period of settlement in British Columbia, Chinese sought opportunity wherever they could, but today Vancouver and Victoria are the only cities with notable Chinatowns. Few Canadians know that large concentrations of Chinese populated Cumberland, Yale, or Quesnelle Forks, which was primarily a Chinese town. In 1884, the three largest urban Chinese settlements were Victoria, New Westminster, and Nanaimo (Lai 1988, 43). Vancouver had yet to be incorporated as a city.

Creating Memory

The younger generation of Canadians of Chinese descent is largely unaware of its history, as demonstrated by a draft script written by undergraduate volunteers for the Vancouver Chinese Cultural Centre's school program on Chinese Canadian history. For example:

> In the past, the Chinese usually gathered and lived in Chinatown. As a result, many cultural activities happened within or around Chinatown. This limited the expansion of Chinese culture in the community. But in recent years, the Chinese population has spread out and are [*sic*] no longer crowded in Vancouver Chinatown. . . . The stability of Chinese culture along with the growth of the Chinese population allowed many organizations and associations to form in the last 20 years, for social, cultural and educational purpose[s]. (VCCC 1996, 4–5)

The first statement implies a lack of understanding regarding the development of the Chinese community. Choice of business and residence was defined by the social milieu of the time, not by one's desire to live in any specific neighborhood or area (see Atkin 1994, 46–57). The second statement suggests that the community flourished only on the arrival of the post-1960s immigrants. Forgotten are the Chinese Theatre and Chinese Opera House of the late 1890s and, in the 1920s and 1930s, the Chinese Tennis Club and Chinese Students Soccer Club (the only nonwhite team that played during those decades) (Yee 1988). District and clan associations, as well as youth clubs, schools, and theatrical groups, provided social and cultural activities before the creation of additional organizations in the 1970s (see Wickberg 1982, Tables 19 and 20, 315–18).

How does one create memory of a community? Of the thousands who came, what *do* we know of them as a collective or as individuals? Average Canadians encounter no Asian Canadian history text at any level of their schooling. In the United States there are many Asian American historical narratives from which to choose, including Ronald Takaki's *Strangers from a Different Shore: A History of Asian Americans,* Sucheng Chan's *Asian Americans: An Interpretive History,* and Gary Okihiro's *Margins and Mainstreams: Asians in American History and Culture.* Peter Ward's *White Canada Forever: Popular Attitudes and Public Policy Towards Orientals in British Columbia* is per-

TABLE 2.2.   Asian-Identified Visible Minorities in
Canada, 1996

All visible minorities	3,197,480	100.0%
Asian visible minorities	2,140,415	66.9
Chinese	860,150	26.9
South Asian	670,585	21.0
Filipino	234,200	7.3
Southeast Asian	172,765	5.4
Japanese	68,135	2.1
Korean	64,835	2.0
Visible minority	69,745	2.2

Source: CSC 1998a.

Note: "Visible minority" includes Pacific Islanders and others not named elsewhere.
"All visible minorities" does not include aboriginal people.

haps the only analogous text. Ward represents three Asian Canadian groups (Chinese, Japanese, and South Asian) from their earliest entry into Canada to the 1940s, in largely ethnic-specific rather than pan-Asian discussions.

One reason for this lack of awareness in Canada is the absence of ethnic studies programs or an equivalent to Asian American studies, in which Takaki's and Sucheng Chan's texts are commonly used. In the late 1960s, the civil rights movement in the United States led the way in the development of ethnic studies programs and centers— from African American studies, Chicano studies, and Native American studies to Asian American studies. Minority groups, not just those whose ancestors had been enslaved, became politicized. As Anthony Chan (1983, 195) noted almost two decades ago, "In Canada there has never been a single dynamic ethnic studies program for research, writing or teaching," a statement that unfortunately remains true.

Population size is a factor. Although Canada boasts an equally large citizenry of Asian origin relative to its general population (see Table 2.2), Canada has one-tenth the total population of the United States (30,750,087 in July 2000). The provinces of British Columbia and Ontario have the largest percentages of inhabitants of Asian origin: 14.4 percent or 531,355 of British Columbians, who make up 13 percent of Canadians, and 8.7 percent or 932,480 Ontarians, who represent about 37 percent of Canadians (CSC 1998b). In Vancouver alone, Canada's third and British Columbia's largest city, 25.6 percent of the population is of Asian descent (CSC 1998c). As the population is now reaching a critical mass, the development of programs such as those that began in 1969 at San Francisco State College and the University of California at Berkeley is possible (see AAAS 1998, i). (British Columbia is similar to California in the relatively large proportion of Asian origin citizens, historically and currently.)

Metropolitan Vancouver is home to two research institutions—Simon Fraser University and the University of British Columbia. Although neither have programs comparable to ethnic studies or Asian American studies, they do offer some analogous courses. Given the diversity of the Asian Canadian population, the number of courses proffered by each institution is limited. Courses tend to focus on economic ties to Asia and issues relating to diaspora or group-specific experience in Canada. But a recently accelerated immigration from Asia is likely to change this picture.

Between 1981 and 1991, Asians represented the largest group of recent arrivals (41.6 percent). In comparison, only 1.9 percent of all immigrants who arrived before 1961 were Asians. Not surprisingly, Canadian-born Asians (East, Southeast, and South Asians and Pacific Islanders) accounted for a mere 1.5 percent of the total population in 1991 (compared to European Canadian-born, 78.3 percent), a result of the prohibitive immigration policies that separated or prevented families from flourishing in Canada (CSC 1998b, Table 2.2, 20)

The undergraduate volunteer's script on Chinese Canadian history shows a skewed sense of time. The students' parents came to Canada after "country of origin" was eliminated as a major criterion to admission to Canada and regulations relied only on a "point system" (Wickberg 1982, 244–45). In this group, memory embraces a more recent time and a more accepting and tolerant Canada, but not the origins of Chinatowns or the franchise restrictions on Asian Canadians that endured until 1947 and 1949 (Ward 1978, 165).[5]

For earlier generations of immigrants, the reality was much harsher. It is a hidden heritage masked even in official documents, as early censuses for several communities on Vancouver Island illustrate. The 1881 census of Victoria identified its minority population generally as individuals, even though names were likely misspelled or incorrect. There was some sense of acknowledging and legitimizing these individuals as a people. In the 1891 census, however, names were generally not recorded or perhaps not asked—of Chinese, Japanese, and Indian (First Nations) individuals. Gender and age were the only identification for 1,931 individuals who were listed as "Chinaman," "Chinawoman," "Chinaboy," or "Chinagirl." In the ten-year interval between the censuses, anti-Chinese sentiment had increased to the extent that the first Royal Commission on Chinese Immigration (1884) had been ordered, and the first Dominion head tax on Chinese had been set at $50 (1885) (CDA 1882, 1893; Morton 1977, 262). The sentiment of the time suggests that anonymity would somehow "eliminate" this "problem" population from the city.

If this is "official" history, what is valued of a community's story? According to Anthony Chan, "Racism and bigotry conceded that the only history that was theirs [Asian Canadians] belonged to the country that they had left behind" (1983, 190). Add to this a shortened sense of presence in Canada and the story of Asian Canadians in general is much abbreviated.

Increasingly, the voice of the past is being realized in a new interest in autobiographies, oral histories, and other cultural forms of personal experience. The success of certain genres, particularly in the United States, has opened the door to increasing support in their production by mainstream publishers. For example, Wayson Choy's *The Jade Peony*, a fictional account of Vancouver's Chinatown in the late 1930s and 1940s, emphasizes generational difference, family history, and the development of self. These voices provide personal validation—to have a history, to find out the experiences of those in the past. For this reason, some are relying on small presses or independent publication, among them, Roy Ito's *Stories of My People: A Japanese Canadian Journal* and Philip Low's *Memories of Cumberland Chinatown*.

The weaving of a so-called objective history with other cultural forms provides a different kind of depth to the reconstruction of individuals' and communities' lives. History is given a personal perspective. For example, Denise Chong's *The Concubine's Children: Portrait of a Family Divided* is a biography of her grandmother that explicitly describes early-twentieth-century Chinese communities in British Columbia, as well as traditional Chinese social structure. History becomes both the recording and resurrection of the past—but also the recycling of it into new replayable forms. Such is the case with Sharon Pollock's *Komagata Maru Incident*. The play chronicles the 1914 incident and circumstances surrounding the departure of the *Komagata Maru* and most of its original passengers ("Hindus," originally numbering 376), who had hoped to land in Vancouver. As time passes, more artistic works like these will develop. In January 2001, Nanaimo's TheatreOne commissioned Denise Chong to adapt her memoir *The Concubine's Children* for the stage and Marty Chan to write a new play about the September 1960 fire that destroyed the city's Chinatown.[6]

Through these stories of events and people, the larger context of British Columbian, or Canadian, history is revealed and remembered. Memoir and literature make Asian Canadian history accessible to a wider audience. An equally effective way to recover and reclaim a history is to do so physically, through archaeological investigations. The evidence lies in the material remains of camps and settlements that established these earliest migrants and immigrants as Asian Canadians.

Chinatown

Vancouver has grown dramatically from its early days as a rough-and-tumble logging town. Land in the 1990s, especially downtown, is at a premium. The area immediately south of Chinatown by False Creek (the former Expo 86 site) has become a prime location for condominium development. In the 1880s, the area at the intersection of Carrall and Pender (formerly Dupont) Streets developed as a Chinese enclave. The wetlands of False Creek abutted the area, so buildings along Pender stood on pilings. In addition, the area was literally and figuratively on the other side of the tracks. The Canadian Pacific Railway and, later, the Great Northern Railway had tracks that terminated in Chinatown. The area was more suited to industrial use, with the Royal City Mill and railway tracks situated nearby, than to residential or business.[7]

Chinese settlement in Vancouver was no different than in other Canadian locales. If a large enough population of Chinese existed, a Chinatown grew up on the periphery of the downtown core. In the eyes of European Canadian society, the Chinese lived in a "warren of tenements" amidst disease and vices of every kind—gambling, opium, and prostitution (Anderson 1991, 82–103). For this reason, Chinatown was viewed as an area that could be moved or removed, as was the case in the late 1960s when its existence was threatened by freeway development (Yee 1988, 133). The Chinese were viewed, accordingly, as an unassimilable race that did not intend to remain in Canada, since their families did not accompany them. Of course, there was no public acknowledgment that their particular circumstances and the lack of family were a result of civic, municipal, provincial, and federal legislation directed against Chinese. From being touted as the perfect workers (for the Canadian Pacific Railway) in building Canada, Chinese became the pariahs of European Canadian society within a few short decades of their arrival.

Although the laws were restrictive, the early Chinatown did expand beyond the intersection of Carrall and Pender Streets—to the west to Shanghai and Canton Alleys, and to the east along Pender Street. It was basically a three- by one-block zone, an area designated in 1971 as a historic site. The blocks were sectioned into twenty-five-foot lots, whose narrow three- and four-story buildings gave the area part of its distinctive appearance.

Today, Carrall and Pender Streets are on the periphery of what had been the core of Chinatown; the bustle and cacophony of shoppers and sellers have moved east and south, allowing for the expansion of residential and business buildings in this section. While visiting the area in 1995, I noticed a developer's sign on what was a parking lot. Unlike most Vancouver residents, I recognized the lot's heritage value and lobbied the city and the developers to allow a planned archaeological excavation. Although no building existed, the parking lot potentially protected a buried heritage. Without intervention, the more common response to such a site in an urban setting would have occurred, namely, archaeology proceeding in a salvage situation (working among heavy machinery with limited data recovery and time), or authorities simply ignoring the need for archaeological work (as has been the case for other development on the same city block).

After I negotiated to excavate one site, the city heritage planner revealed that another lot was to be developed as well. I supervised two excavations on Pender Street during the summer of 1996. The street is an active thoroughfare and the excavation attracted passersby who stopped, looked, and commented. Their comments were for the most part based on either stereotyped images or a general lack of knowledge about Vancouver's Chinese community and its historical development within wider Canadian society. Their stereotypes even included the way I, an archaeologist, was identified. Even though English is my first language, passersby regularly assumed that I was Chinese rather than Canadian. Several complimented me on the fact that I spoke English so well; others referred to me as "another one of *those* immigrants," even though my family has lived in Vancouver for three generations.

Other individuals who proffered an opinion often did so based on stereotypes. On more than one occasion, someone shouted from a vehicle, "Found any tunnels?" or asked about the animal bones recovered, which were assumed to be from some kind of illegal activity. One television producer wanted to do a program that would exoticize the residents of Chinatown by focusing on differences in family social structure, specifically, multiple wives. Rather than providing context—that only wealthy merchants were able to afford more than one wife, not the average laborer—the viewer would be led to believe this was a common occurrence. Personal experience confirmed media interest in producing "tabloid pieces" or recirculating past stereotypes of Chinese (such as prostitution and opium dens) instead of accurately recovering history. For example, the Gim Lee Yuen Company is a homegrown import/export business in existence for more than a hundred years, older than the city itself by one year. The newsworthiness of this fact was of no interest to the producer when it was suggested as an alternative to his proposed exposé of Chinese multiple wives.

Chinatown was familiar to Vancouver residents as a place for shopping and dining. For many, the heart of Chinatown's history, as well as the oldest section, was Canton and Shanghai Alleys. (In fact, the area was not the oldest; addresses for the alleys first appear in 1905 [Henderson 1905].)

The archaeological investigation and its incumbent research dispelled common thinking about Chinatown. Many people believed that tunnels for clandestine activity ran beneath the buildings, that prostitution was rife, and that Chinese were the sole occupants. (In a number of communities throughout North America, Chinatowns reputedly had tunnels leading from buildings and under streets.) While excavation went on, particularly in the lot referred to as the Gim Lee Yuen Building, at least one passerby daily would ask whether we had yet found the tunnels (including a self-identified psychic). As noted, early Chinatown was marshy along East Pender (between Carrall and Columbia Streets) and as the excavation proved, tunnels would have been seriously affected by the tides. At some two meters below surface, the ground was moist; we reached the water table before we had dug three meters. As one informant who had lived in the building noted, the basement was quite wet after a heavy rain. Our own experience indicated that water did not easily drain away after a downpour. In the Pacific Northwest, rain is a common occurrence, and tunnels beneath Chinatown would certainly be hazardous under those conditions, especially in areas adjacent to the filled-in False Creek.

Tunnels? The evidence is not convincing. In Victoria, the excavation of the storm drain system in the late 1950s became the "discovery" of Chinatown's "secret tunnels" (Lai 1991, 35). Unfortunately, rumors quite often have a way of outliving fact, particularly when they serve the purpose of maintaining a mystique that already exists in the minds of European Canadian society.

The tunnel myth appears to be unfounded and is based on misinformation and early misconceptions held by those outside the Chinese community (Wegars 2000). Why is this myth so widespread, and what is its basis? Two points arise from examining architectural details and early fire insurance maps of the area. As noted, the building lots were twenty-five feet wide. The first point is that few structures ran the length and width of each lot during those early days; more than one structure was often built on a lot, and not necessarily adjoining another. Therefore, as the area became increasingly developed, passageways were created to allow access to the various buildings. When buildings were torn down and built over, a passageway (or doorway) was often left, a remnant of an earlier construction. Passageways served as internal alleyways (or entries) between buildings. For those who did not live in Chinatown, seeing a person enter a building and mysteriously reappear from some other street might suggest secret tunnels.

These byways were passageways, not tunnels, and secret only perhaps to those unfamiliar with the community: "Underneath Chinatown is a perfect maze of secret passages designed for the escape of the white and yellow gamblers. . . . Since the Chinese own all the land on which they build, the authorities can do nothing to prevent this burrowing, with all its dangerous possibilities" (see Lai 1991, 34).

The second point about tunnels is the presence of former delivery-access passages beneath the sidewalk. Sidewalk openings were fitted with metal doors, and often glass blocks were inserted to provide natural lighting. Priscilla Wegars in her research on this topic has been shown these regularly as evidence of tunnels. In addition, there is one Vancouver building that is often mentioned as having tunnels—the Sam Kee Building. It is perhaps more distinguished as the narrowest building in the world (less than five feet wide). The lot was once twenty-five feet across, but after the city expropriated the land to expand Pender Street, Chan Doe Gee (Sam Kee) was left with only a sliver of property. As an act of defiance and resistance to the powers that were, Sam Kee built in 1913 the building that bears his name. In order to maximize the little space available, he constructed bay windows on the second floor (creating an additional two feet). The space gained by the bay windows was charged an annual encroachment fee until 1998 (MacQueen 1998). Beneath the first floor was an excavated area that became a bathhouse (Kalman 1974, 51). Again, glass blocks lined the sidewalk to provide light. It was a creative use of space—more a basement than a tunnel.

The other image associated with Chinatown and its residents was that of a den of iniquity. Chinatown was reputedly a haven for three vices: gambling, opium, and prostitution. The latter image was more the result of the area's being home to prostitutes—not necessary Chinese or Chinese Canadian women but European Canadians. Chinatown and the red-light district were one and the same. An examination of the 1889 fire insurance map of East Pender (formerly known as Dupont) shows no fewer than six houses of "ill fame" on one block (Dakin 1889). An examination of the 1893 street section of *Williams' Official British Columbia Directory* confirms this point (see Table 2.3). Of the twenty-one addresses along the north side between Carrall and Westminster Streets, four were vacant and nine were occupied by women with European Canadian names. The women were not the only non-Chinese, as one address identified a group of three men.

This area continued to be recognized as the red-light district through the 1890s into the early twentieth century. Although prostitution was active in other areas, its occurrence in Chinatown was viewed in a sinister light by the city fathers. Civic officials decided to clean up the area, and legislation forced prostitutes to move out in 1906 (Anderson 1991, 97). An examination of the street section of the *City of Vancouver Directory* illustrates this transformation (see Table 2.4). Addresses that had been occupied by women became vacant in 1907. The process was presumably completed with a name change from Dupont to East Pender Street (a change noted in the 1908 *City of Vancouver Directory* [Henderson 1908]).

The evidence for European Canadian women living in Chinatown is strong; the presence of Chinese or Chinese Canadian women is less apparent. The majority of Chinese

TABLE 2.3.   Occupants of Dupont Street, North Side, 1893

#	Name	#	Name
1	Follis, Joseph	117	Vacant
	Taylor, John	119	Jones, Miss Annie
	Hudson, Robt		Sinclair, Alice
5	Kwong Truck & Co.	121	Willis, Nellie
11	Thomas, Miss Fanny	121	Russell, Kitty
	Stewart, Miss Addie	123	Lawrence, Miss
	Kelly, Miss Jennie	125	Smith, Miss Nellie
15	Hong Wo & Co.		Miller, Minnie
17	Vacant	127	Eaton, Bessie
21	Vacant		Mansfield, Lottie
23	Vacant		Russell, Miss Low
25	Kwong Man Lung		Fay, Miss Minnie
29	Wing Sang & Co.	131	Rena, Dora
33	Hung, Hing & Co.		Shaffer, Jessie
39	Lock Kee		Hill, Lillie
43	Lai Kee	131	Goldsmith, Miss Terry
45	Graves, Miss Alice	133	White, Jennie
	Johnson, Miss Lizzie		Gray, Nellie
			Hill, Miss Pearl
			Sheppard, Cora
		133	Heatley, Miss Stella
			Hains, May

Source: Williams 1893.

names listed in the street directory were identified as businesses, such as merchant, druggist, tailor, or jeweler. None appeared to be a listing of Chinese names that might suggest a brothel, as in the case of the European Canadian names. Undoubtedly there were Chinese women involved in prostitution but certainly not to the same extent as European Canadians (see Chong 1994). This was in part due to the onerous cost of coming to Canada, as well as the legislation.

Yet the misconception of "Chinese prostitution" remains. That Chinatown and the red-light district had been one and the same was disbelieved. To be specific—during the excavation, many bits and pieces of footwear were found. One of the earliest was a whole boot. After careful loosening of dirt and cleaning, what was initially thought to be a man's boot was identified as a woman's high-top ankle boot whose copper eyelets dated it as turn-of-the-century footwear. It appeared to be the equivalent of a woman's size eight, which would have been unusually large for a Chinese woman at that time. In all likelihood this belonged to a European Canadian woman—a prostitute. The context suggests that conclusion.

For public relations purposes, the media chose to report only sensationalized depictions of the Chinese community. With "the boot," prostitution and Chinatown once more were associated; unfortunately, contextual details were omitted. The battle to rehabilitate and to reveal a misrepresented and hidden history was not yet won.

TABLE 2.4. Occupants of Dupont Street, North Side, 1904–7

#	1904	1906*	1907
1	Wing Chung Yuen	Wing Chung Yuen	Wing Chung Yuen
5	Chinese barbershop	Occupied	Vacant
5½	*Whitner, Mamie*†	Not listed	Not listed
7	Quong, Chin	Quong, Chin	Not listed
7½	*Malay, Ida*	Not listed	Not listed
9	*Livingston, Gertie*	*Hall, Charman*	Vacant
13	Yam Yiok Lung	Yick Wo Co.	Yick Wo Co.
15	*Brown, Mable*	Vacant	Vacant
17	Lun Chong Co.	Lun Chong & Co.	Lun Chong & Co.
19	*Rosenhale, Mattie*	*de Barr, Ida*	Vacant
21	*Jones, Ruth*	*Jones, Ruth*	Vacant
23	Kwong On Chong Co.	Hing Chong	Hip Tuck Lung & Co.
25	Mee Wo	Wo Me	Me Wo
27	Not listed	Not listed	Chinese barbershop
29	Not listed	Vacant	Vacant
31	Hing Kee & Co.	Yuen Yuen Co.	Yuen Yuen Co.
31½	Not listed	Kee Hing & Co.	Not listed
33	*Duchange, Jane*	*Plotton, Loise*	Vacant
37	Lee Yune & Co.	Lee Yune Co./Lee Kee	Lee Yune Co./Lee Kee
41	Barber shop	Kwong Tai Lung Co.	Yuen Sang Co./ Kwong Tai Lung Co.
43	Not listed	Japanese restaurant/ Homma, T.	Vacant
45	Sang Lung & Co.	Sang Lung & Co.	Sang Lung & Co./ Lee On & Co.
49	Chinese barbers	Chinese barbers	Yuen Lay
51	Wing Sang & Co./ Charlie Yip Yem	Wing Sang & Co	Wing Sang & Co./ Yip Yow
53	Not listed	Long Wo	Long Wo
57	Chinese barbers	Not listed	Not listed
59	*Hill, Grace*	*Compan, May W.*	Vacant
61	Wing Hong On & Co.	Loy Tai & Co.	Tai Loi & Co.
63	Chinese	*Osborne, Georgie*	Vacant
67	Kwong Wo Yuen	Kwong Wo Yuen	Kwong Wo Yuen
69	Chinese	*Rollins, Ruby*	Vacant
71	*Minna, Julia*	Not listed	Not listed
73	*Allice*	*Allice*	Vacant
75	Tai Wo Chung Co.	Portland Restaurant	Jo Lee
77	Kong, C.	Kong, C.	Nong Fu
79	*Wilson, Louise*	Hing, Sam	Sun Lee & Co.
83	*Mina, Julia*	*Dewat, Thelma*	Kwong Hung & Co.
85	Not listed	Poodle Dog Restaurant	Lee Wo Cafe
93	Chinese restaurant	Not listed	Not listed

Source: Henderson 1904–7.

*No street directory available for 1905.

†Names in italics are Euro-Canadian.

Canada touts itself as a multicultural nation, but does its citizenry truly accept and live that reality? The excavation in Chinatown allowed for a discussion of attitudes (and myths) associated with this "town within a city" and Chinese in Canadian history. Current references to Vancouver as "Hongcouver" or "Asia Town," and the suburb of Tsawwassen as "Little Rhodesia" (Cernetig 1995; North 1996), confirm the need to acknowledge that Canadian history included others besides those who arrived from Europe or who had a European heritage.

Giving Voice

On one occasion, a man of Chinese descent in his sixties (who had emigrated in the 1950s) approached me to talk about the excavation. He expressed his appreciation of the project and the publicity it generated, specifically its detailing of the historical context of the Chinese community in Vancouver and in British Columbia. With his voice almost trembling, he noted that there was a need for recent Asian immigrants, primarily Chinese, to know that the social environment of the 1990s was very different, that freedoms and rights assumed today were unavailable to the Asian pioneers who arrived in the years before and after the city's incorporation in 1886.

As population demographics change, the urgency to tell the stories of Asian Canadian pioneers grows, especially as the climate of anti-Asian sentiment appears to be on the rise. The Lims are no more foreign or immigrant than the Owenses (the mayor of Vancouver) or Chrétiens (the prime minister of Canada). Whose history is acknowledged? Why have the sites and objects associated with early Chinese settlement in the Americas been lost to the larger community in which they lived? Part of the answer lies within the community.

Most Chinese came to the Americas without family. Family socializes and creates a degree of stability; it provides community. Without the continuity of family and community, historical memory disappears. That bachelor society is gone, and whatever value its community recognized in sites (i.e., physical layout or particular buildings) and objects disappeared with the inhabitants. Some of those early Chinese communities are all but ghost towns (Cumberland and Quesnelle Forks, among others). Who is to give voice then? Family provides not only the continuation of memory, but a sense of history. In comparison to China's thousands of years, British Columbia's history may seem insignificant. For those early Chinese pioneers, survival in this foreign land was all that mattered. It was not marked by monumental architecture or mass movements of people claiming an area for the nation-state. Although the Chinese were identified as a group, each acted individually. Accomplishments were, therefore, about individual men or families rather than a people. Some measured success by their ability to return to China, but many did not.

Only in the last two decades have the voices from the past begun to be heard through published oral histories (see CCNC 1992; Marlatt and Itter 1979). Few exist, for remembering can be painful and difficult to reveal. For some, these histories are within living memory. As one individual stated, she wants to remember only the positive; another said simply, "The time was hard; I don't want to relive it."

A comprehensive account of the contributions of non-Europeans in the larger context of this developing province and country has yet to be written. One looks for a Canadian history with a perspective comparable to Takaki's *A Different Mirror,* that is, one that gives voice to all those people previously left out of the historical canon— some consider this revisionist history. We are a nation of immigrants. Each immigrant group responded to the other in its own particular fashion, as well as by establishing social structures and customs adapted and modified to a new and different cultural context. The silence of Chinese Canadian (or Asian Canadian) history helps to maintain the myths of the dominant society. Archaeological projects like the Vancouver Chinatown excavation can break that silence. The students who participated in the field school discovered a portion of local history by unearthing muddied and encrusted artifacts, by listening to the comments around them as they labored, by being in Chinatown on a daily basis, and by recovering the actual names of individuals and businesses from archival material. What began as an opportunity to excavate in Vancouver's Chinatown became the unearthing, literally and figuratively, of a history once silent—of individuals, of families, and of businesses that were rarely acknowledged. That history is one that nurtures the Pacific century begun by Asian pioneers to North America and their descendents, as well as the one marking the entry of a revitalized Asian population a hundred years later. The archaeology of Chinatown provides a bridge between "old" and "new" Canadians of Chinese descent—those from one Pacific century to the next.

Notes

1. Rather than refer to "Asian Americans and Asian Canadians," I will use the generic "Asian American" to encompass both groups as nationals of North America.

2. In 1788, Captain John Meares brought seventy Chinese laborers as part of his crew. They landed on the west coast of Vancouver Island—the first documented case (in the English language) of Chinese in western North America. Reputedly, some of these laborers settled among the native population (Wright 1988, 2, 15).

3. Newfoundland joined Canadian Confederation in 1949, while Hawai'i was admitted as the fiftieth state only in 1959.

4. The 1996 Vancouver excavation of two locations, Canton Alley (DhRs-27a) and the Gim Lee Yuen Building (DhRs-27b), was undertaken as part of a five-college consortium field school. There had been salvage work in the area during the construction of Expo 86.

5. Canadians of Chinese and South Asian origin regained the vote provincially and federally in 1947, Canadians of Japanese descent, in 1949.

6. The first public reading of Marty Chan's play occurred 23 June 2001 at Global Connections, Nanaimo, B.C.

7. See Dakin 1889 and *Goad's* 1912; copies are available at the Vancouver City Archives.

Works Cited

Anderson, Kay J. 1991. *Vancouver's Chinatown: Racial Discourse in Canada, 1875–1980.* Montreal: McGill-Queen's University Press.

Association for Asian American Studies (AAAS), comp. 1988. *Directory of Asian American Studies Programs.* Ithaca: Asian American Studies Program, Cornell University.

Atkin, John. 1994. *Strathcona: Vancouver's First Neighbourhood.* Vancouver: Whitecap.

Bowen, Lynne. 1982. *Boss Whistle: The Coal Miners of Vancouver Island Remembered.* Lantzville, B.C.: Oolichan.

Canada Department of Agriculture (CDA). 1882. *Census of Canada, 1881.* Ottawa.

———. 1893. *Census of Canada, 1891.* Ottawa.

Canada. Statistics Canada (CSC). 1994. *Canada's Changing Immigrant Population.* Census 1991. Catalogue No. 96-311E. Ottawa: Ministry of Industry, Science, and Technology.

———. 1998a. "1996 Census: Ethnic Origin, Visible Minorities." *Daily,* 17 February. Online at <http://www.statcan.ca:80/Daily/English/980217/d980217.htm> (3 July 2001).

———. 1998b. "Population by Ethnic Origin, 1996 Census." *Census 1996.* Online at <http://www.statcan.ca/english/Pgdb/People/Population/demo28b.htm> (3 July 2001).

———. 1998c. "Single and Multiple Ethnic Origin Responses, 1996 Census, Census Metropolitan." *Census 1996.* Online at <http://www.statcan.ca/english/Pgdb/People/Population/demo28h.htm> (3 July 2001).

Cernetig, Miro. 1995. "White Flight, Chinese Distress." *Globe and Mail,* 30 September.

Chan, Anthony B. 1983. *Gold Mountain: The Chinese in the New World.* Vancouver, B.C.: New Star.

Chinese Canadian National Council (CCNC). 1992. *Jin Guo: Voices of Chinese Canadian Women.* Toronto: Women's Press.

Chong, Denise. 1994. *The Concubine's Children: Portrait of a Family Divided.* Toronto: Viking.

Choy, Wayson. 1995. *The Jade Peony.* Vancouver: Douglas and McIntyre.

Dakin. 1889. *Fire Map of Vancouver.* San Francisco: Dakin. (Vancouver City Archives Map 338)

Goad's Atlas of the City of Vancouver. 1912. Vancouver: Goad. (Vancouver City Archives Map 342)

Henderson. 1908. *City of Vancouver Directory.* Vancouver: Henderson.

Ito, Roy. 1994. *Stories of My People: A Japanese Canadian Journal.* Hamilton: S-20 and Nisei Veterans Association.

Kalman, Harold. 1978. *Exploring Vancouver 2: Ten Tours of the City and Its Buildings.* Rev. ed. Vancouver: University of British Columbia Press.

Lai, David Chuenyan. 1988. *Chinatowns: Towns within Cities in Canada.* Vancouver: University of British Columbia Press.

———. 1991. *The Forbidden City within Victoria: Myth, Symbol, and Streetscape of Canada's Earliest Chinatown.* Victoria: Orca.

Low, Philip C. P. 1993. *Memories of Cumberland Chinatown.* Vancouver: P.C.P. Low.

MacQueen, Ken. 1998. "Chinatown Building Wins, Old Feud Dies." *Vancouver Sun,* 12 December.

Marlatt, Daphne, and Carole Itter, comps. and eds. 1979. *Opening Doors: Vancouver's East End.* Sound Heritage Ser. 8, Nos. 1 and 2. Victoria: Province of British Columbia.

Morton, James. 1977. *In the Sea of Sterile Mountains: The Chinese in British Columbia.* Vancouver: Douglas.

North, Sam. 1996. "Asia Town." *Vancouver* 29, 7: 46–58.

Pollock, Susan. 1992. "The Komagata Maru Incident." In *Six Canadian Plays,* ed. Tony Hamill. Toronto: Playwrights Canada.

Roy, Patricia E. 1989. *A White Man's Province: British Columbia Politicians and Chinese and Japanese Immigrants, 1858–1914.* Vancouver: University of British Columbia Press.

Sandmeyer, Elmer Clarence. 1991. *The Anti-Chinese Movement in California.* 1939. Urbana: University of Illinois Press.

Takaki, Ronald. 1993. *A Different Mirror: A History of Multicultural America.* Boston: Little, Brown.

Vancouver Chinese Cultural Centre (VCCC). 1996. "Chinese Canadian history." Typescript. Draft copy held by author.

Ward, W. Peter. 1978. *White Canada Forever: Popular Attitudes and Public Policy toward Orientals in British Columbia.* Montreal: McGill-Queen's University Press.

Wegars, Priscilla. 2000. "Ongoing Research: Chinese Tunnels." Asian American Comparative Collection. April. University of Idaho. Online at <http://www.uidaho.edu/LS/AACC/research.htm #tunnels> (3 July 2001).

Wickberg, Edgar, ed. 1982. *From China to Canada: A History of the Chinese Communities in Canada.* Toronto: McClelland.

Williams' Official British Columbia Directory. 1893. Victoria: Williams' British Columbia Directory.

Wright, Richard Thomas. 1988. *In a Strange Land: A Pictorial Record of the Chinese in Canada, 1788–1923.* Saskatoon, Sas.: Western Producer Prairie Books.

Yee, Paul. 1988. *Saltwater City: An Illustrated History of the Chinese in Vancouver.* Vancouver: Douglas and McIntyre.

Randall Rohe

3   Chinese Camps and Chinatowns: Chinese Mining Settlements in the North American West

While perceptions have changed somewhat over the last ten or fifteen years, most North Americans, including many Chinese Americans, associate Chinese settlement in the nineteenth century with urban places—infamous Chinatowns with poor sanitation, overcrowding, gambling, opium smoking, tongs, and prostitution—places that non-Chinese avoided at all costs. Further, they associate these Chinatowns only with a few large cities and think of them as places where immigrant Chinese replicated the culture of their homeland, including constructing buildings in a traditional Chinese fashion. They often believe that Chinatowns came into existence simply because Chinese settled together and formed tight-knit communities to preserve their culture during their sojourn in North America and had almost no interaction with the surrounding non-Chinese community.

Most North Americans do not associate the Chinese with rural settlement or know the important role that the Chinese played in mining the Far West. While few Chinese migrated to the United States before the California gold rush, they came in great numbers after that event—18,000 to 20,000 a year by 1852. As the mining frontier moved eastward, the Chinese followed, becoming a ubiquitous element of the mining West. By 1870 they represented more than 25 percent of all miners, and in some states, they accounted for one-half to almost two-thirds of the mining population. Wherever they settled, the Chinese grouped together in Chinese camps or Chinatowns (see Rohe 1982).

Eventually, most of these Chinese returned home, and their settlements associated with mining, both urban and rural, gradually disappeared. Since few nineteenth-century Chinese immigrants left written accounts, we know relatively little about them or their settlements. Available studies of Chinese immigrant communities fall into two categories: those that treat Chinatowns as a special type of community with features distinct from Anglo-American ones, and those that describe facets of particular communities. In both instances, communities are analyzed mainly in terms of their institutional structure; the

FIGURE 3.1.   The large immigration of Chinese into California in the early 1850s coincided with their mass entry into placer mining. While most Chinese worked for themselves or Chinese companies, the Chinese pictured here at Auburn Ravine in 1852 apparently worked for or with Euro-American miners. (Courtesy of California History Room, California State Library, Sacramento, California)

impression created is that all Chinatowns in the West were merely smaller replicas of the one in San Francisco and that Chinese historical experience was quite homogenous. Further, most studies of Chinese settlement have concentrated on the Chinatowns of large, nonmining communities like San Francisco. Few studies have specifically examined the Chinatowns associated with mining towns like Helena, Montana; Nevada City, California; Deadwood, South Dakota; and Idaho City, Idaho, or the smaller Chinese camps that once dotted the landscape of the mining West in the United States and Canada (Fig. 3.1). We therefore know little about the morphology, layout, structures, locations, architecture, and other characteristics of the settlements associated with Chinese mining.

Because of the passage of time, a study of Chinese mining settlement requires the use of a wide variety of sources and an interdisciplinary approach. Geographers typically employ such an approach, and the study of settlement, both urban and rural, has been a traditional area of inquiry. Since ethnicity usually influences both the forms and components of settlement, geographers have often examined the relationship between ethnicity and settlement. Indeed, spatial identity is a prerequisite of ethnicity, so the study of ethnic groups is inherently geographical. While the topics considered in such studies vary, morphology, layout, structures, location, and architecture are among the ones most commonly considered. Analysis of such topics provides insight on how the ethnic mosaic came to be and how ethnic groups leave their imprint on the landscape.

Geographers have examined such rural settlement features as house types, barns, farmsteads, farm villages, and hamlets, as well as the size, alignment, and spatial arrangement of roads, fields, and buildings. Geographers study such settlement elements and their distribution for the light they throw on origin and the sequence of change, and the information they provide on functional relationships. Structures are designed and grouped to serve specific purposes and therefore carry functional meanings. Their exterior forms reflect the architectural styles of the day and often the culture of their origin. Their distribution provides discernible patterns on the land. Typically, they outlast both their original function and the architectural fashions of their time. Thus they reflect changes in the occupancy of the land and often constitute the only elements of the past that survive in the present landscape.

Geographers are interested in urban settlement because cities are distinct places that have economic, social, and political importance out of all proportion to the areas they occupy. Geographers may examine the city as a part of the fabric of settlement as a whole and consider the interrelationship between the forms and functions of buildings, street patterns, and layout/plan, and trace the forms and patterns of today to their origin in the past. They may consider such topics as the factors in city location, the functions that influence city growth or decline, and the role of the city in the economy of its hinterland. A number of geographers have focused specifically on ethnic settlement in cities and have examined the origin and evolution of ghettos and ethnic neighborhoods and considered such topics as assimilation, sequent occupancy, social interaction, reinforcement of ethnic identities, and cultural preadaptation.

The sources for writing Western mining history are as widely scattered and often as elusive as the gold for which the miners searched. This is especially true of material on the Chinese. Glimpses of Chinese activities in the mining areas of the West are found in gold rush period diaries and newspaper accounts; an occasional article, thesis, or dissertation; some local histories; and the U.S. Census. Some documents in Chinese have survived, but these provide only episodic evidence on Chinese economic and social life. Moreover, it is difficult to judge how representative these may be. As a result, archaeological and visual records are used to supplement and corroborate the documentary record.

Chinese Mining Camps

A Chinese mining camp was a temporary settlement of Chinese miners, typically consisting of fewer than thirty-five structures and an almost entirely male population of not more than a few hundred. The size of Chinese mining camps varied according to time, the success of mining, and the existing social and political conditions. Period accounts mention camps ranging in size from as few as a half dozen Chinese to as many as four hundred or more. If the Chinese camp was of any size, it commonly had some commercial buildings, usually at least a store (Williams 1971, 40; Minnick 1988, 15; Chinn 1977, 31; *Downieville* [Calif.] *Sierra Citizen*, 1 April 1857). Fredlund hypothesizes that for every hundred Chinese there would be some ten businesses, including at a minimum one store, possibly a blacksmith, shoemaker, restaurant, and/or butcher shop, plus several opium dens and gambling establishments (1991, 206). At times, a centrally located blacksmith shop, gambling hall, or store might serve a number of surrounding Chinese mining camps. The camps had few, if any, permanent institutional buildings and often consisted of structures erected for a few years' use. Many of them fell into ruin after the Chinese moved on or died.

Chinese Mining Camp Structures

The first Chinese in the California goldfields organized relatively small camps characterized by small tents and brush houses near their claims, generally on the banks of a stream. McLeod noted that "as time went on, no river bar, creek, or mining camp was complete without a Chinese camp on its outskirts" (1947, 43). The manuscript census of 1850 showed a conspicuous lack of large Chinese camps in the mining areas of California. Later, in groups of a hundred or more, the Chinese banded together in short-lived villages throughout the mining region or occupied camps deserted by white miners. The 1852 manuscript census revealed almost one-third of the Chinese living in large camps, and only a few hundred residing in localities with large foreign, non-Chinese populations (Chiu 1963, 11, 13).

Typically, the Chinese located their camps away from Euro-American camps to lessen contact between the two and the possibility for hostility. For the same reason, Chinese usually located their camps in areas thought unproductive or abandoned as worked out by white miners. While the Chinese often located their earliest camps right next to a river adjacent to the placer diggings, they invariably located their later camps on a flood-free terrace (Barth 1964, 114; Minnick 1988, 15).

Apparently for the most part, the early Chinese mining camps in California consisted of small tents or brush houses, sometimes described in period accounts—such as those in the *Elko (Nevada) Independent* for 7 August 1869 and the *Downieville (California) Sierra Citizen* for 30 December 1854—as wigwams or bowers built out of whatever vegetation happened to be at hand. Irish miner James Galloway noted that the Chinese put up "brush tents . . . with posts and poles, and brush thrown over them" (Shay 1876, 155). Shaw described the construction of one of these: "The Chinese carpenter and ourselves speedily felled some young saplings, and driving two strong posts in the ground, we fixed a long spar longitudinally; on this spar rested the saplings and branches in inclined position; then placing turf at the bottom, our bush-hut was finished that night" (1973, 80–81). LaLande suggests that the brush hut of the Chinese miners may have been derived directly from the summer "crop-watching huts" of rural Kwangtung. These "little booths, some of them overrun with climbing vines," provided farmers shelter from the sun while keeping watch on their crops to prevent their destruction by bandits or rival clans (1981, 300–301).

The simple A-frame (or walled) Euro-American canvas tent was another shelter adopted by the Chinese. Such a structure fit in well with the short-term, migratory nature of much early Chinese mining. Borthwick mentions a company of Chinese miners at Mississippi Bar, California, in 1852. "There were about a hundred and fifty of them here, living in a perfect village of small tents, all clustered together on the rocks." Later he encountered a Chinese camp in a gulch near Angels Camp. Here about a hundred Chinese had pitched their tents on a rocky eminence by the side of their diggings (1948, 215, 261). On 2 May 1853, the *Oroville (California) Butte Record* recorded Chinese tents scattered in all directions on the flats near Bagdad, California. A circa 1870 Harhart lithograph of a Chinese camp shows a cluster of white canvas tents, about five by eight feet in size and about four feet high. The small cloth tent, with a pole supporting each end, probably resembled the four-foot-high straw-mat tent sometimes used by the poorest class of Kwangtung peasants (LaLande 1981, 299–301). Apparently, many Chinese who arrived in California in 1852 brought with them tents of coarse cotton duck and poles of large bamboo canes, as the *San Francisco Alta California* reported on 5 May. In the 1850s, journalists described the banks of some California streams as dotted with numerous white tents of Chinese miners (*Sacramento Bee,* 28 April 1857; *San Francisco Evening Bulletin,* 7 May 1857; *Marysville (Calif.) Herald,* 2 May 1852; *Downieville (Calif.) Sierra Citizen,* 30 December 1854).

Some fairly large Chinese mining camps apparently consisted almost entirely of tents and cloth houses. According to the *Shasta Courier* for 3 December 1853 and 23 December 1854, Hong Kong, located near Shasta, California, for example, consisted entirely of such structures, had a population of four or five hundred, and supported a hotel, gambling saloon, several stores, and other businesses. A single Chinese camp, too, might contain a variety of structures (Fig. 3.2). Borthwick in 1852 described one camp as consisting of a dozen or so small tents and brush houses (1948, 117). The *Oroville (California) Butte Record* on 2 May 1857 reported that the Chinese mining camp at Rancheria (Hullulipa or Columbus) consisted of "quite a village of wooden houses besides the hundreds of smoked and dirty tents." In the late 1860s, a large group of Chinese who camped on the outskirts of Elko, Nevada, used tents and bowers constructed of green willows, according to the *Elko Independent* for 7 August 1869. Archaeologists have identified small level areas at Chinese mining sites in various parts of the West as pads for tents or brush shelters (Smith, 1983, 6; Stevens 1992, 14).

In some areas of the West, especially along parts of the Snake and Salmon Rivers in Idaho, the Chinese used rock shelters or dugouts. These usually consisted of a one-room chamber formed by erecting a wall along the front of a natural rock overhang or the cavity beneath one or more large boulders. Canvas or sacking probably covered the entrance. Along the Lower Salmon River, Chinese miners excavated rectangular pits that used the face of the canyon walls as one side of the structure, then constructed rock walls of angular basalt and dirt along the inside of the pits. The rock walls often extended above the pit, and the Chinese piled dirt against the outside of the rock wall

FIGURE 3.2.   Some Chinese mining camps consisted of both tents and wood structures. (Courtesy of Bancroft Library, University of California, Berkeley, BANC PIC 1905.15024-PIC)

for support. The inside area averaged about ten square meters (see James 1990, 1, 4, 7–8; Sisson 1993, 50; Kingsbury 1989, 5–7; Free 1991, 78, 95, 115–16, 119).

The Chinese recognized the advantages of the easily built American log cabin and used the design in California, Oregon, Montana, Idaho, British Columbia, and elsewhere (Fig. 3.3). The *San Francisco Herald* noted on 25 November 1857 that in California, "upon the banks of the rivers and in the ravines and canyons throughout the mining counties, companies of twenty and thirty Chinamen are found inhabiting close cabins, so small that one of them would not be of sufficient size to allow a couple of Americans to breath in it." Undoubtedly, the Chinese occupied some of these log cabins after their original Euro-American occupants abandoned them. Further, records from various mining districts show that the Chinese fairly often purchased mining claims, including cabins, from Euro-Americans. But the Chinese also built their own cabins, using Euro-American techniques. Whether the Chinese modified Euro-American building techniques to any degree or added any elements of their own is unknown. Their log cabins varied from full-sized structures to small crude lean-tos or half-log, half-dirt cabins (see Sisson 1993, 54, 58; Fredlund 1991, 209; LaLande 1981, 298; Wynne 1964, 44; and Wikoff 1972, 109).

The Chinese-built log cabins had various roofs—canvas, shake, logs and brush, and so on. Whatever the roof construction, the cabins often had no ceiling or only a par-

tial loft. Later Chinese miners erected cabins of lumber at their camps, sometimes from
the boards of abandoned flumes. Some Chinese mining companies built structures of
both logs and lumber. A company that worked at China Gulch, Oregon, erected ten
log or frame buildings, including four cabins. In later years as the Chinese began
hydraulic mining, they probably quite often constructed a number of log and frame
structures to house their employees and support their operations. When a Chinese company bought a hydraulic claim near Trinity Center, California, in 1881, for example,
it erected a boarding house for its laborers as well as a house, barn, poultry house, and
blacksmith shop (see the *Shasta [Calif.] Courier,* 15 December 1866; Chin 1977, 20–21;
LaLande 1981, 186, 299; and Yancey 1960, 16).

Although rammed-earth structures were apparently much more commonly associated
with Chinatowns, the Chinese did build some in their mining camps. Most supposedly
functioned as stores. The technique of rammed-earth construction is common throughout China. Earth was dug and piled into V-shaped or H-shaped wall supports. It was
then pounded with rammers until compacted. Additional earth was piled on top and
the ramming process repeated. When the filling was completed, the supports were
removed, leaving a compacted earth wall (Tordoff and Seldner 1986, 5–41; Sisson 1983,
38; LaLande 1981, 293).

FIGURE 3.3.   These log cabins used by Chinese railroad laborers probably resembled
those built by Chinese miners in various parts of the West. (Courtesy of Vancouver
Public Library, Special Collections, VPL 210)

In some cases, white mining companies employed Chinese laborers. While many provided dwellings for their Chinese workers, others did not, and the Chinese built their own. A case in point is the Great Western Quicksilver Mine near Calistoga, California, which employed 200–250 Chinese (Goss 1954, 292).

> The camps themselves were a mere jumble of huts of the rudest construction, completely lacking in sanitation and surrounded by so much filth and debris that the odors were almost overpowering even to a passerby. A few of the structures were barracks-like buildings made of rough lumber, but the bulk of the houses were a rambling hodge-podge of shacks built by the men themselves of anything they could lay their hands on—scraps of lumber, old shingles, broken-up packing boxes, and flattened-out kerosene cans. (Goss 1954, 293)

Several archaeologists and anthropologists have investigated the possible use of geomantic principles by the Chinese in the western United States. Geomancy or *feng-shui* is the practical art of positioning and designing cultural features in harmony with the features of nature. In practice, decisions ranging from building orientation and position in relation to water and mountains, to arrangements of door and windows, and even to certain moveable furnishings within buildings could be determined with reference to geomantic principles. While Chinese immigrants undoubtedly carried the concepts of feng-shui with them, it is unclear whether the Chinese felt that what happened in America had any geomantic consequences or that only the environment of China had cosmological significance. The principles of feng-shui represented the ideal. When divergence from the ideal proved unavoidable, planting trees, building an embankment, or placing a board with charms painted on it in the proper location countered any potential catastrophe. Moreover, some feng-shui principles represent practical considerations that most miners, regardless of ethnicity, would consider in locating their camps (see Praetzellis et al. 1987, 44; LaLande 1981, 306–7; Sisson 1993, 39; Mueller 1987, 9–10).

As yet no documentary evidence has surfaced that the Chinese miners adhered to feng-shui. A number of archaeologists, however, have suggested that this possibility exists for a number of sites. An excellent example is George Mead's study of a small mining settlement of a hundred Chinese along Tanner Gulch in the Blue Mountains of Oregon. Sometime between 1870 and 1890, Chinese built twenty-five major structures here and occupied the site for two to five years. Detailed analysis of the settlement pattern indicates that the overall site structure reflects a traditional Chinese cultural worldview as embedded in the concept of feng-shui (Mead 1994).

A distinct possibility exists that Chinese mining camps were segregated along district or dialect lines. The Chinese came mainly from fourteen counties on the Pearl River Delta in Kwangtung and displayed chain migration, a stream from a few villages in China to specific places in the Far West. Chen and others have reported that some Chinese immigrants came in groups from specific districts and maintained these groups as working and social units in the new land. Membership in such groupings might have been a major factor affecting mining camp structure, since some long-standing animosities between Chinese ethnic groups seem to have been transplanted to California and from there to the rest of the West (Chen qtd. in Smith 1983, 7; Bowen 1982, 67; Wright 1987, 37–38).

Chinatowns

By the mid-1850s, one of every five miners in California was Chinese, and Chinese settlements developed within the larger mining towns. In fact, major mining towns such as Oroville, Auburn, and Weaverville had as high a percentage of Chinese in their population as San Francisco. Some mining towns by ordinance restricted the Chinese to a certain section of town; other towns by accepted practice achieved the same result. In a few towns like Nanaimo, British Columbia (a coal-mining town), and Silver Creek, California, a wall, a gate, or both formalized this segregation (Rohe, 1982, 6; Minnick 1988, 17; Bowen 1982, 127; Pricer 1991, 2).

Most of the larger settlements associated with Chinese mining consisted of distinct enclaves (Chinatowns) within larger Euro-American mining towns. In a few cases, however, Chinese mining operations produced fairly large towns completely separate and distinct from any white settlement. The Lava Beds, which flourished from 1873 to 1882 near Oroville, California, was the largest such settlement. By the fall of 1873 the town contained about 150 buildings, a dozen canvas tents, and a single brick store. Another couple of dozen shanties surrounded the town proper. At its peak, the Lava Beds contained a population of between five and eight thousand (Rohe 1991, 2–4).

As the Chinese population of the goldfields grew, the white population often declined as well, and some Euro-American mining towns became essentially Chinese communities. By 1852 Auburn and its environs supposedly contained more Chinese than did any other mining district in California. "The streets of that village swarm with them, there [their] hieroglyphics stare one in the face on almost every building, and these 'children of the sun' are almost monopolizing the 'small trade' of that flourishing town" (*Sacramento Union*, 11 October 1852).

In 1876 the *Chico (California) Butte Record* for 29 January stated that "Oroville, once the queen of mining camps and the home of two thousand miners, has degenerated into a village of a few hundred inhabitants, the Mongolian element largely predominating." By the 1870s Timbuctoo, California, had experienced a similar transformation: "Timbuctoo has no store, only a post office and a saloon. A few miners stay there with their families, and work over the tailings for the company which owns them, otherwise the town is occupied by Chinese. Chinese gardens on the hill, Chinese children in the dust of the street, Chinese signs and paper invocations and spells on lintel and door post, Chinese blue blouses moving through the scrub pines on the hill side" (*San Francisco Evening Bulletin*, 2 July 1879)

Most descriptions of mining Chinatowns differ only in detail. A visitor to Upper Calaveritas in 1856 wrote: "Viewing the camp from 'first appearances,' it looked like a badly posted bill on an inclined bulletin board; the narrow streets seemed to be short blank lines, and the irregular rows of unpainted tenements, lower-case and capital (shaded, condensed and extended) houses; we noticed, down near the creek, a row of Chinese italic and back-slope thatched cottages" (*San Andreas [Calif.] Independent*, 15 November 1856). The editor of the *Oroville (California) Mercury* on 11 September 1873 described Oroville's Chinatown as "a narrow street, about a quarter of a mile long, on each side of which is built one-story light wooden shanties and here and there an occasional brick house. The houses are built closely and solidly together, and there is no vacant lots to this extent of street. In front of each house hangs one or more lanterns, and the sidewalks and center of the street are crowded with Chinese."

Except for the Chinese signs hanging on storefronts and the concentration of Chinese residents, the streetscape of Chinatown often differed little from the other parts of a mining town (*Crescent City Courier,* 13 February 1873). At San Andreas, however "scrolls and cupolas gaudy colored red and trimmed in gold, gave the scene an appearance typical of old China" ("Chinese in Calaveras" 1973, 3).

Smith in the late nineteenth century characterized the villages of China as unplanned. "They 'just growed like topsy.' Paths of varying widths and alleys traditionally used for access between the structures and the outside world constituted the 'streets'" (qtd. in Ritchie 1993, 338). Many period descriptions of Chinese settlements in the West evoke similar images. One writer noted that the Chinese built the Lava Beds "solidly so as to accommodate a larger population without infringing largely upon the mining ground" and laid out the streets parallel to each other without any cross streets to allow more building room (Rohe 1991, 14). When the Chinese established a new town half a mile from Coulterville, California, however, they "laid out a village with broad streets, squares etc., a là Melican." A description of the founding of a Chinese town near Mariposa, California, reported the Chinese staking off lots, implying some degree of planning (see *Stockton [Calif.] San Joaquin Republican,* 28 August 1858; *Sacramento Union,* 21 August 1858; *San Francisco Alta California,* 27 April and 24 August 1858; and *Auburn [Calif.] Placer Herald,* 8 May 1858).

Locations

The Chinese quarters of mining communities were generally situated in the oldest part of town or along the nearest waterway (or both), some distance from the more prosperous residents of the community. In some towns, however, they were barely separated from the main settlement. In Silver City, Idaho, only Dead Man's Alley separated whites from Chinese (Derig 1972, 18). The Chinatown at La Porte, California, developed in the very center of the town between the business section and the residences of most of the whites (*La Porte Mountain Messenger,* 4 July 1863). The same thing happened at Shasta. The buildings stood along Main Street for a distance of 250 feet and faced west. The white inhabitants had direct contact with the Chinese every time they traveled the main road through Shasta (Hart 1970, 2). Other Chinatowns developed on a town's outskirts or as much as two miles away. Sometimes, as in North Bloomfield, California, towns had several Chinese quarters (see *Sacramento Union,* 26 April 1858, 22 July 1859; *Nevada City [Calif.] Daily Transcript,* 23 October 1881; *Stockton [Calif.] San Joaquin Republican,* 31 October 1857; *San Francisco Alta California,* 29 October 1857; and *Survey* 1979, 39, 47–48). At Pierce, Idaho, the Chinese did not even live in a separate enclave. There the Chinese dominated the population at an early date and controlled much of the business and trade of the town (Stapp and Longenecker 1984, 6).

Architecture

Typically, the Chinese "jammed" their houses together and cut each house into small rooms "after the Chinese style," "affording means of easy communication, and providing many avenues of escape in time of need." "Though there are some exceptions to the rule, the construction of buildings they consider ventilation, light, comfort or neatness unnecessary." "In many of their dens the apartments are dark, cold and damp, but they are generally cleanly in their persons." The structures of at least some Chinatowns, in fact, consisted "of windowless cabins not much larger than dog houses." Although often exaggerated by the racism of the period, these descriptions appear to be fairly accurate (see *Nevada City [Calif.] Daily Transcript*, 12 January 1870, 30 September 1877, 25 February 1888; *San Francisco Herald*, 7 January 1858; and MacDonald 1966, 48).

Chinese often built a three-walled house, which they attached to an already standing structure. The process continued until the connected houses extended a block long. The editor of the *North San Juan Press* vividly described the procedure: "The process by which John builds is like the gradual accretion of barnacles upon a ship or floating timber, one shanty sprouting out from another in most irregular fashion, until the whole Celestial village presents as many angles as a huge mass of crystallized quartz." The Chinese should not be held completely accountable for the compact, cramped conditions of Chinatown. Often they owned neither the buildings nor the lots on which they stood. The whites, who built structures to rent or sell to the Chinese, often constructed them so as to maximize the profits (*North San Juan [Calif.] Hydraulic Press*, 30 October 1858; *San Francisco Alta California*, 7 November 1858; *Weaverville [Calif.] Trinity Journal*, 26 November 1859).

Generally, except occasionally for some stores and temples, the Chinese built single-story structures. At North San Juan, however, unable to expand horizontally, the Chinese built up and constructed some two-and-a-half-story buildings (*North San Juan [Calif.] Hydraulic Press*, 1 October 1858). As in many of their undertakings, Chinese construction often displayed great use of manual labor. "The Chinese have all hands and on a few buildings one is reminded of the cackling and appearance of a flock of black birds to see them at work" (*Nevada City [Calif.] Daily Transcript*, 17 November 1863). As China-towns grew, they often did so at the expense of the streets on which they stood. At Deadwood, South Dakota, the Chinese reduced the street through their quarter from fifty feet wide to about fifteen feet (*Deadwood [S.D.] Black Hills Daily Times*, 19 September 1879).

During 1849 and into the early 1850s, Chinese imported some prefabricated "camphorwood" structures to California from Hong Kong. These one-story, windowless, two-bedroom buildings measured from about twelve feet square to about twelve by twenty-four feet. Sometimes the Chinese connected several of these structures to form a single building. While these imported buildings saw use mostly in San Francisco, a few did reach the mining region. More commonly, however, the structures of mining Chinatown consisted of log or frame lumber buildings of local construction. Log structures generally were common only during the early years of some Chinatowns (LaLande 1981, 289; *San Francisco Pacific News*, 27 September 1849).

FIGURE 3.4.   Typical Chinatowns consisted of attached, narrow, gable-roof structures like these at Yreka, California. (Photo courtesy of Siskiyou County Museum, Yreka, California)

The majority of the Chinese quarters display a similar pattern: rows of attached, narrow, one- to one-and-a-half-story structures with forty-five-degree-pitch roofs (Fig 3.4). The siding is often of unpainted vertical boards and the roof is usually covered with wood shingles or shakes. Some two-story buildings might have a rail-enclosed balcony across the front elevation. In contrast to the often similar Euro-American structures, few of them have false fronts or large windows. Usually a few of the larger structures were of brick or adobe (LaLande 1981, 290).

Although Chinese often rented dwellings from white owners, many relied on their own ingenuity in constructing dwellings and used whatever was available (see Fig. 3.5). Virginia City, Nevada, offers an excellent example:

> On the northwest corner of I and Union streets John has created a marvelous affair. It is built out far enough to occupy a third of the roadway. The front elevation (height 5′) is composed of odds and ends of stone picked up in the neighborhood. The one window is formed of three oil cans—two up right and the other laid across the top. The roof of this edifice—which has a frontage of about 25′ and a depth of 30′ or more—would make a handsome playground for a school as it is perfectly flat and composed of earth. The interior, which the reporter doubled himself up to enter, is divided into numerous little dens and one spacious saloon with earthen floor and one oil-can window. (*Virginia City [Nev.] Virginia Evening Chronicle*, 20 December 1875)

FIGURE 3.5.   The China-town in Virginia City, Nevada, apparently included some subter-ranean structures. (Courtesy of Nevada Historical Society)

Other Chinese quickly adopted the use of oil cans for building material, and soon Virginia City had numerous such structures.

> Underground residences are also popular. A big square hole is dug into the hillside, covered in with sticks, straw, and an occasional plank. The door is naturally furnished by the eastern slope. Although such trifles as light and air are left out of consideration, the bomb-proof character of the underground structure has a charm for the Chinese inhabitant. (*Virginia City [Nev.] Virginia Evening Chronicle,* 20 December 1875)

Still other Chinatowns contained "rag" houses, adobe, and half-tin and -wood structures. As a result of fire, the Chinese sometimes replaced their wooden structures with fireproof brick or adobe ones. As an added precaution against fire, they often constructed special iron-doored storage cellars covered with earth (see *San Francisco Alta California,* 23 January 1856; Magnaghi 1981, 132; *Candelaria [Nev.] True Fissure,* 10 July 1880; Bragg 1976, 21; and "Chinese in Calaveras," 1).

FIGURE 3.6.   In Barkerville's Chinatown, as in most mining-town Chinatowns, the majority of structures consisted of log or frame buildings. (Courtesy of Provincial Archives of British Columbia, C-09748)

Seldom did the structures of mining Chinatowns bear much resemblance to today's popular image of a Chinatown (see Fig. 3.6). Oroville, however, became a center of Chinese mining, and the Chinese built it "in Oriental splendor," the city's *Butte Record* reported on 6 December 1873. "Celestial carpenters have essayed two and three story buildings, and circular covered porches with elaborate railing front the winding street, and present an imposing appearance. An occasional brick supposed to be fire proof, intervenes, and gives an appearance of stolidity to otherwise light and ephemeral shake buildings."

Generally, however, embellishments such as upturned corners, decorative roof tiles, and elaborate millwork associated by the general public with large Chinatowns like those in San Francisco and Los Angeles had few counterparts in the Chinatowns of mining towns (Fig. 3.7). Moreover, even the distinctively Chinese appearance of these Chinatowns apparently developed only in the twentieth century, sometimes even designed by non-Chinese (Greenwood 1993, 397).

Like their rural counterparts, the houses of Chinatown usually held a number of people—anywhere from five to twenty and sometimes more. Seldom do period sources mention the size of these structures. Those at the Lava Beds, California, were twelve by thirty feet in size; those at Idaho City, Idaho, eight by twelve feet; and those at Oro

Fino, Idaho, ten by twenty feet. Probably in urban settings, the Chinese were more likely to rent or buy structures owned and originally built by Euro-Americans (see *North San Juan [Calif.] Hydraulic Press,* 2 April 1859; *Nevada City [Calif.] Daily Transcript,* 7 May 1884; *Weaverville [Calif.] Trinity Times,* 31 March 1855; Derig, 1972, 18; Rohe, 1991, 14; and Stapp and Longenecker 1984, 5). As the *Weaverville Trinity Times* reported on 31 March 1855: "We wish to call attention to the large and rapidly increasing number of Chinese among us, who are continually crowding themselves into every vacant spot they can find. No sooner is some old, miserably clapboard tenement vacated by a white occupant than the owner receives an offer from a Chinaman of a monthly rent nearly equal to the value of the building, and of course John is immediately installed in possession."

In some cases, in fact, Euro-Americans erected buildings expressly to rent to Chinese. Those in Nevada City's Chinatown rented for six, eight, and ten dollars a month in the late 1870s, depending on size (*Nevada City Daily Transcript,* 2 December 1879). Sometimes a Euro-American owned most of a Chinatown, and buildings changed hands between Chinese and whites on many occasions (see *Jacksonville Oregon Sentinel,* 17 July 1878; Sachs 1982, 72; *Virginia City [Nev.] Territorial Enterprise,* 12 July 1873; *Auburn [Calif.] Placer Herald,* 18 April 1857; and *San Francisco Herald,* 13 July 1855).

FIGURE 3.7.   Barkerville's Chinatown, with a streetscape typical of many Chinatowns, differed little from the other parts of Barkerville. (Courtesy of Provincial Archives of British Columbia, C-09303)

Businesses

Typically the Chinese leased buildings in the cheapest and roughest blocks, and there, surrounded by white saloons and brothels, they established their own stores, restaurants, and gambling dens; often temples, opium dens, theaters; and sometimes drugstores, stables, blacksmith shops, laundries, hotels, bakeries, doctors' offices, barbershops, shoeshops, butcher and fish markets, brothels, slaughterhouses, pawnshops, and other structures. Even the smallest Chinatowns contained a variety of commercial buildings. Often, little except size distinguished them from residences. In some Chinatowns, however, large coal-oil lanterns hung in front of each business (see Mann 1979, 399; *Helena Weekly Independent,* 6 April 1876; *Virginia City [Nev.] Territorial Enterprise,* 25 June 1872; *North San Juan [Calif.] Hydraulic Press,* 27 November 1858; *Yreka Journal,* 13 July 1864; *Sioux City Daily Journal,* 23 June 1877; *Weaverville [Calif.] Trinity Journal,* 13 March 1875; *Nevada City Daily Transcript,* 9 January 1879; *Chico [Calif.] Northern Enterprise,* 6 February 1874; and Magnaghi 1981, 138).

The types and number of businesses found in a Chinatown varied by time, geography, population, type of mining, and other factors. In 1858 North San Juan's Chinatown had a population of only a few hundred yet contained several stores, two restaurants, a barbershop, a bakery, a doctor's office, a butcher shop, and numerous gambling establishments (*North San Juan [Calif.] Hydraulic Press,* 2 November 1858). Silver City, Idaho, with a Chinese population of about seven hundred in 1874, had a Masonic temple, two Joss houses, four stores, three or four restaurants, two laundries, two lotteries, five gambling establishments, and many warehouses. In most mining Chinatowns, stores or temples were the most prominent structures (Derig 1972, 18).

Chinese Stores

Because the Chinese preferred traditional food, every mining Chinatown invariably contained one or more stores that featured dried fish, rice, and tea as staples. While the Chinese constructed many of their stores of logs or lumber, as they had their residences, the value of the goods and merchandise that they contained resulted in the construction of more formidable and more fireproof structures of brick or adobe. For example, in 1878 Quong Tre John built a store twenty-six by seventy feet in size of adobe with iron doors and shutters at Dutch Flat, California (*North San Juan [Calif.] Times,* 5 January 1878). After fires, Chinese merchants in several mining Chinatowns constructed stores of rammed earth. These rammed-earth buildings incorporated a heavy ceiling with a foot of dirt between the ceiling and the roof timber, with heavy iron doors and shutters to the outside (*Jackson [Calif.] Amador Dispatch,* 30 May 1868; Brott 1982, 2, 74; Tordoff and Seldner 1986, 5–41). Some merchants constructed small fireproof buildings or cellars at the rear of their stores. The *Deerlodge New North West* of 6 April 1872 described one such building at Deerlodge, Montana: "We noticed yesterday the fireproof building in course of construction in the rear of the store of Al Kane & Co.

(Chinamen.) We have never seen anything like it. The walls are constructed exclusively of clay, which is packed and pounded until it has almost the solidity of brick or stone and the finish of plaster. We dare not venture a description of the process, but if any of our citizens wish to see a novel and apparently substantial structure, they are invited to inspect for themselves. The workmen are all Celestials."

In 1870, the *Auburn [Calif.] Stars and Stripes* described a "Chinese Fire-Proof" at Dutch Flat in detail in the 1 December 1870 issue:

> It is about twelve feet wide, eighteen feet deep and eight feet high in the clear, with walls and roof three feet in thickness. It is built of the red clay that abounds in mines of that vicinity, which was laid up in a softened state into solid, rough walls, which, after hardening some what, were trimmed down with sharp instruments so that they present a surface almost as smooth as glass, and the whole now constitutes a structure than which it would be difficult to conceive one that could be more impervious to heat. In fact, it is constantly becoming harder and more solid, and a fire would have the effect of transforming it into one immense hollow brick. Possibly there are some very devout Christians who might profitably study this piece of "heathen Chinese" mechanism.

Probably the best-documented example of a Chinese rammed-earth store is the Chew Kee store, which still stands, in Fiddletown, California. About 1850, Yee Fan Chung, a herbal doctor, had local Chinese laborers construct a combined herbal store, office, and residence using rammed-earth construction. The resulting building was thirty-four feet long and twenty-one feet wide, with walls twenty-two inches thick. It had centrally located front and rear doors and two front windows, all closed by iron shutters (Costello 1988, 29, 39).

Temples or Joss Houses

Although completely surrounded by an alien culture, the Chinese did not abandon their religion, and a Chinese temple or Joss house often represented the most important or prominent structure in a mining Chinatown. Most period writers referred to the Chinese temples as the Joss or Josh house. "Joss" in pidgin English means idol or deity. It is a corruption of the Portuguese word "Deos," or God, the term that they applied to Oriental idols in the East Indies during the sixteenth century (Wells 1962, 22, 136–37, 157).

While quite ornate in China, Joss houses in western mining towns often showed no or little exterior sign of their religious function. "We have said that the Temple presents a magnificent appearance; so it does as we view the apparently costly fixtures in the interior; outside however, it present the appearance of a very ordinary building no finish, no style, a plain brick with a plainer wooden addition" (*Oroville [Calif.] Mercury,* 20 March 1874). Sojourner temples varied from "mere lean-to's and sheds," to horizontal log structures, to two-story, wood-frame structures with a loft, constructed of board-and-batten sides and a shiplap-sided front, to rather elaborate brick structures. They ranged in size from "one horse Chinese temple" one story high and ten by twelve feet in size to two-story structures twelve by sixty feet or larger with the second story arched. Some had auxiliary structures nearby, but apparently most consisted of a single, one-room building (see Chace 1991, 17–18; Magnaghi 1981, 144; Chinn 1969, 73; Hart 1970, 3, 7; and Derig, 1958–59, 3). Many, like those at Yreka and Shasta, California, had only minor exterior ornamentation. Perhaps paintings on heavy silk hung along each side of the entrance, painted panels with Chinese lettering, or carved wood panels (Hendryx and Rock 1990, 98). At least one, at Eureka, Nevada, had a "gaudily decorated ensign" with an inscription in Chinese character surmounted by the Stars and Stripes. Others, like the one built at Virginia City, Nevada, in 1864, had a pagodalike style with an intricate gate that led into a courtyard. Some had a long front porch, others had none; many had a recessed entrance. The fronts were painted, most commonly blue and white, to resemble light-blue glazed brick or tile with white mortar (see *Nevada City [Calif.] Daily Transcript*, 14 May 1869; *Nevada City [Calif.] Herald*, 26 August 1879; *Eureka [Nev.] Sentinel*, 23 January 1876; and *Virginia City [Nev.] Virginia Evening Chronicle*, 3 and 21 November 1876).

The size and prosperity of a given Chinatown seemed to strongly influence the number and character of temples. Some of them, like those at Virginia City, Nevada, and Weaverville, Oroville, and Dutch Flat, California, "fixed up in the highest style of oriental art," recalled the native form (see *Virginia City Virginia Evening Chronicle*, 21 November 1876; *Oroville Mercury*, 11 September 1873; Christopher 1975, 54; and Goodyear 1973, 3).

In 1874 Duncan MacKenzie described the "Chinese temple" at Dutch Flat: "It is enclosed with a high fence and is facing the sun [south]. It is painted and gilded all over on the outside with oriental figurines. There is a yard about an acre and a half in front of it which is made as smooth [*sic*] as it can be" (qtd. in Christopher 1975, 54). It stood on an eminence near town. The Chinese "painted the building blue, with green and red finish, richly embellished with handsome carvings and an immense amount of gold leaf" (*Auburn [Calif.] Placer Herald*, 13 June 1874).

Geomancy

Conceivably, the Chinese had more freedom of choice about planning and siting their mining camps than they had in a Chinatown, yet some scholars suggest that even here the Chinese applied geomantic principles. Mueller, for example, contends it influenced the laying out of the Chinatown at Yreka, California. In the 1850s a Chinese quarters developed on the east side of Yreka, north of Center Street and fronting Main Street on the east and west. At the juncture of Main and Center Streets, Main cants to a truer northern direction. The Chinese buildings shift even slightly more toward north, noticeable in a corner protruding onto Center Street. "This places Chinatown into a relatively standard and traditional orientation. There is north-south placement of structures and the main avenue is similarly aligned, but east-west auxiliary passages are not definite. Courtyards are not evident. The broadest building exposure is again east-west, and south appears to be the logical means of access" (Mueller 1987, 20).

A second Chinatown, begun in 1889, occupied land south of the eastern end of Center Street.

> Once again traditional north-south orientation and attendant siting principles can be observed. Of particular interest here, however, is that following the 1890 flood a row of locust trees was planted west of the boardwalk. Here is an unequivocal feng shui remedy for the effects of Yreka Creek. The terrain of both Chinatowns is fairly flat, with only a slight rise towards the west. From a distance, the surrounding mountains form an almost complete horseshoe with an opening facing south. This is traditionally the ideal feng shui formation, strengthened even more by the higher peaks west and north (yang), the gentler slopes east (yin), and an unobstructed southern vista. In considering the vast amount of mountainous terrain surrounding this locale, it is notable that there are no ridges directed at the town. In feng shui such a situation would constitute a "straight arrow" and be indicative of *sha* [malign currents] within the vicinity. (Mueller 1987, 20)

Using historical photographs, Mueller further examined the roofline of buildings. He found the pitched roofs had variable heights with no two adjunct roofs having equal dimensions. Thus, according to Mueller, Yreka had an irregular skyline and avoided "straight arrows" that might induce *sha*.

Contrary to the principles of feng-shui, Sanborn maps show Chinese buildings in city after city as contiguous in straight lines, not square, often in areas subject to flooding, not facing south, and so on. We cannot know whether the Chinese used mirrors, trees, or other talismans to offset the effect of bad feng-sha or whether they simply did not observe the principles of feng-shui. Moreover, feng-shui includes many principles that almost anyone would consider desirable when siting residences, shops, stores, et cetera. Further, the Chinese showed great resourcefulness in using whatever building materials were at hand and practicality in reusing existing habitations. The Chinese apparently set aside feng-shui principles when the socioeconomic situation required them to do so. If the Chinese continued their practice of feng shui in North America, perhaps where they were most likely to do so was in their religious structures. Chace found that the surviving temples in California apparently reflect both a traditional Chinese religious philosophy and geomantic view. Each appears to be situated with respect to flowing water near the edge of the settlement and to stand as a spiritual barrier to evil (Greenwood 1993, 384–86; Chace 1991, 17–19).

Conclusion

While our knowledge of Chinese mining camps continues to increase yearly, especially as the result of the work of archaeologists, it remains possible to compare them with Euro-American camps only in the most general way. Indeed, Maniery and Tordoff characterized Chinese mining camps as appearing "similar to those used by Anglos with the addition of Chinese materials" (1988, 5). It seems that while the physical characteristics of a site affected how both Chinese and Euro-American miners located and laid out their camps, culture in the form of feng shui played an important role in what the

Chinese did, at least in some areas. It appears likely that Euro-American mining camps had a more homogeneous appearance. While Euro-American miners almost always built log or frame structures, the Chinese used a great variety of building material (logs, lumber, rammed earth, adobe, stone, earth, branches, etc.). The Chinese apparently made much greater use of tents and as a result constructed more cobblestone and earthen hearths for cooking outside. Chinese mining camps typically had a somewhat higher number of residents per dwelling, and the dwellings were placed closer together.

Because Chinese miners seldom voluntarily abandoned a site as long as it provided subsistence, and they had strong cultural ties that united them (common surnames, speech, or place of origin), it is possible that Chinese mining camps had a longer duration and more stable population than their Euro-American counterparts. Euro-American mining camps typically contained a polyglot population—Americans, English, Irish, Germans, Cornish, French, and others. The Chinese camps contained not only solely Chinese but also Chinese who typically came from one village or several adjacent villages in China and often consisted of family or clan associations. They invariably had fewer women and children than Euro-American mining camps. Euro-American mining camps seem to have supported a larger number and greater variety of businesses. Some Chinese mining camps consisted almost entirely of residences with a common eating-place that shared a centrally located store, blacksmith shop, and Joss house with several adjacent Chinese camps. The stores in Chinese mining camps typically served a greater variety of functions than those of Euro-American camps; included areas for opium smoking, gambling, eating, praying; and served as news outlets and social centers and sometimes as banks and interpretation centers.

Chinese mining camps often show the use of terraced building sites and gardens. In addition, the Chinese commonly planted a particular plant, Tree of Heaven (*Ailanthus altissima),* at their camps. Euro-American miners apparently had no similar tradition. Today, the sites of Chinese mining camps can often be easily distinguished from Euro-American ones by an artifact assemblage that includes food remains and food preparation utensils characteristic of traditional Chinese diets, parts of opium containers and opium-smoking paraphernalia, Chinese liquor bottles, gaming pieces, and many artifacts showing adaptive reuse.

The Chinese quarters of mining towns resembled more than differed from those of nonmining towns, especially if they were of comparable size. There were, however, some differences, and the most obvious ones resulted from the larger size of the nonmining Chinatowns. The larger Chinatowns might contain a population consisting of a number of clans and dialect groups, while the Chinese quarters of mining towns typically contained only one or two. Usually, the larger the Chinatown, the greater the number and variety of businesses it contained. They also more likely had more permanent structures of brick or stone, more multistory buildings, more buildings that looked distinctly Chinese, and a population that included more women and children. The larger nonmining Chinatowns were more likely to have a Chinese school, hospital, theater, district association headquarters, Masonic Hall, Chinese dead house (for storage of bones awaiting shipment to China), and a great number of and more elaborate temples.

Reflecting the cultural and physical environment of the American West, the structures of mining-town Chinatowns and Chinese mining camps typically bore little resemblance to those of South China. Most reflected the economic and social status of the sojourners who built them. Since few immigrants brought their families or intended to stay in North America, they had little need or desire to try to replicate the villages of South China. The Chinese showed great resourcefulness and ingenuity in the adaptive reuse of Euro-American structures and their employment of available construction materials.

Though subtle, the camps and Chinatowns did show the culture of their inhabitants' homeland in some ways. Chinatowns, for example, showed maximum use of space, blocks divided by alleys and passageways, door and lintel inscriptions, structures sharing a wall, the use of geomancy (feng-shui), and rammed-earth (*hang-t'u*) construction. Most Chinatowns and some of the larger Chinese mining camps contained the distinctly Chinese Joss house or temple, some of which resembled almost exactly those of China. Their dominantly Chinese male populations, their distinctive occupational structure, their compact and often uniform residential structures, and their Joss houses, opium dens, stores, and restaurants gave Chinatowns a distinctive visual quality. Though Chinese were typically denigrated by whites for their noise, smelly filth, and vices, whites often owned the land, if not the buildings, and white racism and discrimination contributed to both the existence of and the conditions found in Chinatowns.

Works Cited

Barth, Gunther. 1964. *Bitter Strength: A History of the Chinese in the United States, 1850–1870.* Cambridge: Harvard University Press.

Borthwick, J. D. 1948. *Three Years in California.* Oakland: BioBooks.

Bowen, Lynne. 1982. *Boss Whistle: The Coal Miners of Vancouver Island Remembered.* Lantzville, B.C.: Oolichan Books.

Bragg, Allen C. 1976. *Humboldt County, 1905.* Winnemucca, Nev.: North Central Nevada Historical Society.

Brott, Clark W. 1982. *Moon Lee One: Life in Old Chinatown, Weaverville, California.* Redding, Calif.: Great Basin Foundation.

Chace, Paul G. 1991. "The Oldest Chinese Temples in California, a Landmarks Tour." *Gum Sann Journal* 14 (June): 1–19.

Chin, Art. 1977. *Golden Tassels: A History of the Chinese in Washington, 1857–1977.* Seattle: Art Chin.

"The Chinese in Calaveras County." 1973. *Chinese Historical Society of America Bulletin* 8 (April): 1.

Chinn, Thomas W., ed. 1969. *A History of the Chinese in California.* San Francisco: Chinese Historical Society of America.

Chiu, Ping. 1963. *Chinese Labor in California, 1850–1880.* Madison: State Historical Society of Wisconsin.

Christopher, Paul. 1975. "Placer County in 1874: The Letters of Duncan MacKenzie." *Pacific Historian* 19 (Spring): 50–57.

Costello, Julia G. 1988. *Archaeological and Historical Studies at the Chew Kee Store, Fiddletown.* Mokelumne Hill, Calif.: Foothill Resource Association.

Derig, Betty. 1958–59. "The Chinese of Silver City." *Idaho Yesterdays,* Winter, 2–5.

———. 1972. "Celestials in the Diggings." *Idaho Yesterdays,* March, 2–23.

Fredlund, Lynn, et al. 1991. *Archeological Investigations in the German Gulch Historic District (24 SB 212): A Historic Chinese and Euroamerican Placer Mining Area in Southwestern Montana.* Vol. 1. Butte: GCM Services.

Free, Jeffrey M. 1991. "A Dragon in the Eagles's Land: Chinese in an Idaho Wilderness, Warren Mining District, ca 1870–1900." Master's thesis, University of Idaho.

Goodyear, Gene. 1973. "The Chinese in Trinity County." Typescript. Shasta College, Redding, Calif.

Goss, Helen Rocca. 1954. "When East Was East in the Old West." *Historical Society of Southern California Quarterly* 36 (December): 292–311.

Greenwood, Roberta S. 1993. "Old Approaches and New Directions: Implications for Future Research." In *Hidden Heritage: Historical Archaeology of the Overseas Chinese,* ed. Priscilla Wegars, 375–403. Amityville, Calif.: Baywood.

Hart, William. 1970. "The Chinese in Shasta and Weaverville." Typescript. Shasta College, Redding, Calif.

Hendryx, Michael, and James T. Rock. 1990. "The Chinese in Siskiyou County: A Glimpse from Yreka." *Siskiyou Pioneer* 6, 3: 1–152.

James, Ron. 1990. "The Mon-Tung Site: Chinese Gold Miners in the Snake River Canyon." Paper presented at the forty-third annual Northwest Anthropological Conference, 22–24 March, Eugene, Ore.

Kingsbury, Lawrence. 1989. "Data Recovery at Ah Toy's Occupation 10-IH-1876: On the South Fork of the Salmon River, Idaho." Paper presented at "Chinese Windows on the Past: A Workshop on the Archaeology of Chinese on the Western Frontier," 22–26 May, Boise, Idaho.

LaLande, Jeffrey M. 1981. "Sojourners in the Oregon Siskiyous: Adaptation and Acculturation of the Chinese Miners in the Applegate Valley, ca 1855–1900." Master's thesis, Oregon State University.

MacDonald, Eileen Hubbell. 1966. "A Study of Chinese Migrants in Certain Idaho Settlements and of Selected Families in Transition." Master's thesis, University of Idaho.

Magnaghi, Russel M. 1981. "Virginia City's Chinese Community, 1860–1880." *Nevada Historical Society Quarterly* 24: 130–57.

Maniery, Mary L., and Judith D. Tordoff. 1988. "Chinese Mining Camps in Northern California." Paper presented at the annual meeting of the Society for Historical Archaeology, 14–16 January, Reno, Nevada.

Mann, Ralph. 1979. "Community Change and Caucasian Attitudes toward the Chinese: The Case of Two California Mining Towns, 1850–1870." In *American Working Class Culture,* ed. Milton Cantor, 397–422. Westport: Greenwood.

McLeod, Alexander. 1947. *Pigtails and Gold Dust.* Caldwell: Caxton Printers.

Mead, George R. 1994. *Two Dragon Camp: A Chinese Settlement in the Camp Carson Mining Area, Union County, Oregon.* LaGrande: Wallowa-Whitman National Forest.

Minnick, Sylvia Sun. 1988. *Samfow: The San Joaquin Chinese Legacy.* Fresno: West.

Mueller, Fred W., Jr. 1987. "Feng Shui: Archaeological Evidence for Geomancy in Overseas Chinese Settlements." In *Wong Ho Leun: An American Chinatown,* 1–24. San Diego: Great Basin Foundation.

Praetzellis, Adrian, Mary Praetzellis, and Marley Brown III. 1987. "Artifacts as Symbols of Identity: An Example from Sacramento's Gold Rush Era Chinese Community." In *Living in Cities: Current Research in Urban Archaeology,* ed. Edward Staski, 38–47. Special Pub. Ser., No. 5. Ann Arbor: Society for Historical Archaeology.

Pricer, Barbara. 1991. "Chinese in Plumas County." *Plumas County Museum Newsletters* 3 (May): 1–5.

Ritchie, Neville A. 1993. "Form and Adaptation: Nineteenth Century Chinese Miners' Dwellings in Southern New Zealand." In *Hidden Heritage: Historical Archaeology of the Overseas Chinese,* ed. Priscilla Wegars, 335–73. Amityville, Calif.: Baywood.

Rohe, Randall E. 1982. "After the Gold Rush: Chinese Mining in the Far West, 1850–1890." *Montana, the Magazine of Western History* 32 (autumn): 2–19.

———. 1991. "Chinese Mining and Settlement at the Lava Beds, California." Paper presented at the annual meeting of the Mining History Association, 5–6 July, Leadville, Colo.

Sachs, Mark. 1982. *Aspects of Chinese Living and Working Spaces in Historical Barkerville.* Barkerville, B.C.: Barkerville Historic Park.

Shaw, William. 1973. *Golden Dreams, and Waking Realities.* New York: Arno.

Shay, Frank. 1876. *Chinese Immigration: The Social, Moral and Political Effect.* Sacramento, Calif.: State Printing Office.

Sisson, David A. 1993. "Archaeological Evidence of Chinese Use along the Lower Salmon River, Idaho." In *Hidden Heritage: Historical Archaeology of the Overseas Chinese,* ed. Priscilla Wegars, 33–63. Amityville, Calif.: Baywood.

Smith, Mary Halderman. 1983. "Chinese Placer Mining and Site Formation Process." Paper presented at the annual meeting of the Society for California Archaeology, 23–26 March, San Diego, Calif.

Stapp, Darby C., and Julia Longenecker. 1984. *1983 Test Excavations at 10-CW-159: The Pierce Chinese Mining Site.* Anthropological Research Ms. Ser., No. 80. Moscow: University of Idaho.

Stevens, Dennis W. 1992. "Cultural Resource Inventory of the North Yuba Trail Project, Sierra County, Downieville Ranger District, Tahoe National Forest." *Report No. 1023.* Nevada City, Calif.: Tahoe National Forest.

Survey of Cultural Resources at Malakoff Diggings State Historic Park. 1979. Sacramento, Calif.: Resource Agency, California Department of Parks and Recreation.

Tordoff, Judy D., and Dana McGowan Seldner. 1986. *Cottonwood Creek Project: Shasta and Tehama Counties, California; Excavation at Thirteen Historic Sites in the Cottonwood Mining District.* Sacramento: Hornet Foundation, California State University.

Wells, Marian Kaye. 1962. "Chinese Temples in California." Master's thesis, University of California, Berkeley.

Wikoff, Melvin D. 1972. "Chinese in the Idaho County Gold Fields, 1864–1933." Master's thesis, Texas A&I University.

Williams, Stephen. 1971. "The Chinese in the California Mines, 1848–1860." Master's thesis, Stanford University.

Wright, Robert T. 1987. *Quesnelle Forks: A Goldrush Town in Historical Perspective.* Barkerville, B.C.: Friends of Barkerville Historical Society.

Wynne, Robert E. 1964. "Reaction to the Chinese in the Pacific Northwest and British Columbia, 1850 to 1910." Ph.D. diss., University of Washington.

Yancey, Anna Larson. 1960. "When the Chinese Came to Trinity Center." In *1960 Yearbook of the Trinity County Historical Society,* 16–17. Trinity, Calif.: Trinity County Historical Society.

Emma J. Teng

4   Artifacts of a Lost City: Arnold Genthe's *Pictures of Old Chinatown* and Its Intertexts

From the moment when you crossed the golden, dimpling bay, whose moods ran the gamut of beauty, from the moment when you sailed between those brown-and-green headlands which guarded the Gate to San Francisco, you heard always of Chinatown. It was the first thing which the tourists asked to see, the first thing which the guides offered to show. . . . Raised on a hillside, it glimpsed you from every corner of that older, more picturesque San Francisco which fell to dust and cinders in the great disaster of 1906. . . . For him who came but to look and enjoy, this was the real heart of San Francisco, this bit of the mystic, suggestive East, so modified by the West that it was neither Oriental nor yet Occidental—but just Chinatown.

      —Will Irwin, "Old Chinatown"

For Will Irwin and his bohemian associates, Arnold Genthe and Frank Norris, Chinatown exerted a unique lure: It was a setting of squalor and romance that made artists and writers of ordinary San Franciscans. With its dark streets, twisted alleys, underground catacombs, and opium dens, Chinatown was a place that the casual tourist dared not enter unguided, and a place where the unchaperoned slummer reveled in mystery and danger. It was the perfect milieu for sensationalist stories and picturesque photographs, for purportedly Chinatown's glittering showy surface covered a hidden realm of darkness.[1] This was the image of Chinatown immortalized in the literary works of Norris and Irwin, and the photographs of Genthe. Genthe, Norris and, to a lesser extent, Irwin were key interpreters of San Francisco Chinatown for the turn-of-the-twentieth-century U.S. reading public. Their artistic works thus helped to shape the popular imagination about the Chinese Quarter and its Chinese American inhabitants.

    The Chinatown of which Irwin writes—"Old Chinatown"—vanished for the bohemians after the 1906 San Francisco earthquake. Gone, along with the old buildings and urban environment, they declared, was the romance. Nostalgic for the old Quarter, they viewed the new Chinatown built in its place as nothing more than a distorted replica. In their eyes, the "true" Chinatown survived only as mimetic artifact—in photographs, literary stories, and recollections. Published in 1908, Arnold Genthe's *Pictures of Old Chinatown* served as a locus for the collective memories of the bohemian slummers who had made Chinatown their haunt before the earthquake.[2] Bringing together Genthe's photographs, Will Irwin's memoir "Old Chinatown" (written to accompany the photographs), and allusions to Frank Norris's short story "The Third Circle," the volume creates an evocative, intertextual reading of this city space.

Frank Norris's "Third Circle" (1897) provides the most powerful trope for structuring this set of collective memories of Old Chinatown. In the famous opening lines of his story Norris writes: "There are more things in San Francisco's Chinatown than are dreamed of in Heaven and earth. In reality there are three parts of Chinatown—the part the guides show you, the part the guides don't show you, and the part that no one ever hears of" (1928b, 1). This last part is the notorious third circle. The trope of the three circles is powerful because it spatializes the types of activities and experiences associated with Chinatown, as well as the outsider's relationship to the Quarter. This trope exerted an enormous influence over the manner in which Irwin and Genthe conceptualized Old Chinatown.

In *Pictures,* Irwin and Genthe mourn not the loss of Chinese life occasioned by the earthquake, but the loss of the Chinatown cityscape. In order to understand the nostalgia for the Old Chinatown, it is necessary first to explore the meanings attributed to this cityscape. In doing so we can begin to see how readings of Chinatown's architectural setting helped to shape the public image of its residents. Indeed, the architectural environment of Old Chinatown was at the heart of its sensationalist reputation and of the mystery that it exerted.[3]

Chinatown was a domain of what Anthony Vidler has termed "the architectural uncanny," architectural or urban space that stages the sensations associated with the uncanny: dread, a sense of lurking unease, suspicion, claustrophobia, and estrangement (1994). The most famous architectural feature of Chinatown was the fabled network of subterranean passageways linking the entire district underground. Cellars were said to have been dug three or four stories down, and to be connected by trapdoors or tunnels. The underground chambers were purportedly used for gambling, prostitution, opium smoking, and other illegal activities. The existence of these deep caverns is most likely apocryphal. The San Francisco Board of Supervisors' Chinatown survey of 1885 reported only the existence of basements and sub-basements (Farwell and Kunkler 1885). Nonetheless, the tunnels formed the stuff of urban legend, much like the sewers of Paris. Popularly imagined as a world of cellars, Chinatown was primed for staging the sensations of the uncanny, for, as Bachelard has shown, cellars are evocative of the irrational and of irrational fears.[4]

A second element of Chinatown's uncanniness lay in its cultural otherness. In Freud's formulation, the uncanny, *das Unheimliche,* literally the "unhomely," has its roots in the defamiliarization of the *Heimliche,* the "homely."[5] With its dark alleys, labyrinthian cellars, unintelligible shop signs, and foreign-looking inhabitants, Chinatown was an "unhomely" space to white Americans both spatially and culturally. It was a space that existed within San Francisco itself, but that seemed somehow to belong to China. Turn-of-the-century writers often described stepping into Chinatown as stepping into another world.

Chinatown space was also uncanny to white Americans, for it represented what Freud termed the "return of the repressed"—that which "ought to have remained hidden but has come to light" (1962, 241). The physical space of San Francisco Chinatown was associated with activities white bourgeois society sought to keep hidden: the dirty secrets of vice and miscegenation. On a more abstract level, Chinatown became a symbol for the darkest aspects of human nature that lie submerged beneath the surface of civilized society. In "The Third Circle," Norris evokes this image of Chinatown as the repressed that threatens to return:

> There are a good many stories that might be written about this third circle of Chinatown, but believe me, they never will be written—at any rate not until the "town" has been, as it were, drained off from the city, as one might drain a noisome swamp, and we shall be able to see the strange, dreadful life that wallows down there in the lowest ooze of the place—wallows and grovels there in the mud and the dark. (1928b, 1)[6]

The architectural uncanny is central to Norris's uncanny tale—as it is to Genthe's pictorial representation of Chinatown. The notion of the architectural uncanny also helps us see how the image of Chinatown as cityscape and the public image of the Chinese as a people were intertwined. Turn-of-the-century writers, guidebooks, and politicians all suggested a connection between the physical setting of Chinatown and its reputed moral atmosphere. The dark spaces of alleys and hidden lairs called to mind the "dark side" of Chinatown life: gambling, prostitution, the trade in slave girls, and opium dens. The Chinese "underworld" of highbinders and tongs was literalized as an underworld of subterranean passages. Chinatown was thus a spatial enactment of moral conditions—crookedness, twistedness, darkness, and concealment.

Chinatown: The Setting

The construction of the original San Francisco Chinatown began in the 1850s after the gold rush. In the 1870s, as white residents began to move out of the original downtown district around Portsmouth Square and up to fashionable Nob Hill, the Chinese expanded into the old commercial center. By 1885, Chinatown came to occupy a twelve-block area centered on Dupont Street. In this district were mostly two- and three-story brick buildings, many with Italianate Victorian or French facades. As Philip Choy (1990) has documented, very few of the new Chinatown buildings were constructed in Chinoiserie style, a decorative style incorporating motifs associated with China (e.g., the pagoda roof). Rather, Chinese residents adapted the existing buildings to suit their lifestyles and need for space. Lanterns, banners, Chinese-character signs, and other decorative elements made the district distinctively Chinese. In the eyes of white American tourists, this sufficed to transform the old commercial center into a Chinese city. Chinatown was frequently called "the Canton of the West," or "a piece of China transplanted" onto American soil.

This idea of transformation is key to the architectural uncanniness of Chinatown. If the uncanny arises from the transformation of the once familiar (the homely), into the unfamiliar (the unhomely), Chinatown was uncanny because it retained the traces of its former identity as San Francisco's business district—familiarly Old World European—but metamorphosed into something foreign and strange. Chinatown was seen as belonging to, yet apart from, the body of San Francisco, a microcosm of the Orient seemingly complete unto itself. Chinatown was thus a liminal space within the larger San Francisco cityscape.

This liminal quality in part explains Chinatown's popularity as a vice resort for working-class whites until the 1890s (see Light 1974, 372). It was this role as a redlight district that initially gave Chinatown its sensational reputation, a reputation that it shared with San Francisco's Barbary Coast as a whole. In the 1880s and 1890s, Chinatown attracted increasing numbers of bourgeois tourists who came to view the vice district and tenements as if it were a type of zoo. In response to this growing tourist trade, certain Chinese entrepreneurs began to capitalize on Chinatown's seedy reputation by hiring whites familiar with the area to serve as guides to show the "secret" parts of the Quarter. They sometimes even went so far as to hire Chinese to stage mock tong battles to cater to tourist expectations of danger and crime. "A favorite show was a knife-wielding scuffle between 'opium crazed' Chinese in dispute over a slave-girl" (Light 1974, 390).

It was this idea of danger that immediately attracted Genthe to Chinatown upon his arrival in San Francisco from Germany in 1895. As he recalled in his memoir: "Like all good tourists I had a Baedeker. A sentence saying, 'It is not advisable to visit the Chinese quarter unless one is accompanied by a guide,' intrigued me. There is a vagabond streak in me which balks at caution. As soon as I could make myself free, I was on my way to Chinatown, where I was to go again and again" (1936, 32).

Ultimately, the bohemian slummers would reject the tour guide version of Chinatown as "inauthentic." Nonetheless, this packaged First Circle served as a foil against which they constructed their own ventures into "those parts the guides don't show you."

The First Circle: Tourist Guidebooks

The guidebook warning that Genthe refers to appears in the 1893 edition of Baedeker's travel handbook for the United States. The San Francisco entry declares: "The *Chinese Quarter* is one of the most interesting and characteristic features of San Francisco, and no one should leave the city without visiting it; . . . the most interesting time to visit it is at night, when everything is in full swing until after midnight, and it is then necessary to be accompanied by a regular guide" (1893, 431). Despite the danger, Chinatown was a must-see: Baedeker gave it a star for noteworthiness. The notion of Chinatown as a place of interest was connected to broader notions of what made San Francisco special as a city: its links to Asia and the China trade; the cultural diversity provided by its numerous ethnic enclaves; and the Gold Rush exuberance and decadence of the notorious Barbary Coast.

A rather more evocative physical description of Chinatown as tourist locale is provided in Samuel Williams's *The City of the Golden Gate: A Description of San Francisco*:

> The Chinese quarter is a system of alleys and passages, labyrinthian in their sinuosities, into which the sunlight never enters; where it is dark and dismal, even at noonday. A stranger attempting to explore them, would be speedily and hopelessly lost. Many of them seem mere slits in the flanks of the streets—dirty rivulets flowing into the great stream of life. Often they have no exit—terminating in a foul court, a dead wall, a gambling or opium den. They literally swarm with life; for this human hive is never at rest. (Williams 1875, 38)

While Baedeker only hints at the perils awaiting the tourist in Chinatown, Williams describes the physical setting of this danger. It is not simply that Chinatown is crime ridden—the actual spatial layout itself, described in terms much like the jungle, poses a threat to the novice.

Chinatown had no architectural landmarks on the level of San Francisco's Mission Dolores or Palace Hotel. Rather, it was a conglomerate of anonymous architectural elements that created a distinct urban environment. Thus, while the tourist might "see" the Mission Dolores or other city "sights," Chinatown was something for the tourist to "do" (Owen 1887, 638). Chinatown was not simply an object to be gazed at, but a space to be moved through, explored.

Michel de Certeau opens his "Walking in the City" with a view of Manhattan from the 110th floor of the former World Trade Center. He speaks of the power of the voyeur, elevated above the walkers below—who are the "ordinary practitioners of the city" (1984, 93)—able to command a view of the entire city, to look down on it like gods. Surveying becomes an act of rational ordering of the space. This panoramic or panoptic view of the city has been the privileged view in Western culture, especially since the nineteenth century. The cityscape of Old Chinatown, in contrast, was not to be viewed with the surveying eye. It was a place for walkers; to see it, one had to move into it, stroll through it. In Chinatown, the tourist is immersed down below in the fabric of the city, with, as de Certeau puts it, one's body "clasped by the streets that turn and return it" (92).

Held within its dark and narrow alleys, the view of the whole always withheld, the tourist wanders through Chinatown's labyrinthine alleys or cellars, perhaps unwittingly observed from above. The tourist is at once a voyeur and one who imagines himself watched by unseen eyes. He experiences not power and control, not the ability to order space, but claustrophobia and a surrender to the possibility of being lost. The possibility of losing oneself is coupled with the possibility of finding some treasure; it is only the walker in the city who can experience the pleasure of random discovery. Therein lies the thrill of Chinatown, an escape from the rational and the ordered. The impulse of the Chinatown tourist is not to climb on high and survey, but to explore its cellars, to submerge himself in the irrational. The thrill is similar to that of the Spooky House at the county fair, where one fumbles through the darkness waiting to be spooked. Indeed, Old Chinatown was a type of amusement park for the bohemian flaneur, that peculiar breed of walker/voyeur.

The Second Circle: Bohemian Slumming

Frank Norris, Arnold Genthe, and Will Irwin were three San Francisco figures whose art was intimately associated with their flaneurie—their observations of and participation in the city's street life. The three men came to know each other through their membership in the San Franciscan Bohemian Club, a prestigious club of writers, artists, theater people, musicians, and other bon vivants founded in 1872, whose members had an avid interest in Oriental art and culture. The three were, furthermore, involved with the weekly publication the *Wave,* founded in 1887. Norris was subeditor of the *Wave* for a time, and many of his most famous short stories and sketches, including "The Third Circle," were originally published in this periodical; Irwin, most renowned as a journalist, succeeded Norris as subeditor; and Genthe published many of his photographs and a few articles in the *Wave*.[7] Like other bohemians of their time, the three were fond of slumming.

Chinatown appealed to bohemian slummers as an escape from Western bourgeois society. It also possessed a mixture of beauty and squalor, of the picturesque and the exotic, that held a particular charm for San Franciscans longing for the patina of the Old World. Will Irwin described Chinatown as a kind of paradise for the would-be artist: "Dirty. . . . But always beautiful—falling everywhere into pictures. . . . From every doorway flashed a group, an arrangement, which suggested the Flemish masters. . . . Such pictures glimpsed about every corner" (Genthe 1913, 45). More bohemian than Orientalist perhaps, Irwin chooses an Old World European allusion rather than the exotica of Delacroix or Gérôme as his artistic point of reference, comparing the Chinatown cityscape to the works of the Flemish masters, known for their naturalistic genre paintings of scenes from daily life.

In the same vein, the tenements of Chinatown provided ample material for naturalist fiction. In "A Plea for Romantic Fiction," a manifesto for his own brand of naturalism, Norris asserts the link between slum squalor and romance. Criticizing those who see romance only in tales of the Middle Ages or the Renaissance, he declares that "this very day, in this very hour, she is sitting among the rags and wretchedness, the dirt and despair of the tenements of the East Side of New York" (1899, 343). For Norris, the Chinatown tenements were similarly home to romance.

Genthe shared with Norris and Irwin this tendency to aestheticize poverty. He articulated this aesthetic pictorially through both content and formal qualities. In a photograph entitled "Where Beauty and Squalor Mingle," Genthe shows a "rags, bottles, sacks man" collecting refuse on a horse cart counterpoised to a Chinese woman and children dressed in festival clothes (Tchen 1984, pl. 8). The mottled messiness of the refuse collector set against the tenement backdrop contrasts with the simplicity of the beautiful figures framed against a black backdrop of shadowed sidewalk: drudgery juxtaposed to refined leisure. This shared aesthetic sensibility, the tendency to see romance in squalor, makes Norris's "Third Circle," and Genthe's *Pictures of Old Chinatown* fitting intertexts.

"The Third Circle"—Norris's Vision of Chinatown

In his highly celebrated depiction of Chinatown's heart of darkness, "The Third Circle," Norris tells the uncanny story of the disappearance of a white woman in Chinatown. The story begins with a flashback, recounting a visit to Chinatown by the young Hillegas and his fiancée, Miss Ten Eck (both easterners). Norris describes Harriet Ten Eck, "Harry," as having the fresh, vigorous, healthful prettiness "only seen in certain types of unmixed American stock" (1928b, 3). The two tourists are charmed by exotic Chinatown and proclaim that they have left both America and the nineteenth century behind. They wander into a deserted restaurant off the tourist track on Waverly Place, the Seventy Moons. Strolling onto a balcony, they spy a fortune-teller on the steps of the joss house below and call him up to tell their fortunes. This man turns out to be not a fortune-teller but a tattoo artist, and Miss Ten Eck decides on a whim to have a butterfly tattooed on her little finger. When the tattoo is completed, Hillegas ventures downstairs to hurry the waiter. He returns to find Miss Ten Eck vanished: "He never saw her again. No white man ever did" (6).

With this abrupt ending of the story within a story, the narrative shifts twenty years forward in time. Curious about the fate of Miss Ten Eck, the narrator seeks advice from a Chinatown "insider," Manning, who tells him that no one had heard word of Miss Ten Eck since Hillegas's detective was finished off by a See Yup "two-knife" hitman from Peking. He suggests visiting Sadie, one of three white women living in an opium-den slave-girl joint, to make inquiries. The two men find the women four stories beneath a hide-tanning room, rolling yen-shee pills from the scrapings of opium pipes, in a room the size of a trunk.

At first the narrator cannot make out that the women, dressed as they are in Chinese clothes and speaking Chinese, are white women. Norris describes Sadie as a picture of human degeneration: "She was smoking a cigar, and from time to time spat through her teeth man-fashion. She was a dreadful looking beast of a woman, wrinkled like a shrivelled apple, her teeth quite black from nicotine, her hands bony and prehensile, like a hawk's claws—but a white woman beyond all doubt" (1928b, 8).

Sadie is mute and regains the ability to speak English only when plied with liquor. The two men interrogate Sadie about why she doesn't return to her "people" or at least to the Mission House. Sadie responds, "Like um China boy better"—for Ah Yee gives her plenty to eat and smoke, and as much yen-shee as she likes (1928b, 9). They ask her whether she has ever heard of Miss Ten Eck, a woman "stolen by Chinamen here in San Francisco a long time ago" (10). Sadie remembers neither having heard the name Harriett Ten Eck, nor how she herself came to the opium den. She finally holds out her left hand and asks, "Say, how did I get that on me?" (10). We see a butterfly tattooed on her little finger. The story ends with this uncanny image of the tattoo, the sign that shows Sadie and Miss Ten Eck to be one and the same, and yet not the same. With this revelation, Norris demonstrates the woman's reversion to an atavistic state of being, aware only of primal needs and desires.

Norris's story plays on the stock pulp-fiction theme of white slavery but gives it a far more complex treatment. Through the device of the three circles, Miss Ten Eck's descent into the most hidden level of Chinatown is figured as a descent into hell. With imagery alluding to Dante's inferno, the third circle is depicted as an underground chamber, the fourth story down in a series of ever-descending levels. As in Dante, a guide leads the narrator through this netherworld, where he is a spectator to horrors while remaining himself immune. Harry Ten Eck is caught in a circle of hell reserved for "fallen" white women who are condemned to ceaselessly roll yen-shee at a frantic pace. In this hell, the fresh-faced girl has reverted to a blackened, shriveled, prehensile "beast of a woman."

The descent away from civilization in "The Third Circle" is also a movement toward a kind of heart of darkness. Here, the primitive in the seemingly civilized emerges from beneath the surface. With its subterranean caverns and its dense tangle of alleys impenetrable by sunlight, Chinatown is an urban wilderness that serves the same function for Ten Eck that the African jungle serves for Joseph Conrad's Kurtz. Having been immersed in the jungle, Kurtz responds to the "heavy mute spell of the wilderness that seemed to draw him to its pitiless breast by the awakening of forgotten and brutal instincts, by the memory of gratified and monstrous passions" (Conrad 1988, 65). Ten Eck, too, submerged in the third circle, has awakened to "forgotten" and "brutal" instincts. In this space, Harry/Sadie is freed from the restrictions of bourgeois society, which forbade her to smoke, drink, spit, take yen-shee, or openly tattoo her arm. As a tale of an urban heart of darkness, Norris's short story is not simply a sensationalist account of Chinatown degeneracy, but also an exploration of the dark forces that lie beneath the veneer of civilization.

Reversion and degeneration constituted two of the main themes of Norris's fiction. For Norris, the idea of reversion was attractive because it explained the presence of the darker passions in human beings, the primal forces that were more compelling to him than ordinary, quotidian life. These forces linked humans to the past, to their ancestors, and to the primitive. Norris's interest in degeneration, and blood and genetics more generally, stemmed from his anxiety that the Nordic and Anglo-Saxon races (which he tended to glorify) were in danger of losing vitality, of becoming exhausted through refinement (Norris 1928a, 101). Harry Ten Eck represents this danger, as a character of "unmixed American stock" who readily reverts to an atavistic state.

Norris's fears of overcivilization and overrefinement were linked to a longing for masculine action that he absorbed from Kipling and others. His fascination with Chinatown arose in part from the notion that this place offered the opportunity for masculine adventure within the urban setting. With the closing of the frontier in the second half of the nineteenth century, Chinatown provided a last space outside the bounds of civilization. Chinatown thus functioned for Norris as a setting where civilized (and hence domesticated) whites could be revitalized through contact with the primitive.

Norris's concern with what he saw as the loss of masculine force in modern life led to his contempt for overrefined, passive, traditionally "feminine" women. The heroines of much of his fiction are large, strong-armed, robust, and sometimes tattooed Aryan women who exhibit "masculine" courage and vulgarity. In "The Third Circle," Chinatown releases the dormant Harry in Harriett Ten Eck, allowing her to revert to a more masculine state. As Lynn Wardley notes in her reading of the story: "A visit to Chinatown offers an occasion for Norris to figure forth the primitive identity housed within every civilized citizen, an identity that includes not only an archaic racial but also an atavistic sexual component" (1993, 229). For a figure such as Harriet Ten Eck, the awakening to primitive instinct is potentially regenerating.

Norris is, in fact, deliberately ambiguous about Ten Eck's disappearance. He plays with the reader's expectations (conditioned by the stereotypical plots of Chinatown pulp fiction) that the white woman has been kidnapped by Chinese highbinders. Yet, all that is said in the narrative itself is that Hillegas returns to find Ten Eck "gone." Her mysterious disappearance draws together the dominant society's various fears about white women in Chinatown. Has she been abducted? Seduced? Or has she, in a moment of moral failure, actually chosen to live with the Chinese? Like the rape fantasy, the Chinatown abduction fantasy expresses Victorian social anxieties about female sexuality and cross-racial desire. As an exploration of an urban heart of darkness, Norris's story is less concerned with Miss Ten Eck's victimization than with the idea of Chinatown as a place where the darker forces within the civilized subject are drawn to the surface.

Genthe's Photographs of Old Chinatown

The notion of Chinatown as a space of dark mystery and adventure held enormous appeal for Arnold Genthe. His fascination with the quaint and exotic Chinese Quarter gave him the impetus to try his hand at the art of photography. He bought a small camera that could be easily hidden and began experimenting with technique. By Genthe's time, the notion that the technology of photography could render faithful images of the natural world had already come to be widely accepted. From the 1850s on, Victorians actively promoted the use of photography for scientific purposes, namely the visual documentation of objects of study (see Ryan 1997). Genthe, however, was interested less in photography's potential for documentation than in its artistic potential. Indeed, Genthe was well aware of the limitations of photography's ability to produce a "perfect copy"; he was particularly troubled by the fact that the camera frequently reduced beautiful women to plainness. Having once aspired to be a painter, Genthe sought to use the photographic medium to create painterly, pictorial scenes after his own vision of the subject. Over time, Genthe took some two hundred photographs of Chinatown.

He published two volumes of them—*Pictures of Old Chinatown* (1908), with the accompanying text by Will Irwin, and *Old Chinatown* (1913), an expanded reprint.[8]

Genthe described his pursuit of photography as his "Chinatown adventure," full of ordeals and dangers. Will Irwin figured Genthe with his camera as a hunter lurking in wait for his game: always on the hunt for the perfect shot, or the ever-elusive Chinese subject. In his memoir, Genthe relates one particularly harrowing night when his photographic activity led him into danger.

> An English photographer whom I had met said he would like to take some night pictures of the "Devil's Kitchen." Had I been alone I would have had no fear, but going there in this instance involved a responsibility, and I asked the Chief to detail a detective to accompany us. We managed to get in without attracting attention as it was pitch dark in the court. But when the flashlight went off like a pistol shot, on the balconies and rushing down the stairways came a shouting, threatening mob. Several shots were fired. "You'd better run for your lives," said the detective, taking us by the arm. Needless to say we beat a hasty retreat. (1936, 38)

The act of photography becomes a battle, the photographers' attempts to "shoot" their subjects drawing gunshots in return. If for Norris Chinatown was a wilderness that called forth atavistic reversion, for Genthe the urban jungle was a site for safari-like adventure. He offered his photographs as documentary evidence of his tenacity and daring. Again we see Chinatown figured as a site for living out particularly masculine fantasies of action.[9]

Genthe's photographs bear a strong intertextual relation to Frank Norris's "Third Circle." On the more superficial level, there is an intertextuality of subject: Places and people that appear in Norris's short story also appear in a number of Genthe's pictures. "In Front of the Joss House" shows the joss house steps on Waverly Place; "The Street of Painted Balconies" shows the balcony of the Fragrant Moon Restaurant on Clay Street between Dupont and Waverly (a place perhaps similar to the "Seventy Moons" of Norris's story).[10] Other shots include "The Street of the Gamblers" (Fig. 4.1), portraits—"Fortune Teller" (Fig. 4.2) and "Pekin Two Knife Man"—as well as shots of St. Louis Alley, a Chinese theater, and the interior of the Chinese Mission (Tchen pl. 97). The coincidence of subject matter is such that Genthe's photographs might even be used to illustrate Norris's story.

A level of intertextuality that goes beyond the use of similar motifs or themes arises from the relation between "The Third Circle" and Genthe's conceptualization of Chinatown space. Like Norris, Genthe viewed Chinatown in terms of light space and dark space, showy surface and hidden depths. While many of his photographs feature prominent "daytime" tourist attractions, or festive scenes of children in their holiday costumes, Genthe claimed that it was the "darker spots"—the Street of the Gamblers, and the Devil's Kitchen—that made for his most interesting pictures.[11] In his memoir, Genthe alludes to "The Third Circle" in describing the pattern of Chinatown life—though he interprets Norris's three circles in a rather more literal, spatial fashion:

> The [theater] building itself was a study in ways Chinese. In it were housed all the strata of life to be found in the district. Above the theater, on the second story, lived the manager

FIGURE 4.1. "The Street of the Gamblers"

and stage director. The first floor underground was the home of the "number two" employees. In the Chinese social code actors belonged in the lower strata. Accordingly they were relegated to the second floor underground. On the third flight down were the opium dens where the smokers in various stages drew their dreams from the long pipes. It was this retreat which was immortalized by Frank Norris in his story, The Third Circle. (1936, 39)

From this statement, and similar remarks by Will Irwin, it seems that this conventional organization of space within Chinatown buildings was the provenance of Norris's three circles. What Genthe does here is reinscribe Norris's trope as physical space: metaphorical circles become architectural structures—three stories segregating classes of people and activities. For Genthe, a building serves as a microcosmic articulation of socio-economic relations in Chinatown society.

The strongest intertextual reading is prompted by Will Irwin's text, which uses "The Third Circle" as a framing device for Genthe's photographs. To Norris's schema, Irwin adds a fourth circle, "the family life and industrial activity of the Quarter," which he locates between the second and third circles (Genthe 1913, 61). Although Irwin claims to be merely "illustrating" Genthe's photographs with his words, his text produces a reading of Genthe's photographs in terms of "The Third Circle." Irwin identifies certain photographs as representative of "the life of the streets," "the prepared show," "the family life and industrial activity," and "glimpses into the third circle." This relation is indicated explicitly by captions to the photographs, by references within the text, and by the organization of the photographs within the book.[12]

The third circle is furthermore given strong visual representation in Genthe's photographs through composition, framing, and lighting. In his study of Genthe's Chinatown oeuvre, John Tchen has shown that these photographs, far from being documentary works, are highly edited and staged artistic creations. By examining original negatives of Genthe's works, Tchen demonstrates that Genthe often cropped his prints, changed

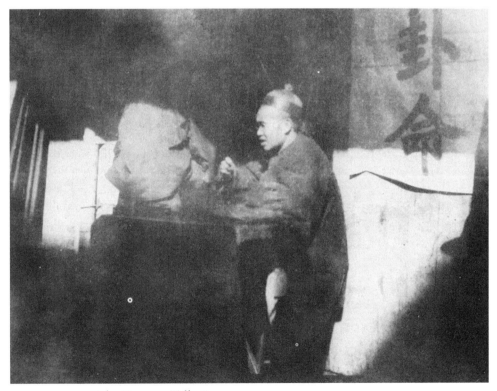

FIGURE 4.2.   "The Fortune Teller"

the exposure, and even retouched photographs with the touch-up crayon or etching tool before making his final prints. Most often, Genthe removed elements such as telephone poles and electric wires, English signs, or figures of white people that interfered with his vision of Chinatown as a "Canton of the West" (Tchen 1984, 14–17). Genthe, after all, considered himself a pictorialist and was, therefore, primarily concerned with achieving his desired artistic effects.

In photographing Chinatown, Genthe was drawn not only to the "picturesque" qualities of its scenes, but also to the chance to realize his artistic vision of "interpret[ing] life after [his] own manner in terms of light and shade" (1936, 43). Indeed, light and shade play important roles in Genthe's photographs. In numerous works, Genthe represents Chinatown as a "dark, shadowy" world. Dramatic shadows or starkly lit night scenes evoke mystery, concealment, and foreboding, all qualities of the spatial uncanny. The streets are narrow, dirty, and in derelict condition. Posters peeling off walls contribute to the sense of squalor and to the atmosphere of "ruins." A particularly dramatic example is the portrait "The Fortune Teller," in which intense shadows darken most of the picture except for a narrow band of light across the center. One figure is obscured by shadow, leaving the fortune-teller alone at the center of the composition. The overall effect is of a sinister creepiness. In other night shots, such as "The Street of Gamblers (by Night)," the isolated spots of bright glare on the dark scene create the impression that Genthe has momentarily uncovered a scene hidden by darkness.

If Norris defines the third circle as "the part that no one ever hears of," then in Genthe's work the third circle is represented as "the part that no one ever sees." In Genthe's photographs, that which lies beyond the frame or remains unpenetrated by the camera's gaze is often as important as the ostensible subject. Architectural elements frequently featured—cellar doors, doorways, alleys, balconies, closed windows—point to spaces that lie concealed behind the picture plane. Thus, these elements are evocative of that space that "no one ever sees," those spaces that no outsider (nor any outsider's camera) ever penetrated. "The Street of the Slave Girls" (Fig. 4.3) is a prime example. Shot on the oblique, the picture shows a white man walking down the street toward a Chinese woman in the foreground, approaching her as if she were perhaps a prostitute. The background is densely patterned by the repetitive elements of shuttered doors and windows, and basement stairwells that tease the viewer with their impenetrability. The photograph thus dramatically represents those spaces that we cannot see, evoking the third circle. "The Cellar Door" (Fig. 4.4) demonstrates Genthe's use of the cellar as a compositional element; a close-up of two boys standing on the street next to some cellar stairs, the photograph's oblique angle denies a frontal view into the cellar door. The "inscrutability" of Chinatown is further conveyed in Genthe's oeuvre by the lack of interior shots, or of shots through open doors or windows.

In contrast to the open scenes of the "life of the streets," which tend to focus on costumes, lanterns, and other decorative elements, Genthe's alley and back-street scenes often rely on architectural details or other elements of the physical space for their exotic effects and compositional dynamism. Genthe's shots are generally taken tight up against

FIGURE 4.3. "The Street of the Slave Girls"

the buildings with a low camera angle, immersing the viewer within the pictorial frame. Shots looking directly down alleys or streets similarly create narrow tunnels of vision. Genthe also tended to crop his published compositions fairly tightly around the central figures, thus eliminating panoramic street views. Many of his street scenes are shot on the oblique with the vanishing point beyond the pictorial frame. The viewer's eye is thus drawn to the edge of the frame, leading the viewer to wonder what lies just beyond the field of vision. Unlike panoramic shots that enable the viewer to step back and survey the scene, in the typical Genthe shot the viewer is unable to command the site, unable to see the whole. The effect is the inverse of panopticism and replicates the experience of the flaneur walking in the city. By the tight controlling of space, the use of dramatic shadows, and the focus on architectural detail rather than entire buildings, Genthe recreates visually the mysterious and sinister atmosphere of the Chinatown cityscape. These techniques are employed even in photographs whose ostensible subject has nothing to do with the Chinese underworld.

FIGURE 4.4.
"The Cellar Door"

"Doorways in Dim Half Tone" (titled "Doorways in Dim Shadows" in the 1913 edition) is a prime example of these techniques (Fig. 4.5). This photograph, taken on Spofford Alley in front of the Guanyin temple entrance, depicts a street lined with five men dressed in black Chinese costume and Homberg hats (see Tchen 1984, 93). A lone figure passes between these men down the alley. The tightening of space as the picture plane recedes gives viewers a sense of increasing enclosure, creating an ominous feeling as we anticipate the figure passing between the men. The picture is taken on the oblique with a strong diagonal dividing the composition. Figures in the distant background can be seen on Washington Street and Church Alley. Other elements of the composition include the lanterns over the temple doors, windows, collection boxes, and various notices pasted on the alley wall. Long dramatic shadows cross the picture plane, obscuring two of the figures in darkness and making deep recesses of the doorways. In *Pictures,* the photograph's caption suggests that it depicts a gambling den: "These lanterns denoted to the Chinese—and never to the police—a big gambling house which was raided monthly, and monthly exonerated 'for lack of evidence' " (Genthe 1908, 32). The words lend ominousness to these "loafers," clad in their anonymous gear, idly smoking cigarettes or reading notices. One imagines them to be lookout men, or bouncers for the gambling den. The importance of the "unseen" to the atmosphere of the photograph is demonstrated in the darkened doorways and in the upper-story windows that stare at the viewer from across the alleyway. These shadowed orifices seem to conceal something; pointing to interiors while refusing transparency, they evoke a sense of mystery or invite discovery.

"The 'Hop Fiend,'" as it appears in *Pictures* ("The Opium Fiend" in the 1913 edition), vividly evokes the spatial qualities of the third circle. A close-up profile of a man reclining on some stairs, the photograph shows only shadowy walls and perhaps a doorway in the background. The steep wood-plank stairs that form the lower right half of the composition suggest basement stairs rather than a stoop, creating the sense of a subterranean space. The photograph is almost overwhelmed by darkness except for the face of the "opium addict." The caption reads: "As the town drunkards to an American community, so were these creeping, flabby slaves of opium to Chinatown" (Genthe 1908, 32). The importance of text to the reading of the photographs is again demonstrated with this picture, for no pipe is shown in the photograph, and the latter-day viewer is hard-pressed to tell that this photograph is of anything more than a man napping on some stairs.

A "glimpse into the third circle" is provided in a pair of photographs of the tenement courtyard known as "the Devil's Kitchen." In "The 'Palace Hotel'" we see a figure descending a staircase into what appears to be a basement containing scattered

FIGURE 4.5.   "Doorways in Dim Half Tone"

refuse, pots and pans, a dog, and a person in the shadows. The shot is taken from a low angle, looking up from the basement through large gaps in the beams, locating the viewer within the subterranean space. A sharp contrast is drawn by the figure who descends from the bright light above into the shadowy hole with its dark little nooks. The viewer's eye descends with the figure, creating a sense of entering some hellish hole. "'The Devil's Kitchen' by Night" (Fig. 4.6) is the same shot, except that the figure is at the bottom of the stairs in the basement itself. The picture is taken at a greater distance, revealing more of the basement. In this night shot, the picture is much darker; the upper floor is obscured in blackness. In the basement we see darkened recesses, perhaps doorways, and long streaks of some mysterious liquid flowing over the floor. This photograph is a provocative image of "Filth," that favorite subject of anti-Chinese invective. The viewer has the impression of being shown some strange, subterranean world to which one is privy only through the camera.

Will Irwin's "Old Chinatown": Nostalgia and Collective Memory

Genthe's photographs of Old Chinatown were published as a collection only after the San Francisco earthquake had destroyed the city. The photographs thus refer to a Chinatown that has ceased to exist and that can be accessed only through memory or through Genthe's pictures. As ghostly images of a vanished place, the photographs serve as uncanny documents, images without referents. Will Irwin's commentary to the collection, "Old Chinatown," transforms this uncanniness into nostalgia (a related, but tamer emotion); indeed, it is nostalgia that structures the text of "Old Chinatown" (Fig. 4.7). Irwin's entire account is written in the past tense. As he explains [to an imagined Genthe]: "It is just that your lenses and plates record only the past; and, I, embroidering your work, have tried to keep in tone" (Genthe 1913, 5). Genthe and Irwin were not the only ones to mourn the passage of the Old Chinatown. In the wake of the disaster, several elegiac or nostalgic pieces appeared in San Francisco magazines, with headlines such as "Chinatown is gone!" (Kessler 1907, 445).

Irwin's travel memoir reveals how Old Chinatown could have vanished so irrevocably in the disaster (despite the immediate rebuilding of the Chinese Quarter). Particularly telling is this passage, in which Irwin laments the replacement of Old Chinatown with the sanitized new version:

> In a newer and stronger San Francisco rises a newer, cleaner, more healthful Chinatown. Better for the city—O yes—and better for the Chinese, who must come to modern ways of life and health if they are to survive among us. But where . . . is the dim reach of Ross Alley, that romantically mysterious cleft in the city's walls? . . . Where are those broken, dingy streets, in which the Chinese made art of rubbish? (Genthe 1913, 8)

Irwin's eulogy for Chinatown's alleys and the other "broken, dingy streets" indicates that above all, it was the physical setting, the architectural environment, that appealed to the bohemian slummers. This was the domain of squalor and beauty that had pro-

FIGURE 4.6.   "'The Devil's Kitchen' by Night"

vided the backdrop for quaint photographs and romantic stories, a place where the exotic gloss of oriental patina transformed ordinary rubbish into picturesque art.

Irwin draws on Norris's "Third Circle" to recreate the atmosphere of the old environment in his memoir, elaborating in particular on the fabled subterranean caverns of the Quarter, "those passageways of the Third Circle" (Genthe 1913, 153). Irwin claims that he devotes so much space to a discussion of the third circle (both as physical locale and sociological phenomenon) only because the crime was so "picturesque" and

FIGURE 4.7. "Old Chinatown."

expressed most clearly the difference between Orient and Occident. The third circle thus embodies the essence of Chinatown. The frequent allusions to Norris's infamous story serve to make Irwin's descriptions highly evocative, connecting his own personal memories to a larger literary context.[13]

The New Chinatown:
"Cleaner, Better, Brighter" Kitsch

The Chinese merchant elite were well aware of the popular association between the physical and moral atmosphere of "the noisome swamp," just as they were aware of the growing call to remove the Chinese presence from the city. After the 1906 earthquake, they sought to build anew a cleaner, more rational, and decorative "oriental city," in

order to improve the public image of Chinatown and its residents. As Philip Choy has documented, Chinatown was rebuilt with Chinoiserie-style large modern structures that were intended both to appeal to tourists and to give the impression of safety and hygiene. Choy calls these design innovations "a tactical response to the constant threat of removal and annihilation of Chinatown by the San Francisco Board of Supervisors and other anti-Chinese forces" (1990, 42)—an attempt to dispel the notion that Chinatown was a breeding ground for disease and crime. The new buildings were sponsored by Chinatown merchants and designed by American architects such as Ross and Burgren, Meyers and Ward, Schroepfer and Bolles, and Julia Morgan.

The vision of a "new Chinatown-beautiful" was initiated by Look Tin Eli and his partners, proprietors of the Sing Chong Bazaar. Look's manifesto for urban renewal was "Our New Oriental City—Veritable Fairy Palaces Filled with the Choicest Treasures of the Orient" (1910). Many of these Sino-American architectural constructions were simply Western brick or stuccoed commercial buildings with Chinoiserie motifs such as pagoda roofs, Chinese brackets, or loggias added as decorative elements. A most stunning example is the Sing Fat and Company Building designed by Ross and Burgren, with its four-tiered pagoda tower gracing the street-front corner. The desired overall effect of this new architecture was, in Look's words, that of "veritable fairy palaces," a type of safe exoticism (1910).

The pagoda became the new symbol of Chinatown architecture, shifting attention from Chinatown's cellars to its roofs. With the elimination of alleys and the addition of electric lighting, the dark spaces of Chinatown were to be conquered by transparency. Look Tin Eli declared that even at night the streets would be bathed by electric lights in "a blaze of glory as bright as midday" (1910). Genthe deplored the "new, cleaner, better, brighter" city, for to him it smacked of commercialism and kitsch. Look Tin Eli, for his part, expressed a deep contempt for the bohemian eulogizing of the old tenement slum. He declared: "San Francisco's new Chinatown is so much more beautiful, artistic, and so much more emphatically Oriental, that the old Chinatown, the destruction of which great writers and artists have wept over for two years, is not worthy to be mentioned in the same breath."

The rebuilding of Chinatown corresponded with merchant efforts to convert the Quarter from vice resort to tourist playground—with the focus on restaurants and curio shops, not gambling dens or brothels—a process that took place between 1896 and 1927 (see Light 1974). Recognizing that the tourist industry could provide a vital source of income to Chinatown at a time when others (mining, railroad work, and manufacture) had declined, the Chinese Six Companies in San Francisco began actively to promote tourism. In 1909, the Six Companies organization published its own guidebook advertising the safety of the new Quarter (Light 1974, 381). The new tourism was to be an entirely new way of viewing Chinatown: Look Tin Eli recommended visiting the new Chinatown-beautiful not under cover of dark but on a "bright, sunny day" (1910). Chinatown would no longer be a domain of dark space, but a domain of Technicolor illumination, famously depicted in the musical *Flower Drum Song*. The Baedeker's of 1909 dropped its warning about visiting Chinatown unescorted; but it also demoted the rebuilt Quarter to "no-star" status. It was thus that Chinatown, in its rebuilding, lost its charm for bohemians.

Notes

Acknowledgments: I thank Stephen Owen, David Palumbo-Liu, Leo Lee, Steve West, Jack Tchen, Edward Baron Turk, Min Song, John Cheng, Yuko Matsukawa, Imogene Lim, Josephine Lee, Stephen Chung, Daisy Ng, and the anonymous reviewers of this article for their comments and suggestions. Thanks also to Bob Broderick, Joanna Levin, Steve Doi, and Teresa Algoso for invaluable research assistance.

1. Chinatown as locale and abstract entity meant many things to many people: To Chinese immigrants it was a safe haven in a hostile environment; to anti-Chinese politicians and moral-

ists it meant vice and a source of disease and moral corruption; to bohemian slummers it was an urban adventure.

2. Irwin represented the memories of Old Chinatown in his text as collective memory, frequently appealing to the audience's shared experiences of the city. The volume was also greeted in the press as an artifact of collective memory (see Franklin 1909, 52).

3. The works of Norris, Genthe, and Irwin, like the guidebooks of their day, are full of references to architectural features, all serving to create a verbal or pictorial atmosphere. The idea of Chinatown as urban landscape was also key to Chinatown literature that featured descriptions of architectural detail, as well as movements through the cityscape, for purposes of plot or atmosphere. The fabled alleys, secret passageways, and trapdoors provided an exotic setting for otherwise hackneyed plots.

4. The association between cellars and the irrational, particularly irrational fears, is described by Bachelard: "[The cellar] is first and foremost the dark entity of the house, the one that partakes of subterranean forces. When we dream there, we are in harmony with the irrationality of the depths" (1994, 18). For Bachelard, the cellar is a space of underground maneuvers, of the diabolical and the sinister.

5. Freud defined the uncanny as that class of frightening elements that arise when the repressed recurs. The uncanny is thus something secretly familiar that has become defamiliarized, alienated from the mind through the force of repression, and then returned (1962).

6. The earthquake of 1906 actually provided an opportunity to see into the lowest ooze of the place. Ironically, when Genthe and Irwin peer into the gaping hellhole left by the disaster, they see nothing of this fabled world. Irwin speaks of this surprise in his account: "Those who knew old Chinatown marveled, when they looked into the gaping cellars left by the fire, to see how little of this mole-work remained" (Genthe 1913, 153).

7. It was through their activities with the paper that Genthe and Norris originally met. In 1897, *Wave* editor John O'Hara Cosgrave asked Genthe to publish some photographs of Telegraph Hill in the magazine and sent Norris along to get material for a story to accompany the pictures. Irwin regarded himself as something of a disciple of both Genthe and Norris, whom he considered to be among the greatest artists of his day.

8. One is tempted to take Genthe's first published collection, *Pictures of Old Chinatown,* as the definitive text. However, the 1913 republication contains almost twice the number (91) of photographs as the older text (47). Moreover, the pictures have been reorganized, reformatted, recaptioned, and in most cases retitled. Will Irwin's account is slightly abridged and is now divided into ten chapters, and there is a new postscript by Genthe. In many ways the reissued edition is essentially a new text. John Tchen's (1984) newly edited compilation contains 130 photographs and is therefore the most complete published representation of the oeuvre.

9. See Wardley 1993 for the masculinized and homosocial images of Chinatown.

10. Genthe's alternate title for this shot, "Before the Big Joss House," indicates that the restaurant was in the proximity of a Joss House.

11. John Tchen notes that of the 159 photographs of Genthe's that he examined, two-thirds focus on children, and almost one-half show Chinese in holiday costume (1984, 13). Genthe seems to have been aware of the great commercial appeal of pictures featuring children.

12. *Pictures* relies more heavily on such captions, while *Old Chinatown* relies mainly on organization to make these connections. The relation between text and photographs is by no means perfect, as indicated by the substantial reorganization of the 1913 edition, which seeks to correlate the photographs more closely with Irwin's text. Irwin's account roughly follows the order "life of the streets," "family and industrial life," "the third circle," and "show places," though

he does not confine himself to these topics. The images that offer a "glimpse into the third circle" are clustered toward the end of the book (particularly in the 1913 edition), where Irwin provides an extended discussion of Chinatown's underworld.

13. Throughout the latter part of Irwin's essay, "The Third Circle" provides a reference point against which Irwin interprets his various experiences in Chinatown. He recalls, for example, watching a Chinese party play a drinking game that "furnished a glimpse into Frank Norris's Third Circle, the underworld" (Genthe 1908, 112).

Works Cited

Bachelard, Gaston. 1994. *The Poetics of Space*. Boston: Beacon Press.

Baedeker, Karl, ed. 1893. *The United States with an Excursion into Mexico: Handbook for Travellers*. New York: Scribner's.

Boyer, M. Christine. 1994. *The City of Collective Memory: Its Historical Imagery and Architectural Entertainments*. Cambridge: MIT Press.

Choy, Philip. 1990. "The Architecture of San Francisco Chinatown." In *Chinese America: History and Perspectives*, 4: 37–66. San Francisco: Chinese Historical Society of America.

Conrad, Joseph. 1988. *Heart of Darkness*. New York: Norton.

de Certeau, Michel. 1984. "Walking in the City." In *The Practice of Everyday Life*, trans. Steven F. Rendall. Los Angeles: University of California Press.

Farwell, Willard B., and John E. Kunkler. 1885. "The Report of the Special Committee of the Board of Supervisors of San Francisco on the Condition of the Chinese Quarter of that City." In *The Chinese at Home and Abroad*, ed. Willard Farwell, part 2, 1–95. San Francisco: Bancroft.

Franklin, Barnett. 1909. Review of *Pictures of Old Chinatown* in "In the Realm of Bookland," by Pierre N. Beringer. *Overland Monthly* 53, 1 (January): 52.

Freud, Sigmund. 1962. "The 'Uncanny.'" Translated by James Strachey. *Standard Edition of the Complete Psychological Works of Sigmund Freud*. Vol. 17 (1917–1919). London: Hogarth Press.

Genthe, Arnold. 1936. *As I Remember*. New York: Reynal and Hitchcock.

Genthe, Arnold, with Will Irwin. 1908. *Pictures of Old Chinatown*. New York: Moffat, Yard.

———. 1913. *Old Chinatown*. New York: Mitchell Kennerley.

Kessler, D. E. 1907. "An Evening in Chinatown." *Overland Monthly*, 2d ser., 49 (May): 445–49.

Light, Ivan. 1974. "From Vice District to Tourist Attraction: The Moral Career of American Chinatowns, 1880–1940." *Pacific Historical Review* 43, 3: 367–94.

Look, Tin Eli. 1910. "Our New Oriental City—Veritable Fairy Palaces Filled with the Choicest Treasures of the Orient." In *San Francisco, the Metropolis of the West*, n.p. San Francisco: Western Press Association.

Norris, Frank. 1899. "A Plea for Romantic Fiction." In *The Complete Works of Frank Norris: Blix, Moran of the Lady Letty, Essays on Authorship*, 341–44. New York: Collier.

———. 1928a. "Among Cliff Dwellers." In *Collected Writings: Hitherto Unpublished in Book Form*, 10:98-101. Garden City, N.Y.: Doubleday.

———. 1928b. "The Third Circle." In *The Third Circle, A Deal in Wheat, and Other Stories of the New and Old West*, 4:1–10. Garden City, N.Y.: Doubleday.

Owen, Juliette A. 1887. "Sundry Observations of an Excursionist." *Overland Monthly*, 2d ser., 10 (December): 636–639.

Ryan, James. 1997. *Picturing Empire: Photography and the Visualization of the British Empire.* Chicago: University of Chicago Press.

Tchen, John Kuo Wei, ed. and comp. 1984. *Genthe's Photographs of San Francisco's Old Chinatown.* New York: Dover.

Vidler, Anthony. 1994. *The Architectural Uncanny: Essays in the Modern Unhomely.* Cambridge: MIT Press.

Wardley, Lynn. 1993. "Bachelors in Paradise: The State of a Theme." In *The Return of Criticism,* ed. Werner Sollors, 217–41. Harvard English Studies 18. Cambridge: Harvard University Press.

Williams, Samuel. 1875. *The City of the Golden Gate: A Description of San Francisco in 1875.* San Francisco: Book Club of California.

Rajini Srikanth

5   The *Komagata Maru:* Memory and Mobilization among the South Asian Diaspora in North America

I try to enjoy the music of the waves
but only the angry Punjabi voices
from the Maru reach my ears
    —Sadhu Binning

A plaque at the Gateway to the Pacific in downtown Vancouver records a brief but telling moment in Canadian immigration history. The text reads:

> On May 23, 1914, 376 British Subjects (12 Hindus, 24 Muslims and 340 Sikhs) of Indian origin arrived in Vancouver harbour aboard the Komagata Maru, seeking to enter Canada. 352 of the passengers were denied entry and forced to depart on July 23, 1914. This plaque commemorates the 75th anniversary of that unfortunate incident of racial discrimination and reminds Canadians of our commitment to an open society in which mutual respect and understanding are honoured, differences are respected, and traditions are cherished.

The *Komagata Maru* was a Japanese ship chartered by Gurdit Singh, an Indian national living in Hong Kong, to help transport his fellow countrymen who wished to immigrate to Canada. The memorial recalls the turn-of-the-century discriminatory immigration regulations adopted by the Canadian government to bring to a stop, specifically, the influx of Indians into Canada. That the Indians aroused such anxiety is surprising, given that in the decade from 1900 to 1910 their presence was only 5,200 strong (Chadney 1985, 60; Judge 1994, 1); by contrast, there were in British Columbia more than 50,000 people of Chinese and Japanese descent (Josh 1975, 11; Ward 1990, 23, 36, 53). The Canadians' racist immigration policies applied to all Asians, but those who came from India were viewed as especially threatening. The *Komagata Maru* incident highlights white Canada's distaste at the time for Indian immigrants.

Although here I rearticulate the salient points of the 1914 event (and in doing so, rely on two books devoted to the voyage of the ship, Josh 1975 and Johnston 1979), I seek to go beyond the actual incident and to examine its significance in the collective memory of the South Asian community in Canada specifically and in North America generally. A recent article characterizes the *Komagata Maru* incident as "the first revolt of immigrants in British Columbia" and declares that the passengers of the ship "still inspire the Indian Canadian community" (Corriea 2000, 24c). On 23 February 2000, Ujjal Dosanjh was sworn in as the first South Asian Canadian premier of British Columbia;[1] here, I speculate on the possible trajectory from the *Komagata Maru* debacle to the climate in which Dosanjh's election to the highest political office of the province became possible. Although his term as premier was short-lived, Dosanjh's election is likely to interest South Asian Americans as well; in fact, at an 8 April 2000 conference organized by Harvard University's South Asian American students, Gurmant Singh Grewal, a Canadian member of Parliament, was a participant on a panel exploring strategies for mobilizing political participation among South Asian Americans. The emotional relevance of the *Komagata Maru* narrative in present times connects with questions of memory—how remembering occurs and how memories are constructed. Here, the *Komagata Maru* affair serves as a springboard to address the intersection of memory, transnationalism, and political participation in diasporic Asian communities in North America.

Anti-Asian and Anti-Indian Sentiment

The plaque at the Gateway to the Pacific lists three Indian religious groups—Sikhs, Hindus, and Muslims. There was much controversy over the wording of the plaque, but the text's meticulous listing of the exact numbers of passengers of each religious persuasion bears little relationship to the Canadian authorities' monolithic reaction to the potential immigrants. The officials were not concerned with the religious affiliation of the passengers but only with the fact that they were all from India. I use "Indian" rather than South Asian because at the time of the *Komagata Maru* incident, the Indian subcontinent had not yet been subdivided into the separate nations that today constitute South Asia.

The *Komagata Maru* incident is significant for three reasons:

1. As a test of the British Empire's rhetoric that its subjects all over the world could travel easily from one part of the empire to another. (In 1914, Canada was a dominion of the British Empire; unlike India, Canada was a self-governing colony.) Johnston writes that Gurdit Singh told an American reporter in Shanghai that he was undertaking the voyage "to test the justice of the British towards all their people" (1979, 30). Upon the ship's arrival, Singh told the press: "We are British citizens and we consider we have a right to visit any part of the British Empire. . . . We are determined to make this a test case and if we are refused entrance into your country, the matter will not end here" (37–38).

2. As irrefutable evidence of Canada's racist policies, that is, as a failure of the "test." Peter Ward observes that whatever might have been the actual motives behind Gurdit Singh's chartering of the ship, the arrival of the *Komagata Maru* in Canada was seen as a "direct challenge to the policy of East Indian exclusion" (1990, 88).

3. As a strong impetus for the forging of a consciousness of resistance among the Indians of North America, a sentiment that had important implications for the British Empire. The Indians saw as a betrayal the silence of the British government at Canada's refusal to let in the passengers of the *Komagata Maru*. The *Komagata Maru* affair convinced many Indians of their second-class membership in the British Empire and quickly dispelled their naïve hope in being able to pursue opportunities in Canada. They became committed revolutionaries in the fight to overthrow British rule in India. There is evidence to suggest that the British government's refusal to intervene in Canada's exclusion of the *Komagata Maru* passengers strengthened the resolve of many Vancouver Indians to join forces with the revolutionary Ghadr party members in California and heightened the fervor of anti-British rhetoric and action in North America.[2] Many Ghadrites returned to India following the outbreak of World War I to accelerate the uprising against British rule (Judge 1994, 87). Darshan Singh Tatla argues that the bloody end that awaited the *Komagata Maru* upon its forced return to India (a narrative we will take up later) fueled "a mood ... of militancy ... supplied by two intellectuals, Taraknath Das and Lala Hardayal, who called for India's liberation [from British rule]. While Hardayal preached to California's Indian students, Taraknath Das was a familiar sight among Vancouver's Sikhs" (1999, 88). Citing a 26 August 1915 interoffice memo on the subject of Indian immigration to Canada, Tatla notes that British officials were aware of the link between immigration grievances and Sikh agitation for India's independence from the British:

> The seriousness of the question, as regards the British empire in India, is that the people of Punjab, the chief recruiting ground for the Indian army, are the class of Indians practically affected, and the grievances of the Sikhs regards Canada have been very skilfully utilised by agitators to excite discontent in the Punjab.... The classes of Indians who go to South Africa are of no military importance; but the Sikhs ... have been a most important element, and the attempts of agitators to tamper with them have been closely connected with immigration grievances. (88–89)

All the passengers of the *Komagata Maru,* and the Indians immigrating to California, were originally from Punjab, a province in North India. The Punjabi Sikhs constituted a large part of the British army in India, and many were stationed in Shanghai and Hong Kong in the service of the empire. They had distinguished themselves as soldiers. For many, the prospects of returning to Punjab were highly unsatisfactory, given the difficulty of making a living on the farms there. Among Punjabi families a tradition existed of sending males out of the country for sojourns elsewhere in the hope that they would send money back home. With the money, those who remained in India planned to increase their land holdings and consolidate their positions in the agricultural economy of Punjab (Ward 1990, 80).

The *Komagata Maru* picked up its 376 passengers from Hong Kong (165), Shanghai (73), and from Moji (124) and Yokohama in Japan (14) before sailing to Victoria and Vancouver. That the passengers had not boarded the ship at an Indian port was a clear violation of a curious Canadian law, the 1908 Continuous Passage Act, which did more to virtually eliminate immigration of Indians than any other piece of immigration legislation. The continuous passage rule stipulated that

> all immigrants were prohibited from entering Canada unless they came from the country of their birth or citizenship by a "continuous journey and on through tickets" purchased in their home country. . . . There being no direct steamship line from India, virtually all Indian immigration was thus eliminated. At the same time the door was shut on the Hawaiian route for Japanese immigrants [although the rule did not apply to Japanese immigrants who sailed directly from Japan]. The order provided effective restriction while avoiding the distasteful and increasingly unacceptable practice of indicating undesirable immigrants by race or nationality. (Ward 1990, 76)

The Reverend Dr. Wilkie, a strong Canadian supporter of immigration from India, perhaps because he had spent twenty years there, pointed to the ludicrousness of the law, especially as it applied to Indians. It meant, he said, that "a Sikh who could not come direct from India to Canada ceased to be making a continuous journey when he walked across the dock at Hong Kong from one steamer to another." Wilkie pointed out that the law "made specially hard and irritating conditions for the Hindu [while] favoring the Jap and Chinaman who can travel direct to Canada." He concluded, "Let us pass no law which will reflect unfairly on this people and if we are going to exclude orientals, let us exclude all of them" (Josh 1975, 7).

Was the *Komagata Maru* a deliberate flouting of Canadian immigration laws, as the officials claimed it was? Was its defiant stance an insult to the paranoia of white Canadians who, since the latter years of the nineteenth century, were beginning to develop a racial consciousness of their whiteness as being separate from other "races"—the Mongolian and, now, the Indians or Hindus? Ward explains that the Canadians' racist and anti-Asian sentiments had less to do with the numbers of Asians who were present in Canada and more to do with the determination of the white immigrants to establish a homogeneous white society. The Indians' arrival in the early part of the twentieth century was the tail end of a stream of immigration from Asia, beginning with the Chinese and followed by the Japanese. They brought to a psychological threshold white Canadians' ability to tolerate nonwhite residents (see Ward 1990, esp. chaps. 2–5).

Of the three nationalities, the Japanese were the most tolerated and the most respected. They were seen as a superior people, almost the equal of whites, but, therefore, all the more necessary to watch, because they could potentially be a formidable competitor to whites. Japan's proximity to the west coast of Canada was also cause for concern: The Japanese fleet was close to British Columbia. In fact, at the end of the nineteenth century, during the Boer War, the British government did not want to antagonize the Japanese, because British resources (of which Canadian forces were a part) were concentrated in South Africa fighting in the Anglo-Boer War. In addition, there existed an informal agreement with the government of Japan that the numbers of

Japanese emigrants would be kept small (similar to the Gentlemen's Agreement between Japan and the United States); the Japanese in Hawai'i defeated this intent, because the government of Japan could not monitor their movements, and it was, in part, to stem the entry of Japanese from Hawai'i that the Continuous Passage Act was passed. This act, however, had its greatest impact on potential immigrants from India and came to be seen by the Indians as especially discriminatory toward them.

The Chinese enjoyed less prestige than the Japanese. They were seen as uncivilized, unassimilable, and unclean. But there was also a grudging acknowledgment that their labor was necessary to the development of the province. The Chinese, because of their greater numbers and longer residence in the western province (since 1858), became the target of more frequent restrictive legislation than other Asian immigrants. In 1903, the head tax (the amount each immigrant had to pay to enter Canada) on Chinese immigrants was increased to five hundred dollars, a figure so high that in a single year, the number of Chinese immigrants dropped from 4,719 to 8 (Ward 1990, 61). In 1908, in response to mounting anti-Asian sentiment in British Columbia, then–prime minister Wilfred Laurier passed a law requiring that *all* Asian immigrants entering Canada possess at least two hundred dollars.

Canadians considered Indians to be more unassimilable than Chinese and Japanese. An editorial in the *Colonist* declared that Indians "are a case more apart even than the Chinese; [t]heir habits of life are unsatisfactory. They do not bring their wives with them, and will not make homes or rear families. They are totally unfitted for a white man's country" (Ward 1990, 83–84). The reaction to Indian immigrants is intriguing. So uneasy were Canadians with the presence of Indians that they even offered to facilitate their relocation to Honduras as indentured laborers. In 1908, two Indians living in Canada—Teja Singh and Balwant Singh—were part of a reconnaissance party that went with J. B. Harkin, private secretary to the minister of the interior, to Honduras to determine its suitability as a potential alternative destination. The report they came back with did not encourage that plan (Ward 1990, 87).

As Sohan Singh Josh points out, during the first two decades of the twentieth century, the Canadian government debated the question of what to do with the Indians. The problem that the Indians posed to the Canadian government was their membership in the British Empire, which gave them, like Canadians, the rights and privileges of British rule. The Indians took seriously the 1858 declaration by the British monarch that Indians would enjoy equal rights with other British subjects in any part of the empire: "We hold ourselves bound to the natives of Indian territories by the same obligations of duty which bind us to all our other subjects" (Josh 1975, 10). It became apparent to them, however, that such was not to be the case, that their brown skin precluded their entry into certain regions of the empire; "because they were *kale admi*—black men—they were the stepchildren of the Empire" (Johnston 1979, 6). But there were also sympathetic whites who saw in the Indians' status as British subjects reason for their being granted entry into Canada, and who drew attention to the legitimacy of their claim to full British citizenship (Josh 1975, 6–8). According to Ward, for example:

Several advocates reasoned that imperial citizenship and past military service entitled these immigrants to special consideration. "It seems to me," argued one staunch champion, "that these Punjabis are entitled to official recognition and protection. Hundreds of these men have been soldiers in our Army and wear medals for their services in the field. They are the subjects of our Empire, and are yet denied the rights of citizenship by a large proportion of their fellow subjects." (1990, 85)

But this legitimacy is precisely what scared white Canadians about the Indians. Their special British subject status made them more of a threat than other Asian immigrants. There was the fear that as subjects of the British Empire, "they had a special claim on entry into Canada" (Ward 1990, 84). It was this perceived special claim that ironically worked to exacerbate the already prevalent anti-orientalism of white Canadians and led them to object vociferously to Indian immigration.

Thus, one can argue that what Indians saw as their claim to rightful entry into Canada, Canadians saw as the very reason to keep them out. The theoretical validity of the Indians' argument made it all the more imperative to safeguard the racial homogeneity of Canadian citizenship. The *Komagata Maru,* in this context, can be seen as the crack in the door, the slim opening that had to be firmly closed to prevent any possibility of the door's being pushed open to let in the "swarms" of Indians from Asia.

Preparing for the Voyage

The process by which the *Komagata Maru* was chartered and outfitted reveals that there was much movement of people among the countries of East, South, and Southeast Asia. We tend to think of transnationalism as a specifically late-twentieth-century phenomenon; the *Komagata Maru* venture tells us otherwise. Gurdit Singh, an affluent businessperson, made his money in Malaya—in the railroad industry and on the rubber plantations. He could speak fluent Malay. He had also spent some time in Singapore and appeared to travel between Hong Kong, India, Malaya, and Singapore with some regularity. The *Komagata Maru* passengers themselves, as we have seen, boarded at different ports in Asia, and the ship was owned by a Japanese company.

There are several explanations for the single-minded determination Gurdit Singh displayed in the matter of the *Komagata Maru's* mission. He is believed to have been deeply disturbed by the condition of the Punjabis in the *gurdwara* (Sikh temple) in Hong Kong as they awaited word from relatives and friends in Vancouver of their chances for immigrating to Canada. Others see his involvement in commercial terms: He wished to trade coal, which he purchased in Japan, for timber in Canada and also hoped to establish a viable travel company, moving passengers from Asia to Canada. One of the most dramatic reasons for his zeal to carry the passengers to Canada has roots in a significant piece of Indian history. In 1857, the sepoys of the Indian Army mutinied against their British officers because of being forced to lubricate their Enfield rifles with grease believed to come from beef or pork fat. The Hindus and Muslims, for whom the cow is sacred and pork a defilement, respectively, began an uprising. The British officers relied heavily on the help of Sikh soldiers to quell the mutiny. So the Sikhs were seen as abetting the rulers during a critical point in Indian colonial history, and Gurdit Singh, a Sikh, appears to have wished to prove to other Indians the loyalty of the Sikhs, to wipe out, as it were, the memory of their helping the British control the rebellion of 1857. He wished to demonstrate convincingly the patriotism of the Sikhs, as Johnston suggests:

> There was a story that he [Gurdit Singh] sometimes told about travelling back to the Panjab with a very spiritual man from his village, returning by way of Madras and visiting temples as they went. In Hyderabad, on the way to the shrine of Hazur Sahib and the place where Guru Gobind Singh was slain, they were mocked by some Mahrattas who referred to the part played by the Sikhs in the Mutiny of 1857. Gurdit Singh replied that the people who helped the British were princes and kings, not the Sikhs, an answer that satisfied the Mahrattas but not himself; at that moment he felt that the Sikhs would have to prove their patriotism so that they could walk with pride. (1979, 25)

Whatever the reasons for his dedication to the voyage, Gurdit Singh gave unequivocal evidence of his revolutionary fervor. At Yokohama, the *Komagata Maru* was visited by two fiery Indian nationalists: Bhagwan Singh Jakh, a fugitive from Victoria who had jumped ship in Yokohama five months before and was still planning his return to North America; and Maulvi Barkatullah, a "militant pan-Islamist from Bhopal State who had just been stripped of a professorship in Hindustani at the University of Tokyo" (Johnston 1979, 34). The two men warned Gurdit Singh that the ship would not be allowed to land in Vancouver. He was undaunted—perhaps because of his determination to disprove the naysayers, perhaps because of his desire to challenge Canadian immigration laws, perhaps because of his mistaken belief that the silence from Canadian authorities upon being informed of the ship's departure from Hong Kong signaled their willingness to let the ship land. (In reality, the wire from the governor of Hong Kong had been overlooked, an error that the Canadians came to regret during the two months that the ship was anchored in Vancouver Harbor.)

At Moji, Gurdit Singh was entertained for dinner by the shipping company's agent and some other Japanese. They might have stoked his revolutionary fervor by saying that "they hoped that India would wake up and be free because the Japanese would help; Japan, India, and China would in combination be strong enough to vanquish the countries of Europe." (This was a conversation that somehow found its way to Malcolm Reid, the hard-line immigration official who saw in it evidence for the seditious collaboration of Gurdit Singh and T. Yamamoto, the Japanese captain of the ship.) Gurdit Singh boasted that the colonial government in India "had been threatened with a revolution led by ten thousand Indian troops if it continued to oppose the sailing of the *Komagata Maru*" (Johnston 1979, 32).

Protagonists in the Drama of Resistance

The passengers, stirred by Gurdit Singh's firm belief in the rightness of their voyage, were equally optimistic. They were not prepared, therefore, for the virulence of the resistance they would encounter from the Canadian government. Both the Indians in Vancouver and the Canadian authorities had been waiting for the *Komagata Maru*. The Canadians wanted to send the ship back to its port of origin. The Indians, who had formed a Shore Committee of multiethnic representation, had lawyers, money, and other provisions ready to help the passengers. The Canadian authorities did not let the passengers leave the boat, claiming they had violated immigration laws. The claim was that the ship had not arrived via direct passage and that most passengers did not have the two hundred dollars required to enter British Columbia. (This second charge was not strictly accurate, because the Khalsa Diwan Society of Vancouver—a Sikh cultural and religious organization that in the early days provided refuge and emotional support to all immigrants from India regardless of religious affiliation—was able to raise the necessary money.)

For two months the passengers of the *Komagata Maru,* the Indians in British Columbia, and the authorities were involved in a heated legal battle. At the end of the two months, only twenty-four passengers, previous residents of Canada, were given permission to stay legally in the country. On 23 July 1914 the *Komagata Maru* was forced to leave and return to Hong Kong.

At Vancouver, the principal Indian players were the members of the Shore Committee—Bhag Singh, Husain Rahim, Belwant Singh, Sohanlal, and Umrao Singh (Josh 1975, 46)—and the Khalsa Diwan Society. The protagonists in Canadian immigration were two officers, Malcolm Reid, the Dominion immigration agent, and William Hopkinson, an immigration inspector. Reid was unequivocally anti-Indian. A few months before the arrival of the *Komagata Maru,* thirty-nine Indians had been allowed entry into Canada on the strength of legal technicalities. In many ways, Reid saw the *Komagata Maru* as an opportunity to settle the score, to prove that he was the gatekeeper, as it were, controlling entry into British Columbia. He openly flouted the process of justice, prohibiting the passengers from appearing before the Board of Inquiry, where they hoped to test the validity of Canadian immigration laws. He deprived them of food and water, sometimes withholding supplies for as long as three days, believing that he could subdue them in this manner and make them leave. He tried to coerce Captain Yamamoto to declare that the passengers were mutinous, a statement that would have given Reid the legal authority to send troops to board the ship and take control. He threatened Yamamoto with a stiff fine when the captain refused to agree with his plan (either because he was sympathetic to the passengers or because he feared the consequences for himself were he to cooperate with Reid; Yamamoto's sentiments are a facet of the narrative that needs further probing).

Although Reid had given the impression that the passengers were a murderous bunch, Johnston remarks that one of the most surprising aspects of the passengers' behavior was their nonviolent demeanor, despite being denied food and water for days at a time and despite having to endure grossly unhygienic conditions. The only show of force they made occurred when Reid sent a tugboat with a police force of 160 officers. The officers were prevented from boarding the ship by the passengers, who "were prepared with piles of coal, fire bricks, and scrap metal which they had brought up from the hold. They stood five meters above the deck of the [tugboat] *Sea Lion* and with that advantage loosed an unanswerable storm on the people" (Johnston 1979, 77). Ultimately, however, Reid won, through a combination of intimidation and psychological harassment. When the *Komagata Maru* finally left Vancouver Harbor, it was "escorted" by a naval vessel whose guns were trained on the ship to ensure that it was truly on its way.

Hopkinson, the immigration officer involved, was a slightly more complicated individual than Reid. He had been born in India in 1880 and had spent several years of his life there before being posted to Canada, perhaps in 1908. Hopkinson could speak fluent Hindi but was less comfortable with Punjabi, the language of most of the immigrants from India. He served as an informant to the colonial government, keeping its authorities in the know about "seditious" activities by Indians in North America and sending them regular reports on the movements and speeches of Ghadr Party leaders and other identified "troublemakers" (for example, Hardayal, Taraknath Das, Guran Ditta Kumar, Balwant Singh, Bhag Singh, and Mewa Singh).

Sharon Pollock, an award-winning Canadian playwright, casts Hopkinson as a central character in her play *The Komagata Maru Incident*. She suggests strongly that Hopkinson's mother was Indian and that Hopkinson was so determined to reject any suggestion of multiracialism in his character that he overcompensated with harsh rhetoric about the inferiority of the brown skinned.

> I know India, and I know its people. When I was a child, my father was stationed in the Punjab—He had only to shout "Quai Hai" to summon a slave—a servant—no, goddamn it, a slave—to summon a slave, to scrawl his initials on a chit, and there was a felt carpet from Kashmir, brass ornaments from Moradabad, silver for pocket money, cigars, a horse, a dog, anything he wanted. . . . My father was a big man, blond curly hair, wonderful moustache he had, looked like a prince in his uniform. A prince—surrounded by little beige people. (1978, 9)

Hopkinson made use of a group of Punjabi immigrants as informants, and through them he learned of the strategies that were being employed by the Shore Committee to gain entry for the passengers. Shortly after the forced departure of the *Komagata Maru*, two of these informants—Harnam Singh and Arjan Singh—were found brutally murdered. No one was arrested, but everyone appears to have known that they had been killed by someone in the Indian community for having betrayed their people. The third informant, Bela Singh, perhaps fearing for his life, is believed to have opened fire at the temple during a large gathering, killing two people. In October 1914, Hopkinson was called to speak in Bela Singh's defense at his trial. While Hopkinson was waiting to be summoned into the courtroom, another Indian, Mewa Singh, shot him for his support of Bela Singh.

There was bloodshed, as well, on the ship's return to India. In all, the *Komagata Maru* affair resulted in the death of twenty passengers (Josh 1975, 77) from the riots that ensued with the British officers following the ship's return to Budge Budge, an industrial port near Calcutta on India's east coast. By the time the ship arrived in Budge Budge, it had become associated with the Ghadr Party, whose members did bring weapons on board the ship in Yokohama, and its passengers were seen as potential enemies of the colonial government. Even Sikh leaders who had sympathized with the passengers as they waited to be allowed entry into Canada and were outraged at the treatment of the passengers dissociated themselves from the ship and its cause when it returned. They believed the official British reports of what had transpired at Calcutta and condemned the passengers' use of arms (Johnston 1979, 107). So, in India, the *Komagata Maru* narrative ended somewhat disgracefully. In the years since India's independence, however, the *Komagata Maru* event has been revisited and an attempt made to tell the "real" story of what happened on its return. Gurdit Singh worked tirelessly to make the actual facts known.

Desire and Memory in Re/Collecting the *Komagata Maru*

In Canada, the *Komagata Maru* incident has been recently rearticulated as a site of emotional empowerment. Charan Gill, a South Asian Canadian activist in Vancouver who is executive director of the Progressive Intercultural Community Services Society (PICSS), observes that there was no commemoration of the *Komagata Maru* debacle for the twenty-fifth or fiftieth anniversary of the event. An immigrant to Canada in 1967 and a man committed to social justice, Gill could not let the seventy-fifth anniversary of the incident go unmarked. He was instrumental in working with the city government to get the plaque erected. Raminder Dosanjh, a community activist and educator (and wife of the ex-premier of British Columbia), helped set up the Komagata Maru Foundation, which financed the production of a documentary film, *Komagata Maru: Voyage of Shattered Dreams*. Numerous articles and editorials have appeared in South Asian Canadian magazines and newspapers (for example, *Rungh, AAJ,* and *MEHFIL*). A play was performed at the progressive South Asian conference held in Toronto, *Desh Pardesh*.[3] A booklet has been written for distribution to South Asian schoolchildren. All of these recoveries of the event emphasize the injustice suffered and call for a vigilant political posture to ensure that such official discrimination is never allowed to recur.

A recent roundtable discussion of South Asian community leaders reveals yet another possible reason for the *Komagata Maru*'s hold on the South Asian imagination. At the roundtable, school principal Sarjeet Singh Jagpal noted:

> In 1914 when the Komagata Maru came here, the federal government wouldn't pay for food and water and other things for the passengers. The Khalsa Diwan Society, which had been formed shortly before the ship arrived and included members from the Muslim and Hindu communities in India, raised close to $70,000 in three months. A $1,000 could buy you any house in town and these guys came up with $70,000 to pay all the expenses incurred by the ship during its two-month stay in Vancouver harbor. (Saeed and Dhillon 1997)

Jagpal is referring to the collective solidarity demonstrated by the early immigrants and immigrant hopefuls in contrast to the individualism that characterizes the current immigrants and offspring of immigrants. In his remarks, one detects nostalgia for the collective sensibility of the earlier time.

But the resurrections of the *Komagata Maru* incident have not been without controversy. The debates have centered on the question of whether the incident marks a specifically Sikh memory or a more general Indian memory. The circumstances surrounding the celebration of the seventy-fifth anniversary of the event reveal the complexities of nostalgia and the intricate workings of identity politics. When the wording of the plaque was being determined, Gill remembers, there were many in the community who wanted to highlight the Sikh identity of the passengers and point to the *Komagata Maru* as a Sikh sacrifice.[4] Their feeling was that the outrage the incident generated both in North America and in India was demonstrated and exhibited largely within the Sikh community, and that its repercussions led to the reinforcement and strengthening of the Sikh resolve to rid India of the British.

Raminder Dosanjh takes issue with such a view. "Listing the numbers of Sikhs, Hindus, and Muslims is an insult to the people who came on that ship, an insult to what they suffered. We are very concerned today about what type of South Asian we are; but back then, in 1914, it was as Indians—not as Sikhs or Malyalis or Gujarathis—that they were denied entry." Although born into a Sikh family herself, Dosanjh points out that to the majority culture, one's religious affiliation or specific South Asian ethnicity is irrelevant: "We forget that if we walk out on the street today, it's because of our brown skin that we get a certain kind of treatment, not because the person insulting us knows enough about us to know what religion we practice or which part of South Asia we come from."

Natasha Singh, a second-generation South Asian Canadian, voices a similar opinion. She finds in the *Komagata Maru* incident hope for healing current rifts in the South Asian community. A creative writer, Singh says that she would like to write a historical novel based on the *Komagata Maru*. About the reasons for her fascination with the event, she explains: "There's little sense of solidarity in the South Asian community today. I feel that the *Komagata Maru* incident will remind us of what we experienced together; it's a memory for *all* South Asians."

One reason for the insistence by some individuals on the Sikh angle of the incident might be found in the circumstances leading up to and resulting from the 1984 assassination of India's prime minister Indira Gandhi by two Sikhs who were part of her own security guard unit. The killing was in retaliation for her orders to Indian troops to storm the Golden Temple in Amritsar, the most holy Sikh sanctuary. Gandhi believed that the Sikh separatist leader was hiding out in the temple with a large cache of arms. Calls for a separate Sikh state had been launched in India since the 1970s by a group of "extremist" Sikhs that, ironically, had been given the opportunity to rise to power by Gandhi and her son Sanjay in their machinations to consolidate power in the State of Punjab (Tharoor 1997, 37–38). Although, according to Judge, the Sikh separatist movement for the independent state of Khalistan appears to have been largely encouraged by Sikhs in the diaspora (1994, 91–93), Tatla points out that this support was by no means universal in the Sikh diaspora (1999, 113–35). The storming of the Golden Temple and the ugly sectarian violence that erupted in India following the assassination of Gandhi, in which many Sikhs were brutally killed, strengthened belief in the need for Khalistan. The events in India of 1984, therefore, polarized the Indian community in Vancouver and, according to Raminder Dosanjh, contributed to the Sikhs' feeling that the *Komagata Maru* should be memorialized as a Sikh event.

Gill, however, is firm in his belief that the passengers were being discriminated against not because of their Sikh identity but because of their being Indian. "In 1914, when the passengers came, they came as brothers, sharing the same voyage, sharing the same hopes. People were thinking less of the differences between them and more of their common dream to start a new life in Canada. Not only did they not think of themselves as Sikhs, Hindus, and Muslims, but also, remember that there was no Pakistan at that time, so they all thought of themselves as Indian." (In fact, surprisingly, the Sikhs themselves used the blanket term "Hindu" to speak of themselves and any other Indian.)

Ujjal Dosanjh's victory in February 2000 for the premiership of British Columbia marked the ascendancy of moderate voices in the Canadian South Asian community. But he did not come by his status easily. In 1985, a year after the assassination of Indira Gandhi and the ensuing sectarian violence against Sikhs in India, Dosanjh was brutally attacked in Vancouver (and required eighty stitches) for speaking out against Khalistan and violence:

> The attempts to promote a division of India or violence associated with those events are not condoned by the overwhelming but silent majority of the people residing abroad. I ask those of us who have raised separatist slogans to reconsider their position and come and join hands with all of us. . . . We have not only the integrity, communal harmony and unity of India at stake but also the credibility and respect of our community in Canada and other parts of the world. (qtd. in Tatla 1999, 132)

But Dosanjh persisted in his message, determined not "to be silenced by fear" (Pais 2000, 24d). His electability had much to do with his appeal not just to moderate Sikhs but also to the South Asian community at large and to other ethnic groups in British Columbia. The Chinese population in British Columbia, almost twice as large as the South Asian population, also played a part in Dosanjh's victory, according to Gill. In our interview on 30 March 2000, Gill, who spoke with great pride about Dosanjh, said he believes that the victory was made possible by the campaign's emphasis on "human rights and social justice for all."

Dosanjh claims that his rise to power came about as a result of his involvement in progressive politics. His early activism took place largely in a working-class context. Pais writes that when Dosanjh "heard about farmers being exploited in British Columbia, [he] got first-hand information by working on the farm disguised as a berry-picker" (2000, 24d). Perhaps Dosanjh's attention to workers' rights has enabled him to reach beyond the South Asian Canadian community to voters in other groups. By contrast, one could speculate on the extent to which the predominantly middle- and upper-middle-class status of South Asian Americans has prevented them from moving beyond celebratory identity politics to engage with urgent issues of voters in other socioeconomic classes.

Vijay Prashad, coeditor of the special *Amerasia Journal* issue titled "Satyagraha in America: The Political Culture of South Asian Americans," believes, like Gill, that identity politics can cause us to run aground of the more immediate and urgent concerns of all solidarity. He, in fact, takes Asian American studies to task for having become a "racial and cultural movement" and for having forgotten its activist roots. Prashad believes that our obsession with narrow ethnic labels—"South Asian," "Asian American"—is counterproductive, and he calls for a renegotiation of the category "people of color" (Prashad 1998, 105). While Prashad acknowledges the deep emotional resonance of ethnic identity, particularly for high school and college students involved in locating themselves in the larger social and cultural world of the United States, he insists that one must go beyond the comfort of the ethnic, religious, or national self to a broader articulation of one's role. Prashad himself is involved in recollecting the forgotten history of the Indian-Black "encounter" in the United States, specifically the place of Mahatma Gandhi in black American culture (see Prashad 2000). His declaration that "youth are in a position to reframe social agendas" reminds us that *how* and *what* we remember—the construction we give to the past—will play a critical role in the messages that young people, the potential leaders of the future, take into their adult lives (Prashad and Mathew, 1999/2000, xiv).

In discussing memory within the context of post-apartheid South Africa, Ingrid de Kok draws attention to three types of articulation. The first, she says, is the language of amnesia, in which one talks about the past in order to get it "out of the way." This is the kind of rhetoric that believes "that life must go on" and "expresses a terror that, if we take one glimpse backwards, we may be dragged back into the apartheid underworld." The second language is that of " 'national catharsis', promoting confession, or some version of 'reliving' that will purge the perpetrators and restore the dignity of the victims" (1998, 59). De Kok believes that this second type of rhetoric "saturates the TRC [the Truth and Reconciliation Commission], with its semi-religious staging, its confessional syntax, and its many clerical commissioners." The third type of articulation "involves a demand for 'reckoning' to resolve the relation between grief and anger. . . . It asks for 'justice' to be added to the requirement for 'truth' and that 'reconciliation' be exposed as an easy sham. It asks for punishments that fit the crime and it sometimes requires a detailed logging of specific crimes, as if they could be added up into a total sum of meanings" (60).

I don't mean at all to suggest that there is an emotional equivalence between South African reconstructions of the apartheid years and remembering what happened to the *Komagata Maru*. De Kok's typology is useful, however, because it illuminates the relationship between why we remember and how we remember.

Why did the year 1989 become a ripe moment for commemorating the *Komagata Maru*? Beyond the obvious fact that it was the seventy-fifth anniversary of the incident, it was a time when two forces coalesced to provide momentum for the effort. First, the South Asian community in Vancouver was sufficiently well established to "work the system," that is, press the local government and, in addition, set things in motion within the South Asian community. Second, the divisiveness among the South Asian commu-

nity that resulted from the 1984 events in India called for a project that had the potential to bring people together both by creating a sense of shared pride in how far the
community had come from 1914 and by reminding the community to remain vigilant
against racism. The plaque marks, as well, the official recognition of and acknowledgment by the majority culture of its racist policies and serves as a reminder to it of the
promise of an open society that must be upheld.

Indian Canadian filmmaker Deepa Mehta, known for her provocative films *Fire*
(1997) and *Earth* (1999), is working on a screenplay for a film about the *Komagata
Maru*. In *Earth,* Mehta revisits the painful moment of the partition of the Indian subcontinent at the end of British rule in 1947, when two nations, India and Pakistan, were
born. This emotionally charged time in the history of India and Pakistan still resonates
deeply for many South Asians; Mehta focuses on what Partition meant for Hindus, Muslims, and Sikhs, giving nuanced portraits of protagonists from each of these communities. If *Earth* is any indication of Mehta's approach to controversial and difficult subjects, it is fair to say that she will probably reconstruct the *Komagata Maru* incident as
an Indian rather than a Sikh memory, privileging no particular religious group.

The *Komagata Maru* affair can easily be remembered as a Sikh affair (the one limi-
tation of Johnston's book is its subtitle—"The Sikh Challenge to Canada's Colour
Bar"), given that the majority of the passengers were Sikhs. But choosing to view the
situation through the lens of a contemporary emphasis on celebrating difference or
through the lens of contemporary national and international politics dehistoricizes the
event and distorts its significance in the historical context of its occurrence.

Raminder Dosanjh emphasizes the larger Indian quality of the narrative. Wider still,
however, is Gill's call for a perspective that takes the *Komagata Maru* as a starting point
for a discussion involving all Canadians, not as an endpoint in remembering only a few.
In his introductory address to the conference he organized for the seventy-fifth anniversary of the event—a conference titled "Beyond the *Komagata Maru*: Race Relations
Today"—Gill issues a plea:

> We ask that while you examine the *Komagata Maru* incident that you also go beyond it to
> review the history since the ship came to Vancouver Harbor. There have been many racist
> incidents in Canadian history such as the systematic discrimination towards native people,
> the head tax on Chinese people, the Jewish refugees turned back to Hitler's Germany to be
> gassed in the gas chambers, the Japanese internment and many more such incidents.
>
> At this conference, our task is to review the past and recommend some positive directions
> for the future. Thousands of visible ethnic minority people have made Canada their home.
> The reality is they are going to stay here. The question is how are we going to get along,
> live harmoniously and make life worthwhile and interesting for all citizens? (1990, 24)

Gill's inclusive vision, like Prashad's sentiments, is a reminder to Asian American
scholars and researchers that as we recover the past we do it with a panethnic sensibility and a transnational vision. The *Komagata Maru* incident is a convincing demonstration of the reality that a single ship with passengers who were primarily Sikh encompassed the history of Chinese and Japanese immigration to Canada, transnationalism

in Asia during the early years of the twentieth century, Indian revolutionary activity against British rule, and resistance among the Indian diaspora in North America to British colonialism. Asian America, it would appear, must move beyond the Asian and the American.

Notes

1. Dosanjh's rise from attorney general of British Columbia to premier was rapid. However, on 16 May 2001, the New Democratic Party, of which he was leader, suffered a crushing defeat in the legislative-assembly elections, losing thirty-eight seats in all, Dosanjh's among them. Nevertheless, Dosanjh does not see his defeat as having an unfavorable impact on the political future of South Asians in Canada. In fact, he points out, eight South Asians were elected to the assembly on the Liberal Party ticket. See Jain 2001.

2. Ghadr ("mutiny") was a revolutionary organization formed in 1913 by Indians in California to organize the struggle against British rule in India. Jane Singh, who teaches in the ethnic studies department at the University of California at Berkeley, has done much primary research on the Ghadr Party and its published material. Some of the poems and songs of the party are anthologized (Cooke and Rustomji-Kerns 1994).

3. Rungh, AAJ, and MEHFIL are all Hindi words; *rung* means "color"; *aaj*, "today"; and *mehfil*, "gathering." Desh Pardesh translates roughly as *desh*, "home country," and *pardesh*, "foreign land."

4. Unless otherwise noted, the quotes from Charan Gill, Raminder Dosanjh, and Natasha Singh in this and the following paragraphs are from my telephone interviews with them between 18 May and 30 May 1998. Gill and Dosanjh live in Vancouver; at the time of the interview, Singh was living in New York City.

Works Cited

Binning, Sadhu. 1995. "The Heart-Breaking Incident." In *No More Watno Dur*. Toronto: TSAR Publications.

Chadney, James G. 1985. "India's Sikhs in Vancouver: Immigration, Occupation, and Ethnic Adaptation." *Population Review* 29, 1–2: 59–66.

Cooke, Miriam, and Roshni Rustomji-Kerns, eds. 1994. *Blood into Ink: South Asian and Middle Eastern Women Write War*. Boulder: Westview Press.

Corriea, Eugene. 2000. "Premier Punjabi." *India Today* (international edition), 6 March: 24c–24f.

de Kok, Ingrid. 1998. "Cracked Heirlooms: Memory on Exhibition." In *Negotiating the Past: The Making of Memory in South Africa*, ed. Sarah Nuttall and Carli Coetzee, 57–71. Cape Town: Oxford University Press.

Gill, Charan. 1990. Introduction to *Beyond the Komagata Maru: Race Relations Today*, ed. Alan Dutton. Vancouver: Progressive Indo-Canadian Community Services, 1990.

Jain, Ajit. 2001. "Dosanjh Wants to Take Time Off to Think." Online at <http://www.rediff.com/us/2001/jun/18can1.htm>.

Johnston, Hugh. 1979. *The Voyage of the Komagata Maru: The Sikh Challenge to Canada's Color Bar*. Delhi: Oxford University Press.

Josh, Sohan Singh. 1975. *Tragedy of Komagata Maru.* New Delhi: People's Publishing House.

Judge, Paramjit S. 1994. *Punjabis in Canada: A Study of Formation of an Ethnic Community.* Delhi: Chanakya Publications.

Pais, Arthur. 2000. "Mr. Nice Guy." *India Today* (international edition), 6 March: 24d.

Pollock, Sharon. 1978. *The Komagata Maru Incident.* Toronto: Theatre Ontario Printing Center.

Prashad, Vijay. 1998. "Crafting Solidarities." In *A Part, Yet Apart: South Asians in Asian America,* ed. Lavina Dhingra Shankar and Rajini Srikanth, 105–26. Philadelphia: Temple University Press.

Prashad, Vijay, and Bijn Mathew. 1999/2000. "*Satyagraha* in America: The Political Culture of South Asians in the U.S." *Amerasia Journal* 25, 3: ix–xv.

Robins, Steve. 1998. "Silence in My Father's House: Memory, Nationalism, and Narratives of the Body." In *Negotiating the Past: The Making of Memory in South Africa,* ed. Sarah Nuttall and Carli Coetzee, 120–40. Cape Town: Oxford University Press.

Saeed, Khurram, and R. Paul Dhillon. 1997. "100 Years." *AAJ Magazine,* November. Online at <http://www.aajmag.com/100yrs.htm>.

Tatla, Darshan Singh. 1999. *The Sikh Diaspora: The Search for Statehood.* Seattle: University of Washington Press.

Tharoor, Shashi. 1997. *India: From Midnight to the Millennium.* New Delhi: Penguin India.

Ward, Peter W. 1990. *White Canada Forever: Popular Attitudes and Public Policy toward Orientals in British Columbia.* Montreal: McGill-Queen's University Press.

Lane Ryo Hirabayashi

---

6   Community Destroyed? Assessing the Impact of the Loss of Community on Japanese Americans during World War II

Community Destroyed?

The glosses of the verbs "to collect" and "to recollect" that this volume's editors offer in the introduction are well worth considering vis-à-vis the fields of Asian American and ethnic studies. In terms of "collect," for example, efforts to "gather, assemble, or accumulate" data for study are highlighted. But immediately one wonders if this is complete. Is this really what we do when we grapple with topics in, say, Asian American history—especially if we are trying to understand a distant past that we have not experienced firsthand? I intend to offer an addendum that acknowledges the importance of actions implied in the verb "recollect" as delineated here; I also propose that a series of antonyms to "cover" are equally relevant: namely, "uncover," "discover," and "recover." To illustrate, I will use my experiences studying the mass incarceration of Japanese Americans in California, and portions of the states of Washington, Oregon, and Arizona, between 1942 and 1945. For the record: I am of part-Japanese descent; my father's family went into various camps or, in one case, to jail; and I was born well after the end of the war.

The impact of mass removal and mass incarceration on prewar communities and communality has received limited attention in the literature on the Japanese American experience (see CWRIC 1982). While there have been assessments of the loss of personal property and of the violation of human and constitutional rights, as well as of the emotional and psychological damage done those who lived through this experience, the bulk of the literature focuses on Japanese American individuals and families. Little attention has been given, comparatively speaking, to the documentation and assessment of collective losses of the group as a whole.

Decolonializing Research Paradigms

I first came to Los Angeles in 1981 in order to carry out a community study. I designed my project in terms of an ethnic studies research methodology that attempted to decolonialize the research process. In other words, mine was not a standard approach to research or one that would be readily accepted by authorities in the traditional social sciences (see Hirabayashi 1995). This is how my project evolved.

After seven years of graduate work, I completed my doctorate in sociocultural anthropology in the spring of 1981. Having become dissatisfied with the top-down, overly officious premises of traditional social science research—especially those that dictated that the researcher alone should determine all aspects of a study—I decided to take a postdoctoral fellowship at UCLA's Asian American Studies Center beginning in fall 1981. One of my central goals was to explore the viability of community-based research designs. In contradistinction to traditional social science research approaches, community-based research rests on the premise that the research problems, as well as the methods for gathering relevant data and analyzing them, can and should be carried out with members of the community—or more precisely, with the members of relevant community-based organizations.

In order to get a feel for this approach, I initiated a number of projects along these lines in Los Angeles between 1981 and 1983. One of the most formative experiences I had came as the result of joining and working with the Gardena chapter of the National Coalition for Redress/Reparations (NCRR).

The NCRR and the Community Fund Concept

Founded in July 1980, the NCRR was a grassroots coalition based primarily in California, with affiliate chapters in Chicago, Denver, and other areas in the Northwest and the Northeast. Basically, the NCRR sought an official apology from the federal government for the mass removal and mass incarceration of more than 110,000 Japanese Americans during World War II, as well as monetary compensation, initially conceptualized at $25,000 per person.[1]

While similar in one respect to another of the major redress/reparations organizations, the Japanese American Citizens League, in terms of its emphasis upon legislative strategies as the primary vehicle for seeking reparations, a number of important features distinguished the NCRR from other groups.[2] These differences included a stronger orientation to grassroots organizing, a more critical assessment of the federal government's role in mass incarceration, as well as a greater willingness to seek linkages to organizations in other communities of color that were also pressing the federal government for reparations. One of the most distinctive differences in terms of goals was the NCRR's specific demand for a community fund.

The NCRR took the philosophical and political position that mass removal and mass incarceration, as well as the War Relocation Authority's policy of dispersal between 1943 and 1946, greatly damaged pre–World War II Japanese American communities. Much like NCRR's approach to individual monetary reparations, the community fund concept was initiated to draw both the Japanese Americans and the larger public's attention to a culturally significant dimension of loss—that is, a collective loss—that seemed to have been forgotten or ignored in the push for reparations. In addition, the original purpose of the community fund was to generate financial support for social service agencies that were dealing with ongoing needs that could be directly or indirectly traced to the long-term effects of mass incarceration (see Mitsunaga 1976; USHEW 1977; Kamikawa 1981).

An innovative dimension of the NCRR's campaign entailed the belief that the federal government should allocate reparation money to compensate for damages to, if not the overall destruction of, pre–World War II Japanese American communities. This compensation, then, was due for damages to the population as a whole, above and beyond damages paid to individuals and their heirs for personal losses and for the personal violation of constitutional and human rights.

JCPA's San Francisco Study

The decision to specify and claim damages for collective losses, which lay at the heart of the NCRR's community fund concept, was not rhetorical or ideological; it was the product of empirical research carried out by members of the Japanese Community Progressive Alliance (JCPA), now defunct, then an affiliate of the NCRR (JCPA 1981).

JCPA's study reported that the Japanese American community of San Francisco was established in its present location after the great earthquake of 1906. Working with the local historian and librarian, Seizo Oka, the JCPA research team made a thorough examination of Japanese- and English-language directories, telephone books, and other sources. This search revealed that, by 1941, there were some 157 business establishments, 116 service-related businesses, 18 cultural organizations, 35 entertainment facilities, 39 health related businesses, 38 religious organizations, and 52 secular organizations operating in San Francisco's Nihonmachi, or Japan Town. By examining the same categories of community businesses and organizations in San Francisco's Japan Town in 1951, the research team was able to establish that small businesses suffered a 30 percent decline. The number of health services and professionals dropped by approximately the same percentage. Service organizations dropped by more than 40 percent, and cultural organizations were reduced to less than half their prewar number. The report concluded that "our community survived" but noted that "the concentration camps had a devastating impact on the entire social fabric of the Japanese community, one that continues today, nearly forty years later" (JCPA 1981, 2).

The Research Task

In 1982, as a UCLA-affiliated researcher and a member of both the Los Angeles and Gardena chapters of NCRR, I was invited by NCRR to do research on the question of World War II and the destruction of Japanese American communities. I decided to define the concept of the "Japanese American community" in the manner proposed by the JCPA study team: with an emphasis upon core populations, community businesses, and institutions. These variables seemed easy enough to work with, since they were important dimensions of the definition of community in a classic social science sense. Here, community revolves around the concentration of people, their interaction within territorial boundaries, and their creation of a range of institutions (see Effrat 1974). Also, this definition lends itself to sociological concepts like "critical mass" and "institutional completeness" that have long been said to be important characteristics of viable ethnic minority communities (see Breton 1964; Fischer 1976).

Inspired by my initial findings on the impact of mass incarceration on prewar Japanese American communities in the greater metropolitan Los Angeles area, I decided to survey all the available literature and see what I might find for the West Coast more generally. My NCRR colleagues reminded me not to forget that some Japanese American communities had been much more dispersed than I was assuming. They also reminded me to try to capture some of the ecological and functional diversity that characterized pre–World War II Japanese American communities. I was advised that at least three different kinds of communities needed to be examined: rural, agricultural, and other more specialized enclaves such as the Japanese American fishing community on Terminal Island, Japanese American communities in midsized regional marketing centers such as Fresno, and Japanese American communities in major metropolitan urban centers.

In terms of conceptualizing the emotional dimensions entailed in the loss of community, both at personal and collective levels, one colleague, Don Nakanishi, suggested that I consider the work of Yale psychologist Kai T. Erikson. Erikson had examined the effects of a major disaster in these terms when he studied the impact on the members of the small Appalachian mountain community at Buffalo Creek after a local dam burst, killing many and destroying "everything in its path" (1976). Erikson defined the resulting emotional impact in terms of the concept of "loss of communality," a collective trauma that especially affects groups of people who have been tightly knit via traditional bonds of kinship and neighborliness. Loss of communality occurs when "a blow to the tissues of social life . . . damages the bonds linking people together." "It is . . . a form of shock—a gradual realization that the community no longer exists as a source of nurturance and that a part of the self has disappeared" (302).

This concept seemed to offer an excellent approach to the sociopsychological functions of community for Japanese Americans on the West Coast before the war, a way to conceptualize and assess their sense of loss when they were removed from their homes and neighborhoods in 1942 and were subject to dispersal away from the West Coast between 1943 and 1945.

Case Studies

As I made my way through the literature, I relied primarily on the excellent collection at UCLA's libraries, specifically the resources in the Asian American Studies reading room (which then had what was in my view the largest and the most comprehensive collection of resources on Japanese Americans on the West Coast), in conjunction with UCLA's University Research Library.

To my amazement, especially given the fact that community studies have been one of the most frequent focuses in Japanese American studies, I could find only a handful of studies that included data on pre– and post–World War II Japanese American communities which would allow the evaluation of the communal impact of mass incarceration. Even more surprising was the fact that I could find virtually no biographical, interview, or oral history materials that would allow me to evaluate individual or familial perceptions, reactions, or emotions having to do with loss of community.

Los Angeles

Perhaps the most detailed information on any single prewar Japanese American community exists in regard to Japanese Americans in Los Angeles. Since few studies compare the pre- and postwar period, however, the focus here will be on the doctoral dissertation of geographer Midori Nishi.[3]

Much like Miyamoto, Nishi found that the prewar community of Japanese in Los Angeles was a tightly knit one, fully adapted to its ecological, economic, and sociocultural setting. Prewar social solidarity found expression in elaborate organizations with varied purposes, including the promotion of economic and social welfare, preservation of the culture, provision of in-group recreational and social activities, mutual-aid and protective services, and maintenance of ties with Japan (1955, 160).

In terms of her assessment of the impact of the wartime events on the traditional Japanese American community, Nishi reports her findings in a section entitled "Postwar Decline in Japanese Social Organization." First, she found that only nineteen of forty-five prewar prefectural associations had been revived. Second, Nishi found that "associations organized along purely Japanese lines . . . have disappeared" although cultural and recreational clubs appeared to have survived (1955, 161). Third, "economic or occupational associations for the general purpose of protecting the business interests of their Japanese members declined markedly in the postwar period" (162). Initially, this included even farmers' and gardeners' associations.

Nishi's general assessment was that the solidarity and internal coherence of the Japanese American community had been effectively undermined due to dispersal and the weakening of ties between mutually reinforcing institutions (1955, 164–65).

For example, in their 1964 article on the changes in residential settlement of Japanese Americans in Los Angeles, Nishi and Kim (1975) found that there were seven identifiable areas of concentration: Little Tokyo, Boyle Heights, the Westside, Olympic Boulevard, Hollywood-Virgil, West Los Angeles, and Harbor. After the war, significant changes took place, and two of the previous areas of concentration did not reemerge at all: Hollywood-Virgil and Harbor.

Other broad trends identified by the authors included: (1) the urban nature of Japanese American residence in the larger Los Angeles/Southern California area; (2) the postwar move of many Japanese Americans to the suburbs; and (3) the decline of the link between the younger generations of Japanese Americans and the traditional "ethno-centered communities" (1975, 30–42).

Seattle

Beyond Los Angeles, perhaps the most extensive social science research on a prewar Japanese American community was carried out in Seattle by S. Frank Miyamoto (1984) and first published in 1939. Miyamoto's research documents the existence of a well-integrated prewar ethnic community with a high level of internal solidarity. Working within a Durkheimian functionalist framework, Miyamoto shows how the individual and family were tightly bound into the network of the larger community through a series of cross-cutting groups and organizations: the *kenjinkai* or prefectural association, the church, vernacular newspapers, various civic and community associations, recreational organizations, and so on (see also LaViolette 1945; Lentz 1947).

Some thirty-three years later, in an article summarizing the development of Japanese American community in America, Miyamoto evaluated the impact of the war on the Seattle community. His findings included: (1) a loss of more than a thousand persons between 1940 and 1950; (2) "large" financial losses; (3) the failure of the business community to regain its prewar level of activity; and (4) a loss in the extent and intensity of the social organization that characterized the community during the era of Issei dominance (Miyamoto 1972; Miyamoto and O'Brian 1942).

A Farming Community in the Sacramento Delta

In the Japanese American community in an anonymous Sacramento Delta agricultural town, anthropologist Richard Beardsley identified four key community organizations that predominated in the prewar period: the Japanese Association, the Buddhist and Methodist churches, prefectural associations, and a businessmen's association (1989; see also Befu 1965). Social relations in the Delta were strictly segregated in those days. Even by the late 1960s, when Beardsley's study was written, he still characterized the community as quite culturally conservative.

Comparing the prewar and postwar community, Beardsley reported the following changes: (1) a reduced population; (2) the failure to reopen or reestablish the Methodist (ethnic) church, the prefectural associations, or the businessmen's association; and (3) the continuing pattern of racial/ethnic segregation. Beardsley also noted the defensive, withdrawn quality of the community in the postwar period. During the 1960s, when Beardsley and two of his graduate students carried out the fieldwork, the economic situation was so bad that in his original manuscript Beardsley referred to the community as a "slum," "a Japanese Ghetto Enclave" (even though he was speaking of both first- and second-generation Japanese Americans), and he argued that the "culture of poverty" concept was useful in understanding the lives of its Japanese American residents. Worst of all, the most promising youth were already leaving the Delta in search of new and better opportunities (1989, 114).[4]

Sacramento

In a study of the Japanese American community in the city of Sacramento, Cheryl Cole gives a detailed outline of the prewar community, including the ethnic economy, churches, prefectural associations, and the Japanese Association (1974, 17–27, 35–42). She also provides details on the return of Japanese Americans to Sacramento, and on changes in the ethnic community after the war. Oral history materials are quoted to illustrate the problems of postwar adjustment, including housing discrimination and lack of housing, the absence of any but the most menial of jobs, and the continuing climate of prejudice and discrimination (63–72).

Cole's evaluation of the effects of evacuation and imprisonment are concise and clear: Community feeling was lost in Sacramento's Japan Town after World War II; in fact, there ceased to be a Japan Town in the postwar period (1974, 72).

Cole's research documents economic losses and the decline in postwar businesses opened by Japanese Americans, loss of farming as an occupation, the decline of ethnic solidarity, and the decline in community organizations. She concludes that much of the effort among Sacramento's Japanese Americans by the early 1970s went "toward restoring the sense of community among Japanese . . . that once lost, was found to be sorely missed" (1974, 75).

Emi Tonooka and Bainbridge Island, Washington

Qualitatively, in terms of strong and clear expressions of loss of communality expressed at an individual level, virtually the only example in 1983 (apart from novels, semi-fictionalized autobiographical accounts, or children's books) was in a video documentary, *Emi* (Uno 1979). This documentary is worth discussing at some length, in this regard, as long as one remembers that at a number of levels, including Emi's exceptional emotional openness, the documentary is a clear exception to the rule.

Issued in 1978 as part of an educational film series on the Asian American experience, *Emi* focuses on a Nisei woman, Emiko Tonooka, who felt so betrayed by the "evacuation" that she suffered from physical and mental difficulties in the Manzanar concentration camp. After the war, she "relocated" to Philadelphia and tried to erase the past from her mind. The film recounts these difficult experiences and shows Emi, some thirty-five years later, returning to the West Coast for the first time to revisit Manzanar. She then returns to Bainbridge Island, in Seattle's Puget Sound, where she lived before she and her family were imprisoned.

Emi's return to the island is very moving. She visits the ruins of her family home and recalls childhood memories that included close, cohesive Japanese American community members who lived, worked, and celebrated together. Then Emi drives down the road to visit her old neighbors, the Nishimoris, with whom her family had been very close. The mother in this family was Emi's mother's best friend. Her daughters were Emi's childhood friends and playmates. The daughters, delighted to see Emi, hug her when she arrives. One of them comments, "We thought you'd never come back!" Their mother, quite old by now, holds Emi's hand, recalling how the two families were best friends. The mother can't get over how young Emi looks and says so repeatedly in Japanese. Emi suddenly realizes that Mrs. Nishimori thinks that Emi is Emi's mother, Mrs. Tonooka. Emi is at once happy but overcome, simultaneously laughing and sobbing with the joy of reunion.

As the film comes to a close, Emi comments: "I don't know how and why it was that I came to be separated from these people, my closest friends before the war. Their mother was like another mother to me. . . . Perhaps in the end, I would have left Bainbridge Island anyway, but this was a decision I should have been allowed to make myself. I should not have had to leave Bainbridge by force."

Analysis

In terms of the indices I used in this research, I found enough empirical evidence to indicate that Japanese Americans did sustain collective losses, although not every Japanese American community was negatively impacted. Although many Japanese Americans eventually wound up reestablishing themselves "back home," especially in areas like Los Angeles, the literature indicated that in many of the medium and smaller cities and towns there were serious damages sustained in terms of population base, ethnic businesses, and community-based institutions. From the documentary on Emi, we can infer that these tangible, organizational losses would reflect profound psychological and emotional trauma for the individuals, families, and communities that experienced them. This much said, why is there such a dearth of information about the impact of the war on Japanese American communities? My analysis suggests that three factors must be considered.

The first has to do with pre–World War II social science analyses, which describe the Issei-dominated Japanese American communities as hampering acculturation, let alone assimilation, to the dominant society. Such analyses were advanced in the earliest Japanese American community studies, and this theme has been repeated over and over (Miyamoto 1984, 69–72). For example, Miyamoto argued for a close causal correlation between social solidarity and "Japanese" tradition:

> In the basic orientation of the Japanese community—*in their tendency to look toward Japan*—we have an explanation of their community solidarity. Had these Japanese discarded their heritage of a collectivistic tradition, in the thirty years and more of their residence here and accepted America more fully, it is doubtful if their community solidarity would be what it is today (15, emphasis added)

By contrast, the historian Yuji Ichioka (1988) proposes that it is crucial to examine Issei's seemingly "Japanese" orientation within the larger context of white racism.[5]

Second, in understanding why there is so little research documenting the impact of the war on Japanese American community, we must also consider what the historian John Modell calls the "Nisei dilemma" (1977). Agreeing with Miyamoto that the prewar Japanese American community in Los Angeles was characterized by a strong level of (ethnic) social solidarity, Modell locates a good deal of that solidarity in ethnic businesses, especially in terms of Japanese Americans' efforts to organize specialized, vertically integrated economic niches. An excellent example of this would be the greater Los Angeles produce industry, in which, from top to bottom, Japanese Americans were the predominant group.

According to Modell, the Nisei dilemma developed as the second generation came of age and found themselves relegated to the "ethnic economy." Nisei had a profound ambivalence about this dependence, as well as about life as young adults under Issei thumbs. Modell noted that Nisei ambivalence also stemmed from value orientations learned in school and the larger society. These value orientations had to do with freedom and a greater degree of individualism, as well as with equal job opportunities that correlated with educational training and achievements (see Modell 1970, 1977). While the Issei counseled patience and accommodation, Modell reports that Nisei exhibited overall impatience to gain access to the mainstream. Stymied in terms of achieving their ambitions, Modell found that the Los Angeles Nisei were terribly frustrated before the war (1977, 114–15).[6]

In short, given assimilatory pressures, the Nisei's occupational constraints imposed by both racial discrimination and the Great Depression, and their general reaction to the tightly knit Issei community during the 1930s, it is perhaps less surprising that it is difficult to find Nisei expressions dealing with "loss of communality."[7]

Third, it is ironic that identical lines of thought are clearly evident in the rulings of the U.S. Supreme Court in regard to the constitutionality of mass incarceration—for example, in *Hirabayashi v. the United States*. In an effort to document that people of Japanese descent were basically loyal to Japan, and thus more likely to be suspect of sabotage and espionage, Chief Justice Victor Stone criticized a number of features of the Japanese American community, including: concentration of Japanese Americans in certain key cities on the West Coast, especially militarily sensitive cities like Seattle, San Francisco, Los Angeles, and Portland; strong group solidarity and a failure to assimilate; alien (i.e., Issei) leadership; the influence of the Japanese consulate; and Japanese-language schools, as well as the practice of sending children to Japan for socialization and education (creating the *Kibei* group within the larger Nisei generation). In Justice Stone's view, these and other characteristics of those of Japanese descent demonstrated "the continuing attachment of members of this group to Japan and Japanese institutions."[8]

In sum, it is extremely difficult to document the full impact, including the sociopsychological impact, of the loss of community, because of a basic lack of pertinent research. Furthermore, this gap is not accidental but systemic, for the following reasons. First, Euro-American and Japanese American researchers, working tacitly from assimilationist premises and biases, underplayed the many positive features of the prewar Japanese American communities (and thus ultimately failed to record the destruction of their ethnic institutions efficaciously). Second, an admittedly undetermined but significant number of Nisei believed that their "American-ness" and access to the mainstream society—which would include its rights and opportunities—were being hampered by traditional values and the dominance of Issei within the ethnic community formation. Thus, Nisei themselves may have undervalued the positive dimensions of the ethnic community formations. Third, the U.S. Supreme Court's majority rulings during the war years subscribed to these positions, at the same time that they used them as justification for supporting the public policies of mass incarceration in 1942, and "resettlement/segregation" between 1943 and 1945.

NCRR's Community Fund and Future Research on Japanese America

NCRR's community fund, as a separate category of monetary reparations, fell by the wayside as negotiations for the Civil Liberties Act of 1988 were carried out. At one level, strategies for getting the 1988 act passed were contingent on keeping the total expense of redress as small as possible. (As I understand it, this is largely why only "survivors" were allowed to file a claim; see Iijima 1998 for a critique of the act.)

Second, from a judicial angle, the U.S. government has never given a monetary award for collective damages having to do with the "loss of community." In the end, supporters of the demand for a community fund had no legal precedent to fall back on, which undermined their case. Nevertheless, despite the ultimate failure of the community fund concept, an important issue was brought out and championed by the NCRR and its local affiliates—that is, that collective damages were sustained by Japanese Americans due to the destruction of their communities, and that the federal government should compensate the group for these damages. My files contain hundreds of pages of notes from NCRR meetings, and notes and documents from talks and conferences organized in whole or in part by the NCRR; I marvel at how I was truly "educated" in the course of carrying out this project.[9]

Most immediately I learned that, as a vehicle to counter the biases and mistaken assertions of academicians and government officials alike, a community-based research paradigm can offer critical resources for new perspectives and new findings in Japanese American studies, especially in terms of the prewar and World War II eras. Not only did my affiliation with and work for the Gardena chapter of NCRR give me an opportunity to try out such an approach; I was able to learn, beyond a doubt, that by working in and with community-based grassroots organizations I could gain access to critical insights not available in the extant literature or anywhere else, for that matter. These insights could then be used to generate research hypotheses that could subsequently be put to the test.

Moreover, my affiliation with and research for GCRR/NCRR allowed me to develop more grounded perspectives on individual and collective dimensions of the Japanese American experience than I could ever have accrued in the academy. As a result, I was in a much better position to be critical of official bureaucratic (especially War Relocation Authority) interpretations of the short- and long-term consequences of mass removal and mass incarceration.

Thus, to return to the questions posed at the beginning of this essay, from my point of view, what I do in terms of Asian American history goes beyond the processes of gathering/assembling/accumulating information for study, (although I acknowledge that one gloss of "collect," that is, "to recover control of emotions and thoughts," is intriguing; it is a special instance of the word "recollect," in the sense of recalling). Since we operate in terms of a world that is framed by conscious and unconscious assumptions and constructions, we must actively and reflexively struggle to achieve a modicum of clarity. We must reread, rethink, reconceptualize, and reconstruct in order to be able to recover our pasts, if only because dominant society hegemony is such a powerful influence. Its premises and biases shape the very intellectual environment through which we view and interpret data, as much as it shapes the form and content of "the data" themselves.

In the final analysis, I think that the words having to do with "cover" (that which is hidden from view) and its antonyms, such as "recovery" ("to regain possession of [something lost or taken away]," in the *Oxford English Dictionary*'s 1989 edition), are relevant to a reflexive understanding of the historical enterprise of people of color in the United States. And it is precisely through a process of asking alternative questions—based in grassroots, vernacular experience—and then constructing plausible scenarios for which there may be no existing dominant society referents, that we can best assess the ideological nature of the data bases we assemble and work with.

Notes

Acknowledgments: I'd like to thank Roy Nakano and Susie Ling, the directors of Asian American Studies Center's "Student/Community Projects" unit at UCLA when I arrived there in 1981. I'm grateful to volunteers at the Gardena Pioneer Project, David Uyekawa, Karen Uyekawa, Gary Uyekawa, George Tanaka, and Gary Tokumoto, who have supported my work over the years. My friends and associates from the Gardena Committee for Redress/Reparations, as well as the members of the NCRR itself, taught me much about the value and the importance of keeping a grassroots base.

James Hirabayashi, Yuji Ichioka, Lloyd Inui, and Don Nakanishi have helped me greatly in formulating this piece. Marilyn C. Alquizola, the editors of this anthology—Josephine Lee, Imogene L. Lim, and Yuko Matsukawa—and Temple University Press series editor David Palumbo-Liu provided critical comments on a preliminary version of this manuscript, for which I am grateful.

1. My overview is based primarily on NCRR meeting minutes, 2 June 1979 through May 1981. Kitayama 1993a provides a useful account of the NCRR and its goals.

2. For overviews of the two other primary redress organizations—the National Coalition for Japanese American Redress and the Japanese American Citizens League—see Daniels et al. 1991 and Kitayama 1993b. Accounts by NCRR and JACL redress leaders include Hohri 1988 and Masaoka and Hosokawa 1987.

3. Prewar studies on Japanese Americans in the Los Angeles area include Mason and McKinstry 1969; Modell 1977; Ogura 1932; Toyama 1926; Tuthill 1924; Waugh 1978; and Kawasaki 1931. For the effect of the evacuation on Little Tokyo, see Matsuoka 1971, 1981. Broom and Riemer 1949 represents the most thorough study of the economic losses of Japanese Americans from the Los Angeles area, including Terminal Island.

4. It is notable (and I think unusual) that, even after the vicissitudes of mass incarceration, and the "cold-war atmosphere of the 1950s and early 1960s, the Japanese were American residents who returned to the town were able, some twenty years later, to organize a successful rent strike to win the right to buy the land that their homes were built on. This fact again raises the issue of variation. Matsumoto 1993 gives us the unusual case of Cortez, California, where the Japanese American residents were able to purchase enough surrounding farmland to start a farming cooperative and corporation. When they were packed off to camp, they had enough responsible colleagues who were not of Japanese descent to keep their farming corporation going. These fortunate farmers came back to their land and business after the war.

5. Miyamoto's arguments are echoed in many of the Japanese American–sponsored Japanese American Research Project tomes; see, for example, Levine and Rhodes 1981.

6. Perhaps future research on the "loss of community" could be more effectively carried out with Japanese-language sources, as the Issei logically would have had stronger feelings of deprivation in this regard.

7. See the interesting reanalysis of interviews with Nisei women in this regard; the interviews were originally carried out by Charles Kikuchi as part of the Japanese American Evacuation and Resettlement Study's "Salvage" research in Chicago (Takagi 1988).

8. See the *Supreme Court Reporter* for a summary of the majority ruling in the case, *Hirabayashi v. United States, 320 U.S. 81 (1943)*. Also see tenBroek et al. 1954 (esp. 265). I don't pretend that this is the entire answer. I would surmise that ideas about the supposedly un-American qualities of Japanese American communities during World War II derived from intelligence reports of the sort carried out on Japanese Americans by the Office of Naval Intelligence, and also very much from "popular" perceptions of the day. See Daniels 1968, 1993.

9. I discuss additional methodological issues that are relevant for cross-checking archival sources in Hirabayashi 1998.

Works Cited

Beardsley, Richard K. 1989. "Ethnic Solidarity Turned to New Activism in a California Enclave: The Japanese Americans of 'Delta.'" *California History* 68, 3 (Fall): 100–15.

Befu, Harumi. 1965. "Contrastive Acculturation of California Japanese: A Comparative Approach to the Study of Immigrants." *Human Organization* 24: 209–16.

Breton, Raymond. 1964. "Institutional Completeness and the Personal Relations of Immigrants." *American Journal of Sociology* 70: 193–205.

Broom, Leonard, and Ruth Riemer. 1949. *Removal and Return: The Socio-Economic Effects of the War on Japanese Americans*. Berkeley: University of California Press.

Cole, Cheryl E. 1974. *A History of the Japanese Community in Sacramento, 1883–1972: Organizations, Businesses, and Generational Response to Majority Domination and Stereotypes*. San Francisco: R&E Research Associates.

Commission on the Wartime Relocation and Internment of Civilians (CWRIC). 1982. *Personal Justice Denied*. Washington, D.C.: GPO.

Daniels, Roger. 1968. *The Politics of Prejudice: The Anti-Japanese Movement in California and the Struggle for Japanese Exclusion*. New York: Holt.

———. 1993. *Concentration Camps: North America-Japanese in the United States and Canada during World War II*. Malabar, Fla.: Krieger.

Daniels, Roger, et al., eds. 1991. *Japanese Americans: From Relocation to Redress.* 2d ed. Seattle: University of Washington Press.

Effrat, Marcia P. 1974. *The Community: Approaches and Applications.* New York: Free Press.

Erikson, Kai. 1976. *Everything in Its Path: Destruction of Community in the Buffalo Creek Flood.* New York: Simon.

Fischer, Claude S. 1976. *The Urban Experience.* New York: Harcourt.

Hirabayashi, Lane Ryo. 1995. "Back to the Future: Re-Framing Community Based Research." *Amerasia Journal* 21, 1–2: 103–18.

———. 1998. "Re-reading the Archives: Intersections of Ethnography, Biography, and Autobiography in Japanese American Evacuation and Resettlement." *Peace and Change* 23 (April): 167–82.

Hohri, William. 1988. *Repairing America: An Account of the Movement for Japanese American Redress.* Pullman: Washington State University Press.

Ichioka, Yuji. 1988. *The Issei: The World of the First Generation Japanese Immigrants, 1885–1924.* New York: Free Press.

Iijima, Chris K. 1998. "Reparations and the 'Model Minority' Ideology of Acquiescence: The Necessity to Refuse the Return to Original Humiliation." *Boston College Law Review* 40: 385–427.

Japanese Community Progressive Alliance (JCPA). 1981. Testimony submitted to the Commission on the Wartime Relocation and Internment of Civilians, San Francisco, California, November. Typescript. National Japanese Library, San Francisco.

Kamikawa, Louise M. 1981. "Executive Order 9066: Its Long-Term Manifestations on the Japanese as an Aging Population." Typescript. Paper submitted to the Commission on Wartime Relocation and Internment of Civilians, Seattle, Washington, 10 September.

Kawasaki, Kanichi. 1931. "The Japanese Community of East San Pedro Terminal Island." Master's thesis, University of Southern California.

Kitayama, Glen. 1993a. "The National Coalition for Redress/Reparations." In *Japanese American History: An A-to-Z Reference from 1868 to the Present,* ed. Brian Niiya. New York: Facts on File.

———. 1993b. "The Redress Movement." In *Japanese American History: An A-to-Z Reference from 1868 to the Present,* ed. Brian Niiya, 289–92. New York: Facts on File.

LaViolette, Forrest E. 1945. *Americans of Japanese Ancestry: A Study of the Assimilation in the American Community.* Toronto: Canadian Institute of International Affairs.

Lentz, Katherine J. 1947. "Japanese American Relations in Seattle." Master's thesis, University of Washington.

Levine, Gene N., and Colbert Rhodes. 1981. *The Japanese American Community: A Three-Generation Study.* New York: Praeger.

Masakoka, Mike, and Bill Hosokawa. 1987. *They Call Me Moses Masaoka.* New York: Morrow.

Mason, William M., and John A. McKinstry. 1969. *The Japanese of Los Angeles.* Contribution in History, No. 1. Los Angeles: Los Angeles County Museum of Natural History.

Matsumoto, Valerie J. 1993. *Farming the Home Place: A Japanese American Community in California, 1919–1982.* Ithaca: Cornell University Press.

Matsuoka, Jim. 1971. "Little Tokyo: Searching for Past and Analyzing Future." In *Roots: An Asian American Reader,* ed. Amy Tachiki et al., 322–34. Los Angeles: Asian American Studies Center, University of California, Los Angeles.

———. 1981. "A Community Destroyed." *Asian American Journey* 4, 1 (September):18–19, 22–24.

Mitsunaga, Geraldine H. 1976. "A Study of the Utilization and Non-Utilization of Social Welfare Services and Needs of Japanese American Elderly in Los Angeles." Master's thesis, University of California at Los Angeles.

Miyamoto, S. Frank. 1972. "The Immigrant Community in America." In *East across the Pacific,* ed. Hillary Conroy and T. Scott Miyakawa, 217–43. Santa Barbara: Clio Press.

———. 1984. *Social Solidarity among the Japanese in Seattle.* 1939. Publications in the Social Sciences. Seattle: University of Washington.

Miyamoto, S. Frank, and Robert W. O'Brian. 1942. "A Survey of Some Changes in the Seattle Japanese Community Resulting from the Evacuation." Japanese American Research Project Collection, Box 49, Folder 15. University Research Library, University of California at Los Angeles.

Modell, John. 1970. "Japanese Americans: Some Costs of Group Achievement." In *Ethnic Conflict in California History,* ed. Charles Wollenberg, 103–19. Los Angeles: Tinnon-Brown.

———. 1977. *The Economics and Politics of Racial Accommodation.* Urbana: University of Illinois Press.

Nishi, Midori. 1955. "Changing Occupancy of the Japanese in Los Angeles County, 1940–1950." Ph.D. diss., University of Washington.

Nishi, Midori, and D. Kim. 1975 "Recent Changes in the Japanese Americans in Los Angeles, 1960–1970." *Journal of the Association of American Geographers* 84: 120–46.

Ogura, Kosei. 1932. "Sociological Study of the Buddhist Churches in North America with a Case Study of the Gardena, California, Congregation." Master's thesis, University of Southern California.

Takagi, Dana. 1988. "Hostility among Nisei Women in 1940s Chicago." In *Reflections on Shattered Windows: Promises and Prospects of Asian American Studies,* ed. Gary Y. Okihiro et al., 184–92. Pullman: Washington State University Press.

tenBroek, Jacobus, et al. 1954. *Prejudice, War, and the Constitution.* Berkeley: University of California Press.

Toyama, Chotoku. 1926. "The Japanese in Los Angeles." Master's thesis, University of Southern California.

Tuthill, Gretchen. 1924. "A Study of the Japanese in the City of Los Angeles." Master's thesis, University of Southern California.

Uno, Michael Toshiyuki. 1979. *Emi.* Pearl Series. Videotape. Seattle.

U.S. Department of Health, Education, and Welfare (USHEW). 1977. Division of Asian American Affairs. *Asian American Field Survey: Summary of the Data.* Washington, D.C.: GPO.

Waugh, Isami Arifuku. 1978. "Hidden Crime and Deviance in the Japanese American Community, 1920–1946." Ph.D. diss., University of California at Berkeley.

Part II

Crossings

Mae M. Ngai

7 From Colonial Subject to Undesirable Alien: Filipino Migration, Exclusion, and Repatriation, 1920–1940

Filipino migration and racial formation during the first half of the twentieth century differed from other Asian immigrations, owing to the Philippines' status as a U.S. territory. The American colonial possession of the Philippines framed the experience of Filipinos who migrated to the United States during the first decades of the century—their aspirations, their reception in America, their suffering and disappointment, and their expulsion.

In a sense, these Filipino migrants were the corporeality of contradictions in U.S. colonial policy and practice. When Filipino laborers began entering the mainland United States in large numbers during the mid-1920s, they forced Americans to confront their colonial subjects, the objects of their tutelage and uplift. The arrival of Filipino laborers in the imperial metropole rendered visible the colonialism that Americans had tried to make invisible through the myths of historical accident and benevolence. These ideas had enabled a powerful amnesia and continue to underwrite American exceptionalism to this day.

Filipino migration laid bare contradictions between the insular policy of benevolent assimilation and the immigration policy of Asiatic exclusion, which had fully matured by the 1920s, and domestic racism generally. These contradictions unfolded in a wave of race riots and labor conflicts that swept California and the Pacific Northwest, leading to decolonization, exclusion, and repatriation during the 1930s. Here, I examine the experience of Filipino migration and exclusion, and the process by which Filipinos transformed from colonial subjects to undesirable aliens.

Benevolent Assimilation and the Colonial Subject

The U.S. annexation of the Philippines in 1898 challenged, from the beginning, deeply held American beliefs in democracy and self-government rooted in the nation's birth that undergirded the rationale for its existence. To be sure, the Philippines was neither the first instance of U.S. conquest nor the nation's first extraterritorial acquisition. Previous acts of expansion, however, had established incorporated territories, that is, future states. But after the Spanish American War the United States established a protectorate over Cuba and acquired the Philippines, Puerto Rico, and Guam as territories—establishing the latter as the first formal colonial possessions in the nation's history. Statehood was not envisioned for these "unincorporated territories"; indeed, such an idea was unthinkable for the Philippines, which lay seven thousand miles from the United States and was inhabited by a population of seven million people of a backward, colored race. As Filipino nationalist leader Manuel Roxas once remarked, statehood would have automatically resulted in fifty Filipino representatives in Congress (U.S. House 1930, 119).

The idea of foreign expansion had gained widespread currency in the United States since the 1880s, as expansionists argued the need for new markets for surplus goods and for relieving domestic tensions and justified their ambitions with Social Darwinism and Anglo Saxonism. But Americans believed their imperialist venture was noble in purpose, unlike old-world colonialism. Some of the most militant expansionists denied that it was imperialist at all. Theodore Roosevelt refused the label; Senator Alfred Beveridge Jr. declared expansion was "for the Greater Republic, not for Imperialism" (Welch 1979, 67; Gossett 1965, 333).

Thus during the Senate debates over the Treaty of Paris, the theme of "moral duty" to protect and civilize the Filipinos emerged to give moral justification to the annexationists' second, more plainly materialist, theme of economic advantage. "Duty" was necessary because Americans did not believe that Filipinos were capable of self-rule, even though the Filipino nationalist movement had defeated Spanish rule and declared an independent republic in 1898. But Americans viewed Filipinos as a motley assortment of uncivilized tribes who lived, according to William Howard Taft, "in a hopeless condition of ignorance, and utterly unable intelligently to wield political control" (qtd. in Healy 1970, 237). While it was common to view all non-European peoples as backward, casting Filipinos as "tribal" was the essential element in this calculus because it denied them the status of *nationhood*. As Oscar Campomanes has pointed out, "denationalizing" the Philippines enabled Americans to deem their mission a benevolent one—the United States had not denied national self-determination because no nation existed (1995, 152–53).

Thus when President McKinley declared U.S. sovereignty throughout the Philippines on 21 December 1899, he found no contradiction in announcing a U.S. commitment to individual freedom for Filipinos but not to their national freedom. "We come not as invaders or conquerors," he said, "but as friends, to protect the natives in their homes, in their employments, and in their personal and religious rights. . . . The mission of the United States is one of benevolent assimilation." He also stated that those who "cooperate" with the United States "will receive the reward of its support and protection. All others will be brought within the lawful rule we have assumed, with firmness if need be" (qtd. in Welch 1979, 163–64n30). That "firmness," of course, was the bloody Philippine-American War (1899–1902), in which more than 125,000 troops—two-thirds of the U.S. Army—were deployed and more than 200,000 Filipinos died. The Americans vastly underestimated the Filipinos, who waged a tenacious guerilla war until the superior military force of the United States and internal division among the Filipino leadership ultimately led to their defeat (Welch 1979, 35, 42).

The policy of benevolence thus rested on violence. It was fraught with other contradictions, as well. Tutelage was based on the concept of "Filipinization," the gradual instruction and transfer of governmental duties to Filipinos. But Filipinization was actually Americanization, because its central premise was that Filipinos had to be trained to act like Americans in order to become civilized. Benevolent assimilation, then, promised civilizing uplift and eventual self-rule, but the concept was inherently paradoxical. As Vicente Rafael has explained, "The 'self' that rules itself can only emerge . . . when the subject has learned to colonize itself" (2000, 22; see also Stanley 1974, 66; Anderson 1995, 10–12).

Other contradictions inhered in the belief that Filipinos were savages. The Philippines' status as an unincorporated territory and Filipinos' ineligibility to citizenship codified Filipinos' alleged racial unfitness for Anglo-American civilization. But if Filipinos were savages, they also had to be deemed educable, because otherwise U.S. tutelage had no purpose. Ultimately, as ideology, tutelage was more about U.S. nationalism than it was about Filipino improvement. Rudyard Kipling's "White Man's Burden" (1899) struck this tone. The point of Kipling's poem was not so much the uplift of the native races but, as Thomas Gossett states, the assumption by white men of a "task which might seem hopeless, but which their manly athleticism and moral rigor would not allow them to evade" (1965, 332–33). Thus the process of denationalizing the Filipino people was the same process by which Americans constructed their own identity as a modern imperialist nation (Brands 1992, 68).

Theodore Roosevelt believed that backward races like the Filipinos would attain the "fitness" required for self-government "only through the slow growth of centuries." But, in fact, colonial policy did Americanize Filipinos, through the imposition of a U.S. school system, political structure, market culture, and other institutions of domination (Gossett 1965, 329; and see Stanley 1994; Rafael 1995). As colonial subjects, Filipinos owed allegiance to no other country but the United States. They were not citizens of the United States, but neither were they aliens. Rather, a liminal status, "U.S. national," was invented to accommodate Filipinos' position under U.S. jurisdiction. Whatever other rights this status curtailed, Filipinos as nationals had the right of free movement within U.S. territory. They were not under the jurisdiction of U.S. immigration law and could not, at least legally, be prohibited from traveling to the mainland United States.

The Filipino as Migrating National

During the first decades of U.S. rule, the territorial government sponsored several hundred students from elite families for university training in the United States. They studied medicine, law, higher education, and politics. By World War I most of these scholarship students, or *pensionados,* returned to the Philippines and assumed positions in the nation-building project (Espiritu 1995, 3–4; Posades and Guyotte 1990, 26–47).

But generally, before the 1920s, emigration from the islands was uncommon. U.S. colonial administrators and U.S. business investors in the Philippines, and the Philippine government (that is, the Filipino legislature under U.S. "training"), all discouraged emigration, citing local labor needs. During the 1910s, however, U.S. sugar producers in Hawai'i recruited Filipinos to break the militancy of Japanese plantation workers (Okihiro 1991, 49–51). This was, in effect, a movement of labor from one site in the colonial periphery to another, a handling of Asiatic labor in the Pacific realm of the United States.

Emigration to the mainland slowly increased during the 1910s. Of the 5,603 Filipinos residing on the mainland in 1920, many were self-supporting students from the middle classes—the first generation educated in the U.S. school system in the Philippines—who had followed in the wake of the *pensionados.* Others were laborers from Hawai'i who ventured to the mainland when their contracts expired. As nationals, Filipinos were not subject to the restrictions imposed in 1907 that prohibited Asiatic migration from Hawaii to the mainland (Lasker 1931, 21; see U.S. President 1907).

Migration to the mainland increased dramatically in the late 1920s. After Congress passed the Immigration Act of 1924 (43 Stat. 153), western agriculture turned to Filipinos and Mexicans to replace European and Japanese farm labor. Between 1920 and 1929 some 14,000 Filipinos migrated from Hawai'i to the mainland, 10,000 of them in the latter half of the decade. Another 37,600 came directly from the Philippines. By 1930 there were some 56,000 Filipinos on the West Coast, more than ten times the number in 1920 (Lasker 1931, 1, 31, 347–48).

Nearly 85 percent of the Filipinos who arrived in California during the 1920s were under the age of thirty, 93 percent were male, and 77 percent were single. In San Francisco and Los Angeles, Filipinos found employment as domestics and in hotels and restaurants as bellmen, cooks, dishwashers, and janitors. Most, however, were migrant laborers who followed the harvest or canning seasons, usually finding work from Filipino labor contractors. They worked in agriculture, cutting asparagus, picking fruit and hops, thinning lettuce, and topping beets, and in lumber mills and canneries in California and the Pacific Northwest. The other major artery in the migrant circuit reached Alaska, where many Filipinos worked on summer contracts in the salmon canneries. There they did the hardest and dirtiest work, such as hauling or cleaning fish. Filipinos were contracted at $250 or more for a four-month season, most of which disappeared in deductions the companies and contractors made for food and supplies, or in gambling (Lasker 1931, 73–75).

As the Filipino population grew, racial violence against Filipinos began to erupt in California and Washington. Contemporaries were quick to attribute the antagonism to job competition with whites. This perception was widespread. In reality, however, Filipinos and whites rarely competed for the same work. By the 1920s there were few native white Americans in California agriculture, especially in fieldwork; most whites had jobs in packing sheds or as ranch foremen. Bruno Lasker, who studied the Filipino population in 1930, reported that Filipinos did not compete with white skilled workers and, in general, were excluded from industrial employment. The few exceptions were in sawmills and box factories. But here, too, Filipinos were hired in unskilled jobs or for seasonal work (see CDIR 1930, 12–13; Lasker 1931, 43–65).

Although labor unions complained that Filipinos undercut the wages of white workers, they did not support Filipino workers' struggles against wage discrimination. For example, in 1927 a Stockton box company hired Filipinos at thirty-five cents an hour, when the wage for common labor had previously been forty cents. When they learned that they were paid at a lower rate, the Filipino workers walked out on strike. However, the union that represented skilled workers was prohibited by its constitution from allowing oriental membership, and the skilled white workers in the factory did not join the strike (CDIR 1930, 72–73).

In a letter reprinted in Stockton, California's *Philippine Advertiser* on 29 February 1928, Filipino farmworkers in the Stockton area petitioned asparagus growers for equal wages: "Filipino workers intended and always do intend to uphold and EMULATE the STANDARD OF AMERICAN WAGES." In 1930, Filipino lettuce workers in Salinas struck to protest a wage reduction from forty cents an hour, the traditional rate, to thirty-five (Lasker 1931, 18–19; see also DeWitt 1980, 14; Melendy 1974, 527–28). The asparagus workers noted that only by "emulating" U.S. wage standards could Filipinos "prove themselves loyal and true to the American most precious TRADITION, thereby becoming most desirable types of people required to remain and live in this country, beyond reproach" ("Martin's Ten Points Warn Contractors, Laborers," *Philippine Advertiser,* 29 February 1928). These were not isolated instances. Indeed, California growers often complained that Filipino workers refused to work for less than forty cents an hour, even as they praised them for being good workers (Woods Papers, file 2.16: 27, 34–35).

During the fall and winter of 1929–30 at least thirty incidents of racial violence against Filipinos took place on the Pacific coast, including two large-scale race riots and several fire-bombings.[1] The first major riot took place in Exeter, in the San Joaquin Valley, in October 1929. Itinerant Italian workers harassed and attacked Filipinos at a local carnival, the latter having brought local white girls to the fair as their dates. For several weeks whites molested or provoked fights with Filipinos on the streets of the town, attacking them with clubs and slingshots made with wire. At the end of the month a mob of two to three hundred whites visited every ranch in the area where Filipinos were employed, demanding their dismissal and destroying the Filipinos' and the growers' property. They destroyed 30,000 trays of fruit at one ranch and burned a barn and ten tons of hay at another. The sheriff did little to stop the rampage; evidence that later surfaced suggested that he had joined, if not led, the vigilantes. Throughout the fall, crudely written signs appeared in Santa Clara and Mountain View: "Get rid of all Filipinos or we'll burn this town down," and "Work no Filipinos or we'll destroy your crop and you too." A Filipino labor camp in Dinuba was firebombed. Similarly, in Arvin, a "committee" of "loafers" presented growers with warnings and petitions and fired shots at the Filipino laborers' bunkhouses. Filipino labor contractors in the valley insisted on carrying guns in the fields to protect their men (see Lasker 1931, 13–14, 18; Woods Papers, file 2.16: 19–22, 34–35; De Witt 1976, 34–36; placards in Woods Papers, file 2.18).

Contemporary observers almost always described the perpetrators as "itinerants," "hoodlums," or "loafers" and often noted that they did not actually want the jobs held by the Filipinos they attacked. Through the late 1920s a labor shortage existed in California agriculture, and whites in rural areas generally had no trouble getting work. E. J. Firebraugh, whose ranch in Exeter was destroyed by rioters, said that "nobody [was] suffering for jobs when trouble occurred. Plenty of work doesn't eliminate the possibility of trouble" (Woods Papers, file 2.16: 22, 32).

At one level, the riots did express anxiety among whites over job competition, even if it was more imaginary than real. White migrant farmworkers who had traditionally worked the fig and apple harvests in Pajaro Valley regarded the increase in the number of Filipinos in the adjoining Salinas Valley's lettuce fields with apprehension and suspicion. But, as the Filipino newspaper the January 1930 issue of *Torch* pointed out: "The lettuce is a new product in the Salinas Valley. No white men thinned lettuce before the Filipinos. Work in the lettuce fields is very hard." Once the Depression started, Filipinos became the target of resentment among unemployed white workers, for whom Asiatics were familiar and convenient scapegoats, even if they did not want the same work.

The perception of job competition was fueled by long-standing racial animus toward Asiatics. The central element of this hostility was the ideology of white entitlement to the resources of the West. That outlook overdetermined race relations and created the problem, both real and imagined, of economic displacement. Filipinos had inherited a tradition of anti-Asian sentiment eighty years in the making. By the 1920s anti-Asiatic politics had fully matured on the West Coast, especially in California, where exclusion had become a staple of the urban and middle-class Progressivist strain of the Democratic Party. When nativists called Filipinos the "third invasion" from the Orient, they placed the problem within a discourse that held maximum political purchase.

But at another level, the anti-Filipino riots evinced dynamics quite different from those that had fueled previous movements for Asiatic exclusion. In fact, orientalist tropes did not easily apply to Filipinos. Filipinos could not be considered heathen or steeped in ancient traditionalism: they were Christians; they went to U.S. schools and spoke English; they wore Western-style clothes; they were familiar with U.S. popular culture. If nativists believed that Chinese and Japanese were unassimilable because they were radically *different* from Anglo-Americans, both racially and culturally, they were discomfited precisely by the extent of Filipinos' Americanization. For Filipinos, of course, the conflicting impulses of nationalism and assimilation were inherent to the colonized identity. The Anglo-American mentality contained a version of the same contradiction. In a sense, the reaction of white Americans to the acculturation of Filipinos was similar to the unsettled response of nineteenth-century Americans to acculturated Native Americans, or of the English to their anglicized colonial subjects in India, whose "partial resemblance" threatened to mock, even as it mimicked (Wolfe 1997, 415–16). Unlike the English, however, white Americans had available to them an avenue for denying the acculturation of their brown-skinned imitators. Because U.S. culture was racially segregated as well as hybrid, white Americans could deny the "Americanness" of Filipinos by ascribing to them attributes that derived from racial representations of Negroes, especially those that depicted black men as sexually aggressive. In fact, this idea neatly bridged the construction of Filipinos as backward savage tribes in the Philippines and the presence of contemporary, acculturated Filipinos in the United States.

By the late 1920s the most common complaint against Filipinos, in addition to their alleged displacement of white labor, was that they fancied white women. Filipino men, it was said, spent all their wages on flashy clothes, cheap entertainment, and white women whom they met at taxi dance halls. The halls were establishments where a dance with a girl cost ten cents. Popular during the Progressive era, the dance hall was a zone of commercialized and sexualized leisure that catered to men of all ethnic groups and was targeted by social reformers as the moral ruin of the young female employees. By the late 1920s the taxi dance hall had become associated with the "Filipino problem," the physical and metaphorical site for the Filipinos' sudden visibility as a social and sexual menace to white society (Cressey 1931, chap. 7).

The notion that Filipino men were oversexed was commonplace. Their sexuality was linked to their primitive development; references to Filipinos' "childlike" nature undergirded claims of both labor docility and sexual promiscuity. The construction of Filipinos' sexuality combined scientific racism and sociology and was not limited to the eugenicists and Asiatic-exclusion lobby. David Barrows, president of the University of California and the first superintendent of education in the Philippines, said the Filipinos' "vices are almost entirely based on sexual passion." Barrows believed that U.S. popular culture "overwhelmed" young Filipinos "who, in most cases, are only a few years removed from the even, placid life of a primitive native barrio" (qtd. in Lasker 1931, 98–99). Bruno Lasker considered the absence of Filipino women and the migrant labor lifestyle causes for Filipinos' social maladjustment and "addiction" to nightlife and sexual vice, although Lasker also noted that Filipinos were "unusually considerate in their dealings with women" (1931, 98–99). Even the liberal Carey McWilliams was susceptible to the influence of racial stereotyping. In his pluralist tract *Brothers under the Skin*, McWilliams wrote that Filipinos' "sexual experiences are, indeed, fantastic" (1948, 237).

Outrage and alarm at the spread of violence pervaded the Filipino community. But Filipinos did not all agree on the source of the problem or the solution. While some defended the dance halls as venues of legitimate leisure activity, many middle-class Filipinos believed that the young laborers who frequented the halls were a small unrepresentative minority whose behavior invited racial hostility toward the entire community. The Rizal Club and Filipino Christian League in Stockton called for the dance halls to be closed (San Francisco *Philippine Advocate,* 1 July 1931). Others blamed the taxi dance hall girls for exploiting young Filipinos and adopted a protective stance toward "our boys," who, they believed, were lonely and impressionable, easy prey for girls with "loose morals" and little education (Woods Papers, file 2.16: 42).

Filipinos deemed both taxi dance hall girls and itinerant European laborers their social inferiors, evincing class bias as well as the belief that they were more Americanized than European immigrants. Hazel Simbe, for example, resented the Croatians who "drove all the Filipinos out" of Aberdeen, Washington, in 1931. "They couldn't even speak English, a lot of them," she recalled. "The Filipinos could all speak English" (Dixon and Koslosky 1981, 14). This sense of superiority contained a sense of bitterness over the failure of Americans to recognize the success of benevolent assimilation, but that bitterness, paradoxically, was nationalist in its thrust. Journalist Jose Bulatao compared Filipino men in the United States, who "take care of their families and will never become social burdens," to the U.S. soldiers going to the Philippines, "[where] they marry our women and then leave their children to be cared for by our government—thousands, tens of thousands of fatherless children are left by the Americans of cultured mentality. . . . And our people are still jungle folk and of Primitive Moral Code?" Bulatao also believed it was regrettable that Filipino men associated with "white women of low breed," but he asserted that Filipinos had the right to do so and that such relationships were understandable because "it is only natural that the demands should be supplied by any means from anywhere" (San Francisco *Philippine Advocate,* 1 July 1931).

These overt claims to Filipinos' social equality infuriated white Americans. Supplementing the violent response, in 1933 the California District Court of Appeals ruled in *Salvador Roldan v. Los Angeles County* (129 Ca. App. 267) that Filipinos were covered by the state's 1901 anti-miscegenation law, section 60 of which proscribed marriage between whites and Negroes, Indians, and Mongolians, ruling that Malay was a branch of the Mongolian race (qtd. in Melendy 1967, 8). Later that year the California legislature amended the law explicitly to prohibit Filipinos from marrying whites. These laws remained in effect until 1948.

Anti-Filipino hostility was thus a site where ideas about gender, sexuality, class, and colonialism intersected in violent ways and, moreover, informed the construction of the racial identities of both Filipinos and European immigrants. Through these conflicts Filipinos were denied U.S. acculturation and reclassified into an identity that combined racial representations of Negroes and Orientals. The same process gave immigrant workers from southern and eastern Europe a purchase on whiteness by which they became American. Anti-Filipino sentiment was thus unlike other strands of orientalism, especially in the gender coding of race. Western colonialism had, of course, feminized the Chinese. On the other hand, Americans gendered the imperialist Japanese as masculine, but in a way that rendered them as virile moderns. By contrast, anti-Filipino racism was animated by the construction of Filipino sexuality as physically base and socially dangerous. That construction served the desire to strip Filipinos of their Americanness and to overturn benevolent assimilation—the colonial policy that had, ironically, led Filipinos to demand wage and social equality in the United States.

Decolonization, Exclusion, and Repatriation

Racial violence at the grassroots level provided empirical evidence for the national nativist lobby's efforts to pass legislation excluding Filipinos from the United States. The California Joint Immigration Committee, American Federation of Labor, and American Legion passed resolutions for Filipino exclusion at their conventions in 1927, 1928, and 1929. The American Coalition, the national umbrella organization of the patriotic societies, which had led the lobby for immigration quotas based on national origin during the early 1920s, gave full backing to the demand for Filipino exclusion (Lasker 1931, v, 34–35, 299).

However, Filipino exclusion continued to be perceived in Washington as a strident regional interest that ran counter to the nation's constitutional principles and standing in the international community. Secretary of State Henry Stimson emphasized that U.S. trade in the Orient depended upon public opinion. "Our reputation in the Orient will depend on fair dealing and good will, and nothing will be judged more sharply than the way in which we have kept our promises to the Filipino people thirty years ago when we said we would govern in their interest and in our interest" (U.S. House 1930, 131).

In order to overcome these obstacles, the movement for exclusion began to identify its interest with Philippine independence. The exclusionists were not motivated, of course, by a desire for freedom for the Philippines; rather, they sought to free the United States of the Philippines and, with it, the Filipino problem. Whatever economic benefits accrued from the insular possession, they were not, in the exclusionists' eyes, worth the price of another Asiatic invasion of the mainland. In fact, neither the eugenicists nor organized labor held much respect for U.S. interests in the Philippines. They believed the sugar industrialists were but the latest incarnation of a long line of monopolists who used cheap labor to undermine U.S. standards (Lasker 1931, 37).

The nativists' entrance into the political debate over Philippine independence brought that struggle to a head. In 1934 Congress passed the Philippines Independence Act, also known as the Tydings McDuffie Act (48 Stat. 456). It set a ten-year transition period to full independence, during which executive powers would be increasingly assumed by the Philippine government and a republican constitution drawn up. The act left open the question of U.S. military bases after independence, although all parties presumed that the United States would continue to have a military presence in the islands (Brands 1992, 156–57).

Independence, under commonwealth status, reproduced many features of the colonial relationship. Citizens of the Philippine Commonwealth continued to owe allegiance to the United States, yet the act declared that "citizens of the Philippine Islands who are not citizens of the Untied States shall be considered as if they are aliens" and that "for such purposes the Philippine Islands shall be considered a separate country" with an annual immigration quota of fifty. Because the minimum quota for all countries under the Immigration Act of 1924 was one hundred, the Philippine quota was a gratuitous gesture meant to degrade Filipinos to a status something short of nationhood, their U.S. "training" placing them just barely above the fully excludable Asiatic races.

Moreover, the act granted U.S. citizens continued unrestricted and unlimited entry into the Philippines, as well as the rights and privileges of Filipino citizens of the Philippines, without the necessity of naturalization. Bidirectional free trade was replaced by a one-sided agreement that subjected Filipino products to the tariff schedules that applied to all other countries, yet granted U.S. capital and products continued free access to the Philippine market. The Salinas *Philippines Mail* for 30 April 1934 called the Tydings McDuffie Act "a bait to entrap us.... It restricts our liberty of action." Indeed, with independence at least a decade away, Filipinos would seem to have been handed a poor bargain.

Decolonization required one additional measure. The catalysts of the crisis that led to independence—the Filipino laborers who arrived in large numbers in the continental United States, bringing U.S. colonial policy home, so to speak—remained a problem. It would not be enough to restrict future immigration to fifty a year. Race conflict, labor militancy, and sexual anxiety continued to attend the Filipino presence on the Pacific coast; in particular, Filipino labor organizing in California agriculture and in the Alaska canning industry intensified during the mid-1930s (De Witt 1980; Friday 1994, 125–48).

The "voluntary" repatriation of hundreds of thousands of Mexicans during the early years of the Depression suggested a method of ridding the country of the remaining Filipino population. In fact, proposals to repatriate Filipinos emerged in the early 1930s, before Philippine independence was enacted. As with the entire colonial experience, proponents of repatriation expressed benevolent intentions to assist Filipinos who had become jobless and homeless during the Depression.

In 1935, on the heels of the passage of the Tydings McDuffie Act, Congressman Richard Welch introduced legislation to repatriate Filipinos. The Welch Bill explicitly provided that Filipinos would be virtually unable to reenter the United States. Section 4 of the Filipino Repatriation Act (49 Stat. 478) read: "No Filipino who receives the benefits of this Act shall be entitled to return to the continental United States except as a quota immigrant under the provisions of [the Tydings McDuffie Act]." The Immigration and Naturalization Service (INS), which was charged with administering the repatriation program, estimated that ten to fifteen thousand Filipinos might "avail themselves of the privilege of returning to Manila" (USINS 1935).

To recruit for the program, the INS issued press releases to Filipino newspapers and posted translations of the act in pool halls, restaurants, and other sites frequented by Filipinos. The service also sent letters to Filipino community organizations, asking them to publicize the repatriation program among their members. Despite these efforts, Filipinos were slow to sign up. Edward Cahill, the San Francisco district director of the INS, blamed a negative propaganda campaign by unnamed agricultural interests who, he alleged, sought to exploit Filipino cheap labor (Coloma 1974, 38, 43).

In reality, however, Filipinos were skeptical of the repatriation program's ostensible benefits. The Los Angeles *Philippine Herald Tribune* acknowledged that there was a "whispering campaign" discouraging repatriation but noted that for Filipinos in America, "shorn of wealth they have earned and acquired; equipped with experiences they

TABLE 7.1. Filipino Repatriations and INS Spending,
1936–1941

Fiscal Year	Number Repatriated	Amount Expended
1936	157	$16,619
1937	585	62,993
1938	497	61,232
1939	391	46,742
1940	391	45,635
1941	42	5,851
Total	2,063	$238,972

Source: USINS, file 55883/412-C.

could not utilize in their own country; possessed of education but no place to fit in; would not these facts explain why the repatriation act has all the earmarks of glaring failure?" Similarly, the *Los Angeles Times* reported that Filipinos believed that they would be disgraced if they returned home as paupers. A Filipino on relief at the Los Angeles County Welfare Office told an interviewer: "I would prefer to stay in America. I would rather go hungry and die here than go home with an empty hand." Although critics faulted Filipinos' prideful nature, Francisco Varona, former labor commissioner to Hawai'i, believed the problem was not so much pride as fear. Filipinos, he said, would "like to return to the islands and follow their trade or practice their profession. But the Filipinos in the United States seemed afraid. They dread the thought of returning home because they fear they may not be able to get work" (Coloma 1974, 43–45, 47–48).

By the end of the first fiscal year of the program, only 157 Filipinos had repatriated under the auspices of the INS. A vigorous effort resulted in 585 repatriations during fiscal year 1937. However, by that time economic conditions had begun to improve, so Filipinos became more hopeful that their luck in the United States would change, and the repatriations continued at only a moderate pace. In all, Congress extended the Repatriation Act three times, allowing it to finally expire in 1940, and allocated a total of $250,000 to the project. According to the INS, from the first sailing in April 1936 to the last in July 1940, a total of 2,063 Filipino nationals returned to the Philippines (Table 7.1) (USINS 1940).[2]

Who were the repatriates? According to data compiled from the manifests of 1,259 passengers who departed between 1936 and 1939, an overwhelming number came from California, reflecting the aggressive efforts made there. Six percent came from Seattle and the Pacific Northwest. Another 11 percent were brought from other parts of the country by the INS (Table 7.2). Ninety-five percent of the repatriates were men. The average age was thirty-five, somewhat older than the general Filipino population in the United States. Twenty-one percent of the men were married; most had wives and families in the Philippines. Of couples traveling together, approximately one-quarter were

TABLE 7.2.   Filipino Repatriates, 1936–1939, by Region

Region	Number	Percent
California	1,044	83.0
Seattle/Pacific NW	94	8.0
NY/Northeast	45	3.5
Chicago/Midwest	56	4.5
South	3	<1.0
Southwest	17	1.0
Total	1,259	100.0

Source: USINS, File 55883/412-A, Manifests of Departing Passengers.

Filipino-American marriages (see Fig. 7.1). More than a hundred children returned to the Philippines with their parents (Cahill 1938).

Forty percent of the repatriates listed Ilocano provinces as their final destination, 23 percent headed for the Visayan region, nearly 20 percent went to Manila, and 16 percent went to other areas on Luzon. This distribution suggests that students and urban middle-class Filipinos were disproportionately represented among the repatriates.

Judging by their baggage, many repatriates do not appear to have been indigent, especially in the earlier sailings. For example, of the 126 passengers who sailed out of San Francisco on the SS *Chaumont* on 9 November 1936, forty-three listed special baggage, including numerous violins, guitars, tennis rackets, typewriters, phonographs, radios, briefcases, boxes of books, bicycles, framed pictures, and the like. Families on the *Chaumont* and other ships brought household furnishings, including cribs, washing machines, dishes, and sewing machines. This suggests that Filipinos who chose to return to the Philippines during the earlier phases of the program were not desperately poor but rather were inclined to return home and took advantage of the free transportation. It also offers a glimpse at the rich cultural life of Filipino laborers, students, and student laborers in the United States.

The desire of Filipino men to repatriate with wives and children who were citizens of the United States posed a problem for the authorities. The legislation provided transportation only for natives of the Philippines. In California, the State Emergency Relief Administration, which had subsidized a substantial portion of the repatriation of Mexicans during the early 1930s, was a logical source to provide passage for family members, especially the children who were U.S. citizens. However, in October 1935, the governor of the Philippines lodged a strong protest at the repatriation of U.S.-born wives and children. He believed such families were destitute and would become public charges in the Philippines, and he threatened to return them to the United States. But by March 1936, the Philippine government softened its position, at least toward the U.S.-born children of Filipinos (Shaughnessy 1935; Murphy 1936).

The "white wives," however, remained a problem. The Philippine government frowned upon their migration, citing their likely indigence, but in truth American women were

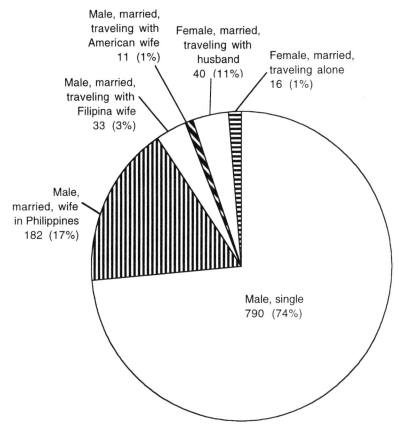

FIGURE 7.1.   Filipino Repatriates, 1935–39: Gender and Marital Status.
Source: Manifests of departing passengers, File 55883/412-A, General Records of the INS, Washington, D.C.

not welcome in Philippine society, which considered them outsiders and of low class. The INS tried to discourage them from traveling to the Philippines by emphasizing the lack of any federal appropriation for their transportation expenses. Yet, as Cahill acknowledged, there was "no way that we can prevent anyone from buying a ticket to go to Manila, and if the white wife of a Filipino purchases a ticket, there is nothing to prevent her from traveling on the same ship with her husband" (1937).

Repatriates also complained that the INS treated them like deportees or criminals. The INS sent officers and guards with each sailing to keep order and to make sure that the ships' managers adhered to a strict food budget (Cahill 1938). That year, sixty of the ninety-nine repatriates aboard the SS *President Jackson* petitioned the authorities for better food and conditions. They protested that they were not allowed to leave the ship when it stopped at ports. A repatriate wrote to the *Philippines Mail:* "The repatriation is supposed to be a Santa Claus gift to Filipinos who want to go home, but have not the money for fare. But in view of the shabby, shameful and almost inhuman treatment we received, the administration of the Repatriation Act reminds us of a CROCODILE's affection and caresses" (qtd. in Coloma 1974, 48).

If the purpose of repatriation was to resolve the contradiction of benevolent assimilation by ridding the country of Filipino laborers and the Filipino "problem," the INS program was only partly successful. Certainly, tens of thousands of Filipinos did not repatriate, as Cahill and Welch had hoped. While some two thousand Filipinos took advantage of the opportunity to return home, many others chose not to go, for reasons involving pride or uncertainty about employment prospects, or simply because they preferred to remain in the United States. Unlike the Mexican repatriation program, which was unofficial and did not, at least theoretically, bar repatriates from reentering the country, the Filipino repatriation act explicitly prohibited Filipino repatriates from returning to the United States. In a sense, Filipinos' lack of participation in and support for the repatriation program constituted an act of resistance against efforts to expel them.

The Filipino problem that exploded on the West Coast during the late 1920s and early 1930s subsided by the late 1930s. As the economy improved, and especially after the start of World War II, rural whites in California moved to industrial jobs in urban areas. As well, young Filipino men became a little older, and in any event mixed marriages were less common after California amended its anti-miscegenation law to include Filipinos. The generation of laboring men who had come to the United States during the 1920s settled, for the most part, into homosocial "Little Manilas" at the margins of Chinatown communities. Labor militancy among Filipino cannery and agricultural workers continued throughout the 1930s, and Filipino trade unionists became important figures in the Pacific Coast labor movement, affiliating with both AFL and CIO unions (Friday 1994, 149–92).

World War II overshadowed the commonwealth status of the islands and the transition period to independence, as the Philippines and the United States were allies in a crucial theater of the Pacific war. The U.S. liberation of the Philippines from Japan served to further ennoble the United States as the protector of the Filipino people; after the war, the Philippines achieved full independence and the United States, in recognition of the role Filipinos had played in the war, made Filipinos eligible to naturalized citizenship with the Magnuson Act of 1946 (60 Stat. 416).

Yet, even as Filipinos who remained in the United States carved out a place in the lower ranks of the working class and in small middle-class enclaves, they seemed to return to a state of invisibility. If the repatriation program had limited numerical success, the cultural impact of the project—and the broader movement for decolonization and exclusion within which it was embedded—was more far-reaching. It restored benevolent assimilation to the status of myth, disembodied and abstracted from its putative beneficiaries. In so doing, it undermined the process of ethnic identification, the "naming" that is invented out of the interplay between immigrants and the larger society. Since ethnicity emerged in the mid–twentieth century as the fundamental building block of the nation, the problem of nonrecognition is tantamount to nonmembership in the national community. It is as though the entire experience of Filipino immigration during the first half of the century was willfully forgotten by a public determined to erase the colonial past from the American imagination.

Notes

1. Lasker counted twenty-six incidents of racial conflict, including three that involved Japanese or Mexicans (13–20); James Woods recorded an additional half dozen incidents (Woods Papers, file 2.16: 19–22, 42, 50).

2. The Filipino Repatriation Acts comprised the original act, 10 July 1935 (49 Stat. 478), extended 4 June 1936 (49 Stat. 1462), 14 May 1937 (50 Stat. 165), and 27 July 1939 (53 Stat. 1133).

Works Cited

Anderson, Benedict. 1995. "Cacique Democracy in the Philippines." In *Discrepant Histories: Translocal Essays on Filipino Cultures,* ed. Vicente L. Rafael, 3–47. Metro Manila: Anvil.

Brands, H. W. 1992. *Bound to Empire: The United States and the Philippines.* New York: Oxford University Press.

Cahill, Edward. 1935. Memorandum to Wagner, 5 July. File 55883/412. USINS Records.

———. 1937. Letter to E. M. Kline, 23 August. File 55883/412-B. USINS Records.

———. 1938. Memorandum to Wagner, 27 January. File 55883/412-B. USINS Records.

California Department of Industrial Relations (CDIR). 1930. *Facts about Filipino Immigration into California.* San Francisco: California Department of Industrial Relations.

Campomanes, Oscar. 1995. "The New Empire's Forgetful and Forgotten Citizens: Unrepresentability and Unassimilability in Filipino American Postcolonialities." *Critical Mass* 2 (spring): 145–200.

Coloma, Casiano Pagdilao. 1974. *A Study of the Filipino Repatriation Movement.* San Francisco: R&E Research Associates.

Cressey, Paul Goalby. 1931. *Taxi Dance Hall: A Sociological Study in Commercialized Recreation and City Life.* Chicago: University of Chicago Press.

DeWitt, Howard A. 1976. *Anti-Filipino Movements in California: A History, Bibliography, and Study Guide.* San Francisco: R&E Research Associates.

———. 1980. *Violence in the Fields: California Filipino Farm Labor Unionization during the Great Depression.* Saratoga: Century Twenty One.

Dixon, DeeAnn, and Nancy Koslosky. 1981. Oral history interview with Roman and Hazel Simbe, 18 January. File PNW82-Fil-030ad/nk. Seattle: Demonstration Project for Asian Americans.

Espiritu, Yen Le. 1995. *Filipino American Lives.* Philadelphia: Temple University Press.

Filipino Repatriation Act of 1935. 1935. 49 Stat. 478.

Friday, Chris. 1994. *Organizing Asian American Labor: The Pacific Coast Canned-Salmon Industry.* Philadelphia: Temple University Press.

Gossett, Thomas F. 1965. *Race: The History of an Idea in America.* 1963. New York: Schocken Books.

Healy, David. 1970. *U.S. Expansionism: The Imperialist Urge in the 1890s.* Madison: University of Wisconsin Press.

Lasker, Bruno. 1931. *Filipino Immigration to the Continental United States and Hawaii.* American Council, Institute of Pacific Relations. Chicago: University of Chicago Press.

McWilliams, Carey. 1948. *Brothers under the Skin.* Boston: Little.

Melendy, Brett. 1967. "California's Discrimination Against Filipinos, 1927–1935." In *The Filipino Exclusion Movement 1927–1935,* ed. Josefa M. Saniel, 3–10. Institute of Asian Studies, Occasional Papers No. 1. Quezon City: University of the Philippines Press.

———. 1974. "Filipinos in the U.S." *Pacific Historical Review* 43: 527–28.

Murphy. 1936. Radiogram to Secretary of War, 6 April. File 55883/412. USINS Records.

Okihiro, Gary Y. 1991. *Cane Fires: The Anti-Japanese Movement in Hawaii, 1865–1945.* Philadelphia: Temple University Press.

Posades, Barbara, and Roland Guyotte. 1990. "Unintended Immigrants: Chicago's Filipino Foreign Students Become Permanent Settlers." *Journal of American Ethnic History* 9 (spring): 26–47.

Rafael, Vicente L. 2000. *White Love and Other Events in Filipino History.* Durham, N.C.: Duke University Press.

Rafael, Vicente L., ed. 1995. *Discrepant Histories: Translocal Essays on Filipino Cultures.* Metro Manila: Anvil.

Shaughnessy, Edward J. 1935. INS Circular Letter. 26 October. File 55883/412. USINS Records.

Stanley, Peter W. 1974. *A Nation in the Making: The Philippines and the United States, 1899–1921.* Cambridge: Harvard University Press.

U.S. House. 1930. Committee on Immigration and Naturalization. *Exclusion of Immigration from the Philippine Islands: Hearings on H.R. 8708.* 71st Cong., 2d sess.

U.S. Immigration and Naturalization Service (USINS). 1935. "Memorandum in re Repatriation of Filipinos." Records. File 55883/412. 2 July. INS Central Office, Washington, D.C.

———. 1940. "Filipino Repatriation Acts." Records. File 55883/412-C. 24 August. INS Central Office, Washington, D.C.

U.S. President. 1907. Executive Order 589. 14 Mar.

Welch, Richard E., Jr. 1979. *Response to Imperialism: The United States and the Philippine-American War, 1899–1902.* Chapel Hill: University of North Carolina Press.

Wolfe, Patrick. 1997. "History and Imperialism." *American Historical Review* 102 (April): 415–16.

Woods, James. Papers. Box 2. Bancroft Library, University of California, Berkeley. [microfilm]

Adam McKeown

8   The Sojourner as Astronaut: Paul Siu in Global Perspective

We overseas people can find no place in China. We can only spend money when we get back to China. No matter how much money we bring home, but as soon as the money is spent, we must come back here.

—Chinese laundryman in Chicago interviewed by Paul Siu

No Chinese laundryman . . . has ever seriously attempted to organize his life around the laundry, saying, "I feel at home in this country and laundry work is my life, my career, and my ambition. I hope to be a prosperous laundryman."

—Paul Siu, *The Chinese Laundryman*

The publication of Paul Siu's University of Chicago dissertation, *The Chinese Laundryman,* as a book in 1987, thirty-four years after its completion, marks its recognition by scholars of Asian America and immigration as a pioneering document by and about Chinese in America in the 1930s. The letters and interviews quoted at length come together with Siu's own sympathetic analysis to produce a portrait of the daily lives of Chinese laundrymen that remains unparalleled to this day. On the other hand, Siu's theoretical contribution to the sociology of immigration, most concisely presented in his article "The Sojourner," has been regarded by recent Asian American scholars with little if any enthusiasm. Although it emerges from the same deep engagement and familiarity with his research as his dissertation, Siu's conceptualization of the sojourner is regarded with discomfort and suspicion by scholars who desire to include Asians as an integral part of American history.

Siu's conceptualization of the sojourner was deeply embedded in the sociological discourse of its time, both as a contribution and as a challenge to some of its assumptions. It was an attempt to describe a social space that transcended the socially and politically constructed boundaries of the United States and China, to fill in the gap between perspectives like those in the epigraphs of this article. In the end, however, Siu was unable to create a viable alternative to the unsatisfactorily monodirectional narrative of migration as a break from the past and transplantation into the new. This was in large part due to his reliance on the methodological frameworks of social types and assimilation theory that legitimized and perpetuated such understandings of migration. Similarly, recent Asian American scholars have also attempted to create an alternative to dominant narratives of American immigration, but in their haste to discredit the idea of the sojourner they have often replicated the hegemonic narratives that they, like Siu, were aiming to transcend. On the other hand, an attempt to disembed Siu's sojourner from its theoretical moorings can recover it as an attempt to develop a transnational perspective on Chinese migration that is as useful and evocative for contemporary Asian American studies as *The Chinese Laundryman*. It would be a perspective of people whose role in U.S. history is precisely their ability to negotiate paths around the dominant boundaries of states and cultures, whether the domination be that of the United States, China, or the international system within which these nations have been constructed as discrete and incompatible entities.

Siu as Sojourner

Paul Siu's life intersected with the trajectory of Chicago sociology in a way that uniquely positioned him to create a work like *The Chinese Laundryman*, which takes pains to replicate the voices of Chinese immigrants as richly as possible within the framework of sociological analysis (Yu 2001, 132–40). He was born in China in 1906 and studied in an American-run missionary school in Canton for several years before moving to St. Paul, Minnesota, at the age of twenty-one to join his laundryman father and enroll as a student in Macalester College (Tchen 1987). He unfortunately did not have the funds to continue as a full-time student and, within a year, moved to Chicago, where he tried to mix night school with day work as a waiter in a chop suey house. This grueling combination seemed to lead nowhere until 1932, when the sociologist Ernest Burgess offered him funding for graduate studies in sociology at the University of Chicago. Siu was one of many graduate students recruited and trained by Burgess and Robert Park. These students were often sent back to do fieldwork in the Chicago communities from which they had come, where their language skills and personal connections were now revalorized as part of the analytic gaze of their professors into a city they had come to think of as a "social laboratory."

Siu had originally intended to stay in the United States only seven years, returning to China after the completion of his studies. He later delayed his return until after he completed his dissertation. When he finally finished the dissertation in 1953, two decades after starting the research, he had put off his trip indefinitely. He made a short visit in 1976, which fell far short of his earlier ambitions to make a career in China. As a student, Siu had continued his involvement with China by taking part in organizations devoted to working against Japanese imperialism. For a while he considered writing his dissertation on why China had not been able to develop modern science, a line of inquiry that then, as now, shaped the research of ambitious Chinese and Western intellectuals who wanted to understand how China had fallen behind in the competition among modern nation-states (Tchen 1987, xxxi). Siu was slightly ahead of his time, however (the rise of postwar area studies would have provided a more accommodating environment), and funding was not available. In order to realize his academic ambitions, Siu had to return to the Chinese immigrant environment he had been trying so hard to climb out of. He lived with relatives in a suburban laundry and worked as a laundry supply agent as part of his new project to create a sociological understanding of Chinese immigrants.

Siu's graduate student experiences hint at the tensions that accompanied the integration of an insider's perspective with "objective" sociological analysis. The ability to communicate within the discursive frameworks of the social sciences requires a level of socialization that transforms the patterns of understanding a student may have originally brought to his education. Any actions or utterances collected during fieldwork and reproduced by the social scientist will necessarily be interpreted within an idiom that is meaningful to the contemporary academic community. It is an idiom that strives for the appearance of penetrating beyond the surface, to highlight trends not readily apparent to the casual observer. This can make practitioners resistant to, or incapable of understanding, material in the way its producers intended. The reinterpretation of material from the field takes place even as it is collected, because the interactions of the social scientist with the objects of his research are always to be mediated through the expectations—both his and those of the people with whom he is interacting—generated by his position and training. Prior categories of understanding and expression may survive in the mind and work of the trained "native" social scientist, but in an altered and recontextualized form. By the time Siu was selling laundry supplies to his relatives, he was as much an extension of the University of Chicago sociological agenda as he was an immigrant making a living among his fellows.

Siu's work did not resolve this tension but grew from it. Like many other sociology graduate students at the University of Chicago, Siu attempted to use his university training in objectivity, generalizing, and the systematic accumulation of detailed data to untangle his own strong yet ambivalent feelings about his life as a Chinese immigrant. Sociological analysis through fieldwork offered a way to simultaneously distance himself from and approach more closely his personal history. The very fabric of Siu's investigations was woven from these lines of stress, generating the special qualities of his work that go beyond its documentary value.

Unfortunately, Siu's inquiries ultimately generated more frustration and alienation than they resolved. The dissertation he produced two decades after he began was subtitled "A Study of Social Isolation." It offers a bleak picture of immigrant life, consistently returning to themes of loneliness, desperation, maladjustment, and "deviancy." Despite the lack of control suggested by these adjectives, *The Chinese Laundryman* still achieves a feeling of closure due to its embeddedness in the concrete language and issues of sociological description. Although his arguments could have been tighter, the progression of the chapters through discrete categories of laundryman life, such as work, leisure, and out-group contacts, provides the framework of a fully consummated and efficiently dispatched research project.

It is in Siu's field notes, stored among the Ernest Burgess papers in the University of Chicago special collections, that the unresolved tensions of Siu's search come to the fore. Some of the documents are papers written to fulfill class requirements. They report on aspects of the local Chinese immigrant community selected to fill the contours of standard sociological categories of the time, such as families, vice, and immigrant associations. Like his dissertation, they have beginnings, ends, statistical tables, and discussions of methodology. It is in the sprawling and unorganized collection of field notes that Siu's personal engagement with his research emerges more strongly through detailed anecdotes and interviews. Again and again, his informants reproduce themes of lust, failed interracial romance, the desperate search for amusement in all corners of the city, and, of course, loneliness.

Although the personalities of individual informants shine through many of the accounts, the collection as a whole comes together as nothing other than Siu's own desperate search for meaning through the possibilities of immigrant life. Encounters with pretty Sunday school teachers, relentless demands in letters from China, lewd comments about female customers, furtive hopes placed in chance flirtations, the lure of gambling and drugs in Chinatown as a solution for Sunday afternoon blues, midnight drives through the South Side in search of prostitutes, and the relentless days, weeks, months, and years of washing clothes in dark, humid laundries make up the texture of Siu's recorded fieldwork. Rather than illuminate his situation with the clear light of knowledge, his attempts to redefine his own life through the collection of sociological data succeeded mostly in elaborating a scene of frustration and unfulfilling human relations.

Siu on Sojourners

Siu's article "The Sojourner," published in 1952, a year before the completion of his dissertation, was much more successful in transcending the tensions of his life and work. In it, Siu attempted to objectify and negotiate both his immigrant and academic lives by proposing an alternative to predominant sociological and nationalistic paradigms. The social type of the sojourner was an attempt to position mobile and transnational people as an analytic center, rather than an eccentricity lodged at the margins of more dominant and geographically stable societies. Although he uses Chinese immigrants as his primary examples, he explicitly extended the category to include Jews, diplomats, international journalists, missionaries, and anthropologists on fieldwork. This attempt to stake out an autonomous identity for Chinese migrants between the expectations of U.S. and Chinese societies was simultaneously an attempt to stake out a personal identity as an academic and immigrant. By appropriating the vocabulary of sociology, he established the terms by which he could control the discourse and involvement with his immigrant fellows. By appropriating the oral narratives of his immigrant fellows, he also challenged the ethnocentric assumptions of Chicago sociology.

Siu borrowed the term "sojourner" from Clarence Glick (1938), a fellow University of Chicago sociology student who was writing a dissertation on the Chinese in Hawai'i. Glick defined sojourners in a more conventional way than did Siu, as immigrants who intended to return home. He placed them in opposition to the settler, who intended to reside permanently in the new country, although he also argued that many sojourners eventually changed their attitudes and became settlers. Siu tweaked Glick's definition by defining sojourners as people who travel abroad to complete a job as quickly as possible before returning. This is only a slight modification of the more conventional image of sojourners as wanting to make as much money as they can as quickly as possible, but it is a shift that provides the basis for a more generalized and less denunciating approach. A job is a much more positive form of interaction with society than the extraction of money. It provides the basis from which to understand sojourners as people who can be defined not only in terms of their orientation toward the lands they came from or went to, but also by their multiple interactions and orientation toward a continued existence between these lands. It was a perspective that began with the migrants, not the societies they traveled between.

Although Siu appropriated the word and basic definition of a sojourner, he did not adopt Glick's narrative of the sojourner trajectory that concluded either in a return to China or transformation into a settler. This conventional plotting of the sojourner in terms of a binary opposition is tied to the assumption that a person can only be identified with one home. It is allowed that immigrants can get homesick, and even return home, but not that they can imagine themselves as belonging to two places at once. It assumes that migration is primarily transplantation from one place to another and ignores the flows of goods, money, information, and people that constantly circulate across social and spatial boundaries. In doing so, it reproduces the dominant and marginalizing historical narratives associated with the perspectives of nation-states, and separates immigrants from the global web of institutions and discourses that transcended these boundaries and made migration possible.

Siu's definition of the sojourner was also an insightful challenge to the assumptions behind the marginal-man type proposed by Robert Park. The marginal man was conceived by Park as a person or group living between two cultures and internalizing the tensions between these cultures (Park, 1937; Stonequist 1937). In many ways, "marginal" was an unfortunate choice of adjective. The word "marginal" evokes the image of people defined mainly by their exclusion from the mainstream, and the marginal man has often been understood as such. "Boundary man," or even "vanguard man," would have been a more appropriate label. As proposed by Park, the marginal man was not at the edges of civilization but was the most cosmopolitan of men, "the individual with the wider horizon, the keener intelligence, the more detached and rational viewpoint" (1937, xvii). The racial hybrid and the culturally hybrid children of immigrants were the prototypical marginal men. Park believed that civilization could only develop through contact and communication between cultures, and marginal men were the leading edge of that development: "It is in the mind of the marginal man—where the changes and fusions of cultures are going on—that we can best study the processes of civilization and progress" (1928, 893).

In his book *Thinking Orientals*, Henry Yu described how the marginal man was a liberating trope for many Asian American academics in the early twentieth century, helping them give meaning to their own lives as translators and mediators at the cutting edge of modernity. At the same time, to inhabit this role of the marginal man meant to participate in the reification of bipolar categories, such as tradition and modernity, or Oriental and American. The early life of these academics had often been an attempt to leave behind their identification as "Oriental," and their hopes for the future entailed some sort of complete assimilation or transcendence of these differences. One of the appeals of sociology was its ability to place all peoples and groups within a universal vocabulary of social processes, rather than isolate them outside the realm of "normal" interaction. Yet any status these scholars were to gain as academic professionals and marginal men (in the progressive sense of this term) was dependent on the still-prevalent idea that Orientals were different, and on their ability to act as a "bridge" between oriental communities and the white sociological establishment.

Siu's own history, lived between missionary school, immigrant laundries and restaurants, expatriate political activism, and academia, should have given him a strong personal history from which to live out the role of marginal man. Nonetheless, he found the "marginal man" an unsatisfactory term for describing both his own experience and the experiences of Chinese immigrants. His article emphasized that the sojourner did not occupy a transitional point on the way to fusion with a dominant society or larger, universalizing civilization: "Psychologically [the sojourner] is unwilling to organize himself as a permanent resident in the country of his sojourn. When he does he becomes a marginal man" (1952, 34). The marginal man, despite being at the edges of two societies, perhaps even despised by them, still defined himself primarily in the terms of these societies and the conflict between them. "It seems that the essential difference between the marginal man and the sojourner is the fact that the former tends to seek status in the society of the dominant group while the latter does not" (Siu 1987, 294).

The marginal man was also a product of Park's concept of migration, which meant "at the very least ... a breaking of home ties," with its accompanying "release" and integration into a new social order (Park 1928, 886, 888). Sojourners, however, were not on the path toward integration. They remained symbiotic to the society in which they resided, not a full social part of it. From Park's perspective, this made them merely nomads, like gypsies who maintained a distance from the societies in which they wandered, their stable, unprogressive relationships with those societies guaranteeing their position on the periphery. For Siu, on the other hand, sojourning was not wandering. It was the creation of an alternative social space that was strongly structured by its ties to two or more larger cultures, yet not totally defined by them.

To put sojourners on center stage as a stable social form woven across the boundaries of dominant cultures, Siu started his article on the sojourner by quoting Simmel's characterization of the stranger as "not the man who comes today and goes tomorrow but rather the man who comes today and stays tomorrow" (1971, 35). Unlike the progressive state of fusion embodied in the marginal man, the stranger had a more stable relationship with a given society through the positive construction of difference. He was the product not of blending, but of the maintenance and imposition of social distance constructed over a period of prolonged contact. It was that very perception of remoteness that made possible many of his activities and was the basis of his social status. For Simmel, traders were prototypical strangers, important to any society because of their connections with the outside, their ability to provide goods and perspectives that could not be generated internally, and as convenient icons of alterity that were useful in the generation of identity. The stranger was not just a wanderer who came "incidentally into contact with every single element but is not bound up organically, through ties of kinship, locality, or occupation, with any single one" (Simmel 1971, 145). Rather, he was part of a system of relationships. It was these relationships with others, and the discourse of difference that surrounded them, that made him a stranger, rather than any qualities internal to him. He was treated not as an individual, but as a sign, a representation of the qualities of outsiders. When he returned home, he was no longer a stranger.

Park had made Simmel's conception more dynamic by drawing attention to fusion, transformation, and ultimate transcendence beyond the two societies in question. Siu, on the other hand, described sojourners from the inside, as a set of attitudes and orientations. He tried to recapture the functional stability in Simmel's description while simultaneously maintaining Park's focus on individuals and their relationship to society. In doing so, Siu lost the focus on change that was at the heart of Park's marginal men, and the focus on interaction that was central to Simmel's sociology. Yet he also offered a perspective that challenged Park's and Simmel's rather tightly bounded conceptions of national cultures by starting with the migrants themselves as the point of departure for analysis.

Siu also goes beyond Simmel in explicitly arguing that the sojourning experience had fundamentally altered the relationship of sojourners to their home. Their lack of orientation to the country they lived in did not imply a more fundamental orientation to the country of origin, as the conventional definition of a sojourner would have it. His trips were often more permanent than originally planned, and when he did manage to return home, his relationships were no longer the same as before he left: "When [the sojourner] gets home he finds it hard to stay and wants to go abroad again" (1987, 297). Both the new expectations developed abroad, and the changed expectations of the people at home about what a person who had made such a journey was supposed to have become, made a return to the past impossible. "As time goes on he becomes, unconsciously perhaps, more of a sharer in the racial colony, developing a mode of living which is characteristic neither of his home nor of the dominant group" (Siu 1952, 42).

Sojourning did mean, however, the existence of a social discourse that valorized home. Even the trips home gained much of their significance in the context of sojourning fellows: "The return trip is the result of a social expectation of members of his primary group as much as of his individual effort, their sentiments and attitudes make his trip meaningful. The trip shows that he is a person to be admired, to be appreciated, to be proud of, and to be envied" (Siu 1952, 39). Whether or not a sojourner actually returned to his home country, or even whether he wanted to, was not so significant as the existence of a home country and the possibility of returning: "The sojourner may make several trips back and forth, he may make only one trip, or he may not make any trip at all. Nevertheless, those who do not make the trip may remain unassimilated just as much as those who do make it" (43). The ideal was a trip back every few years, but all the same, "[t]he mere fact that one has never made the return trip is by no means proof that he is not a sojourner" (42).

Sojourner as Social Type

The marginal man and the sojourner were both produced as contributions to the sociology of social types. As a methodological tool, social typing helped Siu create an abstraction of sojourning that could transcend the more limited usage of directly linking the term to physical movement. Types were intended to be ideal formulations, tools to help understand the relationship between society and personality, in part by describing "the mind ... as the result of activities" (qtd. in Siu 1952, 294). In practice, however, the vocabulary of attitudes that was conveniently used to describe social types suggested the inverse: that social activities were the result of the mind. Social-type formulations tended to be ahistorical generalizations, unlinked from any social or institutional context. These abstractions were too easily projected onto concrete individuals, resulting in stereotypes, inflexible conceptualizations of social groups, and an ultimate inability to dislodge sojourners from the larger perspectives that marginalized them.

Within the scope of this social type, Siu's sojourners offered a complex array of personal orientations that went far beyond the mere attribution of intention to return home. Nonetheless, he made little attempt to describe the institutional and social bases of sojourning. A discussion of the family strategies, business networks, native place associations, remittances, and investments that made migration, in and of itself, a source of profit and site of self-reproducing transnational circulation would provide a much better context from which to understand individual actions (McKeown 2001). Instead, his sojourners appear trapped in perpetual isolation, through both personal choice and host society prejudice.

Siu's awareness of this shortcoming can be seen in his comment that he had not found the "cause" of the sojourners' attitude, which would require a fuller study of the "white man" (1987, 295). The second chapter of his dissertation does analyze the attitudes of Americans toward Chinese immigrants, but it is not well integrated into the rest of the work. It was precisely these sorts of intergroup relations that were at the core of Simmel's typologizing. For Simmel, the stranger was only relevant within the context of certain social situations and was not inherent in the individual. Siu's tactic of centering the analysis on the migrants themselves was unable to account for the socially imposed aspect of that identity. Thus, fifty years later, Siu's success in transcending the unhappy internal conflicts of the marginal man and in freeing Chinese immigrants from subjection to either U.S. or Chinese culture appears only partial. He placed migrants at the center of analysis but did not manage to critique the forces that generated perceptions of eccentricity.

The Sojourner and Assimilation

Siu's acceptance of assimilation as a natural trajectory further hindered him from fully developing the critiques implied by the sojourner type. It restricted him to suggesting that the sojourner was an exception to the rule, rather than a new approach to migration and culture in general. This could be seen in his frequent use of the word "deviant" to describe sojourners (1987, 295). It could also be seen in the off-handed suggestion in his dissertation that the race relations cycle could be modified from "contact, conflict, accommodation, and assimilation" to read "contact, conflict, accommodation, and isolation" (1953, 3). On one hand, this formulation was a recognition that assimilation was not inevitable, underlining Siu's insistence on the creation of a new identity. On the other, it takes a step back from his migrant-based transnational perspective and returns to the perspective of territorial national cultures setting the terms by which participation and isolation are understood.

As an explanation of social change, the idea of assimilation is inextricable from perspectives and institutions of locally dominant societies. This bias was made even more totalizing by the way that many theorists understood integration into modern U.S. cities not merely as assimilation into a dominant culture, but as emancipation into a modern society organized on rational and individualistic principles. This individualism was set in opposition to "tradition" and "culture," which they understood as those bonds that shaped life in the lands from which immigrants came. Park, in particular, spoke of migration as a step toward liberation from the bonds of culture, often using the word "emancipation" where others might say "assimilation." Writing of life in U.S. cities, Park asserted: "The breaking-up of the isolation of smaller groups has had the effect of emancipating the individual man, giving him room and freedom for the expansion and development of his individual aptitudes" (1914, 607). In this way, he reified the individualist rhetoric of the United States into a universalistic statement on human nature and rationality.

Thus, when Siu used the image of unrealized assimilation to describe sojourners, he obscured any relevance that sojourners may have had not only in terms of local narratives, but also in terms of universal processes. A different conclusion was possible and could have been reached by following up on his inclusion of people like anthropologists, colonial officials, and diplomats as sojourners. Such people were clearly at the forefront of many social changes (including the increasingly common definitions of peoples into discrete, bounded cultures), and their transnational movement could be a viable and prestigious social alternative. More attention to their examples could have led to a more complex understanding of the relationship of power and ideology to trajectories of sojourning and assimilation. Siu's concentration on the relatively impoverished and marginalized Chinese migrants as his main example, however, made it difficult to see sojourning as a viable alternative to integration in a nation-state.

The Sojourner in Asian America

One of the most significant agendas of contemporary Asian American studies has been to transcend hegemonic and racially prejudiced narratives of integration into U.S. society—in the words of Ronald Takaki, to " 're-vision' history to include Asians in the history of America" (1989, 7). The introduction to a recent collection of essays entitled

Claiming America elaborated on this goal by asserting: "Mere inclusion ... is not enough. Rather, we must write corrective histories—accounts that simultaneously ... supplement and replace the established histories" (Wong and Chan 1998, viii). Asian American studies has indeed succeeded admirably in writing peoples of color into the national history. This recasting of U.S. history, however, has primarily entailed a reinterpretation of the role of Asians in the United States as conforming to, and even exemplifying, the dominant ideals of its history. Gary Okihiro put forth this agenda explicitly in *Margins and Mainstreams,* which

> contends that the core values and ideals of the nation emanate not from the mainstream but from the margin—from among Asian and African Americans, Latinos and American Indians, women, gays and lesbians. In their struggles for equality, these groups have helped preserve and advance the principles and ideals of democracy and have thereby made America a freer place for all.... Asian American history is suffused with optimism: of belief in the human spirit, of certitude in human agency, of an abiding faith in the individual, however mean, and in the power of human will however fragile. (1994, ix, 3)

As such, Asian American history has appropriated the dominant narrative tropes of U.S. history rather than used the experiences of Asian immigrants to replace or challenge them. This can be seen clearly in the resistance of Asian American scholars to the possibilities of Siu's conception of the sojourner. Siu's sojourner suggested identities and heritages that stretch beyond the boundaries of nationalist cultures, and a way to transcend the interplay of center and margin that accompany those boundaries. In rejecting the sojourner, many of the assimilationist and nationalist assumptions that have constructed sojourning as an undesirable and alien phenomenon are reconfirmed.

At the simplest level, much of the resistance to Siu's idea of the sojourner can be traced to his unfortunate use of a word that carries an enormous amount of negative historical baggage. Since the 1850s, the word "sojourner" has been unable to transcend its widespread appropriation in the United States by racist anti-Chinese agitators. In polemics against Chinese immigration, sojourners were understood as wanting to enter the country to make as much money as they could, as quickly as possible, and then return home. This definition was inseparable from claims that Chinese immigrants were unassimilable, that they created unfair competition by their ability to work for low wages because they had no family to support in the United States, and that, as bachelor societies, their settlements were dens of vice, disease, and corruption.

Asian American historians anxious to counter these stereotypes have often done so by denying the applicability of the sojourner label. Any correspondence between the behavior of Chinese immigrants and the negative implications of sojourning have been explained as a result of discriminatory treatment. In short, it is argued that the imposition of racist barriers, rather than the behavior of the Chinese themselves, has marginalized them in the United States. Anthony Chan has perhaps gone furthest in calling the sojourner an orientalist construction with little basis in reality (A. Chan 1981). Sucheng Chan has remained neutral on the actual motivations of the Chinese in coming to the United States but has still rejected the application of the word "sojourner" to Chinese immigrants because it serves to "exclude them categorically from American immigration history" (1986, xx).

L. Ling-chi Wang is one of the few recent Asian American scholars to accept the applicability of the label to pre–World War II Chinese immigrants, but he takes pains to condemn what he calls the "sojourner mentality" as an "acquired value . . . both racial and cultural and . . . at times ethnocentric, chauvinistic and racist" (1991, 195). That is to say, he condemns it as precisely the misguided orientation that made Chinese ready to accept discrimination in the first place. Franklin Ng has attempted to recontextualize the Chinese sojourner with the observation that most European migrants also engaged in return migration (1987). This helps to put Chinese on a par with other migrant groups but does not necessarily lead to a revalorization of sojourning within U.S. history. Indeed, return migration has been recognized and even researched by immigration historians but rarely incorporated into the histories of particular immigrant groups in any meaningful way. The return migrants are treated as people who drop out of the story, rather than as links beyond the border of the United States into wider patterns of transnational circulation and identity (Wyman 1993).

All of these attitudes toward sojourning (with the possible exception of Ng) accept the negative assessment of sojourning developed by anti-Chinese agitators. Rather than rethinking or revalorizing the idea of sojourning, they reject it as an incorrect description or as an undesirable orientation. This is a rejection of the racism inherent in its historical usage, but also an implicit acceptance of the tendency to reject as undesirable anything that cannot be encompassed within standard narratives of U.S. history. Moreover, sojourning is still understood primarily as a personal value, rather than as a social structure that makes continued migration and transnational connections possible. Understandings of sojourning are still firmly embedded in U.S. traditions of individualism, as a choice to belong or not to belong to the United States, despite the thorough criticism of attitudes that might block free exercise of this choice.

In their conceptualization of migration narratives, most Asian American histories have followed Park in seeing migration not merely as movement, but as a break from the past and the necessary first step toward emancipatory transformation in a new land. The drama of this perspective has been fully exploited by Ronald Takaki in *Strangers from a Different Shore:*

> In their trans-Pacific odyssey, [Asian immigrants] "crossed boundaries not delineated in space." Their migration broke the "cake of custom" and placed them within a new dynamic and transitional context, an ambiguous situation "betwixt and between all fixed points of classification." They reached a kind of geographical and cultural margin where old norms became detached, and they found themselves free for new associations and new enterprises. . . . Energies, pent up in the old country, were released, and they found themselves pursuing urges and doing things they had thought beyond their capabilities. (1989, 18)

Takaki's "betwixt and between all fixed points of classification" is later explained more clearly as situated between the binding cultural ties of the homeland and the racial categorizations of "New World" capitalism that justify the exploitation and degradation of Asian immigrants. It is very different from the betwixt and between inhabited by Siu's sojourners. Whereas Siu trapped his sojourners within a new set of relationships that wove back and forth between the larger entities, Takaki's immigrants have found a small but significant space of liberation.

Takaki parts ways with Park, however, in suggesting that the drama of immigration was inherent not only in the experience of immigration, but also in the very cut of the people who would make the choice to migrate:

> [They] felt their hearts tugging them toward an alluring America as they separated themselves from the graves of their ancestors and from a world where there were common points of cultural reference. . . . Hunger and want were not what essentially defined the migrants. . . . The migrants were unique in a felicitous way: they were dreamers. They could imagine what they could do in an unformed America, and their dreams inspired them to take risks. They wondered what they could become, unfurled before the winds of change and challenge. (1989, 66)

Whereas Park's focus on the race relations cycle and marginal man almost imperceptibly transforms the process of adaptation to U.S. culture into a narrative of cosmopolitan emancipation, Takaki doubles back and more forcefully highlights the United States as the privileged site of emancipation by drawing into its borders a self-chosen group of unique individuals, united by the vision of freedom. His work is an uncompromising celebration of the self-valorizing myths of U.S. history.

Takaki's book was produced for a popular market steeped in such narratives, but even a historian of Asian immigrants like Sucheng Chan, who has a much more cautious narrative style, still depends on the construction of migration as a break. In order to describe adaptation and change among Chinese immigrants in the United States, she takes care to create firm borders against the continued relevance of China. She imagines life in south China as one of parochial villagers, characterized by a subsistence existence, a lack of encounters outside the village and family, and little experience with sophisticated economic activities and social organization. Thus, in her book *This Bittersweet Soil,* life in China provides little precedent by which to explain the successful adaptation of Chinese laborers to the demands of California agricultural organization: "The Chinese arrived as peasants, but they quickly became capitalist farmers and agricultural wage laborers" (1986, 79). Her descriptions of the organizational sophistication of the Chinese, which she uses to criticize stereotypes of Chinese laborers as merely docile, long-suffering, and cheap, do not trace it to organizational precedents in China, because "belonging to clubs was definitely not a habit they brought from the homeland, where kinship formed the basis of virtually all aspects of social life, but they readily became joiners in the New World out of necessity" (1991, 78). It was a transformation from tradition-bound being to rational man: "Though Chinese traditionally have valued the land for non-economic reasons, . . . Chinese immigrants in America had to be more rational and treat the land primarily as a factor of production" (1986, 222).

Chan's rejection of the role of cultural precedents in the experience and adaptation of Chinese immigrants is rooted in critiques of essentialized conceptions of culture as bounded and unchanging, which can easily lead to the idea of Chinese as rigid and unadaptable. Nonetheless, her depiction of China as primarily the site of familism and subsistence labor is informed by those same narrow conceptions. Such understandings have often been embedded either in an evolutionary trope depicting China as an earlier stage in human development, or in an orientalist perspective constructing China as essentially incompatible with modern Western society. Chan's depiction of migration as a break, and of immigrant adaptation as unprecedented change, challenges the idea of culture in the United States yet reproduces it in a far distant land, where it can be bracketed off and denied any claim it may have on U.S. history.[1]

The Sojourner as Astronaut

Even though the claims of Asian American scholars and anti-Chinese agitators appear quite different on the surface, they still share many assumptions about nations as the fundamental units from which to begin an evaluation of human society. Words like "emancipation" and "adaptation" appear to bridge nations but only succeed in reproducing a construction of cultural difference as the indispensable foil to American universality. Asian American studies has done pathbreaking work in understanding the racializing discourses that have excluded Asian immigrants but has still reconfirmed the boundaries that produced those discourses in the first place. It need not stop there, however, because these attempts to call racial discourse into question have also provided tools to recover Siu's migrant-centered perspective from the assumptions of assimilation theory. Even if the word "sojourner" itself is beyond salvage, the activities and orientations of the people described by Siu are not.

Any label used to describe mobile people—be it "sojourner," "immigrant," "expatriate," or "transnational"—is simultaneously a description of concrete processes and a prescriptive category that is inseparable from the historical context in which it is produced. A careful interrogation of the relationships of labels to those contexts can recover valuable insights that have been lost under outmoded theory and subsequent reinterpretations. Siu's sojourners inhabited an essentially transnational space, but, in an era when identity was inseparable from inclusion in a national culture, Siu was unable, or unwilling, to transcend narratives of relocation and assimilation and depict his sojourners as a satisfactory alternative.

Despite many critiques of early sociological thinking about Asians in the United States, much contemporary scholarship still hesitates to follow networks of migration beyond national boundaries. Henry Yu's *Thinking Orientals* (2001) analyzes the relationship of Chicago sociology and Asian Academics in more depth than I have been able to do in this essay. Our basic arguments are broadly similar: that Chicago sociology was both liberating and limiting for Asian American intellectuals, that the focus on "attitudes" and lack of attention to institutionalized behavior was one of the critical shortcomings of Chicago sociology, and that Asian American studies, despite its critiques of the "Oriental problem," still perpetuates some of its basic assumptions. Yet, we draw different lessons from our analyses. Yu's book is ultimately a statement that racism continues to exist deeply in structures and institutions that are beyond the reach of human intentions, and a critique of early sociologists for failing to perceive this. Even though he is aware of the emphasis on movement in early Chicago sociology, the transnational implications of Siu's work are not seen as relevant to his main argument.

In recent years, a vocabulary of diaspora, multiplicity, mobility, flows, and shifting identities has arisen to challenge visions of Asian America based on tropes of mono-directional immigration and "cultural nationalism" (Hsu 1996; Kim and Lowe 1997; Koshy 1996). The Chinese "astronauts," wealthy and middle-class businesspeople who are so named because of their constant orbiting between homes and workplaces located around the globe, are a prominent subject that drives some of these new conceptualizations (Ong 1999). The implications of a diasporic perspective are still controversial and sometimes seen as a dangerous distraction from pressing issues of local politics and identity (Dirlik 1996; Wong 1995). Understandings of diaspora on both sides, however, have tended to see it as a transformation in migration that has occurred over the past thirty years, roughly contemporaneous with the rise of the new vocabulary used to describe it. Asian America before this period is still described as primarily shaped by policies of "containment and exclusion" (Koshy 1996, 319).

On the other hand, Siu's description of sojourners shows that Chinese migrants have long had a transnational orientation that reached beyond local situations. A recovery of those sojourners suggests that astronauts and diaspora are not new challenges to narratives of Chinese American identity, but links to a thread of the Chinese American past that has been submerged under nation-based assimilationist narratives. They are links that can direct us beyond the historical myths of the United States to identities that flow through and across boundaries rather than identities that are marginalized by them.

Note

1. A large literature has emerged on the social and economic organization of south China. Three works well situated in the context of migration are Goodman 1995, Mazumdar 1998, and Ownby and Heidhues 1993.

Works Cited

Chan, Anthony. 1981. "'Orientalism' and Image Making: The Sojourner in Canadian History." *Journal of Ethnic Studies* 9: 37–46.

Chan, Sucheng. 1986. *This Bittersweet Soil: The Chinese in California Agriculture, 1860–1910.* Berkeley: University of California Press.

———. 1991. *Asian Americans: An Interpretive History.* Boston: Twaine.

Dirlik, Arif. 1996. "Asians on the Rim: Transnational Capital and Local Community in the Making of Contemporary Asian America." *Amerasia Journal* 22: 1–24.

Glick, Clarence. 1938. "Chinese Migrants in Hawaii: A Study in Accommodation." Ph.D. diss, University of Chicago.

Goodman, Bryna. 1995. *Native Place, City, and Nation: Regional Networks and Identities in Shanghai, 1853–1937.* Berkeley: University of California Press.

Hsu, Ruth. 1996. "Will the Model Minority Please Identify Itself? American Ethnic Identity and Its Discontents." *Diaspora* 5: 37–63.

Kim, Elaine, and Lisa Lowe, eds. 1997. *New Formations, New Questions: Asian American Studies.* Special issue of *Positions* 5: 2.

Koshy, Susan. 1996. "The Fiction of Asian American Literature." *Yale Journal of Criticism* 9: 315–46.

Mazumdar, Sucheta. 1998. *Sugar and Society in China: Peasants, Technology, and the World Market.* Cambridge: Harvard University Asia Center.

McKeown, Adam. 2001. *Chinese Migrant Networks and Cultural Change: Peru, Chicago, and Hawaii, 1900–1936.* Chicago: University of Chicago Press.

Ng, Franklin. 1987. "The Sojourner, Return Migration, and Immigration History." In *Chinese America: History and Perspectives,* 53–71. San Francisco: Chinese Historical Center.

Okihiro, Gary. 1994. *Margins and Mainstreams: Asians in American History and Culture.* Seattle: University of Washington Press.

Ong, Aihwa. 1999. *Flexible Citizenship: The Cultural Logics of Transnationality.* Durham, N.C.: Duke University Press.

Ownby, David, and Mary Somers Heidhues, eds. 1993. *"Secret Societies" Reconsidered: Perspectives on the Social History of Modern South China and Southeast Asia.* Armonk, N.Y.: Sharpe.

Park, Robert. 1914. "Racial Assimilation in Secondary Groups: With Particular Reference to the Negro." *American Journal of Sociology* 19: 606–23.

———. 1928. "Human Migration and the Marginal Man." *American Journal of Sociology* 33: 881–93.

———. 1937. Introduction to *The Marginal Man: A Study in Personality and Culture Conflict,* by Everett Stonequist. New York: Scribner's.

Simmel, Georg. 1971. "The Stranger." In *On Individuality and Social Forms,* ed. David Levine, 143–49. Chicago: University of Chicago Press.

Siu, Paul C. P. 1952. "The Sojourner." *American Journal of Sociology* 58: 34–44.

———. 1953. "The Chinese Laundryman: A Study of Social Isolation." Ph.D. diss., University of Chicago

———. 1987. *The Chinese Laundryman: A Study of Social Isolation.* Edited by John Kuo Wei Tchen. New York: New York University Press.

Stonequist, Everett V. 1937. *The Marginal Man: A Study in Personality and Culture Conflict.* New York: Scribner's.

Takaki, Ronald. 1989. *Strangers from a Different Shore.* Boston: Little, Brown.

Tchen, John Kuo Wei. 1987. Editor's introduction to *The Chinese Laundryman,* by Paul Siu. New York: New York University Press.

Wang, L. Ling-chi. 1991. "Roots and Changing Identity of the Chinese in the United States." *Daedalus* 120: 181–206.

Wong, K. Scott, and Sucheng Chan, eds. 1998. *Claiming America: Constructing Chinese American Identities during the Exclusion Era.* Philadelphia: Temple University Press.

Wong, Sau-ling C. 1995. "Denationalization Reconsidered: Asian American Cultural Criticism at a Theoretical Crossroads." *Amerasia Journal* 21: 1–28.

Wyman, Mark. 1993. *Round-Trip to America: The Immigrants Return to Europe, 1880–1930.* Ithaca: Cornell University Press.

Yu, Henry. 2001. *Thinking Orientals: Migration, Contact, and Exoticism in Modern America.* Oxford: Oxford University Press.

Guanhua Wang

9 Between Fact and Fiction: Literary Portraits of Chinese Americans in the 1905 Anti-American Boycott

In the summer of 1905, tens of thousands of Chinese in more than twenty cities and towns launched a boycott against U.S. products. The boycotters were outraged by U.S. exclusion laws against Chinese and by the mistreatment of their compatriots in the United States (see Salyer 1995; McClain 1994; McKee 1977). In just two months, from late July to early September, no fewer than thirteen thousand individuals and stores published their boycott pledges in Shanghai's *Shibao* alone. The boycott quickly developed into "the largest anti-foreign movement in China between the Boxer Incident and the May Fourth Movement of 1919" (Tsai 1976, 95). Only after U.S. intervention and the Qing government's suppression did the boycott movement fade away in 1906.

The immense popularity of the movement is partly attributable to a successful campaign against exclusion. Financed by overseas Chinese funds, writers and publishers in Shanghai and other boycott centers in China produced and distributed an enormous number of handbills, poems, pamphlets, essays, and news reports, and half a dozen novels (see A Ying 1960).[1] A thematic analysis of anti-exclusion materials can be found in my study on boycott ideology (Wang 1995). Here, I focus on boycott novels and show that they contain valuable information on an important dimension of the movement—the roles played by Chinese Americans in the boycott. Three particularly informative novels, *The Bitter Society* (1905), *The Golden World* (Host 1907), and *Extraordinary Speeches on the Boycott* (China's 1906), are, I argue, works of collaboration between Shanghai writers and their overseas Chinese informants. As such, they reflect shared Chinese views of social justice and the unique roles overseas Chinese might play in the country's future.

Conventional wisdom attributes the origins of the boycott primarily to the rising nationalism in China (see Zhang Cunwu 1966). Recent scholarship, however, stresses the important roles played by overseas Chinese in this event (McKee 1977, 1986; Chan 1991, 96–97; Salyer 1995). Delber McKee, in particular, has convincingly shown that Chinese Americans initiated the boycott in America in response to the harsh U.S. exclusion acts of the early 1900s (1977, 216–17). Legal historian Lucy E. Salyer's 1995 study, which lends support to this view, shows that the Chinese were losing their only institutional protection in the United States—the courts—in the early 1900s. Indeed, the struggle for equal immigration rights had only symbolic meaning for most Chinese participants in the movement because only a tiny fraction of the people had ever been to the United States. (According to Shih-shan Henry Tsai, 99 percent of Chinese immigrants to the United States were from Guangdong Province [1971, 200]).

Yet the struggle was critical for the very livelihood of Chinese Americans. There is ample evidence to show that Chinese Americans constantly watched the boycott drama and tried to play a role as it was unfolding in China, collecting funds for boycott organizations there. When President Theodore Roosevelt issued an order in June 1905 giving Chinese in the United States more courteous treatment, the encouraging news was immediately telegraphed to China by overseas Chinese (McKee 1977, 127).

Whatever the contributions to the movement made by Chinese in the United States, China was the theater where the boycott drama was played out. The challenge is to show how overseas Chinese worked together with their compatriots in China to force changes in U.S. racist laws. This requires crossing conventional disciplinary divisions to use new analytical categories. Nation-states, for example, should be replaced by transnational territories as our analytical focus (Duara 1997).

Given the complexity of U.S. laws, one wonders what specific role Chinese Americans played in China to help define goals and strategies of the movement by sharing their knowledge of exclusion laws and of U.S. politics with local activists in Shanghai, Guangzhou, and other boycott centers. Previous studies give the impression that Chinese Americans contributed to the movement only from afar, rallying support in the United States and wiring funds across the Pacific. In fact, the idea of sending coordinators back to China to instigate a boycott had been suggested well before the mass movement began. As early as 1903, Chen Yikan, editorial columnist for the reformist Chinese newspaper *New China Daily (Xin Zhongguo bao)* in Honolulu, first laid out a plan for the boycott. He suggested that boycott headquarters be established in the United States and representatives be sent back to major cities in China to help with communication and fund-raising (1903, 596–97).

Were representatives sent to China two years later when the boycott broke out? Contemporary newspapers, various boycott publications, and government documents provide clues but no details.[2] The activists returning from the United States might have kept a low profile in China. The movement was presumably a spontaneous outburst of Chinese public discontent. Besides, the returned Chinese Americans might well have connections with exiled Chinese reformers in the United States who were on the Qing government's wanted list (McKee 1986). Yet, considering that the immigration disputes were so critical for the Chinese in America, it is almost certain that there were indeed Chinese Americans who returned from overseas to join the boycott in China. Significantly, the boycott novels provide detailed accounts of anti-exclusion activities by the returnees in Shanghai and other boycott centers in China.

But how reliable are these novels as historical sources? The original publishers, editors of the later editions, and literary historians tend not to question their authenticity. Lai Fangling (1988), who published the only study on these novels, for example, cites descriptions in the novels as historical facts. Her study assumes a natural, linear, and unproblematic link between (literary) text and (historical) context. Little has been said about the intermediaries—the authors, the cultural milieu of novel production and consumption of the period, and the ways in which these novels fit into the contemporary public discourse on issues and problems related to Chinese emigration. The English translators of *The Bitter Society* underscore its historicity by noting that the novel "seems to be partly autobiographical and partly based on stories related to the author by others" (Mei and Pang Yip 1981, 34). Reflecting the biases of Asian American scholarship, which focuses almost exclusively on Asian experience in the United States, the translators do not bother to translate chapters that feature the protagonists' activities in China. The question therefore remains: How should we read these novels as historical evidence?

Between Fact and Fiction: The Boycott Novels

The definition of "novel" is historically specific. At the turn of the century, Chinese readers and writers did not make a sharp distinction between fiction and nonfiction (Zhao 1995). This is also true in the West. In the nineteenth-century United States, as Richard D. Brown notes, novels served at once as historical sources and educational and entertaining materials (1989, 232). Not until the late nineteenth and early twentieth centuries did censorship, boredom, and the limited ability of journalism to do justice to the complexity of the world drive Mark Twain, Theodore Dreiser, Ernest Hemingway, and some others to literature (Fishkin 1985). Similarly, late Qing novelists wrote for the daily press. Novels (*Xiaoshuo*) of the era contain much factual information for historians. Contemporary critics complained that many novels contained too much political discussion to be novels anymore (Lee and Nathan 1982, 378–92; Link 1981, 125–40). The boycott novels, like many other creative writings of the era, are actually admixtures of a variety of modes of writing, including news reportage, travelers' accounts, history, and political essays, as well as fictitious stories.

The rise of commercial journalism in early-twentieth-century China further strengthened the factual tendency of fiction. Like novelists in general, authors of boycott fiction based their stories on newspaper reports, among other sources (Zhao 1995, 27). *The Bitter Society* is typical in this regard. Virtually all the stories about the mistreatment of Chinese under U.S. exclusion laws can be found in contemporary newspapers, pamphlets, diaries, travelers' accounts, and official documents. Regarding the author and the authenticity of the stories, Sun Yusheng, a well-known Shanghai novelist who wrote the preface to *The Bitter Society,* explains:

> It was written by a Chinese laborer in America about his experiences there. The feelings are realistic and the language is deeply personal. In this, it cannot be matched by purely fictional novels. Starting from chapter 20, nearly every word contains tears and blood, so much so that it is almost impossible to stop reading. Indeed, the entire novel is just as impossible to put down. After the novel was written, [the author] traveled across the ocean and brought it to China. (1905)

Since three thousand copies were quickly sold (A Ying 1960, 14), not a small number for a first edition at the time, the novel was probably well received. But was the author really a returned Chinese laborer from America? Based on the fact that the protagonists were all well educated, A Ying (1900–77), a prominent literary historian, decided that the novel might have been written by an intellectual who was familiar with the lives of Chinese merchants and laborers in the United States (14). The English translators of the novel similarly believe that the novel might be autobiographic, though "there is also a possibility that the novel was written collectively by a group of friends whose experiences it relates" (Mei and Pang Yip 1981, 34). Although reliable evidence on authorship is not available, enough information warrants a bolder hypothesis, namely, that *The Bitter Society* is likely a work of collaboration between Shanghai writers and their Chinese American informants. At the turn of the century, the production and consumption of novels was essentially a Shanghai phenomenon. All boycott novels were published in the treaty port city, which also claimed most of the country's newspapers and almost all the literary journals. Not surprisingly, while most Chinese Americans were from Guangdong Province, the protagonists of the novel were from the Yangzi Delta region and spoke the Wu dialect used in the Shanghai and Suzhou regions. Besides, Chinese Americans were not known at the time for using fiction to express themselves. They preferred poems instead (Hom 1987).[3]

While Shanghai writers were likely authors of the novels, returned Chinese from the United States undoubtedly played important roles as informants. The sections on Chinese experiences in the United States bear striking resemblances to Lin Qianfu's anti-exclusion speeches published in *Shibao,* (13 and 23 May 1905). Lin, a former official interpreter who worked for Chinese customs, had lived in the United States for eleven years (*Shibao,* 23 May 1905). Similarly, other boycott novels show signs of cooperation between writers in China and their overseas collaborators. In these novels Shanghai is typically the setting where returned Chinese from the United States join local boycotters in their struggle for justice. What is striking is that the boycott novels tend to be sympathetic to the Chinese Americans' insights on various boycott issues. Stories are often told from the Chinese Americans' perspective. They are the protagonists who explain the origins and practices of the exclusion laws and who propose boycott strategies. It is not an exaggeration, therefore, to say that these novels are themselves evidence of direct Chinese American involvement of the boycott movement.

Informative as they are, the boycott novels are nevertheless romanticized accounts of historical reality and must be read as such. *The Golden World* (Host 1907), the second-most important novel of this genre, is a good example. Compared to the realistic style of *The Bitter Society, The Golden World* is a tragedy that ends like a fairy tale. When it becomes clear that the heroic efforts on the part of returned Chinese and their comrades in China are about to crumble, the protagonists find refuge on Snail Island, an imaginary place near the South Pole. Available sources make it clear that numerous details in boycott novels, including *The Bitter Society,* are simply untrue or impossible to verify. There is no doubt that the boycott novelists took full advantage of their privilege as creative writers to manipulate time and space so that their boycott heroes and heroines would miraculously appear in the right place at the right moment.

For example, *The Bitter Society* (1905) unfolds from the Suzhou region to Peru to the United States to Shanghai, between the 1850s or 1870s and the 1900s. *The Golden World* (Host 1906) follows a similar but more complex pattern: Guangdong to Cuba or the United States to Snail Island to Shanghai, between the 1850s or 1870s and the 1900s. A less well-known novel, *The Tears of Overseas Chinese,* adopts a comparable structural scheme: Guangdong or Fujian to Singapore to Indonesia to Manila to Hawai'i to San Francisco, between the 1870s and the 1900s. This panoramic view of the Chinese diaspora, I believe, is intended to show the fundamental commonality of Chinese emigration—economic hardship in China and the inhuman treatment that the Chinese received in foreign countries, including the United States. "Novelists do not merely show us characters," as Catherine H. Zuckert points out, "they show them in particular circumstances of the novelists' own choosing" (1992, 144). In order to present a panoramic view, boycott novelists let their characters in Peru, Cuba, the United States, and many other places meet (often on ships back to China) and share their stories.

The fictitious aspects of the novels, however, do not make them any less significant. These novels tell us a great deal about the ways in which boycott activists in China, those in the lower Yangzi region in particular, idealized their compatriots overseas, and how overseas Chinese portrayed themselves as a unique group with a special historical role to play in China's future. As Zuckert notes: "Novels both reflect and reflect on the political communities they depict. They reflect the communities for which they are written because, like any other writers, novelists must speak in terms their readers understand" (1992, 126). Among many memorable characters portrayed in the boycott novels, Li Xinchun in *The Bitter Society* stands out for his extensive personal experience in the United States and his sophisticated analysis of a sound boycott strategy.

Literary Portraits of Chinese Americans in the Boycott

The Bitter Society (A Ying 1960) tells of social dislocation in nineteenth-century China, emigration, and the Chinese struggle for equal treatment. Li Xinchun, a grade school teacher in Suzhou (a city in Jiangsu Province known for its numerous literary figures rather than its emigrants) is one of several poor intellectuals in the novel who could not eke out a living in the turbulent years of late Qing China. Natural disasters and corrupt officials force them to migrate, first to Shanghai then overseas. While Li's friends answer an ad in a Shanghai newspaper and become coolies in Peru, Li is luckier. He establishes a small business in Shanghai and later decides to try his fortune in the United States. All the events witnessed by Li in the United States could have happened, but clearly Li is a literary composite of many personalities.

The novel exposes the arbitrariness, harshness, and absurdity of the exclusion laws through Li's eyes and through a series of episodes. For years the Chinese in the United States had pointed out that the exclusion was against *all* Chinese. These episodes, not incidentally, involve individuals of all social backgrounds, ranging from merchants, students, and officials to laborers. In one episode, for example, a worker in charge of machinery at Xinchun's garment shop in San Francisco's Chinatown becomes drunk and loses his identity paper. He is thrown into jail and released only when he agrees to go back to China with his wife and children (Chaps. 37–38). Another episode involves a merchant who presumably belongs to the exempt class. At issue is his wife's legal right to join him. She arrives at a time when U.S. immigration had introduced wooden barracks to hold incoming Chinese whose immigration status was uncertain. The wife is detained in a barrack simply because she has misspoken one part of a street name where her husband has his business. While the case is under investigation, the wife falls ill and becomes disoriented, out of fear, humiliation, and anxiety. Despite the merchant's high social status, the immigration inspector does not allow bail but agrees to have the wife released as soon as the merchant declares his intention to go back to China with his family. Physically and emotionally exhausted, the merchant auctions his business at a ridiculously low price and leaves the United States (Chaps. 39–40).

The wife could have died if she was detained any longer, as happened to a student accused of violating the new immigration regulations. As Xinchun hears it, the student is locked up in the barrack for several months and becomes ill because the place is filthy and damp. By the time he is sent to a hospital, it is too late. He dies soon afterward (Chaps. 41–42).

The most shocking case, however, involves a Chinese military attaché, Tan Jinyong. According to Li Xinchun, who allegedly witnesses the incident, one night Tan is taking a stroll under the full moon after dinner at Xinchun's store. A patrol officer stops him, suspecting that he is doing something illegal at midnight. Asked for identification papers, Tan explains that he is a Chinese diplomat and that the Chinese consulate is minutes away, where his identity can be easily verified. The officer is not convinced and attempts to have him arrested. Tan protests the violation of his diplomatic immunity and refuses to be taken away. The officer whistles for help and several police officers rush over. Accusing Tan of resisting arrest, they beat him up and arrest him despite the protests of Xinchun and some other bystanders who confirm to the officers that Tan is indeed a Chinese diplomat. Humiliated, Tan hangs himself from his bedpost one day after the Chinese consulate secures his release (Chaps. 43–44).[4]

All the cases involve people who have a legal right to be in the United States, even under the exclusion laws. The author's point reflects a fear widely shared in U.S. Chinese communities: The real purpose of the exclusion laws was to drive all Chinese—laborers, merchants, students, and officials—out of the United States. The narrative of painful experiences thus laid the foundation for Li Xinchun's return to China and his plan for a boycott.

On the return voyage, as *The Bitter Society* continues, Li Xinchun meets several Chinese students who are turned back from the United States for violating aspects of the complicated and unreasonable exclusion laws. Together they explore the pros and cons of various strategies of combating U.S. racism. The students suggest that the boycotters publicize to the world America's ill treatment of the Chinese and force the Chinese government to petition the Hague International Court of Justice for arbitration. Li Xinchun, the merchant, turns out to be much more politically sophisticated. He points out that the Dutch do not have a better record in their colonies as far as the treatment of Chinese laborers is concerned, and that it is naïve to expect great powers to be on the Chinese side.[5] The students then propose to lobby U.S. politicians and missionaries. They are again cautioned by Li Xinchun. He doubts that Americans, whomever they might be, would help the Chinese against their own people, despite differences of opinion among themselves.

Naturally, the boycott as a retaliatory strategy becomes the next topic of discussion. The students think that economic sanction is a simple matter. They suggest that merchants mobilize to identify and list U.S. products, which would then be declared contraband in public meetings. They further propose to seek cooperation from Chinese porters, who will be told not to unload the banned merchandise. When the boycott forces U.S. factories to shut down and U.S. workers onto the streets, the students predict optimistically, the discriminatory policy of the United States will have to change. In hindsight, we know that the boycott, though quite effective in slowing down the sales of U.S. goods, was unable to force bankruptcy of any U.S. business firms in China or manufacturers in the United States; serious trade interruptions were reported by U.S. consulates in Guangzhou, Amoy, and Shanghai, however (USDS 1905–6; and see Remer 1933). But the kind of chain reaction predicted by the students was highly publicized in numerous boycott materials at the time (A Ying 1960).

The students' optimism is not shared by Li Xinchun, who is not convinced that the proposed boycott strategy will work as simply as they suggest. What if merchants of other countries take over the sale of U.S. goods when the Chinese merchants launch a boycott? What if the consumers, who are both numerous and scattered, cannot recognize U.S. products? These and many other questions concern Li Xinchun. The novel does not, however, portray the merchant hero as a defeatist, nor does it suggest that the boycott will never work. Rather, it creates a patriotic and thoughtful character—a Chinese American merchant—who reminds people that the boycott is a double-edged sword that has to be used with care. The boycott "is a serious matter," Li Xinchun cautions others, "which cannot be done with two or three of us and with a single strategy.

The three suggestions that merchants do not trade with Americans, consumers do not buy American goods, and workers do not unload American merchandise should not be carried out without considering both [positive and negative] sides. And we must do all three and stick to the very end" (Chaps. 47–48 [A Ying 1960, 110]).

Unlike other boycott materials, which focus almost exclusively on the proposed economic sanction, the boycott novels seriously contemplate other ways of alleviating the pains of overseas Chinese, especially those in the United States. In *The Bitter Society*, Li Xinchun proposes that arrangements be made for tens of thousands of Chinese in the United States to be shipped back home. None of the previous studies on the boycott movement has mentioned this important suggestion. But this view has historic roots, and some boycotters in Shanghai enthusiastically advocated this alternative.[6] The suggestion indicates some ambivalence among overseas Chinese and their supporters at home who were fighting for equal immigration rights. Yet, Li Xinchun's rationale seems quite sound and consistent with the novel's detailed portrait of the painful experiences of overseas Chinese. Through a conversation between two Chinese merchants in America, the novel implies that emigrant life is actually much worse than that in China:

"After returning to China, we shall tell others about our personal experiences and many years of hardship here."

"The people back home just think that once abroad, success will follow."

"How could they know that of those who are in business here, six or seven out of ten lose money. And the laborers here who lost their jobs suffer much more than they would have in their own country." (Chaps. 45–46 [A Ying 1960, 107])

Li Xinchun supports the idea of return from both humanitarian and nationalistic viewpoints: The Chinese are miserable in the United States anyway, and the money that Chinese merchants make is mainly from the Chinese population in the United States, not from Americans. With the money that they invest in the United States, he reasons, they could establish businesses in China. As to the impoverished Chinese in the United States, Li Xinchun asks for donations to pay their ship fare home (Chaps. 47–48). He even believes that the "going back movement" could itself be a blow to U.S. interests: "If all the Chinese actually leave," Li says, "American businesses will suffer and large factories and companies will be especially hard hit. In time, [the Americans] may change their stand and abolish some of these harsh regulations to accommodate the Chinese requests" (Chaps. 45–46).

The idea must have enjoyed some popularity at the time, because it is also mentioned in other boycott novels. In *The Golden World*, a merchant returned from the United States proposes to bring back unemployed Chinese laborers first, then other laborers and eventually merchants (Host 1906, Chap. 14).[7] There is no solid evidence, however, to show that Chinese communities in the United States actually contemplated or planned a "return to China" movement.[8] Nevertheless, we should not dismiss the idea as simply springing from the novelist's imagination. If Chinese Americans in fact feared that exclusion laws were aimed at driving all Chinese out of the country, it would be quite reasonable for them to contemplate the option of returning (or going elsewhere). Historical actors, as Paul Cohen reminds us, faced numerous uncertainties (1997, 61). The information contained in these novels certainly offers a more complicated picture of Chinese American thinking during a critical moment of their lives.

Unfortunately, *The Bitter Society* stops short of providing more details on both the boycott movement and the grand plan of building China's nationalist industries. Although the novel was intended to have a sequel, it was never written, perhaps because the movement itself ended too soon. *The Golden World* (Host 1906) both supplements and forms a sharp contrast to *The Bitter Society*. (Could it be the promised sequel?)[9] It starts where *The Bitter Society* leaves off, with the boycott movement just beginning, but the two novels differ in important ways. While *The Bitter Society* was characterized by realism, *The Golden World* shows an idealism typical of many contemporary political novels at the time. It speculates on a golden future for the Chinese. *The Bitter Society* tries to convince the reader that it tells a true story about real people, whereas *The Golden World* does not conceal the fact that it is fiction. The author fictionalizes his characters, who act in vastly different periods and imaginary places, as mentioned earlier. The novel creates two memorable characters who have ideas for both the boycott movement and visions for China's future. One is a merchant named Xia Jiawei who has a business in New York and whose wealth is as legendary as the man himself. The other, simply called Ms. Zhang, is a doctor among a group of the Ming loyalist descendants.

The Golden World begins with Xia's return to Shanghai upon his learning the news of the boycott. On the ship he miraculously meets a Chinese couple, two of a group of Ming loyalists that has been hiding on an (imaginary) island near the South Pole for more than two hundred years. The husband is the democratically elected head of the island and the wife, a doctor—Ms. Zhang. After the Qing troops drove their ancestors from their home in mainland China centuries before, the Ming loyalists have lived a democratic and peaceful life on an insulated island far away. Their fairy tale–like life collides with reality when several islanders discover an unconscious Chinese woman drifting in the ocean. It turns out that she is on her way to Cuba with her husband, who becomes a contract laborer after failing to pay his gambling debt. The woman was beaten up and thrown into the sea for her defiance against humiliating treatment and sexual advances by foreigners on the ship. The islanders rescue her, and Ms. Zhang and her husband decide to help find her husband in Cuba, or wherever he might be. The search takes them to the United States and eventually back to China, where they find themselves in the middle of the anti-U.S. boycott (Chaps. 1–4).

As a merchant coming back from America, Xia Jianwei has intimate knowledge of the exclusion laws and is eager to guide pubic enthusiasm in the right direction with tangible accomplishments. "Otherwise," as Xia says, "[the movement] would thaw like ice" (Chap. 5 [A Ying 1960, 137]). He attends several boycott meetings and is disappointed that few participants understand the real issues at stake. Many public gatherings resemble theatrical shows; the speeches have little substance. Speakers advocate either reform or abrogation of China's immigration treaty with the United States, which, according to Xia, will have little effect on the current situation; it is the exclusion laws, not the treaty, that do the greatest harm to Chinese communities in the United States. Even if the immigration treaty is abolished, he believes, the exclusion laws will continue to be in effect. Xia therefore argues that the boycotters should demand the nullification of the exclusion laws to obtain real benefits for Chinese people (Chap. 10).

As convincing as he sounds, however, Mr. Xia cannot persuade the local organizers of the boycott meetings, who have real concerns about going beyond what is politically safe for them in China. They reject Xia's suggestion on the ground that they have neither the ambition nor the power to force changes in U.S. domestic laws.

Xia's setback sets the stage for Ms. Zhang to continue the effort among her female compatriots. Urban and small-town Chinese women began to form organizations in the late nineteenth and early twentieth centuries to address various gender-related issues, foot binding in particular. The boycott provides them with the first opportunity to participate in national politics not as individuals but as a distinct social group. They hold meetings exclusively for women and pass resolutions of their own. These novels pay specific attention to women's boycott activities, as well as to their emigrant experiences.

Unlike Xia, who is courteously treated as a guest by the local boycott organizers, Ms. Zhang is actively involved in organizing women's boycott meetings, despite her background as an overseas Chinese. From other sources, we know that the novelist might have based part of the story about Ms. Zhang on a real historic figure, Zhang Zhujun, a doctor of Guangdong origin. When the boycott broke out, Zhang Zhujun had just moved from Guangzhou to Shanghai for about a year and was active in setting up women's schools and handicraft workshops. In real life, however, she did not distinguish herself as a boycott leader, though she did on several occasions denounce the exclusion laws and called upon the Chinese in the United States to return to China rather than stay in the United States as slaves (*Dalu bao,* 17 May 1905, 4). Nevertheless she is featured in several novels, probably because she was considered by many contemporaries to be the most learned and enlightened contemporary female reformer (Kobayashi 1976).

As a fictitious character in *The Golden World,* Ms. Zhang is a close comrade of Xia Jiawei and shares many ideas with him. After Xia fails to change the views of the male boycotters, Ms. Zhang continues her cause among women. At a woman's boycott meeting, she makes a keynote speech in which she stresses the futility of amending the treaty between the two countries and advocates the abolition of the exclusion laws. She makes the argument from a woman's perspective, though, which generates tremendous sympathy for the lower-class Chinese—the laborers. (*The Golden World* apparently does not have the "pro-merchant bias" that some find in *The Bitter Society* [Mei and Pang Yip 1981, 36].) An amendment of the treaty, says Ms. Zhang, "will benefit the upper classes only, such as merchants and students, but not the workers who are also human beings" (Chap. 11 [A Ying 1960, 176]).

As important as it seems, the controversy over the goal of the mass protest is not the immediate cause of its abortive ending. The boycott might have lasted longer if it had not encountered stiff opposition from the merchant interests of the Shanghai foreign trade business. In *The Golden World,* the concerned merchants not only find excuses to sell the U.S. goods they have in stock but also secretly order more such commodities. When it appears that no significant changes to the exclusion laws can be achieved and the boycott movement is in jeopardy, Xia Jiawei and his comrades, just like Li Xinchun in *The Bitter Society,* begin to explore long-term solutions. As mentioned earlier, they discuss ways to bring their fellow Chinese back from the United States (Chaps. 14, 17). Unlike the heroes in *The Bitter Society,* however, Xia Jiawei and his friends realize the magnitude of the task of bringing 100,000 people back and providing them jobs. The difficulty is solved when all the main characters in the novel leave China for the imaginary island, where they establish a republic and live happily ever after (Chap. 20).

If *The Bitter Society* and *The Golden World* are novels that address issues of contemporary politics, *Extraordinary Speeches on the Boycott* (China's 1906) is a political essay disguised as a novel. Although the work has little literary value, it contains some of the most sophisticated discussions on boycott politics. The novel centers on an eccentric individual called "Sick Man." While the setting is again Shanghai, the protagonist—not a native—speaks various dialects and even foreign languages. Is the mysterious character from abroad? The novel leaves the answer to the reader's imagination. There is little question, however, that the man has intimate knowledge of the Chinese exclusion laws and shares much of Xia Jiawei's view on the boycott movement, as evidenced by his extraordinary and compelling speeches.[10]

The boycotters debated three objectives for the movement, as mentioned earlier: modification of the treaty, termination of the treaty, and abolition of the exclusion laws. In his speeches, Sick Man addresses all three. He first makes clear the futility of revising the treaty:

> Let me ask you gentlemen. Did our merchants and students suffer humiliation in the United States because of the treaty or because of the exclusion laws? If it is because of the treaty, there is little to be asked for change because the treaty not only allows the merchants and students to enter [the country] but also grants them the same privilege as nationals of the most favored nations. If it is because of the exclusion laws, then the reform of the treaty will have no effect on the laws.... If we want to settle the dispute once and for all, we must demand the abrogation of the exclusion laws. (A Ying 1960, 238)

Having said this, however, Sick Man acknowledges that the treaty and the exclusion laws are indeed related. He then goes on to explain why even the total abrogation of the treaty would not help Chinese Americans. "As long as the exclusion laws continue to be in effect, our fellow countrymen will suffer the humiliation as they did before" (Chap. 2 [A Ying 1960, 238]).

The controversy over the treaty and the laws is after all a matter of formality. Behind this controversy is the debate over what the boycotters really want: some modification of the existing exclusion laws and their abusive implementation, or the end of the exclusion entirely? Sick Man is by no means simplistic and sentimental in this regard. He spells out the dilemma before his audience: To request mere correction of current abuses would continue to disfavor Chinese laborers in the United States and leave loopholes for the extension of discrimination to other Chinese classes. Yet, to demand equal privileges for the laborers would be almost impossible, since the United States had practiced the exclusion laws for more than thirty years. What then was the solution? He proposed that the boycotters should simultaneously work on two fronts: internally, to persuade the government not to renew the treaty so that the Americans would have no excuses to promulgate new exclusion laws; and externally, to demand abolition of the exclusion laws (Chap. 2).

If, as Sick Man argues, the exclusion laws should be the target, on what ground can the Chinese demand a sovereign country to change laws made to protect its own border? There is a real concern among boycott participants that the exclusion laws are beyond their reach. While the treaty is a matter of bilateral interest, it is argued, the exclusion laws are purely a domestic matter. To this view Sick Man gives a brilliant rebuttal: "Were the harsh exclusion laws promulgated for regulating Americans or for Chinese?" "If they were for Americans," he reasons,

> then, they are indeed domestic matters and there is no reason for us to interfere. But these laws are exercised against the Chinese. Furthermore, are they promulgated against immigrants to America in general or exclusively against the Chinese? If they were against all the rest, . . . then we could sit still waiting for other countries to complain and denounce them. But they are used exclusively against the Chinese. Since the exclusion laws discriminate against only the Chinese not against immigrants in general, they are domestic laws with international implications. (Chap. 4 [A Ying 1960, 247])

Sick Man is indeed eloquent in justifying the demand to end the exclusion laws. The real difficulty, however, is to persuade sophisticated urban consumers not to buy cheaper and better U.S. goods, which might have little, if any, effect upon the U.S. economy, let alone on its exclusion laws. Given that U.S. exports to China were insignificant to the U.S. economy ($53,384,000 or 0.3 percent of total U.S. exports in 1905), many better informed Shanghai urban dwellers had doubts about the effectiveness of the boycott (Chao 1986, 105; USDC 1975, 885). At this, the mysterious speaker, as the readers may anticipate, once again expresses his unique view. He deals with the issue not with a passionate call for sacrificing patriotism but with a realistic assessment of the situation. Admitting that the boycott will not be able to bring Americans to their knees in the short run, he proposes a long-term plan that centers on the idea that "Chinese buy Chinese [products]" (Chap. 7 [A Ying 1960, 263]). The story ends with Sick Man becoming an entrepreneur who establishes a huge farm in northern Jiangsu, where hundreds of workers raise chickens, sheep, and other animals, and cultivate tea, mulberry trees, and various other crops. They also work in textile factories (Chap. 8).

Is this outcome totally fictitious? As early as 1895, Zhang Jian (1853–1926), a well-known Confucian scholar, became an entrepreneur. His textile enterprise in Nantong, northern Jiangsu, earned him much fame and prestige. Like other boycott novels, *Extraordinary Speeches on the Boycott* fascinates its readers by maintaining a tension between fact and fiction.

Beyond the Boycott

U.S. racial discrimination against Chinese in the nineteenth century did not simply force them into ethnic ghettos—Chinatowns—it also made them turn to their homeland. Not only were they more interested in changes in China, but also they attempted to facilitate and define the changes. The 1905 Chinese anti-U.S. boycott was the first such attempt.

Their outrage against racist U.S. immigration laws was shared by millions in China—mainly in Guangdong, Fujian, and Shanghai, the hub of commercial transactions and information exchange. As is often the case, participants of the movement responded not to facts but to images, symbols, sentiments, and ideas presented through various media, including fiction. Unlike conventional materials for mobilization, fiction offers multiple perspectives and expresses mixed feelings—confusion, ambivalence, hope, and aspiration. While the writers' sympathy toward their overseas compatriots is obvious, their central concern was China, which they understood from their vantage point in Shanghai. For people in the Yangzi Delta region, where the budding national industries were centered, emigration rights had only symbolic significance, not immediate economic and social benefits for the country. If the boycott symbolizes Chinese political connection across the ocean, the abortive end of the movement indicates the degree to which they were separated.

Yet, despite the boycott's ending with no significant accomplishments, the bond between Chinese communities in the United States and their compatriots in China was strengthened. Many Chinese in the United States turned into revolutionaries after 1905; they contributed significantly to the 1911 revolution and continued their support for China's struggle toward independence and modernization.

Notes

1. Some materials in the novels analyzed here are briefly touched upon in my book *In Search of Justice: The 1905–1906 Chinese Anti-American Boycott* (Cambridge: Harvard University Press, 2001) in the Harvard East Asian Monographs series.

2. *Shibao* (26 May 1905) for example lists eleven returned Chinese merchants in Guangzhou. The newspaper also mentions several returned Chinese students, government staff, and others who gave speeches at Shanghai's boycott meetings. One medical student allegedly told his stories of America in English, which presumably were translated by someone (*Shibao,* 22 May 1905).

3. Students and exiled reformers and revolutionaries in America and other countries might have written novels that were published in Hong Kong and Shanghai. *The Wretched Student* (Qi Youzi 1905), for example, was very likely written by a returned student.

4. The novel's version differs only slightly from that of a pamphlet published in Shanghai a little earlier, "Records of Sufferings of Our Brethren" (*Tongbao shounue ji*) (qtd. in A Ying 1960, 523–52). In the pamphlet, Tan commits suicide by turning on the gas in his bedroom.

5. Mistreatment of Chinese laborers in the Dutch East Indies as well as elsewhere in the world was well known to urban readers in early-twentieth-century China, thanks to numerous

newspaper and journal reports (see Wang 1995). *The Bitter Society* portrays Li Xinchun as a well-informed Chinese merchant with extensive overseas experience.

6. When news reached China of the horrendous working and living conditions of Chinese laborers in Peru in the early 1870s, the Qing government refused to sign a treaty with the Peruvian government that would legalize the recruitment of Chinese laborers, until Peru agreed to send all the Chinese in its country back home at its own expense.

7. Some boycott novels mention real difficulties for Chinese Americans returning to their home country. *The Wretched Student,* for example, quotes a wealthy Chinese merchant who longs to return to his home country but decides not to because of the local custom of squeezing the returned overseas Chinese (Qi Youzi 1905, Chap. 8). *The Golden World* tells stories of a legal battle between a returned Chinese American merchant and his greedy relatives in China (Host 1906, Chap. 6). Similarly, *The Bitter Society* shows the dilemma Chinese Americans face: To stay or to return is not an easy choice for them. Nevertheless, the boycott novels make clear that some Chinese Americans, along with the boycotters in China, contemplated the option of "going home."

8. On the contrary, some sources and studies have shown that Chinese Americans actually began consciously to change their sojourner image to that of permanent resident in order to secure their stay in the United States (Zhang Qingsong 1994).

9. Li Xinchun optimistically predicts toward the end of *The Bitter Society* that with the development of China's resources, the country "will become the Golden World in ten or twenty years" (A Ying 1960, 111).

10. Unlike *The Bitter Society* and *The Golden World, Extraordinary Speeches on the Boycott* (China's 1906) conveys some unique ideas on the boycott movement directly, through Sick Man's public speeches. In mass gatherings, boycott speakers could not possibly discuss subtle points. In a novel, however, it is possible. The novel not only spells out in print what otherwise could only be heard, but also provides sophisticated analysis rarely seen even in nonfiction.

Works Cited

Ai Hua. N.d. *The Tears of Overseas Chinese* (in Chinese). *Xiaoshuo Yuebao* 4, 3. Reprinted in A Ying 1960, 419–32.

A Ying. *Collected Literature on Opposition to the American Treaty Excluding Chinese Laborers* (in Chinese). Beijing: Zhonghua shuju, 1960.

The Bitter Society (in Chinese). Shanghai: Tushu jichen, 1905. Reprinted in A Ying 1960, 15–113.

Brown, Richard D. 1989. *Knowledge Is Power: The Diffusion of Information in Early America, 1700–1865.* New York: Oxford University Press.

Chan, Sucheng. 1991. *Asian Americans: An Interpretive History.* New York: Twayne.

Chao Hang. 1986. "The Chinese-American Textile Trade, 1830–1930." In *America's China Trade in Historical Perspective: the Chinese and American Performance,* ed. Ernest R. May and John K. Fairbank, 103–27. Cambridge: Harvard University Press.

Chen Yikan. 1903. "On Strategies of a Boycott against the Exclusion Laws" (in Chinese). Reprinted in A Ying 1960, 588–97.

China's Cold-Blooded Man [pseud.]. 1906. *Extraordinary Speeches on the Boycott* (in Chinese). Shanghai: Qizhi shuju. Reprinted in A Ying 1960, 230–73.

Cohen, Paul. 1997. *History in Three Keys: The Boxers as Event, Experience, and Myth.* New York: Columbia University Press.

Duara, Prasenjit. 1997. "Transnationalism and the Predicament of Sovereignty: China 1900–1945." *American Historical Review* 102 (October): 1030–51.

Hom, Marlon K. 1987. *Songs of Gold Mountain: Cantonese Rhymes from San Francisco Chinatown*. Berkeley: University of California Press.

Fishkin, Shelley Fisher. 1985. *From Fact to Fiction: Journalism and Imaginative Writing in America*. Baltimore: Johns Hopkins University Press.

Host of the Green Lotus Mansion [pseud.]. 1907. *The Golden World* (in Chinese). Shanghai: Xiaoshuo lin. Reprinted in A Ying 1960, 113–230.

Kobayashi, T. 1976. "Chang Chu-chun for Women's Rights." *Journal of the Oriental Society of Australia* 2: 62–80.

Lai Fangling. 1988. *Late Qing Novels on Overseas Chinese Laborers*. In *Studies on the Late Qing Novels* (in Chinese), 155–83. Taipei: Lianjin chubanshe.

Lee, Leo Ou-fan, and Andrew J. Nathan. 1982. "The Beginnings of Mass Culture: Journalism and Fiction in the Late Ch'ing and Beyond." In *Popular Culture in Late Imperial China*, ed. David Johnson, Andrew J. Nathan, and Evelyn S. Rawski, 360–95. Berkeley: University of California Press.

Link, E. Perry, Jr. 1981. *Mandarin Ducks and Butterflies: Popular Fiction in Early Twentieth-Century Chinese Cities*. Berkeley: University of California Press.

McClain, Charles J. 1994. *In Search of Equality: The Chinese Struggle against Discrimination in Nineteenth-Century America*. Berkeley: University of California Press.

McKee, Delber L. 1977. *Chinese Exclusion versus the Open Door Policy, 1900–1906: Clashes over China Policy in the Roosevelt Era*. Detroit: Wayne State University Press.

———. 1986. "The Chinese Boycott of 1905–1906 Reconsidered: The Role of Chinese Americans." *Pacific Historical Review* 55: 165–91.

Mei, June, and Jean Pang Yip, with Russell Leong, trans. 1981. "*The Bitter Society: Ku Shehui*, A Translation, Chapters 37–46." *Amerasia Journal* 8, 1 (Spring/Summer): 33–67.

Qi Youzi [pseud.]. 1905. *The Wretched Student* (in Chinese). Shanghai: Xiuxiang xiaoshuo. Reprinted in A Ying 1960, 273–310.

Remer, C. F. 1933. *A Study of Chinese Boycotts with Special Reference to their Economic Effectiveness*. Baltimore: Johns Hopkins University Press.

Salyer, Lucy E. 1995. *Laws Harsh as Tigers: Chinese Immigrants and the Shaping of Modern Immigration Law*. Chapel Hill: University of North Carolina Press.

Sun Yusheng. 1905. Preface to *The Bitter Society*. Shanghai: Tushu jichen. Reprinted in A Ying 1960, 15.

Tsai, Shih-shan Henry. 1971. "Chinese Laborers and American Diplomacy." *American Studies* (in Chinese) 3 (September): 197–221.

———. 1976. "Reaction to Exclusion: The Boycott of 1905 and Chinese National Awakening." *Chinese Historian* 8, 14 (November): 95–110.

U.S. Department of Commerce (USDC). Bureau of the Census. 1975. *Historical Statistics of the United States: Colonial Times to 1970*, pt. 2.

U.S. Department of State (USDS). 1905–6. *Consular Dispatches*. Canton: M-101, roll 19–20; Hong Kong: M-108, roll 21; Shanghai: M-112, roll 51–53.

Wang Guanhua. 1995. "Media, Intellectuals, and the Ideology of the 1905 Anti-Exclusion Boycott." *Chinese Historian* 15: 1–48.

Zhang Cunwu. 1966. *The Storm in 1905 over the Sino-American Labor Treaty* (in Chinese). Taipei: Institute of Modern History, Academia Sinica.

Zhang Qingsong. 1994. "Dragon in the Land of the Eagle: The Exclusion of Chinese from U.S. Citizenship, 1848–1943." Ph.D. diss., University of Virginia,

Zhao, I-heng. 1995. *The Uneasy Narrator: Chinese Fiction from the Traditional to the Modern.* Oxford: Oxford University Press.

Zuckert, Catherine H. 1992. "The Novel as a Form of American Political Thought." In *Reading Political Stories: Representations of Politics in Novels and Pictures,* ed. Maureen Whitebrook. Lanham: Rowan and Littlefield.

Catherine Ceniza Choy

10   From Exchange Visitor to Permanent Resident: Reconsidering Filipino Nurse Migration as a Post-1965 Phenomenon

The international migration of Filipino nurses is often characterized as a post-1965 phenomenon, primarily because in the late 1960s the Philippines became the world's largest exporter of nurses, with significant numbers working in the Middle East, Germany, and Canada, for example (Arbeiter 1988, 57). When at least twenty-five thousand Filipino nurses migrated to the United States between 1966 and 1985, their increasing numbers ended decades of domination by foreign-trained nurses from European countries and Canada (Ong and Azores 1994, 164). In the United States during those decades, "it could be argued that a discussion of immigrant Asian nurses, indeed of foreign-trained nurses in general, is predominantly about Filipino nurses" (165).

In their explanations of this phenomenon, sociologists, immigration historians, and Asian American Studies scholars have pointed to contemporary government policies. The U.S. Immigration Act of 1965, for example, encouraged the immigration of Filipino nurses through its new occupational preferences, which favored the migration of professionals with needed skills (see Ong, Bonacich, and Cheng 1994). With the establishment of the Marcos dictatorship in 1972, the Philippine government focused on the development of an export-oriented economy that included the export of labor as well as goods (see Abella 1979; Hawes 1989). Contemporary government policies, however, do not explain why so many Filipinos have become nurses or why tens of thousands of Filipino nurses have decided to work abroad. As the migration of Filipino professionals to the United States has increased, why have Filipino nurses in particular comprised such a significant percentage of them?

Very few works have acknowledged the roles of early-twentieth-century U.S. colonial education in the Philippines and mid-twentieth-century U.S. exchange programs in the development of this late-twentieth-century phenomenon (see Ong and Azores 1994; Ishi 1987; Choy 1998). In general, Asian American historians have adopted a post-1965 framework when writing about Filipino nurse migration to the United States and have marginalized its connection to early-twentieth-century U.S. history (see Takaki 1989; Chan 1991). While the "pre- and post-1965" framework in Asian American studies is useful when describing general sociological and demographic changes, its emphasis on immigration legislation to organize Asian American histories marginalizes the roles of sojourners, exchange students, and temporary workers in shaping these histories.

Here, I focus on the yet unexplored effect of the U.S. Exchange Visitor Program of the 1950s and 1960s on contemporary Filipino American immigration history. As participation in the program created a space in which persons, goods, images, and ideas circulated across U.S. and Philippine national boundaries, the transnational movement of Filipino exchange nurses and American hospital recruiters combined with the circulation of advertisements, letters, and packages to change the culture of Filipino nurse migration abroad. Instead of earning U.S. educational credentials and returning home to work, Filipino nursing graduates aimed to live abroad indefinitely. For young Filipino women, nursing opportunities abroad became motivations for studying nursing in the first place.

I emphasize that these transnational movements are multi-directional and interdependent because, until very recently, Asian American immigration studies have tended to focus on the unidirectional movement of immigrants to the United States. However, as I interviewed Filipino American nurses, I was struck by the ways in which much of their work and study experience could not be understood within that paradigm. Many had worked and studied in the United States temporarily, returned to the Philippines, and then immigrated to the United States. One had worked for several years in Saudi Arabia and then returned to the Philippines before coming to the United States. Another had worked in Canada previously, and another in the Netherlands. Among the forty-three Filipino RNs I interviewed, fifteen, or approximately one-third, had entered the United States during the 1950s and 1960s as exchange visitor nurses (see also Espiritu 1995, 84–85; Vallangca 1987, 167–68). These experiences create social, cultural, economic, and political linkages that defy national contextualization and traditional immigrant narratives.

A Dynamic Measure

Study and work experience abroad, and specifically in the United States, has been an important component of Filipino nurses' training since the early twentieth century, when U.S. scholarship programs for Filipino nurses functioned mainly as vehicles for occupational mobility in the Philippines.[1] The few Filipino nurses who participated in these programs became part of an elite class of Filipino professionals with U.S. educational credentials, eventually returning to the Philippines to replace the U.S. nursing administrators and educators in the colonial government. For the majority of Filipino nurses in the early twentieth century, the opportunity to study or work abroad was an elusive one or, as for Filipino nurse Patrocinio Montellano, a "dream" (Montellano 1962, 235).

However, in the mid–twentieth century, several exchange and work programs acted as vehicles for transforming nursing into an international profession. While new international work programs in Germany and Holland, for example, also recruited Filipino nurses to work outside the Philippines, the U.S. Exchange Visitor Program (EVP) facilitated the first wave of mass migration of Filipino nurses abroad by providing several thousands of Filipino nurses with the opportunity to work and study in the United States. Between 1956 and 1969, more than eleven thousand Filipino nurses participated in the EVP (Asperilla 1971, 52). In the Philippines, it transformed the experience of going abroad from one reserved for the few into one available to any Filipino registered nurse.

The U.S. government through the U.S. Information and Educational Act established the Exchange Visitor Program in 1948 "to promote a better understanding of the United States in other countries and to increase mutual understanding between the people of the United States and the people of other countries." However, the motivations for establishing the program were rooted in cold-war politics. According to Senate reports, "[H]ostile propaganda campaigns directed against democracy, human welfare, freedom, truth, and the United States, spearheaded by the Government of the Soviet Union and the Communist Parties throughout the world" in the post–World War II period called for "dynamic measures to disseminate truth" (U.S. Senate 1948, 4). One of the "dynamic measures" that the Senate proposed was an educational exchange service that would involve the interchange of persons, knowledge, and skills. Like the Fulbright and Peace Corps programs for example, the EVP masked its political and ideological motivations with a rhetoric of educational opportunity and progress.

Exchange Visitor Program participants from abroad received a monthly stipend for their work and study in their sponsoring U.S. institutions. Although the Senate discussions of the exchange program did not refer to the U.S. health care system specifically, several thousand U.S. agencies and institutions were able to sponsor EVP participants, including the American Nurses Association (ANA) and individual hospitals. The U.S. government issued EVP visas for a maximum stay of two years. The U.S. and the sending countries' governments expected the EVP participants to return to their countries of origin upon completing the program.

In certain respects, the EVP's objectives and effects were similar to those of early-twentieth-century U.S. colonial education programs in the Philippines.[2] The program aimed to re-create a type of sojourner elite class of Filipino professionals who would study in the United States for a limited time period, earn U.S. educational credentials and gain U.S. work experience, and eventually return to work in the Philippines. It perpetuated the construction of a labor force of young Filipino women who studied U.S. professional nursing (Choy 1998, 8). It also reconstructed a global, cultural, and intellectual hierarchy in which U.S. institutions—educational, political, and medical—were superior to those of other countries, such as the Philippines. Like previous colonial programs, it maintained this hierarchy through the U.S. sponsorship and training of foreign students, in which foreign nurses played a unique role. As one U.S. nursing study of exchange visitor nurses proposed:

> What better persons can communicate our achievements to other countries than the nurse with her high code of ethics? What better ambassador can we expect to have? The nurse belongs to an honorable, dignified profession. It is she, who on her return home will mingle both with the average and the influential people of her country. She will tell them about the way of life in the United States. (Broadhurst 1958, 201)

The Philippines and Filipino nurses were not the sole participants of the Exchange Visitor Program. U.S. institutions sponsored exchange visitors from a number of foreign countries in Europe, as well as Asia. The occupational backgrounds of EVP participants also varied. Furthermore, U.S. nurses participated in the program as exchange visitor nurses in foreign countries. Yet the international migration dynamics of exchange nurses (to non-U.S. countries, as well as to the United States) were highly unequal. Throughout the 1950s, nursing exchanges between the United States and northern Europe dominated the exchange visitor arrangements made by the ANA. According to Barbara Brush, between 1949 and 1951, Danish, Swedish, British, and Norwegian nurses comprised the majority of exchange nurses in the United States.[3]

Statistics of ANA-sponsored foreign exchange nurses from the late 1950s offer a lens through which to view their countries of origin as the program continued (ANA 1959–1961). From 1956 to 1960, Australia sent the highest number (159) of new ANA-sponsored exchange visitor nurses (961 total). The numbers of exchange visitor nurses from Denmark (115), Great Britain (89), and Sweden (80) surpassed those from the Philippines (77).

However, once Filipino nurses and the Philippine government became actively involved in the EVP, they began to dominate participation in the program. Although the EVP began in 1948, it was not until 1951 that the Filipino Nurses Association began assisting Filipino nurses with exchange arrangements. Philippine president Ramon Magsaysay created an Exchange Visitor Program Committee only in 1956 to screen applicants. According to Purita Asperilla, by the late 1960s, 80 percent of EVP participants in the United States were from the Philippines (53). And nurses comprised the majority of Filipino exchange visitors. Between 1956 and 1969, nurses comprised more than 50 percent (11,136) of the total number (20,420) of exchange visitors from the Philippines (Asperilla 1971, 5).

Filipino nurses were able to obtain EVP sponsorship from a variety of institutions: the ANA, U.S. hospitals, and the U.S. Public Health Service. However, the overwhelming majority of Filipino exchange nurses arranged their exchange placements with individual U.S. hospitals and travel agencies (see Capulong 1965, 77; also Asperilla 1971, 141).[4] Travel agencies expedited the placement of Filipino nurses on the exchange program because they profited from the airline tickets purchased by Filipino nurses going abroad and particularly from the payment plans for these tickets, popularly known as "fly now, pay later" plans. While these plans allowed Filipino nurses to purchase an airline ticket for an initial minimal amount, they charged high interest on the remaining balance. In the 1960s, Pan American and Northwest Airlines were among the many air carriers targeting Filipino nurses for "fly now, pay later" plans in advertisements in the *Philippine Journal of Nursing*. As one Northwest Airlines advertisement beckoned in the July–September 1969 issue: "189.40 pesos is all the cash you need to fly to the USA on Northwest Orient's 'Fly Now—Pay Later' plan. The balance may be paid in as many as 24 monthly installments. The arrangements are simple."

Complex Adjustments

Upon their arrival in the United States, Filipino exchange nurses faced culture shock, financial difficulties, and hospital exploitation that further complicated romanticized narratives about life in America. Travel agencies may have expedited the placement process for Filipino exchange nurses, but they had little interest in the quality of work conditions and educational programs of sponsoring hospitals. Many Filipino exchange nurses placed by travel agencies encountered poor work conditions and inadequate orientation programs (see Castillejos 1966).

Some U.S. hospital administrators offered little, if any, assistance to new Filipino exchange nurses. Even when sponsoring hospitals attempted to provide temporary lodging for newly arrived exchange visitors, at times these provisions were poorly planned. In 1964, Fortunata Kennedy arrived in the United States with fifteen other exchange nurses. A representative of the Chicago hospital that had sponsored them met them at the airport and accompanied them to a YWCA. As Fortune (as she preferred to be called) explained to me in a letter dated 27 February 1995: "When we got there, the clerk denied ever receiving reservations for us. We ended up with 3 nurses sharing one small room. The next day, one of the nurses was able to contact a friend who had been in Chicago for over a year. Through her, we were able to find a place to stay. No one really helped us settle in the U.S. Our initiative and determination made us survive the first few difficult years."

Aside from providing inadequate settlement assistance, some U.S. hospital administrators abused the educational component of the EVP by assigning exchange nurses the work of nurses' aides (see Alinea and Senador 1973). Other hospitals did not offer any orientation or educational programs. As Josephine Abalos told me in our interview 18 March 1995, "to be a hospital accepted in the Exchange Visitor Program, you were supposed to give training to these foreign grad nurses to enhance their previous education. . . . But a lot of us didn't have any orientation. They just . . . said, 'Look, this is the med-surg unit. We have eighteen patients here. They're all yours. Okay?' That's the kind of orientation."

Other U.S. hospital administrators also took advantage of the exchange status of these nurses by assigning them the work of registered nurses and then compensating them with a minimal stipend. Christina Hing told me in our interview on 7 February 1995 that in 1962 she earned $46.50 per week as an exchange nurse in a Philadelphia hospital. ANA statistics reveal that in 1960, a general-duty nurse in a Philadelphia nongovernmental hospital averaged $71.50 per week (ANA 1961). Extrapolating from these examples, a sponsoring hospital could exploit the exchange nurse by having her perform general nursing duties and then compensate her with about two-thirds of a general-duty nurse's average salary.

While some Americans expected exchange nurses to popularize U.S. nursing achievements in their countries of origin, many sponsoring U.S. hospitals used exchange nurses primarily to alleviate growing nursing shortages in the post–World War II period.[5] In 1961, the ANA conducted a spot check of nonfederal general hospitals and found the need for general duty nurses particularly critical; 23 percent of these positions were vacant (ANA 1962–1963, 28). By the mid-1960s, the use of exchange nurses as employees appeared to be more the rule than the exception. A study committee of the Philippine Department of Labor characterized the EVP as "a handy recruitment device" and "a loophole for the circumvention of United States immigration laws" (qtd. in Asperilla 1971, 54).

Some Filipino exchange nurses themselves were well aware of this. According to former exchange nurse Priscilla Santayana in our 19 November 1994 interview, the Exchange Visitor Program "was work. The 'exchange' was a misnomer. When you came here, you were working as a staff nurse with a stipend. They didn't call it salary because if they call it a salary that means you are a permanent employee. . . . Everybody knew that."

According to some Philippine reports of the exchange program, there were few if any redeeming qualities about the program. In 1966, Philippine congress member Epifanio Castillejos visited the United States to survey the situation of Filipino exchange nurses and severely criticized the exchange program: "Almost every Filipino nurse I met had problems which ran the gamut from discrimination in stipend, as well as in the nature and amount of work they are made to do, to the lack of in-service or specialized training in the hospitals they work in. . . . I have seen with my own eyes the extent and the seriousness of their helplessness and hopelessness" (1996, 306–7).

While one might surmise that such reports of discrimination and exploitation would discourage further Filipino nurse migration to the United States through the EVP, my interview with Lourdes Velasco on 6 February 1995 revealed the opposite. She arrived in the United States in 1964, after negative reports of the exchange program had already been publicized. According to Lourdes, she and her best friend were in "a rush to apply" to the Exchange Visitor Program. They were certainly not the only ones. More than three thousand Filipino nurses participated in the program between 1967 and 1970, after Representative Castillejos declared that the situation of Filipino exchange nurses was one full of helplessness and hopelessness (Asperilla 1971, 52). Why then were these young women in such a "rush to apply"?

The Politics of Desire

Reports of hospital exploitation, inadequate educational programs, and minimal stipends in the United States may have compelled some Filipino nurses to rethink their idealization of the EVP. However, Filipino nurses' dissatisfaction with their work schedules, opportunities, and salaries in the Philippines also motivated them to take a chance on a new work environment. Several former exchange nurses I interviewed had used their exchange placements to leave unfavorable work conditions in the Philippines. For example, Milagros Rabara applied for an exchange placement to avoid an evening work shift. As she explained to me on 21 March 1995: "The place I was working in as an industrial nurse, they tried to change my time and I didn't like it, my schedule time. . . . I used to work morning and then they let me work in the evening, which was very difficult for me to go home. I had to take a bus, maybe a ride of an hour. . . . So I left the company. . . . And I found this agency and they said we have an [exchange] opening for November." The limited number of days off at her hospital in the Philippines was another motivating factor for Lourdes Velasco to apply to the exchange program. As she recalled in our 1995 interview: "We heard that here [in the United States] you're off two days a week. . . . We were off [in the Philippines] only two days a month. Because when, in 1963 after graduation, one of my close relatives was getting married, I could not attend the wedding because I did not have the day off. I missed that important wedding."

Additionally, Filipino nurses working in the Philippines suffered from low wages and little professional respect. Some government agencies employing nurses paid them lower wages than their janitors, drivers, and messengers. In the mid-1960s, Filipino nurses earned approximately two to three hundred pesos monthly for working six days a week, including holidays and overtime if necessary (Quijano). These low nursing salaries contributed to their desire to go abroad to countries like the United States where, in the mid-1960s, general duty nurses earned four to five hundred dollars per month (Bureau of Labor Statistics 1966, qtd. in ANA 1969, 124). Even if Filipino exchange nurses earned a fraction of U.S. nursing salaries with their stipends, the amount was often greater than their nurse salaries in the Philippines.

Seemingly contradictory narratives about the EVP emerged from my interviews. While many exchange nurses characterized their exchange nurse duties as exploitation, several of the nurses I interviewed found their work experiences rewarding. Josephine Abalos praised the collaboration between the exchange nurses and medical students during her exchange visit at the University of Pennsylvania: "It was fun working with medical students too and exchanging ideas." Fely (Ofelia) Boado in an interview on 6 February 1995 reminisced about her exchange visit at the Children's Hospital in Washington, D.C., with great excitement: "I liked it very, very much. All children, no adults. We were really working at emergencies [with] very sick children. I really enjoyed it. We had asthma. We had overdose of aspirin. We had, they call it, wringer injury, when children put their hands in the washing machine. . . . The work was rewarding, very rewarding."

Furthermore, several political, social, and economic contexts illuminate why thousands of Filipino nurses applied to the exchange program. While work conditions and salaries in both the Philippines and the United States influenced Filipino nurses to go abroad, Filipino nurses were also attracted to the prestige attached to studying and working in the United States, a prestige partly created by the U.S. colonial scholarship programs of the early twentieth century. The Filipino Nurses Association contributed to the reconstruction of this idealization of U.S. work and educational experience through news stories in the *Philippine Journal of Nursing*. Simply participating in the program was newsworthy. In 1960, the *PJN* published the names and alma maters of the more than one hundred Filipino exchange nurses leaving for the United States every two to three months ("104," 1960; "122," 1960). The journal also began recognizing Filipino nurses for the professional success they had obtained in the United States. When Chicago's American Hospital honored Filipino nurse Juanita Jimenez as "Best Nurse of the Year," the *PJN* called her "a silver lining in our profession" (Bacala 1962).

Travel agents working with sponsoring U.S. hospitals attracted Filipino nurses with enticing advertisements and bonuses for exchange placements. In the September– October 1964 issue of *PJN,* an advertisement for Philippine Airlines featured a picture of a Filipino nurse with the caption, "Training abroad?" The ad continued: "Free placement service: PAL will assist you with the choice of a U.S. hospital. You get complete information on employment requirements, terms, living expenses, wardrobe, etc. This is a special service extended by PAL to U.S.-bound Filipino doctors and nurses." Other travel agency placement perks included free hotel accommodations in Hong Kong and Tokyo, and a sightseeing stopover in Honolulu.

Travel advertisements further enticed Filipino nurses with opportunities for international sightseeing and employment beyond the United States as well. In one *PJN* advertisement in the September–October 1965 issue, Manila Educational and Exchange Placement Service featured a basket, decorated with the Philippine flag, that held brochures titled USA, Canada, and Europe. The caption read: "Dear Nurse: . . . Now we have placed over 8,000 nurses to different parts of the world. . . . So, if you're not happy wherever you are right now, why not take the easy way out and go some place else. We can't promise you'll find happiness, but we can help you chase it all over the place. . . . We'll do the worrying and you do the travelling and earning too." Exploitive hospital employers commodified Filipino nurses as units of labor, but Philippine travel and placement agencies refashioned Filipino nurses' work abroad into a very different kind of commodity, often representing it as a simple route to fun, adventure, and personal contentment.

Furthermore, working abroad could offer Filipino nurses "personal" transformation, a literal and figurative makeover. Commercial Credit Corporation of Greater Manila Travel Department targeted Filipino nurses in its September–October 1966 *PJN* advertisement: "Visit those far-away castles, climb those dazzling mountains, taste exotic foods and indulge in fabulous shopping bargains. . . . And like a dream, you can fly to all those interesting places, meet interesting people, and come back, a more interesting you!"

In a different country and among new networks of colleagues and friends, the EVP experience provided an opportunity for a new socioeconomic way of life. As Josephine Abalos explained in our interview: "See, in the Philippines, if you were rich, you were rich. If you were poor, you were poor. Here [in the United States] it equalizes everybody. The work and the salary equalizes. Your status becomes lost. . . . So you were somebody in the Philippines? Too bad. You are somebody here but everybody else is somebody too, see?"

Filipino exchange nurses augmented their socioeconomic status through their earnings in U.S. dollars, accumulation of material goods unobtainable in the Philippines, and new forms of leisure unavailable there as well. In addition to wage differentials between nurses working in the Philippines and the United States, the devaluation of the Philippine peso exponentially increased the earning power of Filipino nurses working in America. The devaluation began in 1946 with the Tydings Rehabilitation Act, which provided much-needed economic aid to a devastated post–World War II Philippine economy, yet at the same time established the exchange rate of the peso-dollar at 2:1. By 1971, one U.S. dollar was equivalent to six and a quarter pesos. A Filipino working as a staff nurse in a New York hospital earned a minimum of 60,000 pesos annually, given this exchange rate. In the Philippines, the Filipino nurse earned an annual salary of approximately 4,200 pesos. In other words, a Filipino nurse working in the Philippines needed to work for twelve years in order to earn what she could make working as a nurse in the United States in one year (Asperilla 1971, 43–44).

Given this neocolonial economic disparity and their exploitation by U.S. hospital administrators to fill nursing shortages, some Filipino exchange nurses manipulated the EVP to serve their own agendas, for example, by working sixteen-hour shifts to earn more money. With their stipends in U.S. dollars, U.S. credit cards, and lay-away plans, Filipino exchange nurses purchased stereos, kitchen appliances, and cosmetics unobtainable for all except the affluent elite in the Philippines. They engaged in forms of leisure completely unavailable in the Philippines: Broadway shows, Lincoln Center performances, travel within the United States and to Europe. They lived in their own apartments and stayed out late at night. According to Fely Boado: "You're very independent. You have your own apartment. In the Philippines, you live in the dorm where everything closes at nine o'clock P.M. Or even if you stay at home, you don't go home late in the night or anything like that."

While some Filipino exchange nurses, like Fely Boado, referred to their new "independence" in the United States, this did not translate into emotional and economic separation from their families in the Philippines. By the time of Philippine independence in 1946, one way in which the Philippine landholding agricultural elite solidified its social status was by sending its sons and daughters abroad for training as doctors, lawyers, and other white-collar professions (Hawes 1989, 27–28). Filipino exchange nurses in the United States could also enhance their families' socioeconomic status by sending home material goods and money. Although the exchange visit temporarily separated Julieta Luistro from her boyfriend in the Philippines, she told me on 25 April 1995 that she also welcomed the opportunity to go to the United States, as it allowed her to shape new social as well as economic relationships between herself and her mother in the Philippines. She observed that other Filipino nurses abroad purchased U.S. goods and sent them back to their friends and family members. Julieta interpreted these material exchanges positively:

I had a classmate in high school who already was a nurse and here in the States at the time [the early 1960s]. . . . My cousin was in Kentucky at that time . . . and she was sending Avon cosmetics to me. . . . And my classmate was sending me Avon cosmetics also. . . . They have products here that we don't have in the Philippines. And . . . I guess I sort of would want that to happen to me too, to be able to send things to my mom at home when I get here. And that's what I did.

Socioeconomic opportunities for Filipino exchange nurses in the United States emerged in these contexts of U.S. neocolonial policies and Philippine social hierarchies. Given these opportunities abroad, Filipino exchange nurses created a "folklore" about America filled with social and economic promise, a folklore that coexisted with their exploitation by Filipino recruiters and U.S. hospital administrators. Through their letters to Filipino nursing friends back in the Philippines, Filipino exchange nurses encouraged others to follow them, with stories of high salaries, liberal working policies, and "good living" in the United States (Asperilla 1971, 15–17, 72).

Going abroad became a trend among Filipino nurses. One study revealed that between 1952 and 1965 an average of slightly more than 50 percent of 377 graduates from the University of the Philippines College of Nursing went abroad (see Ignacio, Masaganda, and Santa Maria 1967). The presence of their nursing friends in the United States motivated some of the former exchange nurses I interviewed to go abroad: "Because most of my friends and my classmates were already here. So they write to me," Luz Alerta said in our 13 March 1995 interview. Milagros Rabara told me that "most of my classmates were already here in the U.S.A., so I wanted to come."

Filipino exchange nurses encouraged not only thousands of other Filipino nurses to go to the United States but also other young Filipino women to enter nursing school. In 1962 there were more applicants for nursing studies than Philippine colleges and schools of nursing were able to accommodate (de la Vaca 1962, 183). And going abroad after the study of nursing figured prominently in their plans. In 1963, the president of the Filipino Nurses Association asked prospective nursing students why they chose that field of study: "This may surprise you but about 80 percent of those asked have answered me that it is because they want to go to the United States and other countries. About 10 percent of them say, because their boyfriends are medical students and they have agreed to go abroad together" (Alvarez 1960, 169).

Opportunities specifically through the Exchange Visitor Program motivated many young Filipino women to take up nursing. In the early 1960s, nursing applicants to St. Luke's School of Nursing in Quezon City, Metro Manila, mentioned the EVP in their statements of purpose.[6] "Many say that nurses have more opportunities to go to the U.S. under the Exchange program," wrote a 1965 applicant. "After finishing my nursing course I am planning . . . to go to the United States to specialize in surgical nursing." A class of 1967 applicant wrote: "I realized that nursing is one of the most profitable professions that a woman could hope to have . . . Furthermore, the profession offers a wide field of employment especially abroad, through the EVP. . . . After a few years of practice, I would like to go abroad through the EVP."

In 1960, FNA president Luisa Alvarez reported that many Filipino exchange nurses in Chicago complained about the length of their visits. According to these exchange nurses, a two-year period was insufficient time to "avail the benefits of the program" (Alvarez 1960, 133). They inquired if it were possible to extend their visit to a period of three to five years. When extensions of the exchange visit did not materialize, some Filipino exchange nurses returned to the Philippines after their two-year stay. However, others attempted to bypass the foreign residency requirement altogether and to change their "exchange" visa status while they were still in the United States.

After having been exposed to the social and material advantages of practicing nursing in the United States and earning U.S. dollars, Filipino exchange nurses employed multiple strategies to avoid returning to the Philippines. Some married U.S. citizens. Others immigrated to Canada. Filipino exchange nurses also exited the United States through Canada, Mexico, or St. Thomas and reentered as students. Some used a combination of requests by U.S. universities, the Philippine consul general, and U.S. hospital employers to petition the Exchange Visitor Waiver Board of the Department of Health, Education, and Welfare for a waiver of the foreign residence requirement. When these strategies failed and the Immigration and Naturalization Service set their dates for departure, some Filipino exchange nurses brought their cases to the U.S. Court of Appeals in an attempt to overturn INS rulings.[7] These court cases reveal that the interests between U.S. hospital employers and U.S. government agencies diverged and often competed with one another. Furthermore, the efforts of Filipino exchange nurses to waive their foreign residence requirement with the support of petitions from their U.S. hospital employers illustrate the contradictory ways in which the interests of hospital employers and Filipino exchange nurses complemented one another, although the former group exploited the latter as a cheap labor supply.

Filipino exchange nurses' desire to remain in the United States became a cause of alarm for Philippine government officials and nursing leaders. They interpreted Filipino nurses' duties as an integral part of Philippine nation building. Since recent Filipino nurse graduates were in a "rush to apply" to go abroad, commencement speeches became one forum for expressing these concerns regarding nationalism and nursing. In her speech to the 1966 graduating class of the Philippine General Hospital School of Nursing, Assistant Secretary for Cultural Affairs Pura Castrence criticized Filipino exchange nurses who refused to return to the Philippines:

> What is relevant is the problem of our nurses' restlessness to go to the United States—and remain there.... Why, you wonder, perhaps, has this problem of nurses become almost a national problem? The reason is simple. The country needs you nurses here. There are in the Philippines only 300 rural health units with a full complement of 1 physician, 1 nurse, 1 midwife, and 1 sanitary inspector; ... there are 112 units without physician or nurse. (1966, 207)

Castrence appealed to a nationalistic sense of nursing, but she conceded that the professional definition of nursing signified commitment to all those in the nurse's care, not primarily to the nurse's compatriots:

I can offer no solution. I looked over the Florence Nightingale pledge and find nothing that would uphold me in persuading you not to want to serve elsewhere than in your own country. True, your pledge says that you are to practice your profession faithfully—does faithfully mean, in your own country, to serve your own suffering fellow-countrymen? . . . True it pledges you to a devotion of yourself to the welfare of those committed to your care, but would that signify that you would think of the welfare of your fellow countrymen first because that dedication would be the deepening and the broadening of your pledge, which might be its intention? You alone can answer these questions when the time comes, dear nurses. (206–7)

Yet when the time came for Filipino exchange nurses to return to the Philippines, the vast majority who did return planned to go back to the United States (Asperilla 1971, 151).[8] If they shared any new skills they had learned from abroad, it was not for very long. They compared their salaries, nursing facilities, equipment, and research in the United States with that of the Philippines and became frustrated and disappointed with the latter. Josephine Abalos explained in our 1995 interview: "The thing that I love about American hospitals is that we have enough supplies and equipment. You have catheters. . . . In the Philippines we boiled our own rectal tubes. You use the catheters over and over. . . . Here you just use it once and dump it out. Supplies and equipment, paper and everything. It was no comparison. [In the Philippines], it was so limited all the time."

The EVP produced many unexpected outcomes. Returning nurses such as Sofronia Sanchez may have confirmed U.S. nurses' expectations that Filipino nurses would publicize the achievements of U.S. nursing when they went home to the islands. In 1963, she wrote to the editor of the *Philippine Journal of Nursing:* "I am a recent arrival from abroad and am now teaching in a school of nursing. One subject I am interested in is Professional Adjustments. In my readings around, I have yet to see a local textbook on the subject. . . . I am almost desperate to find out that after all these years, we have no local products beyond the mimeograph notes. Is this how backward we are?" (1963, 100; see also Capulong 1965, 86).

Such acknowledgments of the superiority of U.S. nursing also led to the development of a prejudice among Filipino exchange nurses against Philippine nursing, a prejudice that contributed to returnees' desire to go back to the United States and to some exchange nurses' refusal to leave the United States at all.

Your Cap Is a Passport

In 1962, the ANA distributed a brochure to professional nursing organizations worldwide appropriately entitled "Your Cap Is a Passport." The cover featured women wearing nursing caps and encircling the globe ("Exchange," 1958, 1667). It illustrated the theoretical underpinnings as well as the physical phenomenon of international nurse migration. Theoretically, the nursing cap, the symbol of professional nursing, enabled these women to practice nursing anywhere in the world. By the 1960s, professional nurses from around the world joined this migration under the auspices of various international programs. For Filipino nurses, their nursing cap was a passport to many parts of the world: Europe, other parts of Asia, the Middle East, and North America. Hospitals in Holland, Germany, the Netherlands, Brunei, Laos, Turkey, and Iran also recruited Filipino nurses to alleviate their nursing shortages.[9]

In the 1950s and 1960s, Filipinos and Americans transformed a program that was supposed to have been a vehicle for cultural and professional exchange. Unlike the early scholarship programs, the Exchange Visitor Program did not function as a path for occupational mobility in the Philippines. It became a means to an end, and that end was across the Pacific Ocean. In 1965, new U.S. immigration legislation would expedite a phenomenon that was already well underway.

Notes

1. For a critical analysis of the rise of professional nursing in the Philippines during the U.S. colonial period, see Choy 1998.

2. These programs included U.S. colonial government–sponsored study programs in the United States, such as the *pensionado* program (see Sutherland 1953), and Americanized hospital training schools for nurses in the Philippines (see Girón-Tupas 1952).

3. Between 1949 and 1951, Danish nurses comprised 54 percent of exchangees; Swedish nurses, 11 percent; British nurses, 9 percent; and Norwegian nurses, 6 percent (Brush 1993, 173, 179).

4. Of my interviewees, seven of the fifteen exchange nurses arranged their placement directly with the sponsoring hospitals, six with travel agencies, and two through the U.S. Embassy.

5. In 1946, the director of the Nursing Information Bureau reported that the U.S. health care system required 41,700 additional nurses. The demand for nursing care was particularly acute in U.S. hospitals, which in 1946 admitted one million more patients than the previous year (Roberts 1946, 3). By 1951, the president of the ANA estimated that current civilian nursing needs required 65,000 additional nurses (Porter 1951, 3).

6. Transcript files, St. Luke's College of Nursing, Trinity College, Quezon City, Philippines. Many other applications mentioned goals of "going abroad" in general, though not specifically through the EVP.

7. Isauro H. Glorioso v. INS, Rosita C. Colinco v. INS, 386 F.2d 664 (1967); Lilia B. Velasco v. INS, Nellie J. C. Morales v. INS, 386 F.2d 283 (1967).

8. In Asperilla's study of 411 Filipino nurse returnees, 97 percent said that they would like to go back if possible, and 86 percent said that they had already made plans to go back.

9. On Holland, see De Guzman (1965, 23–27, 29) and "In Our Mail" (1965, 111–13); on Germany and the Netherlands, see Lastrella (1967, 143–47) and Diamante (1967, 249–58). In the 1960s, there were several hundred Filipino nurses working in Holland, Germany, and the Netherlands. In 1953, the Filipino Nurses Association sent five Filipino nurses to work in Brunei (see *PJN* 29, 1 [January–February 1960]: 56). In November–December 1966, an advertisement titled "Nurses Wanted for Brunei" (*PJN* 35, 6: 360) offered gratuities on top of salaries and free transportation to Brunei. A Filipino nurse working in Turkey wrote *PJN* that there were at least three Filipino nurses in Iran (Sy 1967).

Works Cited

Abella, Manolo J. 1979. *Export of Filipino Manpower.* Manila: Institute of Labor and Manpower Studies.

Alinea, Patria G., and Gloria B. Senador. 1973. "Leaving for Abroad? . . . Here's a Word of Caution." *PJN* 42, 1 (January–March): 92–94.

Alvarez, Luisa A. 1960. "By the President." *PJN* 29, 3 (May–June): 132–38.

———. 1963. "The President's Page: Words to Student Nurses." *PJN* 32, 4 (July–Aug.): 168–69.

American Nurses Association (ANA). 1959–69. Nursing Information Bureau. *Facts about Nursing.* New York: American Nurses Association.

Arbeiter, Jean S. 1988. "The Facts about Foreign Nurses." *RN* 51, 9: 56–63.

Asperilla, Purita Falgui. 1971. "The Mobility of Filipino Nurses." Ph.D. diss., Columbia University.

Bacala, J.C. 1962. "This Issue's Personality: Juanita J. Jimenez, a Silver Lining in Our Profession." *PJN* 31, 3 (May–June): 192–93.

Broadhurst, Martha Jeanne. 1958. "Knowing Our Exchange Visitors." *Nursing Outlook* 6 (April): 201.

Brush, Barbara. 1993. "'Exchangees' or Employees?: The Exchange Visitor Program and Foreign Nurse Immigration to the United States, 1945–1990." *Nursing History Review* 1, 1: 171–80.

Capulong, Purificacion N. 1965. "An Appraisal of the United States Exchange-Visitor Program for Filipino Nurses." Master's thesis, Philippine Women's University.

Castillejos, Epifanio B. 1966. "The Exchange Visitors Program: Report and Recommendation." *PJN* 35, 5 (September–October): 306–7.

Castrence, Pura S. 1966. "Challenge to the Filipino Nurses." *PJN* 35, 4 (July–August): 205–7.

Chan, Sucheng. 1991. *Asian Americans: An Interpretive History.* Boston: Twayne.

Choy, Catherine Ceniza. 1998. "'The Usual Subjects': Medicine, Nursing, and American Colonialism in the Philippines." *Critical Mass* (spring): 1–28.

De Guzman, Genara S. M. 1965. "Report on Holland." *PJN* 34, 1 (January–February): 23–27, 29.

de la Vaca, Tomas Antonio. 1962. "Should Filipino Students Take Their Basic Nursing Studies Abroad?" *Santo Tomas Nursing Journal* 1, 3 (December): 183–84.

Diamante, Rosario S. 1967. "Glimpses of Hospitals and Nursing Schools in Germany and Netherlands." *PJN* 36, 5 (September–October): 249–58.

Espiritu, Yen Le. 1995. *Filipino American Lives.* Philadelphia: Temple University Press.

"Exchange for Education." 1958. *American Journal of Nursing* 58, 12 (December): 1666–71.

Girón-Tupas, Anastacia. 1952. *History of Nursing in the Philippines.* Manila: University Book Supply.

Hawes, Gary. 1989. *The Philippine State and the Marcos Regime.* Bloomington: Indiana University Press.

Ignacio, Teodora, Marlena Masaganda, and Leticia Santa Maria. 1967. "A Study of the Graduates of the Basic Degree Program of the University of the Philippines College of Nursing Who Have Gone Abroad." *ANPHI* (October): 50–68.

"In Our Mail." 1965. *PJN* 34, 3 (May-June): 111–13.

Ishi, Tomoji. 1987. "Class Conflict, the State, and Linkage: The International Migration of Nurses from the Philippines." *Berkeley Journal of Sociology* 32: 281–95.

Lastrella, Ida F. 1967. "The Filipino Nurses at the Academic Hospital, Leiden, Nederland." *PJN* 36, 3 (May–June): 143–47.

Montellano, Patrocinio J. 1962. "Years That Count." *PJN* 31, 4 (July–August 1962): 235–36, 255–57.

"104 Young Nurses Off to U.S." 1960. *PJN* 29, 3 (May–June): 195–96.

"122 Young Nurses Departed to U.S." 1960. *PJN* 29, 4 (July–August): 267–68.

Ong, Paul, and Tania Azores. 1994. "The Migration and Incorporation of Filipino Nurses." In Ong, Bonacich, and Cheng, 164–95.

Ong, Paul, Edna Bonacich, and Lucie Cheng, eds. 1994. *The New Asian Immigration in Los Angeles and Global Restructuring*. Philadelphia: Temple University Press.

Porter, Elizabeth K. 1951. Preface to *Facts about Nursing*. ANA Nursing Information Bureau. New York: American Nurses Association.

Roberts, Mary. 1946. Preface to *Facts about Nursing*. ANA Nursing Information Bureau. New York: American Nurses Association.

Sanchez, Sofronia S. 1963. Letter. "In Our Mail." *PJN* 32, 3 (May–June): 100.

Sutherland, William Alexander. 1953. *Not By Might: The Epic of the Philippines*. Las Cruces, N.M.: Southwest.

Sy, Magdalena. 1967. "In Our Mail." *PJN* 36, 2 (March–April): 90.

Takaki, Ronald. 1989. *Strangers from a Different Shore: A History of Asian Americans*. New York: Little, Brown.

U.S. Senate. 1948. "Promoting the Better Understanding of the United States among the Peoples of the World and to Strengthen Cooperative International Relations." *Senate Miscellaneous Reports I.* 80th Cong., 2d sess. S. Rpt. 811. Washington, D.C.: GPO.

Vallangca, Caridad Concepcion. 1987. *The Second Wave: Pinay and Pinoy (1945–1960)*. San Francisco: Strawberry Hill Press.

Fabiana Chiu-Rinaldi

---

11   China Latina

After I had finished a presentation on the history of Chinese in Peru at the American Museum of Natural History in New York, a member of the audience stood up and commented that he had been to Peru and indeed had not seen any Chinese there. His assertion took me by surprise, especially because it is estimated that 15 percent of Peru's population, or 3.5 million Peruvians, have some Chinese blood.

What could his assertion mean? What are the implications of not being counted, of being invisible to some and overly visible to others? As I considered the possible responses to his statement, five generations of my family's history in Peru flashed before my eyes. Was my one-hour lecture, accompanied by more than eighty slides, not enough? As a Chinese Peruvian, I realized that with a story as little told and considered as ours, it is almost as if we do not exist. Our lives have not been lived, our contributions not recorded or appreciated by ourselves or anyone else.

I left Peru at age twenty-one with little knowledge about the hows and whys of my own family's history. Nothing I had packed prepared me for what was to come. In the United States I faced a set of questions to which I had never been subjected to in Peru. Latinos were asking me how I came to speak Spanish so well, and everyone else wondered why I didn't speak a word of Chinese—questioning my strong sense of "Latinidad" and heightening a growing interest in my Asian background. Unfortunately, retelling the miniscule piece of history I was taught in Peru about my own community invited questions for which I had no answers.

Most of the information one finds about Chinese Peruvians is limited to research conducted by non-Chinese Peruvians on the "coolie trade," a phenomenon that brought hundreds of thousands of Chinese to work Peru's difficult terrain in the 1850s. Their arrival came at the end of slavery and provided the Peruvian elite with a way to maintain their status. Thousands of Chinese lost their lives picking guano, the rich organic fertilizer that seabirds left behind in many of Peru's coastal islands; building Peru's Ferrocarril Central, the railroad into the high sierras of the Andes mountains; and working the vast coastal sugar and cotton plantations. Beatings and whippings were commonplace for those who didn't perform as required by their eight-year contracts.

The Chinese were often vilified, seen as untrustworthy, stupid, dirty, ugly, and racially inferior. They staged revolts and uprisings, and many reputedly fled to the United States looking for better treatment. Present-day reminders of those harsh experiences persist. Phrases like *Chino cochino*—a derogatory sing-song rhyme that means "filthy Chinese," and *No me Chine-es,* a phrase that means "Don't try to make a fool of me," giving the word *chino* the connotation of fool—can still be heard in Lima's streets. That's how the Chinese Peruvian community started—at the bottom, looking up at all they had to accomplish and gain.

Growing up in Lima, I remember how uncomfortable I used to be when the history teacher would discuss the only chapter in Peruvian history where we Chinese are mentioned. There we were, frozen in time as indentured servants or "coolies," and there I was, suffering from a seemingly communitywide amnesia, with no known connection to a history no one seemed to want. This changed recently, when I met Humberto Rodriguez Pastor, a researcher of Chinese Peruvian history, who suggested that according to the date of my great- grandfather's arrival in Peru, there was a good chance that he had been a "coolie." "A coolie?" I asked, alarmed. "Well, an ex-coolie," he explained. I became determined to uncover a more personal history that would help me explain a period that started with but moved beyond the "coolie" chapter. So I began to look into the photographs, family albums, letters, and diary journals my father had saved for more than fifty years. Wanting to reclaim a difficult past, I was looking for clues and for answers that would help me respond to those questioning my community's history.

Faded Photos, Blurred Memories

I have been around photographs since I can remember. By the time I was born in Lima in 1964, three generations of our family's history there had passed, and my father's photographs and journals served as the only tie to people I had never met. Dad has been a photographer at heart and by profession. Born Victor Lizardo Chiu Yipmantin in Lima's El Barrio Chino on 10 October 1926, he has spent more than half a century documenting his life and times. No gathering was ever complete until his tripod was set up and the camera's timer had begun its countdown. Whether they were studio photographs or snapshots, they were all carefully orchestrated by Dad, who often managed to position himself deftly in the right spot before the timer could trigger the shutter. Without his keen desire to capture his family on film, much of this story would be hard to tell today.

Surely, many of the photos were taken to be sent back to China to tell paternal great-aunt Chiu Kam Lin, whom Dad had never met, that he and the family were doing well. In the last letter my father received from her, she writes in Chinese: "The photos you sent were taken quite a long time ago and their colors are blurred and fading. I hope you can send me some recent ones so that I can look at them as if we met." Sadly, all contact with our Chinese family was lost in the 1960s. "It's because we no longer knew people who we could ask to write for us in Chinese," Dad explained.

From China to Peru

One hundred and fifteen years ago, my paternal great-grandfather, Agustin Yipmantin, set sail from Nanhai, Canton, for Lima. In the oldest photograph I've seen of him, he is seated in a studio with his two daughters: my grandmother Rebeca and great-aunt Manuela. These two sisters were born in different worlds, one in China, one in Peru. Their mother, Rosa Michelena, remains a mystery. Was she Chinese? Indigenous? Black? Or none or all of the above? Furthermore, no one in the family seems to know much about my great-grandfather, what his occupation was, or why, of all places, he ended up in Peru.

My grandfather Lizardo Chiu Jim, the eldest son in his family, was born in Nanhai, Canton, in 1887 to a family of potters. He married my grandmother Rebeca in Lima in 1919 and had three boys and two girls: Maria Luz, Rebeca Paulina, Rodolfo Andres, Victor Lizardo (my father), and Agustin. According to Peruvian custom, their last name, Chiu Yipmantin, reflected both their paternal and maternal lineage, although no one seems to know why the official last name that appeared in their early records was not Chiu Yipmantin but the puzzling Avila, a Spanish surname.

Grandfather did everything he could to make ends meet. He was a cook at Hacienda Boza in Huaral, a locale north of Lima, and he sold Chinese vegetables from the *chacra,* a vegetable garden he rented in Lima. He was also a tinsmith and a doctor of Chinese medicine. Dad also recalls the many times when his father would wake up in the middle of the night to bake Chinese pastries he would later sell out of a street cart in Lima's Mercado Central. From cook to tinsmith, my grandfather never really talked about China or those he left behind. When he died, he had twenty dollars to his name, all of which was sent to his family in China.

Baptized in the Catholic Church as Fabiana Leonor Chiu Cheon, I am the third of four daughters. Some of my earliest memories are of sneaking into my parents' bedroom while they were out at work and climbing onto a stool to reach for the old family photo albums stacked high up in their closet. Since Mom and Dad seemed to be always working, I spent many afternoons secretly reading Dad's journals and matching his detailed entries to the corresponding photographs, many of which were also carefully annotated.

In a picture taken in August 1967 during a family outing (Fig. 11.1), I am the three-year-old wearing a poncho decorated with llamas. My sister Vilma is holding the portable National short-band radio brought for us to dance and sing along to hits like "La Bamba," "Guantanamera," and mambo master Perez Prado's "El Taconazo."

Together with Mom, Dad, and Laura, my eldest sister, we are all pointing our left foot out, angling our knees to create a more "pleasing" pose, waiting for the camera to click. The mountains behind us add an exclamation point to another slightly chilly August winter in Peru.

Boarding the old Chevrolet, we would drive for two hours, the Central Andes beckoning us, only to stop short of the foothills in Chaclacayo, a town that was home to the Centro Vacacional Huampani, a modest country compound with a swimming

FIGURE 11.1. August 1967, Chaclacayo, Peru. Victor Lizardo Chiu Yipmantin and Maria Leonor Cheon de Chiu with children *(from left)* Vilma Celinda, Fabiana Leonor, and Laura Matilde Chiu Cheon at the Centro Vacacional Huampani beneath the foothills of the Andes.

pool, and plenty of clean air. It was a change from polluted Lima, a chance to experience a sunny day.

In the photo, Mom is five months pregnant with our younger sister Milagros. Mom and Dad were always hoping for the arrival of *el varoncito*, or baby boy, the Chinese son who would carry the family's name and legacy. Since he never materialized, we daughters were taught the many things Dad would have passed on to his son, from how to fix appliances and splice wires to how to take photographs. Pushing us to accomplish what they had only dreamed of for themselves, Mom and Dad worked tirelessly so that each of us could go to college in Peru.

While many of Dad's old photos show his family dressed in their Sunday best, the pictures seem to depict the success they imagined for themselves. Extreme poverty and limited access to education more accurately described their situation. Between world wars, his family lived in El Barrio Chino, Lima's old Chinatown, in a *callejon de un solo cano,* an alleyway where dozens of other Chinese Peruvians lived, sharing a makeshift sink and a faucet. Rebeca Yipmantin, my grandmother, who was born in Lima in 1899, was a seamstress and a teacher of Spanish to Chinese immigrants. She had

FIGURE 11.2.   February 1950, Hacienda Arona, Cañete, Peru. *Una Cadenita* (little chain links), *left to right,* Lucy Wong Chiu, Victor Lizardo Chiu Yipmantin, Sergio Chuypon Chiu, and Rodolfo Andres Chiu Yipmantin.

two older siblings, both born in China: Augusto and Manuela. During the world depression of the 1930s, Manuela and her husband went back to China. Grandmother was devastated. She feared she would never see her sister again. She was right.

A photograph that my father titled *Una cadenita,* "little chain links," was taken in February 1950 at Hacienda Arona, a coastal plantation near San Vicente de Canete, south of Lima. It shows my oldest cousin, Lucy Wong Chiu, my father, my cousin Sergio Chuypon Chiu, and my uncle Rodolfo (Fig. 11.2). Already third- and fourth-generation Chinese Peruvians, they pose against the sky, holding hands, forming a determined and solid human chain. What they might not have known was that had this picture been taken a hundred years earlier in the same location, it would have depicted real chains and the widespread mistreatment that the Chinese endured as indentured servants in Peru.

In the almost cinematic shot, *Una cadenita* symbolized the hopes and dreams my family members had for themselves. United, they took control of their destinies. They were young and healthy and had found freedom in Arona.

Hacienda Arona in the 1950s produced mostly cotton and corn and was being rented by Wing On Chong y Compania, a prosperous import company headquartered in

Lima's Barrio Chino and run by Cantonese from Nanhai, our family's ancestral village. Since the 1940s, my father had worked at Wing On Chong's store on Plateros de San Pedro, a street next to Lima's historic Plaza de Armas. During the day, he sold silk, porcelain, and cloisonné gift items. At night, he arranged the display windows and kept the store's inventory. In his free time, he studied to be a radio repair technician and moonlighted with his best friend, Carlos Unyen, who owned the Casa Musical Babalu, an outfit that rented sound equipment also known as "pick-ups" for dance parties.

El Barrio Chino

To be born in Peru and not in China, Dad recalls, was sometimes considered an automatic demotion within the ranks of Chinatown's class structure. At Chinese-owned businesses, many Peruvian-born Chinese were denied access to upper management positions. In El Barrio Chino, Peruvians of Chinese descent were and are still known as *injertos*, a term that in its worst connotation could mean "half-breed." Spread over many square blocks in the shadow of Lima's legendary Spanish-colonial government buildings, members of the Chinese community opened countless Chinese restaurants; *encomenderias*, or small grocery stores; print shops for community newspapers; fraternal organizations, schools, and temples; and fine import stores that sold the latest porcelain and silk products from China.

Although Dad had never been to China, he learned to speak such good Chinese that in school language contests he would win over many Chinese-born students. Through hard work, he also managed to be trusted as one of their own at Wing On Chong and qualified for many of the special benefits reserved for those born in China. On special occasions, such as El Dia de la Independencia Nacional del Peru on 28 July, he would secure permission from his bosses and rally the family for a three-hour trip in a hired car for a weekend of rest and relaxation at Hacienda Arona.

Dad's journal entry of 9 February 1948 details one of these visits. "This morning we rode some horses through the wide cotton fields which are almost ready to be harvested. On the way back to the 'Casa Grande,' we took several photos posing as 'jockeys' and 'cowboys.' In the evening we all gathered around the radio to listen to 'El Programa Coca Cola' featuring 'Xavier Cugat y su Orquesta,' who played 'La Bamba,' 'Tio Tico' and 'Chio Chio Chon.' "

The next day, according to the diary, they boarded a truck to go into town to see an American movie titled *Our Very Own*, starring Ann Blyth, Farley Granger, and Jane Wyatt. The amateur movie critic in Dad writes, "*Una pelicula donde se reflejan el sentir y las costumbres del pueblo americano, incluyendo un baile con algunos pasos nuevos de Bugui Bugui* [a film that reflects the feelings and customs of the American people, including a new dance called the boogie-boogie]." ("*Bugui Bugui*" is his phonetic translation of what he understood the name of the dance to be.) For Dad, these movies were not only entertainment but also a way to learn more about a culture that had captured his imagination.

Jackson Studios

Although it had been Dad's original intention to go into the radio repair business, he decided to put his life's savings toward what already was an established family business. His robust, tall, and China-born uncle Augusto Yipmantin had founded the Fotografia Yipmantin in Lima in the late 1920s. His son Arnaldo ran the Instituto Fotografio Yipmantin out of it. It was a school where many Peruvian would-be photographers learned their craft. Arnaldo gave his cousins two scholarships so that they too could learn the business.

After six years at Wing On Chong, Dad cashed in his company stock and, together with uncle Rodolfo, opened Jackson Studios in Lima's El Porvenir neighborhood. The year was 1951 and Dad was twenty-five years old.

Jackson Studios got its name from Dad's feeling that a U.S.-sounding name would carry extra cachet and bring more business. The other stores on the block followed suit and became Tienda de Repuestos de Automovil Wilson, which sold auto parts, and the Sastreria Boston, a tailor shop. The studio's customers reflected Peru's diverse population of chinos, mestizos, mulattos, and *blancos,* many of whom came in to discover that "Mr. Jackson" looked very Chinese.

Soon, Dad recalls, Jackson Studios became the *fotografos casi oficiales de la Colonia China,* the unofficial photographers of the Chinese community. One finds evidence of this by examining the names of some of the people they photographed: Don Alfredo Tay Chy, Felipe Chang, Julio Ching, Don Alberto Yip Chen Yui, Rodolfo Lock, Carlos Pun, Luis Chang Ji, Don Aurelio Chang Tac, and Francisco Lam—tongue-twister names born out of the encounter of two cultures. Among other achievements, Jackson Studios enabled Dad and Uncle Rodolfo to move their recently widowed mother out of the cramped and unsanitary living conditions of the Calle Huanta tenement in Chinatown, near the city's busy Mercado Central.

Lima in the 1950s was a sprawling city that attracted U.S. businesses and tourists alike. Firms such as the Grace Company, Dupont, Sherwin Williams, Kodak, and Sears, Roebuck established solid footholds in Peru. Film companies like Warner Brothers, Paramount, Metro-Goldwyn-Mayer, and Twentieth Century Fox owned lavish movie theaters in Lima. In addition, magazines such as *Life, Popular Mechanics,* and *Reader's Digest* offered Dad a glimpse of progress "American- style."

Jackson Studios became the perfect place to implement his own vision of prosperity, shown in a December 1952 photo (Fig. 11.3) in which a large sign he made wished his customers *"Muy Felices Pascuas y Prospero Ano Nuevo, Desean a Ud. Jackson Studios,"* a "very Merry Christmas and a prosperous New Year from Jackson Studios." To the left of the counter, a blonde, blue-eyed cardboard beauty wearing a swimsuit and a Kodak camera around her neck invited shoppers to buy Kodak film and cameras.

In the photo, Jackson Studios employee Manuela Soplin, my father, and my cousin Lucy are surrounded by the caramel-colored wooden paneling and cabinets that Dad designed for the store. Whether in the darkroom or on the studio set, he always added

FIGURE 11.3.   Christmas 1952, Lima, Peru. Interior shot of Jackson Studios. *Left to right:* employee Manuela Soplin, studio co-owner Victor Lizardo Chiu Yipmantin, and his niece Lucy Wong Chiu.

his special touch. One year he painted a life-sized Jesus handing out a piece of holy bread. He drew it, cut it out, and placed it strategically so that parents would bring their kids to get their first-communion pictures taken. The studio also transformed sepia-toned photos into full-color works of art, hand coloring hair, eyes, and dresses in colors requested by the customers. While Uncle Rodolfo stayed at the store, Dad took the camera on the road, hoping to bring in extra *soles*, the Peruvian currency. He photographed weddings, social dances, baptisms, and many store openings. While at it, he witnessed a whole generation of Chinese Peruvians getting married. As he took pictures at Julio Kuangfung's wedding, Dad fell in love with Maria Leonor Cheon Salas, one of the maids of honor and the bride's youngest sister. He figured that if he took beautiful pictures of this shy twenty-year-old, she would fall in love with him. He was right.

My mother's story echoes those of many other Chinese Peruvians. With few China-born women in Peru, many Chinese men formed families with local Peruvian women. Born in Arequipa, Peru, in 1931, my mother was the youngest of Manuel Cheon's and Maria Salas's three daughters. When asked why she married a Chinese man, Maria, known to us as Apocito (a name that combines the Cantonese word for grandmother with a Spanish ending), replied that after witnessing the physical abuse her own mother, Juana Aldecoa Arrospide de Salas, had endured from her Peruvian husband, she hoped that a Chinese man would make a kinder husband. While spousal abuse knows no ethnic boundaries, her intuition paid off.

As time went by, Mom and Dad began to put in seven-day workweeks. Family outings became infrequent, so photographing them became a way to make cherished moments last longer. Some trips, however, remain vivid in our memories for other reasons. During a family trip to Ica, a sunny city south of Lima, some men around the Plaza de Armas started calling us *chinos* to our faces. The first two letters of the word seemed to be coming out of their mouths angry, deliberately harsh. While the word *chino/a* means nothing more than Chinese man or woman, they were using the word as an insult. Dad's indignation was such that he said we should have worn big signs saying "Si, *somos* chinos,"—"Yes, we *are* Chinese." I was eight years old. Incidents of this sort made me suspect that a *china* was perhaps not an ideal thing to be.

From Peru to the United States

My memories of Peru are both sweet and sour. More than half of my life in Peru was spent under two military dictatorships. One of the dictators, General Juan Velasco Alvarado, was a man who, like many Peruvians of indigenous descent, had "slanted" eyes and was widely referred to as "El Chino Velasco." In 1990, Peru gained world attention by electing Alberto Fujimori, the first national president of Asian descent outside of Asia. Ever since, I have been teased, being called President Fujimori's cousin, daughter, or niece. In fact, in Peru, as in many Latin American countries, Chinese, Koreans, and Japanese, are all called *chinos*.

Still, I remember proudly raising our Peruvian flag during holidays and singing the national anthem. Despite displaying the racism and stereotyping that overseas Chinese faced in many countries they emigrated to, Peru is also a place where my presence was never questioned, where my proficiency in Spanish and things Peruvian was never doubted, where the flavorful Latin American and Chinese cuisines come together at the *chifas*—the popular Chinese Peruvian restaurants, named from the Spanish pronunciation for "eat rice" in Cantonese.

As Peru's economy sharply declined in the 1980s and Shining Path terrorism became rampant, each of my sisters, my parents, and I moved to the United States. Although we are immigrants for the first time in our lives, our arrival here feels strangely like a continuation of the journey my great grandfather Agustin Yipmantin started more than 115 years ago when he left Canton. And it seems that our story is not much unlike that of others who continue to immigrate to Peru from China. Many may be on their way to the United States through a smuggling route connecting Asia to the United States via Latin America. By the time they get to the States, possibly on their third or fourth family migration, they face the daunting challenge of defining their identity.

When I applied for a new Social Security card in Brooklyn, the form instructed me to check only one racial/ethnic category. I decided to be accurate and checked both Hispanic and Asian. Minutes after I turned in my form, the clerk and later her supervisor called me to their desks to try to persuade me to choose between the categories. After my tiresome recitation about who my parents were, what language we spoke, and what our last names were, they—fully confused—shrugged their shoulders and left the form unchanged. Unwilling to give in, I wanted every part of my identity, China/Peruana/Asian/Latina/American, to be counted and accounted for.

Today, with a 150-year legacy in the Americas, Asian Latinos represent a unique link between two of the largest immigrant groups in the United States. We, like the photos in our family albums, offer a window into our little-known history.

Part III

Objects

Jeanette Roan

12 Exotic Explorations: Travels to Asia and the Pacific in Early Cinema

The Fascination of the Faraway

In an article published in 1907 the French critic and essayist Rémy de Gourmont proclaimed: "I love the cinema. It satisfies my curiosity. It allows me to tour the world and stop, to my liking, in Tokyo and Singapore. I follow the craziest itineraries" (1988, 48). A number of film companies of the time capitalized upon this fascination with the faraway by using some version of the phrase "the whole world within reach" as their motto, highlighting the ability of cinema to make images of distant lands immediately accessible (Gunning 1995, 28). This curiosity, however, must be situated in relation to larger debates of the time concerning economic expansion, racial and cultural difference, and colonial conquest. The naming of Tokyo and Singapore by de Gourmont as examples of "the craziest itineraries" not only contrasts the exoticism of Asia to the more prosaic destinations of a European Grand Tour, but also suggests the manner in which cinema could provide remarkably easy passage to such previously remote lands.

A particularly privileged manifestation of the fascination with the faraway within the larger industry of travel images was the illustrated travel lecture. Illustrated travel lecturers were generally upper-class white men who traveled to different parts of the world, took images of these locales, then returned and presented them to audiences at elite institutions such as the Brooklyn Institute for Arts and Sciences. The lectures appealed to relatively wealthy patrons in search of both education and entertainment, and their cinematic component should be distinguished from the more commercial, mass-oriented films of the time. One of the most popular illustrated travel lecturers of the early twentieth century was E. Burton Holmes. Especially notable about Holmes's early lectures is their relationship to the historical era in which they were situated. Holmes has written of the first fourteen years of the twentieth century as "those happy years" when "I was almost alone in the then peculiar field of showing Americans what the world, outside of America, looked like" (1953, 199). But at this very moment, the means for "showing," as well as "America" as a nation and its relationship to the world outside, were undergoing dramatic redefinition. Donna Haraway suggests that we understand biography as "woven into and from a social and political tissue," and the life and work of E. Burton Holmes bear out the complex truth of her insight (1993, 249).

Holmes's predecessor, John L. Stoddard, held a nostalgic view of travel and lamented the advent of railroads, steamships, and telegraphs, accusing them of robbing the earth of its romance. Holmes took a radically different approach to travel, proudly taking on the title of "Everyman's tourist." Stoddard's lectures were composed primarily of slides. As one of the first illustrated travel lecturers to incorporate film into his presentations, Holmes combined the well-worn conventions of the travel lecture with the visual and dramatic possibilities offered by cinema. Thus, Holmes's early embrace of film may be seen as emblematic of his difference from Stoddard, a difference that symbolized a new era of travel, and a new kind of traveler. Another equally important distinction between the works of the two men may be found in the kinds of destinations to which they traveled.

In 1892, Holmes and Stoddard met onboard a steamship bound for Japan. Stoddard, who was already famous for his lectures on European subjects, was embarking on his first trip around the world, gathering material for future lectures. Holmes, then twenty-two years old, was on a vacation funded by his family. As Stoddard's son later recalled: "The older man found Japan queer, quaint, comfortless, and almost repellent. To the younger man it was a fairyland" (qtd. in Wallace 1977, 16). This trip to Japan would eventually provide the material for Holmes's first professional lectures. David Palumbo-Liu has written of how U.S. expansion into East Asia and the Pacific region was an essential part of the project of American modernization, and he notes a growth of interest in Asia in turn-of-the-century U.S. culture (1999, 17, 19). Images of Asia both resulted from and were a constitutive part of the development of this project. In this socio-historic context, Holmes's enthusiastic embrace of the exotic, the importance to his work of certain Asian and Pacific nations—including Japan, China, Korea, the Philippines, and Hawai'i—and his use of moving-picture technology all had important consequences for the store of representations of Asians and Pacific Islanders in the American imaginary.[1] In addition, the fact that Holmes began his career at the historic moment of the "birth" of U.S. overseas imperialism provides an opportunity to examine the question of how the representation of faraway lands was implicated in the literal traversal of space in geopolitical expansion, and how the political dimensions of this expansion shaped the conventions of the developing medium of film.[2]

Although Holmes is a relatively obscure historical figure today, he was immensely popular at the height of his career. The historian Arthur M. Schlesinger Jr., who attended the "Burton Holmes Lectures" with his mother at Boston's Symphony Hall in the 1920s, opens a recent essay on Holmes with a paean: "Burton Holmes!—forgotten today, but such a familiar name in America in the first half of the 20th century, a name then almost synonymous with dreams of foreign travel" (1998, 24). Schlesinger concludes that the reprinting of Holmes's lectures, in a series aimed at children aged nine to twelve and titled "The World 100 Years Ago," will "show new generations how their grandparents learned about a world that has since passed away but remains a fragrant mem-ory" (9). But traces of that complex past linger, as often in the form of disturbing mem-ories as of fragrant ones. Holmes's photographs, films, and lectures from the turn of the century are indeed fascinating glimpses of the world one hundred years ago. Yet many of his images and narratives also evoke complex and ambivalent responses that exceed their status as mere records of a bygone era. From a contemporary perspective, the lectures on Hawai'i and the Philippines, for instance, serve as a reminder of the his-tory of U.S. overseas imperialism and colonial conquest. Remembering this history is crucial to understanding the present. Thus, Holmes's lectures are not merely historical artifacts, as Schlesinger suggests, but products of the (colonial) intersection of technol-ogy, representation, and the international balance of power that remain in play, albeit in an updated form, in the (postcolonial/neocolonial) present.

Images and Imagination

Holmes's first trip abroad took him through Europe with his grandmother when he was a teenager. But it was the five-month-long visit to Japan in 1892 that served as the point of departure for his extended and productive career as one of the most popular givers of illustrated travel lectures in the United States. Upon his return from Japan, he found his hometown of Chicago busily preparing for the 1893 Columbian Exposition. In his biography Holmes writes of the exposition with great enthusiasm: "I found in that great exposition an epitome and a foretaste of the great world that I longed to see. I trav-elled around the world within the gates of the Chicago Fair." Furthermore, "the Fair had so intensified my love for things foreign, exotic, far-away and unfamiliar that I resolved, before going back to work, to try to find a way to keep on going places, see-ing things, indulging my *wanderlust*" (Holmes, 1953, 135–37). Irving Wallace provides the exact moment of Holmes's vocational epiphany, quoting Holmes: "The photo sup-ply house offered me fifteen dollars a week to return. But I didn't want to work. The trip to Japan, the Oriental exhibits of the Exposition, were still on my mind. I thought of [John L.] Stoddard. I thought of the slides I'd had hand-colored in Tokyo. That was it, and it wasn't work. So I hired a hall and became a travel lecturer" (1977, 16).

Holmes's first professional lectures, presented in the recital hall of the Auditorium Building in Chicago, were "Japan—The Country" and "Japan—The Cities." The invi-tations to "The E. Burton Holmes Lectures," printed on oblong Japanese "poem cards," deliberately played upon the refined aesthetic associated with all things Japanese, as did the lectures themselves.[3]

For the spoken text of these first lectures, Holmes consulted written works on Japan ranging from guidebooks to untranslated writings by the well-known French author Pierre Loti. But even in later years, when his experience allowed him to compose more original lectures, he still recognized that "in writing of Japan it is hard not to quote or misquote, unconsciously or even consciously, Pierre Loti or Lafcadio Hearn" (Holmes 1953, 138). Yet Holmes's actual visit to Japan was mediated by the same influential authors. In writing of it, Holmes rhapsodized, "Through that land of magic pictorial beauty I travelled ... feasting my eyes on scenes that had for me the charm of something *deja vue* (already seen) as Pierre Loti put it" (1953, 90). It is telling that what Holmes sees of Japan conveniently organizes itself into "scenes," and scenes from Pierre Loti at that. That Loti's term "deja vue" itself refers to some precedent serves as an illustration of Ali Behdad's analysis of travel narratives as necessarily reiterations of earlier texts that come between travelers and their travels (1994, 26). This repetitive and referential structure of travel narratives is, of course, a key mechanism of what Edward Said has famously theorized as "Orientalism."

In her analysis of the relationship between the writings of Lafcadio Hearn and the films of Cecil B. DeMille, Sumiko Higashi cites Said on the way that travel involves a situation where what he calls a "textual attitude," or a preference for "the schematic authority of a text to the disorientations of direct encounters with the human," is likely to prevail, lending travel books an authority greater than the actuality they describe (1978, 93). Higashi adds that cinema, because of its "reality effect," would be attributed with even greater authority than the written text (1996, 347). Holmes's lectures, as a practice that employed both the older conventions of the written travelogue and the emerging technology of cinema, allow further insight into how cinema reinscribed as well as rearticulated preexisting representations of the cultural differences involved in the experience of travel. In other words, at issue here is the manner in which cinema visualized cultural difference as compared to other forms of representation.

The program for Holmes's 1899–1900 season, the first season in which films were shown during the course of the lecture rather than only at their conclusion, stated that films were "to be projected during the lecture at moments when movement is essential to complete and vivify the impressions produced by the spoken words and colored illustrations." Exactly what Holmes felt the films added to his lectures, aside from "mark[ing] the beginning of a new epoch in the treatment of the illustrated lecture," is an important question (qtd. in Musser 1991, 125). Paradoxically, it is the desire for the as yet unavailable technology that is most revealing of the uses to which Holmes envisioned cinema to be best suited.

Holmes wrote of an imperial garden party he attended during his first trip to Japan: "Bustles are funny. As worn in Japan in 1892, they were a scream. The dainty Japanese ladies, who would have looked so charming in kimono, had adopted western fashions but not western manners. When they bowed, they bent forward at the waist, again and again, jack-knife fashion. As their heads went down, up came the bustles. Oh, that the movies had been invented then!" (1953, 123).

Holmes's anecdote assumes an absolute and irreconcilable difference between East and West that is apparent in the ludicrous attempts of the Japanese to assimilate Western fashions while retaining traditional forms of greeting. The movies, Holmes surmises, could have captured this contradiction in a way that a still image or words could not. In a photograph, the Japanese might appear westernized, but moving pictures would reveal the superficial nature of this resemblance by showing the disjuncture between appearance and actuality. In other words, despite the efforts of the Japanese to look Western, moving pictures would affirm the extent to which they nevertheless remained

Japanese. The insistence that kimonos constitute the only appropriate dress for Japanese women thus belies a larger ambivalence about Japanese modernization.[4]

As an example of the use of cinema to "complete and vivify the impressions produced by the spoken words and colored illustrations," film historian Charles Musser quotes the following excerpt from "Japan, Land of Flowers," a review of Holmes's lecture on Japan published in the 6 January 1900 edition of the *Brooklyn Eagle*:

> Photographs of some of the girls were shown and demonstrated instantly their right to the claim of beauty and fascination that is made for them by so many travelers. Then in motion pictures they went through many of their dances for the express edification of the motion picture machine and the audiences which it was to reach. Always they were graceful, always picturesque and quaint, always there was about them an atmosphere of unreality as if they were characters out of a fairy tale and not real persons dancing in a real [world] and before a real camera. (1990, 125)

This review is intriguing because it suggests some of the possible implications of film technology for images of an exoticized, eroticized Orient as embodied, in this example, by the geisha girl.[5] However, although cinema is generally heralded for bringing an increasing "realism" to the screen, the filming of the dances of the geishas had the surprisingly contrary effect of dematerializing and derealizing them. Where the still photographs communicated beauty and fascination, the film was characterized by "an atmosphere of unreality." In this representation of the geishas, who occupy an eroticized space of fantasy in the Western imaginary, it seems that film served to make the dream real by making the reality dreamlike.

Or did it? "Realism" is always conditioned by the expectations of the perceiver, and in the case of Japan, the "atmosphere of unreality" pervades the travel accounts of both Holmes and Stoddard. It is, in fact, the blurring of reality and fantasy that characterizes their subjective experience of Japan, which Holmes compared to "living in a land of exquisite old Japanese prints" (1953, 90). Stoddard, recalling a moonlit moment in Japan, writes, "At such a time, the scene recalled a painting in some cyclorama,—so difficult was it to discern where fancy ended and reality began," and elsewhere he exclaims: "What pictures thus disclose themselves at every turn throughout this marvelous country? Anywhere else you would pronounce them stage effects" (1910, 30, 120). It is, after all, the reality of the fantastic, timeless, traditional Japan that is revealed on the screen in the dances of the geishas, via what Behdad (1994) calls a "fantasmatic intertext"—Japan as it has been imagined through the centuries by generations of travelers. Since representations—old prints, cycloramas, and stage effects—so consistently serve as the point of reference for the actuality of Japan, it seems only logical that cinema would confirm the mixture of reality and fantasy that seems to characterize the culture. Thus, the reception of this early film of dancing geishas suggests not only that the verisimilitude of cinema can be used toward fantastic ends, but also that the belief in the reality of film lends to film the very capacity to shape the "real" itself.

These examples from the lectures on Japan suggest the need for a more nuanced understanding of the rationale for using films in the illustrated travel lectures. For Holmes, cinema was no less than the ideal means of recording life. An unusually explicit statement of Holmes's thinking on the topic may be found in the lecture "Seoul, the Capital of Korea." In a brief digression from his descriptions of the city, Holmes proposes the founding of a Library of Cinematographic Records that would preserve the cultures of people of all lands for future generations and thus "bring into close and intimate comparison the personality of individuals and the manners and peculiarities of multitudes separated from one another by a long lapse of years" (1910, 10:65).[6] He concludes: "Time and space are not barriers to vision; for example, have we not shown upon the magic screen in the great cities of America, the Korean crowds of hundreds of our fellow-creatures reenacting their unconscious little comedy of customs as they had played it many months before, eight thousand miles away, on the other side of the world, in the streets of a city few of us had ever seen?" (65–66).

The condescending description of Korean culture as an "unconscious little comedy of customs" underscores the way in which the comparative nature of Holmes's vision of a Library of Cinematographic Records is founded upon a belief in the hierarchy of the races and Anglo-Saxon superiority. At the beginning of the lecture, Seoul is introduced as "three hundred thousand folk, so strangely dressed, so unlike us in thought and custom, that nowhere in the world is there a population more congenial to the lover of the curious and picturesque," while in another lecture a Peking street crowd is found to be "so Asiatic and so picturesque" that "only the magic of the motion-picture can reveal the peculiar fascination of the scene" (1910, 10:15, 162). In China, where "the common, continuous passing throng is in itself enough to hold the attention for hours at a time" (1977, 89), the inhabitants become the objects of a knowing gaze that marks the difference between Holmes's world and "the world outside."

London, on the other hand, is described as "the most important place on earth. It is not only the most populous, it is the greatest of great cities," while "whoever you may be, whatever things attract you, you will be at home in Paris; you will find there the very thing you seek—Paris is all things to all men" (1977, 64, 60). Western Europe clearly served as the cultural ideal to which Holmes and his audiences aspired, while their relationship to the rest of the world was more equivocal. Ironically, while the technological advances represented by cinema supported its claims to a greater realism, in practice, cinema often further reified stereotypical notions of non-Western cultures, including those of Asia and the Pacific. The fact that, as Holmes noted, few of his audience members in the United States would have had any direct experience of Seoul—since Korea was, after all, "eight thousand miles away, on the other side of the world"—suggests the significance of his work to notions of Asians and Pacific Islanders in the turn-of-the-century United States, and the importance of understanding its effects.

Holmes's entertaining narratives and picturesque images of foreign lands, which presumed a clear demarcation between "America" and "the world outside," should also be seen in relation to domestic debates over immigration and racial and ethnic difference. As Ella Shohat and Robert Stam argue in relation to Hollywood films:

> Since all Americans, except for Native Americans, trace their origins to other nations or continents, Hollywood's geographical and historical constructs have a visceral impact for "America's" communities. And since immigration is at the core of the official master-narrative, the

sympathetic portrayal of certain lands of origin and the caricaturing of others has indirectly legitimated links to Europe while undermining links to Asia, Africa, and Latin America. (1994, 221)

While the history of Asian exclusion laws and anti-immigration sentiments around the turn of the century is beyond the scope of this essay, surely Holmes's insistence upon the curious and picturesque nature of Japanese, Chinese, and Koreans further reinforced the rhetoric of Asians as unassimilable foreigners used to legitimize racist acts. However, in other lectures Holmes's work also recorded the effects of such beliefs and the violence of the military practices that allowed him access to the distant lands where he sought the picturesque and the quaint.

Travel and Possession

Holmes begins his autobiography, *The World Is Mine,* with his motto, "To travel is to possess the world." He intended the phrase metaphorically rather than literally, adding, "I know that through travel I have possessed the world more completely, more satisfyingly than if I had acquired the whole earth by purchase or conquest," and he observed that one advantage of possessing the world through travel is that "one may enjoy all the satisfactions of possession without the responsibilities of ownership." Yet despite his care in setting apart travel, which "takes naught from any man," from the more brute political and military realities of conquest, Holmes's remarkable career as a professional traveler was made possible, in many ways, by these very practices (1953, ix–x).

Historian E. J. Hobsbawm has designated the years 1875–1914 the "age of empire" due to the processes of colonization, annexation, and administration that took place at the time, and that had the effect of partitioning much of the world among a handful of nations (1987, 57). In 1898 the United States engaged Spain in a war, ostensibly to free Cuba from its Spanish oppressors. In the aftermath of the war, the United States, a country in which expansion had been conceived of as nothing less than manifest destiny, joined European nations such as Great Britain and France in the development of an overseas empire, with the annexation of Puerto Rico and Guam, and the purchase of the Philippines from Spain. This was also the year of the annexation of Hawaiʻi, which was the result of a separate, though related, history. Actuality films, or films of actual events, reported these exploits, serving as a kind of "visual newspaper" (Musser 1990, 225). Illustrated travel lectures, however, offered a different kind of education about empire. Holmes's lectures, which were well positioned to take advantage of the outgrowth of interest in "the world outside" occasioned by the war, allowed his audiences a leisurely reflection upon the pleasures of colonial power, the benefits of territorial possession, and the rationale for imperial expansion. As a result, the lectures may be seen as one effort, among others, to negotiate a new understanding of U.S. identity during a historic moment of imperial expansion. Unlike Stoddard, who "photographed only what had nothing to do with present reality, and remained forever on the alert for perfect, unspoiled sites," and who "refused, in his photographs at least, to acknowledge the effect of his own culture on those of other countries," Holmes in his lectures provides a view of history in the making (Fabian and Adam 1981, 335–36).[7]

In 1898 Holmes was traveling in Hawai'i at the very moment the nation was officially annexed in Washington. At the opening of his lecture on the Hawaiian Islands, Holmes writes of the "two thousand miles of peaceful ocean . . . between our coast and the palm-fringed shores of the Republic of Hawaii." But, he notes, by the end of his trip, this ocean will have been transformed into an American channel, and what were previously transpacific steamers will become nothing more than "mere 'ferries,' running from San Francisco, Cal. to Honolulu, United States of America" (1910, 5:5–6, 10). The lecture concludes with Holmes and two entrepreneurial American coffee planters learning of the annexation from a passing stranger: "At his next words, 'Annexation is an accomplished fact,' we fix our feet more firmly on this lava shore, for we, who a moment since were as strangers in a strange land are now at home—Hawaii has become part of the United States" (5:112). The dramatic impact of this final sentence of the lecture derives from the significance of the erasure of the distinction between "home" and "a strange land," which redefines the U.S. presence in Hawai'i as a permanent and proprietary one. Holmes endows the annexation with a celebratory sense of pride. From the perspective of the native Hawaiians, the change of ownership must be understood as a forced expropriation with continuing repercussions to the present day.

Edward Said locates the struggle for empire in the space between "the idea of what a given place was (could be, might become), and an actual place" (1994, 78). Holmes's description of Pearl Harbor in his lecture as both an ideal site for a naval station and a place of exotic adventure is one example of this imagination of empire:

> As the haunt of man-eating sharks and as the scene of many an exciting chase, Pearl Harbor is famous in Hawaii; but it has, as we know, a wider fame, as the only available site for a naval station in all that vast watery desert between California and Asia, between Alaska and the Antarctic seas. It is not only the sole safe harbor of Hawaii, it is as perfectly adapted to the needs of a modern naval power as if it had been planned and dredged and blasted out by naval engineers. (1910, 5:67)

Holmes then goes on to describe the physical characteristics of the harbor in more detail. However, these facts concerning the military value of Pearl Harbor are an aside, woven into a section of the lecture devoted to describing a shark-hunting expedition, and accompanied by serene images of the harbor, portraits of the members of the expedition, and two views of the unfortunate shark. Nestled among the illustrations of the hunt is an unremarkable image of four people dressed in suits and dresses, standing with their backs to the camera and looking out over a landscape. The image is captioned "Our future naval harbor." In this section of the lecture, composed of no more than a handful of pages, multiple identifications and appropriations are put into play. The picturesque aspects of travel are emphasized through the narrative of the shark hunt, complete with exotic details such as the use of a goat for bait. The visual representations of the tranquil harbor are lovely and inviting, suggesting just the kind of place one might visit for a relaxing vacation. The information about the strategic configuration of the harbor acknowledges U.S. national interests in the area and foresees a time when the harbor will be known for its naval base rather than as "the haunt of man-eating sharks." This is a Hawai'i conceived entirely in relation to the fulfillment of U.S. needs and desires, as an idyllic tourist paradise filled with "local color," and as a mid-Pacific military command post. What is extraordinary about Holmes's lecture is the way in which it recognizes the former status of Hawai'i as a sovereign nation, even as it participates in the project of transforming Hawai'i into one of the United States.[8]

The lecture on the Hawaiian Islands was accompanied by a series of films on "Hawaiian life and customs and the visit of the United States Manila Expedition to Honolulu." The book version of the lecture does not reproduce any films of "Hawaiian life and customs," although there are several frames from films that show U.S. soldiers marching. In fact, one of the highlights of Holmes's visit to Honolulu was the brief stopover of U.S. military personnel on the way to Manila. The effect upon the locals was, in his estimation, a significant one: "Cheered by the populace, followed by children of every age and color, stared at by Chinamen and Japanese and natives, who thus receive an object-lesson in the strength of the United States, our boys march on at a swinging pace" (Holmes 1910, 5:31–32). In these films, the camera is turned upon "our boys" while "the populace" is relegated to the background; the interest in bringing foreign lands to life is exchanged for the spectacle of military maneuvers. Amy Kaplan observes a similar phenomenon in early films of the Spanish-American War: "The appeal of these war films lay less in their exhibition of exotic foreign lands and people, who were rarely visible, or in the battle scenes than in the spectacle of American mobility itself—in the movement of men, horses, vehicles, and ships abroad and in their return home. The films celebrate the capacity of military power and the camera to encompass the globe" (1968–79, 1069).

The representation of U.S. military capabilities would be even more pronounced in Holmes's lecture on Manila, where, unlike the case of Hawai'i in which annexation took place on the floor of the Senate, the United States had to engage in a brutal three-year war before finally taking "ownership."

At the opening of the lecture on Manila, Holmes summarized the situation as follows: "In 1899 America was looking with anxious interest toward the Philippines. Admiral Dewey, his work accomplished, had left Manila; General Otis, as military governor, was in command; the Filipinos under Aguinaldo were successfully defending themselves, and all the American forces were confined to the immediate surroundings of Manila" (1910, 5:227).

Holmes, like many Americans, may well have been curious to learn more about "our new Oriental city" (1910, 5:227), though he was explicit in stating his intent to relate his experiences as a traveler rather than to cover the military campaign. Nevertheless, during this trip he witnesses a minor drama of the war. Near the town of Baliuag, the farthermost outpost held by the U.S. forces, a telegraph wire is cut in an apparent act of sabotage. The colonel in charge orders a native house to be burned as a warning to the villagers. But despite the efforts of the officer in command to uncover the identity of the culprit, no evidence of guilt can be found. However, as Holmes relates, "the wire was cut and a house must be burned." The dilemma facing the captain, of course, is which house to burn, since he has found no one in particular to punish. The captain solves his problem by asking Holmes to pick out the house that will make the most effective film as it burns. "Fortunately," Holmes relates, "the one lending itself best to artistic necessities was an abandoned nipa dwelling—a pretty little affair with a neat little garden around it" (1910, 5:321). According to the lecture, Holmes does in fact proceed with the filming, even though no corresponding images accompany the text. That the logic of reprisal stood unquestioned is disturbing enough. But the way in which Holmes, as a filmmaker, was interpellated as a colonizer is even more astounding.

The illustrated travel lecture on Hawai'i participated in the imperial project by contributing to the imagination of empire. In the Baliuag scenario, the political power represented by the camera and the destructive force of its gaze are literalized in a spectacular manner. Holmes's story, despite its tone of bemusement and worldly sophistication, exposes the kind of tactical strategies used by the U.S. Army in the Philippines that led historians decades later to compare U.S. intervention in Vietnam to the war waged in the Philippines at the turn of the century. In the context of the shared history of cinema and imperialism, this anecdote is especially striking, in that filming the burning of a nipa hut combines the picturesqueness of foreign lands with a rare glimpse of the brutality of warfare in a show of force that was literally staged for the camera. As a foreshadowing of the spectacular images of violence characteristic of media coverage of the Vietnam War, this incident uncannily foreshadows the future of U.S. intervention in Asia.

Exotic Explorations

When the Boxer Rebellion broke out in Peking (now Beijing) in 1900, proponents of U.S. overseas expansion noted the relative ease with which troops could be transferred from the battle in the Philippines to Peking. In mid-August the United States contributed five thousand soldiers to an international force of sixteen thousand that crushed the antiforeign uprising, drove the imperial family from the Forbidden City, and exacted a heavy indemnity from the Chinese government. Holmes was among the foreigners who took advantage of the terms of the resolution of the Boxer Rebellion to visit the Forbidden City.[9] He was quite conscious of the political circumstances of his visit, noting that "what we have already done and are about to do in Peking, are things which a year before no foreigner would have dared to dream of doing. The traveler who reached Peking in the first year of the twentieth century was fortunate indeed. Doors that had been closed for hundreds of years, stood open" (Holmes 1910, 9:256–57). Throughout the lecture the descriptions of many of the images are appended with the phrase "hitherto unseen," or some variation of it. Holmes was not exaggerating the staggering significance of the mass dissemination of images of the Forbidden City to his U.S. audiences. At the conclusion of his lecture on the Forbidden City, when Holmes again pondered the immensity of what he, and in the context of an actual lecture, his audience as well, had just seen, he reminded them that "on the 17th of September, 1901, the American detachment retired from the gate and turned over to the Chinese troops the violated sanctum of China, which has again become, though in a sense less absolute, 'forbidden' to the foreigner. Never till war shall bring another foreign army to Peking, will foreign eyes look upon its courts and palaces" (1910, 9:306–8).

Many decades later, in a very different political context, the international cast and crew of Bernardo Bertolucci's Oscar-winning film *The Last Emperor* (1987) labored to bring the Forbidden City to life for a Western audience. Once again, access to the Forbidden City was an issue of some importance. According to Bertolucci: "The major hurdle was getting permission to use the locations. I was particularly nervous about the Forbidden City; I knew that it was the heart of the movie from the production standpoint. We finally cleared it, and we're the first foreigners who have been allowed to shoot there" (qtd. in Rayns 1987, 35). The negotiations over permissions presumably did not involve the threat of military force, but Bertolucci's use of the word "shoot," although it is a standard term for filming, is especially ironic considering the history of filming in the Forbidden City. Bertolucci's claim to have been the first foreigner to have filmed the Forbidden City is clearly untrue. But pointing out the error of his statement is not meant simply to prove him wrong, but to call attention to the history the statement obscures. Like Holmes, Bertolucci strove to represent the Forbidden City to foreign eyes, but with considerably less historical self-consciousness than had his predecessor.

Regardless of the circumstances of Bertolucci's access to the Forbidden City, the fact of shooting on location lent his film undeniable legitimacy. The popular film critic Gene Siskel described *The Last Emperor* as "the best way to see China without going there" (1987, 5), while professional historian Paul G. Pickowicz of the University of California, San Diego, though generally critical of the film, allows that its first portion is "both visually stunning . . . and of considerable ethnographic interest" (1989, 1036). That such an eminently cinematic film as *The Last Emperor,* with its fantasmatic vision of a mysterious, exotic, and erotic Orient, could be seen so literally, and by such a wide range of critics, testifies to the lingering legacy of a long history of cinematic fascination with China. This fascination is, of course, still with us, as is apparent in the title of the 1995 *New York Times* special travel section on Asia and the Pacific, "Exotic Explorations."

Ali Behdad, in describing the project of his book *Belated Travelers,* writes that "postcolonial archival work, in short, ought to restore to the science of colonialism its political significance in the current global setting. What would emerge out of such a reading is not a specialized erudite knowledge of Europe's guilty past but the provoking rediscovery of new traces of the past today" (1994, 9). Similarly, looking back at Holmes's illustrated travel lectures at the turn of the century involves a recollection of the history of U.S. overseas imperialism, the symbolic and ideological underpinnings of that project, and the continuing implications of the emergence of cinema in the United States at that moment in history. To remember this history is to trace the genealogy of the present.

Notes

1. See Robert Lee (1999) and James Moy (1993) for broader discussions of the representation of Asians in American popular culture. Dorothy B. Jones (1955) and Eugene Franklin Wong (1978) focus on the representation of Asians in U.S. film.

2. The analysis of Holmes's lectures in this essay is based on a ten-volume published version of the illustrated travel lectures, which reportedly reproduces the spoken text in full but includes only a selection of the accompanying slides and films.

3. Neil Harris (1976) provides evidence that Holmes's interest in Japan was hardly an idiosyncratic one.

4. A number of films since have used the trope of Asian women and their (failed) attempts to clothe themselves in Western garb. See, for example, Gina Marchetti's analysis of *The World of Suzie Wong* (1960) and *Love Is a Many-Splendored Thing* (1955) (1993, 109–124).

5. This figure has lost none of her popularity, as the recent success of Arthur Golden's novel *Memoirs of a Geisha,* soon to be a Steven Spielberg film, demonstrates.

6. See Fatimah Tobing Rony (1996) for an analysis of Félix-Louis Regnault's similar aspirations for an ethnographic film archive. Her study offers an important critique of the writing of race in cinema that is relevant to the argument of this essay.

7. The photographer Arnold Genthe, like Stoddard, practiced a similar kind of editorial license in his efforts to represent San Francisco's Chinatown as a timeless, self-enclosed ethnic enclave. See Tchen 1984 and Moy 1993, especially Chapter 6, for discussions of Genthe's work. See also Chapter 4, "Artifacts of a Lost City: Arnold Genthe's *Pictures of Old Chinatown* and Its Intertexts," by Emma Teng, in this volume.

8. By the time of World War II, the U.S. claim upon the harbor was so completely naturalized that the bombing of Pearl Harbor not only propelled the U.S. entrance into the war, but also justified Japanese American internment in the name of U.S. "national interests."

9. The American Mutoscope and Biograph Company produced at least two films of the Forbidden City, *The Forbidden City, Pekin* (no. 1765) and *The Forbidden City* (no. 1766), at this time. Other related films include Siegmund Lubin's staged reenactments on the topic from June 1900, *Chinese Massacring* [sic] *Christians* and *Beheading a Chinese Prisoner,* and the Edison film of 1902, *A Chinese Mystery,* which alluded to the Boxer Rebellion within the genre of the "trick film."

Works Cited

Behdad, Ali. 1994. *Belated Travelers: Orientalism in the Age of Colonial Dissolution.* Durham, N.C.: Duke University Press.

de Gourmont, Rémy. 1988. "Epilogues: Cinematograph." In *French Film Theory and Criticism,* ed. Richard Abel. Vol. 1: 1907–1929, 47–50 (Princeton: Princeton University Press). First published in *Mercure de France,* 1 September 1907, 124–27.

Fabian, Rainer, and Hans-Christian Adam. 1981. *Masters of Early Travel Photography.* New York: Vendome Press.

Gunning, Tom. 1995. " 'The Whole World within Reach': Travel Images Without Borders." In *Cinéma sans frontières, 1896–1918,* ed. Roland Cosandy and François Albera, 21–36. Lausanne: Editions Payot.

Haraway, Donna. 1993. "Teddy Bear Patriarchy: Taxidermy in the Garden of Eden, New York City, 1908–1936." In *Cultures of United States Imperialism,* ed. Amy Kaplan and Donald E. Pease, 237–91. Durham, N.C.: Duke University Press.

Harris, Neil. 1976. "All the World a Melting Pot? Japan at American Fairs, 1876–1904." In *Mutual Images: Essays in American-Japanese Relations,* ed. Akira Iriye, 24–54. Cambridge: Harvard University Press.

Higashi, Sumiko. 1996. "Touring the Orient with Lafcadio Hearn and Cecil B. DeMille: High-brow versus Lowbrow in a Consumer Culture." In *The Birth of Whiteness: Race and the Emergence of U.S. Cinema,* ed. Daniel Bernardi, 329–54. New Brunswick, N.J.: Rutgers University Press.

Hobsbawm, E. J. 1987. *The Age of Empire, 1875–1914.* New York: Pantheon.

Holmes, E. Burton. 1910. *Burton Holmes Travelogues.* 10 vols. New York: McClure.

———. 1953. *The World Is Mine.* Culver City: Murray and Gee.

———. 1977. *The Man Who Photographed the World: Burton Holmes: Travelogues, 1886–1938.* Compiled and edited by Genoa S. Caldwell. New York: Abrams.

Jones, Dorothy B. 1955. *The Portrayal of China and India on the American Screen, 1896–1955.* Cambridge: MIT Press.

Kaplan, Amy. 1999. "The Birth of an Empire." *PMLA* 114, 5: 1068–79.

Lee, Robert G. 1999. *Orientals: Asian Americans in Popular Culture.* Philadelphia: Temple University Press.

Marchetti, Gina. 1993. *Romance and the "Yellow Peril": Race, Sex, and Discursive Strategies in Hollywood Fiction.* Berkeley: University of California Press.

Moy, James S. 1993. *Marginal Sights: Staging the Chinese in America.* Iowa City: University of Iowa Press.

Musser, Charles. 1990. *The Emergence of Cinema: The American Screen to 1907.* Berkeley: University of California Press.

Musser, Charles, with Carol Nelson. 1991. *High-Class Moving Pictures: Lyman H. Howe and the Forgotten Era of Traveling Exhibition, 1880–1920.* Princeton: Princeton University Press.

Palumbo-Liu, David. 1999. *Asian/American: Historical Crossings of a Racial Frontier.* Stanford: Stanford University Press.

Pickowicz, Paul G. 1989. Review of *The Last Emperor,* dir. Bernardo Bertolucci. *American Historical Review* 94: 1035–36.

Rayns, Tony. 1987. "Model Citizen: Bernardo Bertolucci on Location in China." *Film Comment* 23, 6: 31–36.

Rony, Fatimah Tobing. 1996. *The Third Eye: Race, Cinema, and Ethnographic Spectacle.* Durham, N.C.: Duke University Press.

Said, Edward. 1978. *Orientalism.* New York: Pantheon.

———. 1994. *Culture and Imperialism.* New York: Vintage Books.

Schlesinger, Arthur M., Jr. 1998. "Burton Holmes." In *Peking,* by Burton Holmes, 24–25. The World 100 Years Ago Series. Philadelphia: Chelsea House.

Shohat, Ella, and Robert Stam. 1994. *Unthinking Eurocentrism: Multiculturalism and the Media.* London: Routledge.

Siskel, Gene. 1987. "Bertolucci in China." *Chicago Tribune,* 13 December.

Stoddard, John L. 1910. *John L. Stoddard's Lectures.* Vol. 3. Chicago: Shuman.

Tchen, John Kuo Wei, comp. and ed. 1984. *Genthe's Photographs of San Francisco's Old Chinatown.* Photographs by Arnold Genthe. New York: Dover.

Wallace, Irving. 1977. "Everybody's Rover Boy." In Holmes 1977, 9–22.

Wong, Eugene Franklin. 1978. *On Visual Media Racism: Asians in the American Motion Pictures.* New York: Arno Press.

Yuko Matsukawa

---

13   Representing the Oriental in Nineteenth-Century Trade Cards

Collecting and Recollecting Trade Cards

The act of recollecting, in its many meanings, is integral to this essay. My collecting ephemera and turn-of-the-century representations of Asian (American) bodies in trade cards—postcard-sized advertisements popular during the last quarter of the nineteenth century—mimics and repeats the collecting practices of consumers targeted by these cards, especially women and children of the 1880s and 1890s (see Garvey 1996). Since the popularity and the production of trade cards as a medium for advertising and items for collecting died out around the turn into the twentieth century, the cards circulating now are mostly those produced between the years 1875 and 1900. My (re)collecting practices may be similar to those of nineteenth-century consumers in that I look for a specific image and accumulate cards that fit that description. However, unlike those who avidly collected trade cards more than a century ago, my recollecting engages in reassessing the technologies that made trade cards possible and popular as well as reviewing the audiences and their social contexts in order to reexamine how and what the Asian (American) body is made to signify.

   Trade cards were small advertising cards that manufacturers and retailers ordered to advertise their products or shops (see Jay 1987; Cheadle 1996; Barry 1993). The cards themselves were free and were most often left on a shop's counters for the clientele to take as they pleased, sent out to consumers in advertising campaigns, or distributed at World's Fairs. In addition to a brightly colored picture of the manufacturer or retailer's choice, typically there would be ad copy on the back of the card that highlighted the strengths of a certain product or listed the name, address, and business hours of the retail establishment. The more established and financially secure organizations who had more money to spend on advertising and wished to initiate a strong tie between product/shop and image had artists create cards especially for them. Those with limited resources went to a printer's shop and selected a stock card—a preprinted generic card with blank spaces on the front or the back so that a business or product name could be inserted—out of the many available. Stock cards were inexpensive, and many buyers chose the same image.

Through examining such cards, now collectors' items, we understand better the development of a particular stereotype with respect to technologies of representation. The rise of trade cards follows the growing awareness of the Chinese immigrant presence in the United States and the political opposition, supported by a vocal part of the white dominant culture, to those Chinese in the last quarter of the nineteenth century. As a precursor to more widespread magazine and newspaper advertising, trade cards provide us with a glimpse of race relations and racial hierarchies in late-nineteenth-century popular culture; furthermore, the images of the Oriental encapsulated in trade cards demonstrate how stereotypes circulated at the time and perhaps give us insight into why they continue to circulate after more than a century.

Such visual images had a strong impact upon the U.S. imagination. In a world devoid of film, television, radio, and the Internet, nineteenth-century American life was irrevocably altered with the advent of chromolithography, the new technology of color printing. This technology also changed the representation of race: By making real the yellowness of the Oriental, chromolithography developed a visual vocabulary of race by reinforcing through color the language of the eighteenth-century racial taxonomies of Linnaeus and Blumenbach. Using this late-nineteenth-century innovation, such a vocabulary could be not only developed with ease, but also marketed and disseminated broadly to middle-class families who were, in the post–Civil War era, attracted to and able to afford store-bought goods and national brands, as opposed to products made locally or at home.

As chromolithography became increasingly inexpensive, large printing houses such as Prang and Bufford were able to distribute stock cards to printers around the nation. The advertising images, internalized and naturalized through consumption, served to instruct their audience in racial hierarchies. Historically speaking, in nineteenth-century America, the "Oriental" referred to the most visible Asian (American) body: that of the Chinese male worker. By producing and reproducing color, trade cards featuring the Oriental managed to fuse anti-Chinese sentiment and scientific discourses of race with everyday consumption.

Some trade cards have an affinity with political cartoons, in that they have been composed with an anti-Chinese bias. Given that the predominant audience for these trade cards was female and that the cards needed to appeal in some way to women who were in charge of households, however, many are more nuanced in their political messages, because they had to relate to the domestic sphere, especially with regard to women's work. The male oriental body on the cards conveys a major fantasy concerning women in the dominant culture: the work fantasy in which "the Chinaman" (rather than a Chinese man) embodies the alien presence in the United States and becomes the surrogate for the laboring woman.

"Color Was the Biggest Attraction":
Chromolithography and Representing Race

Chromolithography arrived in the United States in the 1840s. The Boston lithographer Louis Prang pioneered the designing and marketing of trade cards in color, as well as color holiday cards, an innovation that endures though the trade cards did not. By the 1870s, printing stock cards in color became economically viable. Earlier trade cards had been meticulously engraved and then printed in black and white; with chromolithography, as Robert Jay declares, "color was the biggest attraction. At a time when color scarcely existed in periodical publishing, lithographic printing in full color was still a novelty for the general public." By the 1880s, Jay notes, chromolithographed trade cards replaced engraved cards in the market and were distributed on an "unprecedented scale by small firms and large industries alike. As more commercial lithographers began to specialize in this aspect of the trade, standards of quality became more competitive while prices for large orders steadily dropped. As production of the cards increased, so did the card craze of the public" (1987, 32).

Most surviving trade cards reflect the overwhelming popularity of the trade card printed in color. Whereas political cartooning provided most of the vocabulary for representing the Oriental or the Chinaman in black and white, chromolithography injected color into this language, representing racial difference by directly showing "yellowness." Though in many cards, racial difference is not necessarily indicated by skin tone but by slanted eyes and queues and baggy clothing, in others, it is the yellowness—or sallowness, the lack of rosy cheeks—that also marks the Oriental. In other words, by foregrounding yellowness, a color associated with jaundice, disease, and contamination, trade cards instruct consumers to see Chinese as different, if not unclean.

The connection between yellowness and Asians derived from eighteenth-century racial taxonomies that made Asian yellowness as well as Native American redness and African blackness fixed ideas in the emergent field of physical anthropology. According to the Swedish naturalist Carolus Linnaeus's classification of *Homo sapiens* (1758), the Asian (*Homo asiaticus*) could be summed up as having lurid skin color, a melancholic temperament, a haughty avaricious character, loose-fitting clothing, and an intellect governed by opinion; furthermore, the Asian was ranked third in a descending racial hierarchy among the four varieties of *Homo sapiens,* after the American Indian (ranked first) and the European and ahead of the African (Broberg 1997, 617). The German anatomist Johan Friedrich Blumenbach developed Linnaeus's classification in *De Generis Humani Varietate Nativa* (On the natural varieties of mankind; 1795) into five categories—Caucasian, Mongoloid, Malay, Ethiopian, American— which were popularized as the white, yellow, brown, black, and red races (Stevenson 1991, 340). Blumenbach ranked the "racial varieties of colour" in the following descending order: white (European), yellow (Mongolian), copper (Native American), tawny (Malay), and tawny-black (Ethiopian). He describes Asians as having skin that is "*yellow, olive-tinge,* a sort of colour half-way between grains of wheat and cooked oranges, or the dry exsiccated [*sic*] rind of lemons: very usual in the Mongolian nations" (1969, 209). Other anthropologists continued variations of these taxonomies through the eighteenth and nineteenth centuries, solidifying the connection between "yellow" and Asian.

Linnaeus's term "lurid" holds the key to connecting the Oriental to not only wanness but also sensationalism. The *Oxford English Dictionary* defines "lurid" in the following ways:

1. Pale and dismal in colour; wan and sallow; ghastly of hue. Said, e.g. of the sickly pallor of the skin in disease, or of the aspect of things when the sky is overcast. . . .
2. Shining with a red glow or glare amid darkness (said, e.g. of lightning-flashes across dark clouds, or flame mingled with smoke). . . .
3. *fig.* (from either of the preceding senses), with connotation of "terrible," "ominous," "ghastly," "sensational," often in phr. *to cast or throw a lurid light on* (a subject).

In Linnaeus's taxonomy, "lurid" indicates a yellowness, but since the word also means ominous and sensational, it is no surprise that visual representations and descriptions in texts of the Oriental, especially the Oriental in the United States, conflate the meanings. Thus, in the U.S. popular imagination, yellow people are lurid: ghastly and ominous.

Many of the trade cards depict the Chinese as monstrous or as associated with vermin. One example of overt political propaganda ties anti-Chinese sentiment in the United States in 1888 to Grover Cleveland's presidential campaign. This campaign card resembles a trade card in size and shape, as well as in its strategy for shocking or amusing the public. One side of the card touts Benjamin Harrison as "China's presidential candidate" with an oddly shaped yellow-and-blue dragon flag. On the other side is the product being endorsed "For President of the United States: Grover Cleveland," with the red-white-and-blue American flag. The anti-Chinese (and hence anti-Harrison) rhetoric is charged with labor issues:

> He [Harrison] voted not only for the unrestricted immigration of Chinese, but favored their naturalization.
> He said in a lecture that the United States had no more right to prohibit the immigration of Chinese than it had to keep out the Irish or German.
> If you want the Chinese flag to displace the American. Chinese labor to take the place of American and a real Chinese candidate
>
> BENJAMIN HARRISON
IS THE MAN TO VOTE FOR.

As we will see, the movement to expel the Chinese is tied directly to anxieties about labor. The same anxiety about who gets to work and who gets to stay in the United States is played out in different ways but with the same result: the expulsion of the Chinese. This equation implicitly drives the cards in question here.

That the Chinese are "lurid" though not imaged (and neither are the presidential candidates) on this card means that the rhetoric depends on contemporary and pervasive images of Chinese to make its point. The yellow of the flag stands in for Chinese and

FIGURE 13.1.   Magnolia Ham trade card. ("That is a plump rat, Chang Whang, but excuse me, I always carry MAGNOLIA HAMS.") (This and following cards from author's collection)

presents itself in stark contrast to the Stars and Stripes. Another card advertising Magnolia Hams also juxtaposes president and Oriental. However, this card (Fig. 13.1), which ostensibly refers to Ulysses Grant's stop in Hong Kong during his post-presidential world tour (May 1877–December 1879), shows a resplendent Grant refusing the bowing Chinaman's offering of a rat on a dish by declaring emphatically and somewhat diplomatically, "That is a plump rat, Chang Whang, but excuse me, I always carry MAGNOLIA HAMS."

U.S. superiority is underscored in several ways in this image. Grant, whose initials remind the viewer that he stands for his nation, is at the center of this card, arms crossed, in an open stance, looming above the bowing Chinaman. Political superiority is deftly linked with gastronomic superiority. In the visual narrative of the card, Grant is superior to the Chinaman, and so Magnolia Hams, endorsed by Grant, becomes the national food. The presence of the African American serving man represents a related aspect of the racial hierarchy. As M. M. Manring argues, in the years following the Civil War, African Americans became a necessary part of domestic identity, especially as incorporated in the image of the plantation, reassuring the primacy of "whiteness" in the United States (1988, 11).[1] The kowtowing Chinese, on the other hand, is debased in a different way, through his alienness.

The impetus to capitalize on exclusion and the image of the Chinaman as vermin is most blatantly evident in Rough on Rats, a trade card for rat poison (Fig. 13.2). This card, circa 1885, does not mention the Chinese in its advertising copy, but the central image of a Chinaman face-to-face with a rat, with the slogan "They must go" above them, conflates the two. His queue marks the man as Chinese and it mirrors the rat's tail; again, it provokes the viewer's emotional response to the situation. The visual narrative suggests that the Chinaman is about to eat a rat, an act sure to be repellant to the viewer. Perhaps he is about to eat a rat that has already ingested rat poison, in which case he will also die. Since this ad equated the Chinese with pests and vermin, we may also read it as suggesting an act of cannibalism, which further emphasizes alienness and barbarism. In a strange twist, the Chinaman is linked not only with the rat but also with the poison, because he serves to exterminate rats as well.

The slogan "They must go" is a variation of "The Chinese must go" attributed to Denis Kearney, a labor reformer who, as head of the California Workingmen's Party, agitated for labor reform after the 1877 depression and the influx of Chinese labor.[2]

FIGURE 13.2. Rough on Rats trade card.

By using the phrase "They must go," the manufacturers and the designer of the trade card equate a household problem with what some perceived as a national one. And as Robert Lee reminds us, "Only when the foreign is present does it become alien. The alien is always out of place, therefore disturbing and dangerous. . . . Only when aliens exit or are 'naturalized' (cleansed of their foreignness and remade) can they shed their status as pollutants" (1999, 3).

The Rough on Rats card, though it has become one of the best-known examples of anti-Asian racist imagery from the turn of the century, is something of an anomaly. Compared with other trade cards advertising the same product that do not employ racist imagery, this card is oversized and delivers a clearly racist message. Contrary to the impression given by this Rough on Rats card, many trade cards using the trope of the Oriental in fact demand a much more subtle, more complex, and therefore more interesting reading. As we will see, because Orientals are never "cleansed of their foreignness and remade" in trade card representations, their only option is to leave.

Work Fantasies: The Alien Chinaman and Domestic Work

Trade cards joined other popular forms of visual grotesquerie. Robert G. Lee, John Tchen, Philip Choy, Lorraine Dong, and Marlon Hom, among others, have shown how images of the "Oriental" proliferated in the political cartoons of the last quarter of the nineteenth century. Thomas Nast and other political cartoonists, along with illustrators for the weekly and monthly magazines so popular in the late nineteenth and early twentieth centuries, constructed the "oriental" body as a representation of geopolitical otherness as well as a contaminant and threat (see Choy, Dong, and Hom 1994). Male writers and male cartoonists constructed a masculine discourse to chart the course of U.S. empire that used the now familiar trope of the emasculated Chinaman to signify racial, cultural, and mental inferiority. Perhaps even more interesting, trade cards portrayals of Orientals brought home political messages; targeted to women, presumably white and middle class, they entered the domestic sphere in a way that antiChinese political cartoons would not. The targeting of women, especially housewives, proved successful in that collecting these small advertisements became a gendered pastime. As Ellen Gruber Garvey has noted, while stamp collecting was seen as a male pursuit, the collecting of trade cards was perceived as a female diversion and hobby (1996, 26).[3]

If representations of the Oriental are found mostly in political cartooning and in the public sphere, the images of Asians that infiltrated the everyday lives of Americans in the late nineteenth century came from trade cards. Both political cartoons and trade cards paint the Chinaman as other and as a threat to the national cohesiveness, in order to make explicit a political agenda; both produce the same sorts of physical caricatured characteristics that are still legible to us today (short, sallow, and slant-eyed, with a queue and baggy blouson and pants). One way to read these trade cards, then, is to see them as a way for women of the house to participate in a national project that had

FIGURE 13.3. David's Prize Soap trade card.

been defined and propelled by men and their interests; in this case, the project is the eradication of the Chinese from the United States.

In the trade cards from that era, one of the most common images of the Oriental is that of the Chinaman as laundryman. In a constellation of cards featuring Chinese laundrymen that mostly advertise laundry soap and celluloid collars, the trajectory from happy worker to out-of-work laundryman returning to China is carefully played out. For instance, the glee that the laundrymen display in David's Prize Soap (Fig. 13.3) turns to alarm in a trade card for waterproof celluloid collars and cuffs, in which a salesman displays an ad for celluloid collars; the advent of celluloid collars, cuffs, and shirtfronts that are waterproof and presumably need no laundering endangers their livelihood (Fig. 13.4).

What is intriguing then is that the Chinaman, long associated with the laundry, is not always deployed in advertising to demonstrate the superiority of a particular laundry

FIGURE 13.4. Water-
proof Celluloid Col-
lars, Cuffs, and Shirt
Bosoms trade card.
("The Last Invention.
Economical, Durable,
Handsome.")

soap or starch. Trade cards use him to show the superiority of a product that would
put him out of business, such as the waterproof collars and certain kinds of starch. It
is a kind of political *schadenfreude* that makes possible cards like those advertising
waterproof linen, such as the "Off for China" card in which the Chinamen say, "No
More Washee Washee, Melican Man Wear Celluloid Collar And Cuff" (Fig. 13.5), that
serves as a terminus for this narrative of exclusion. Both cards feature relatively
prosperous-looking white men testing out the virtues of the celluloid clothes items,
much to the dismay of the Chinese laundryman.

This narrative of exclusion is remarkably dissimilar to the advertising campaigns for
soap in Great Britain in the nineteenth century. In her book *Imperial Leather*, Anne
McClintock discusses the Pears Soap advertising campaign of the late nineteenth century
as offering "an allegory of imperial progress as spectacle." (214) She states that "Pears'

FIGURE 13.5.   Waterproof linen trade card. ("Off for China.")

distinction, swiftly emulated by scores of soap companies including Monkey Brand and Sunlight, as well as countless other advertisers, was to invest the aesthetic space around the domestic commodity with the commercial cult of empire" (1995, 214, 213).

McClintock goes on to discuss the four fetishes in British soap advertising: the soap itself, white clothing, mirrors, and monkeys (1995, 214). In the late-nineteenth-century British context, the crisis of how to represent domestic work without representing women at work was resolved in the case of Monkey Brand soap by aligning monkeys simultaneously with "the dangerous classes: 'the apelike' wandering poor, the hungry Irish, Jews, prostitutes, impoverished black people, the ragged working class," and with metamorphosis, to signal "the transformations of nature (dirt, waste and disorder) into culture (cleanliness, rationality and industry)" (216–17).

In a U.S. context, the course of empire is not as straightforward. Unlike Pears Soap, which delights in constructing an advertising campaign that is in and of itself a campaign to colonize and take over the world via soap, U.S. soap manufacturers are more concerned with appealing to U.S. consumers by first transposing labor onto oriental bodies and then, in concert with celluloid collar manufacturers, eliminating those oriental bodies altogether. Unlike the British ads, which chart the course of empire by civilizing monkeys, whitewashing black bodies, and generally bringing undesirables up to the standards of the Victorian middle class in terms of cleanliness and whiteness, the U.S. ads make no gesture toward removing yellowness or "civilizing" a Chinaman. Though the advances of empire are mediated through capitalism and better products, in the U.S. soap ads, empire is policed by exclusionary processes, as indicated by the advent of the

FIGURE 13.6.   Muzzy's Starch trade card.

celluloid collar. Though the laundryman figure seems to take the place of the monkey in the British ads because it represents women's work without representing women, the changes that the monkey undergoes as he transforms himself into a more civilized creature do not have a parallel in U.S. soap ads. The bodies are alien, the workplace is alien, and there are rats there.

Earlier I posited that reading trade cards in a political context engaged women in political debates and allowed them to participate in a national project. But what about the cards that feature Orientals that are not as easily read as bodies to exclude, exterminate, and exile?

For instance, in the trade card for Muzzy's Starch, the Chinese laundryman, though he has the markings of the racial other (queue, clothing, slanted eyes), is not so much caricatured as seen as a happy participant in a family tableau (Fig. 13.6). Instead of the laundry as an alien, sordid, unspeakable site, it is light and clean and a place that welcomes family visits. A middle-class family—father, mother, and little girl—are gazing at the shirt that the laundryman is ironing. The husband looks toward his wife, while his daughter (whose outfit mirrors her mother's) and his wife look intently at the shirt, in which the wife's face is reflected. The family is clearly delighted by the handiwork of the laundryman and appreciates his efforts. The overt anti-Chinese message in previously discussed cards is not there.

One of the ways to understand this card is to look at women as the potential audience for products and at how advertisers might entice them to buy specific goods.

Advertisers targeted women by suggesting labor-saving practices and time-saving products to them, which, in an ideal world, would free the women to enjoy other activities. The Chinese laundryman, then, is an ally of sorts because he understands the tedium and difficulties of women's work. That the woman of the house sees herself in the shirt implies that it is as if she had done the work herself; hence the laundryman stands in for the housewife and so is considered good, benevolent, and useful.

The key difference between these cards and those with an overt political agenda is that these center on the mistress of the house and her work. It is no coincidence that the Muzzy's Starch card has at its center the image of the housewife and her reflection. Other cards that operate in a similar way include the tea shop stock card used by "G. Rossler, Dealer in Staple and Fancy Groceries, Crockery and Glassware" (Fig. 13.7) and a card advertising Lavine Soap (Fig. 13.8). The tea shop stock card features a

FIGURE 13.7. Trade card for G. Rossler, dealer in staple and fancy groceries, crockery, and glassware.

FIGURE 13.8. Lavine Soap trade card.

Chinese man looking at boxes of tea and other groceries as the proprietor stands by, ready to wait on him. The usual characteristics of the Chinaman are present, but there is none of the demeaning caricature that accompanies other cards. In this card, we see again the figure of the oriental stand-in for the woman, evaluating tea as a shopkeeper looks on, a scene that mirrors women's own experiences.

The Lavine Soap trade card reinforces the idea that the Chinaman encourages and helps the woman as she deals with household chores. This card has miniature China-men happily dancing around a gigantic box of Lavine Soap, ostensibly because it is such a wonderful product. The Chinamen may mirror the woman of the house's delight in finding a superior product, but they also serve to encourage her to transform the time-consuming and tedious job of laundry into one that is more lighthearted.

The connection between Chinamen and women's domestic work is echoed in another trade card that miniaturizes people, in this case, women. In a card for Agate Ironware entitled "The Crowning Triumph," women of different races and ethnicities dance around a coffeepot. The only exception is a Chinaman on the far right, who forces us to recognize this ring as comprised of housewives and servants; furthermore, the presence of the Oriental propels us to reconsider the relationship between domestic work and gender, as well as race.

This is not to say that there was a clear-cut gendered difference in how Orientals were perceived by the dominant white culture but rather that from a woman's point of view, the anti-Chinese political agenda that aligned some trade cards with political cartoons was not the only message that those cards could convey. And conversely, cards that featured Chinamen as profoundly alien or ridiculous reminded women that Orientals were, after all, other. For instance, in the stock card for "Millspaugh and Co., Books, Paper, Magazines" (Fig. 13.9), an annoyed well-dressed woman walking her dog is looking disdainfully at the Chinaman who is happily addressing her. He is shorter than she, dressed in baggy clothing, sporting a top hat and a queue, and bowing to her as he declares, "Me mashee alle samee Mellican man," which we may take to mean "I can excite you sentimentally and sexually [i.e., mash] just as well as an American man." However, even as he speaks, he fails to attract the admiration of the woman, and a schoolboy thumbs his nose at him while the tiny dog seems to be on the verge of attacking him. His outward appearance coupled with his heavily accented speech mark him as inconsequential and unworthy of attention. The woman again is the center of the card and is instructed on how to treat a Chinaman: with disdain.

Because of these competing readings of the political and the domestic, there is a triangulation of the white man, the white woman, and the Chinaman. In the political readings, it is the white man against the Chinaman, with the implied presence of the white woman on the side of the white man. In domestic readings, it is the Chinaman who is aligned with the white woman because he understands her labor and takes it over from her, against the white man who is the beneficiary of the labors of both the white woman and the Chinaman, though he does not acknowledge that work.

However, as mentioned earlier, these readings are not mutually exclusive. With that in mind I return to some of the cards to reconsider how they might attract the attention

FIGURE 13.9.   Trade card for S. W. Millspaugh and Company. ("Me mashee alle samee mellican man.")

of female consumers by means other than an invitation to participate in a project of Chinese exclusion. The political narrative is clear—make new products that render the Chinese superfluous so that they have to leave; it projects, furthermore, a bloodless victorious battle. The domestic narrative, I believe, is just as compelling, especially to women. If we regard these cards in light of women's work, the political agenda and the Chinese recede into the background, and in the foreground is displayed the triumphant image of the white man resplendent in his celluloid collar. If Botticelli's painting of Venus rising from the sea is seductive to men, then these middle-class men in bright white celluloid collars and cuffs and shirt bosoms rising from the ocean may be just as exciting to U.S. women worn out from laundering, starching, and ironing the shirts of their fathers, brothers, husbands, and sons, in addition to their other work in the home.

This product promised to rally the dominant white culture against the Chinaman without relegating to white women the work that the Chinaman used to do. In that sense, the advertising for these celluloid products satisfies dual desires, effecting the disappearance both of certain kinds of women's work and the Chinaman.

Less directly commenting on the exclusion of the Chinaman, the card for New Process Starch also shows a housewife besting a Chinese laundryman (Fig. 13.10). The left side of the card has the Chinese laundryman laboring in a windowless room and saying, "Old process starchee no goodee. It smellee rots & makee shirts yellee." The young mother on the right side of the card is happily ironing in a room with a window and nice carpet, declaring, "I will never use any other but the New Process Starch," while her young, clean son helpfully holds out the starch box. If sending out the laundry is going to make shirts yellow (like the Chinaman, lurid and unhealthy), then a product like New Process Starch, by implication, eliminates the Chinaman while simplifying women's work, keeping her home and children tidy, orderly, clean, and white.

Naturalizing Orientalist Ideology

The logic that makes the advertisements for celluloid collars or starch so compelling depends on the triangulated relationship of white men, white women, and Chinese men mentioned earlier. Lee notes that "the presence of the Chinese male disrupts the fragile balances between sexes within the household . . . the employment of the male Chinese servant to do 'woman's work' destabilized the gendered nature of labor" (1999, 104). The Chinese male laborer, caricatured as a Chinaman, who undertook women's work embodied and encapsulated in these images the tension between the necessity for labor (and the accompanying debasement of the Chinese) and exclusion.

How are these images "naturalized" in late-nineteenth-century U.S. households? The trade cards reveal that ideology not only is invested in the fiery satire of political cartoons played out in public spaces but also permeates domestic spaces of prosperity and everyday home life. As seen in the trade cards that illustrate this essay, the ideological message of Chinese otherness and exclusion is naturalized through everyday acts such as ironing, washing, and shopping. The cards, an easily obtainable bit of colorful amuse-

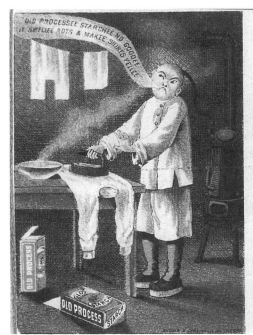

FIGURE 13.10. New Process Starch trade card.

ment in a world that has yet to be saturated by color, inform and instruct, even as the images debase the Chinese.

From our contemporary perspective, that such demeaning representations of the Chinese circulated in not only political but also domestic discourses seems strikingly incongruous. However, we are reminded how easily the unproblematic juxtaposition of the domestic and the political persists by the opening paragraphs of a popular children's book of the time, *Polly Oliver's Problem* (1893), by Kate Douglas Wiggin. Here Denis Kearney's exclusionist slogan that we saw echoed in the Rough on Rats card is seamlessly incorporated into domestic discourse:

> "I have determined only one thing definitely," said Polly Oliver; "and that is, the boarders must go. Oh, how charming that sounds! I've been thinking it ever since I was old enough to think, but I never cast it in such an attractive decisive form before. 'The Boarders Must Go!' To a California girl it is every bit as inspiring as 'The Chinese Must Go.' If I weren't obliged to set the boarders' table, I'd work the motto on a banner this very minute, and march up and down the plaza with it, followed by a crowd of small boys with toy drums."
>
> "The Chinese never did go," said Mrs. Oliver suggestively, from the sofa.
>
> "Oh, that's a trifle; they had a treaty or something, and besides, there are so many of them, and they have such an object in staying." (Wiggin 1893, 7–8)

Like many other Wiggin heroines, Polly is spirited, smart, and willing to work her way out of any difficulty. Her artless and offhand reference to "The Chinese must go" and her "charming" and "inspiring" version, "The Boarders Must Go," discloses how naturalized representations hidden in everyday life are ever-present and percolate to the surface of the collective consciousness.

In the end, the Chinese were not Polly Oliver's problem, though certainly they were made to seem so in the building of late-nineteenth-century U.S. national identity. These Chinese men simultaneously supported and threatened national order through their work in the domestic sphere. Accordingly, their visual representation in these trade cards conveys a mixed, surprisingly complex, message about the representation of race in the domestic sphere and underscores the importance of reading even ephemera when recollecting early Asian America.

Notes

Acknowledgments: Many thanks to the Museum of American History at the Smithsonian Institution, the Boston Athenaeum, the Boston Public Library, the Strong Museum, the Wilson Library of the University of Minnesota, and trade card dealers across the country, who provided me with primary and secondary materials for this essay. All images reproduced here come from cards in my personal collection. Special thanks go to Josephine Lee for her most helpful advice in rethinking how to read gender in these trade cards.

1. Manring 1998 discusses in detail the advertising campaigns that sustained this kind of ideology.

2. Appel 1991 catalogues many trade cards that feature this slogan and images of the Chinaman but does not mention this card.

3. Garvey further notes how in nineteenth-century discourses, "inextricably bound with the gender of the children who took up collecting stamps and trade cards was the relative value assigned to the economic activities they recapitulated—participation in the marketplace as traders and as sellers on the one hand, or as shoppers and tasteful arrangers on the other. The result was that stamp collecting was valued while trade card collecting was largely disregarded" (1994, 26).

Works Cited

Appel, John, and Selma Appel. 1991. "Sino-Phobic Advertising Slogans: 'The Chinese Must Go.'" *Ephemera Journal* 4: 35–40.

Barry, Kit. 1993. *Reflections: Ephemera from Trades, Products, and Events.* Brattleboro, Vt.: Iris.

Blumenbach, Johann Friedrich. 1969. *On the Natural Varieties of Mankind.* 1795. Reprint, New York: Bergman.

Broberg, Gunnar. 1997. "Linnaeus' Anthropology." In *History of Physical Anthropology,* ed. Frank Spencer. Vol. 2. New York: Garland.

Cheadle, Dave. 1996. *Victorian Trade Cards: Historical Reference and Value Guide.* Paducah, Ky.: Collector Books.

Choy, Philip, Lorraine Dong, and Marlon Hom, eds. 1994. *The Coming Man: 19th Century American Perceptions of the Chinese.* Seattle: University of Washington Press.

Garvey, Ellen Gruber. 1996. *The Adman in the Parlor: Magazines and the Gendering of Consumer Culture, 1880s to 1910s.* New York: Oxford University Press.

Lee, Robert G. 1999. *Orientals: Asian Americans in Popular Culture.* Philadelphia: Temple University Press.

Jay, Robert. 1987. *The Trade Card in Nineteenth-Century America.* Columbia: University of Missouri Press.

Manring, M. M. 1998. *Slave in a Box: The Strange Career of Aunt Jemima.* Charlottesville: University Press of Virginia.

McClintock, Anne. 1995. *Imperial Leather: Race, Gender, and Sexuality in the Colonial Contest.* New York: Routledge.

Stevenson, Joan C., ed. 1991. *Dictionary of Concepts in Physical Anthropology.* Westport, Conn.: Greenwood.

Tchen, John Kuo Wei. 1999. *New York before Chinatown: Orientalism and the Shaping of American Culture, 1776–1882.* Baltimore: Johns Hopkins University Press.

Wiggin, Kate Douglas. 1893. *Polly Oliver's Problem.* Boston: Houghton Mifflin.

Tina Chen

14   Dissecting the "Devil Doctor": Stereotype and Sensationalism in Sax Rohmer's Fu Manchu

In the introduction to *The Big Aiiieeeee!*, Jeffrey Paul Chan, Frank Chin, Lawson Fusao Inada, and Shawn Wong attempt to counter what they see as a dangerous propensity: the emphasis of "belief over . . . fact, and the fake over the real, until the stereotype has completely displaced history in the white sensibility." This assessment of stereotype, which is motivated by concern about the emasculation of Asian American men in "mainstream" U.S. culture, identifies Fu Manchu as the "worst" image in the "white liberal American" imagination, a figure who surpasses an "effeminate closet queen like Charlie Chan" to become a full-blown "homosexual menace" (1991, xiii).[1] These critics' anxiety involves not only the perception of stereotype but also the detection of its boundaries, a process requiring the vigilant policing of parameters to demarcate the good from the bad and "the real" from "the fake." While Chan and his fellow editors voice a desire for "authenticity"—constituted as "history," "fact," and "the real"—the vehemence with which they make such distinctions marks the impossibility of ascertaining such differentiations. As Daniel Kim asserts, the "intent to establish a neat binary between 'how we are seen' and 'how we are' . . . is always turning against itself" (1998, 275). The fear of perception becoming "the real" demands a retraining of how we see, an insistence on ferreting out the "fakes" among us.

Chan and his colleagues essentially charge that Fu Manchu is a "fake" who perverts Asian American masculine expression. Significantly, Fu Manchu's "fakeness" raises the issue of how stereotype is not only an important context for but also, in some unsettling ways, inextricably tied to the "authenticity" of Asian American identity formation. Although the "Devil Doctor" constitutes a problematic image for Asian Americans, his vexed textual and visual representation must be interrogated more systematically if his sway over the public imagination is to be addressed. Doubtless, Sax Rohmer's Fu Manchu books catered to the racist and sensationalistic proclivities of their intended audience. While the racism and formulaic nature of the books seems to render nuanced criticisms

FIGURE 14.1. Dr. Fu Manchu, from "The Mask of Fu Manchu" in *Collier's* magazine in 1932. This illustration by J. R. Flanagan reveals the Doctor's Caucasian features and stages Fu Manchu in the kind of museological setting so important to the series.

of them absurd, I propose in this essay a reevaluation of Dr. Fu Manchu and, by extension, a critique of the stereotype that he has come to represent for Asian Americans. Recognizing stereotype's capacity to be ideologically ambivalent in its formation if not always in its deployment is critical as Asian Americans seek to counter the representational legacy of stereotypes that have been produced about them by non-Asians.

Homi K. Bhabha reminds us that "the stereotype is a complex, ambivalent, contradictory mode of representation, as anxious as it is assertive, and demands not only that we extend our critical and political objectives but that we change the object of analysis itself" (1994, 70). According to Bhabha, an integral part of "chang[ing] the object of analysis" involves "construct[ing the stereotype's] regime of truth, not . . . subject[ing] its representations to a normalizing judgment" (67). In that vein, my essay seeks to strategize stereotype by reading against its surface and probing for the fissures and contradictions that are always embedded in such representation. By focusing on Rohmer's original depictions of Fu Manchu—particularly, his construction of Fu Manchu as a creolized character, his investigation of imperial desire even as he succumbs to it, and his exploitation and critique of museological practice—I hope to expose the blindness of Rohmer's white protagonists, his contemporary reading audiences, and Asian American literary critics who have decried Fu Manchu as "nothing more" than a stereotype.

Introducing the Mysterious Dr. Fu Manchu

As the story goes, deep in the forests of colonial Burma, Sir Denis Nayland Smith narrowly escapes the poisoned tip of an arrow and steals his first glimpse of "the most malign and formidable personality existing in the known world" (Rohmer 1970, *Insidious,* 15). Although Scotland Yard's finest operative is ostensibly the protagonist of one of the most widely read series of books published in the twentieth century, he was not the series' chief attraction. That role was reserved for the man he characterized as "the yellow peril incarnate," known to millions as Dr. Fu Manchu. Fu Manchu's status as a transnational popular icon granted him a material presence that would dictate the series evolving politics.[2] While the early novels pit Smith's "British" intelligence against the "Chinese cunning" of Dr. Fu Manchu, later books reframe their conflict in more expansive geographical and cultural terms. Reflecting the emergence of the United States as a world power, many of the post-1933 books pair Smith with young American partners, thereby enacting an ethnocentric transfer of not only global responsibility, but also the burden of representation. Benedict Anderson has convincingly demonstrated how print culture works to establish the formation of communities across time and space. Although Anderson discusses the emergence of an "imagined community" in the context of nationalism, the Fu Manchu stories created an Anglo-American alliance between England and the United States, cementing them into a cohesive Western unit in the battle against the Eastern forces commanded by the "Devil Doctor." (From the beginning, the Fu Manchu books were published simultaneously in London and New York.) The "alliance" has proven formidable: The series's popularity in both countries has established Fu Manchu as one of the most enduring stereotypes of Asian villainy.

In his study of Chinese American images in U.S. fiction, William Wu grants Fu Manchu the status of "archetypal Asian villain" in the U.S. consciousness because of the character's warm reception by the U.S. reading public. Rohmer's textual accommodations to his U.S. audience included making his younger protagonists American, setting several of the later novels in New York, and writing a book about Fu Manchu's attempt to take over the U.S. presidency. Consequently, "the Fu Manchu character [was] the first Asian role of prominence in modern literature to have a large American readership" (Wu 1982, 164). Don Hutchinson writes that the Fu Manchu novels "were, if anything, even more popular in the U.S. than they were in Britain" (1991, xxviii). In fact, Rohmer's exploitation of Yellow Peril fears proved so compelling to U.S. audiences that when the series ended after the first three books with the Doctor's apparent demise at the end of *The Hand of Fu Manchu* (1917), readers of *Collier's* pressured the magazine to commission the revival of both the series and its lead character (see Lee 1997). Despite his British origins, Fu Manchu was quickly adopted into U.S. popular culture, appearing in television, newspaper comics, movies, and pulp fiction.[3]

West versus East: A Study in Mythic Opposition

The series pits Sir Denis Nayland Smith against the diabolical genius Dr. Fu Manchu, the head of a secret organization aiming to wrest world control from the West. At its most basic level, their adventure is a tale of conflict cast in racialized terms. Smith, who initiates his struggle against Fu Manchu while a Burmese colonial official, literally represents the British Empire.[4] According to Smith's rhetoric, the British Empire stands for race as well as nation: He cautions his partner, Petrie, a medical practitioner who narrates the first three novels, "I have traveled from Burma not in the interests of the British Government merely, but in the interests of the entire white race, and I honestly believe—though I pray I may be wrong—that its survival depends largely upon the success of my mission" (Rohmer 1970, *Insidious*, 6). Just as Smith metonymically figures both the British Empire and the "white" race, Fu Manchu and the organization he represents are the Yellow Peril, a threat to (inter)national security figured in racial terms. In the most famous description of the Doctor, Smith tells Petrie:

> Imagine a person, tall, lean and feline, high-shouldered, with a brow like Shakespeare and a face like Satan, a close-shaven skull, and long, magnetic eyes of the true cat-green. Invest him with all the cruel cunning of an entire Eastern race, accumulated in one giant intellect, with all the resources of science past and present, with all the resources, if you will, of a wealthy government.... Imagine that awful being, and you have a mental picture of Dr. Fu-Manchu, the yellow peril incarnate in one man. (17)[5]

Figured in these terms, the story is an old one. It is the fight between self and other, the West and the rest, a political conflict cast in mythic terms of opposition. Yet, while such clear distinctions lend themselves well to the genre Rohmer was writing, they were not always appreciated by his critics. According to Christopher Frayling, "Rohmer's books have always had bad Press . . . it be[ing] a critical commonplace to categorize [them] as the lowest form of racist propaganda, a humourless version of the mid-Victorian penny dreadfuls" (1977, 66).[6] Such criticisms reflect the tendency John Cawelti identifies in his study of formula fiction to brand the generic conventions of formula stories as inferior to "more serious" literature.[7] Focusing largely on the series' sensationalist and racist properties, critics of Rohmer's writing have generally overlooked the ways in which the texts complicate received conventions of racial representation in early twentieth-century popular literature. As we shall see, Rohmer's writing often problematizes the clear distinction between "good" and "bad" that scholars perceive to be the defining characteristic of popular fiction (Watson 1979, 109).

"The Devilish Doctor Is the Reason Why . . ."

Much of Fu Manchu's popularity as a character did seem to depend upon the exaggerated struggle between "good" and "bad" that his conflict with Smith symbolized. To that end, his countless appearances in other contexts, command performances capitalizing on his "evil" nature, gradually distorted Rohmer's original characterizations of the Doctor. Fu Manchu's name usually conjures up images of the feminized, long-clawed, bearded visage of the character's popular reincarnation in other media. Rohmer's own writing style, tailored toward the melodramatic and repetitive, abetted this transformation by giving the public several reductive labels for the Doctor. Ironically, the author who believed himself the reincarnation of a Nile dweller as well as a Caribbean pirate would watch the popular imagination reincarnate his creation, sometimes to such an extent that he deemed it unrecognizable.[8]

During the course of the novels, Rohmer himself resurrected Fu Manchu several times, thereby enhancing his awesome appeal. Despite popular assumptions about his "sinister," "Satanic," and "loathsome" character, Fu Manchu did not remain the mysterious, wholly evil personality that Smith and Petrie first encountered. Unlike the mass media representations of the Doctor, the reincarnations of Fu Manchu in Rohmer's later texts tended to develop and complicate the simple villainy Fu Manchu evinced in the earlier books. Although the Doctor was originally depicted as the head of a "yellow octopus . . . whose tentacles were dacoity, thuggee, modes of death, secret and swift," Smith's increasing reliance on Fu Manchu's sense of honor and the inviolability of his word recast him as the undeniably majestic "Emperor of Lawbreakers." As the series evolved, Smith's repeated characterizations of Fu Manchu as Satan provided a dark counterpoint to later assessments of the Doctor's appearance. Time transmuted the Satanic visage into "a most wonderful face" that was "aged, yet ageless" (Rohmer 1933, 112). Changing political situations also caused younger protagonists to read different qualities into the Doctor's countenance. In *The Drums of Fu Manchu,* the Doctor attempts to prevent the eruption of a second world war by threatening to kill any government leaders who agitate against international stability. As a result, Smith and Fu Manchu find themselves working toward the shared goal of world peace, a situation reflected in protagonist Bart Kerrigan's impression of the Doctor:

> [His face] might have been the face of an emperor. I found myself thinking of Zenghis Khan [*sic*]. Intellectually, the brow was phenomenal, the dignity of the lined features might have belonged to a Pharaoh, but the soul of the great Chinese doctor lay in his eyes. Never had I seen before, and never have I seen again, such power in a man's eyes as lay in those of Dr. Fu Manchu. (Rohmer 1939, 107)

This description echoes the observations of Alan Sterling, the protagonist who falls in love with Fu Manchu's chosen bride and who thinks that the Doctor's "wonderful face ... might once have been beautiful." Eventually, even Fu Manchu's association with the unrelenting evil symbolized by the devil mellowed into a reminder that Satan was once "Lucifer, Son of the Morning: an angel, but a fallen angel" (Rohmer 1966, 97).

Smith, doomed to forever being the same hyperactive criminal investigator introduced in the first book, could not compete with the Doctor's mesmerizing evolution. During the course of almost a half century, Fu Manchu undergoes a host of transformations: from a representative dispatched by a secret organization to "pave the way" into a leader of the Si-fan, the most powerful secret organization in the world; from an unmitigated force of evil intent on the destruction of Western civilization into a powerful ally in the fight against Communism; from a diabolical enemy into a godlike being whose abilities to transcend the laws of time and man set him "above good and evil"; from a master criminal into a "mighty instrument of vengeance" aimed at warmongers; and from the harbinger of death into "the supreme physician." Speaking for contemporary readers, Alan Brien, in an article criticizing Rohmer for being a "dedicated righty," concludes that "the devilish Doctor is the reason why we can still read Rohmer, one of those great good-bad writers" (1985, 32).

Staging Race

Rohmer's flair for creating such a memorable character can be traced to his theatrical background and the lessons it taught him concerning the conjunction of race and "authenticity" in popular representation. Christopher Frayling has argued that "many of the incidents, characters, and stylistic trademarks of the first three Fu Manchu stories ... are strongly reminiscent of the music hall world in which Rohmer was mixing" (1973, 67). The popularity of the music hall as "imperial theatre" denoted a pervasive interest in melodrama and the staging of cultural and racial difference (Mackenzie 1984, 41). In addition to escapist musicals set in the Orient, the music hall of Rohmer's time also hosted variety shows billing rival magicians Ching Ling Foo ("Court Conjurer to the Empress of China") and Chung Ling Soo ("a rare bit of old China"). The representational issues at the heart of Chung Ling Soo's stage show appeared only at the moment of his death. After Soo was shot in the chest while performing his popular

"Defying the Bullets" act in 1918, surgeons discovered that Soo, despite using interpreters and Chinese assistants for more than ten years, was actually a Euro-American named William E. Robinson. Robinson's death exposed the complex issue of "authenticity" that authorized performances such as his.

The idea of performing authentic "Chineseness" on the music hall stage was a product of the "institutional culture of the gaze" operating at the end of the nineteenth century to represent the unknown in prescripted ways (Moy 1993, 8). As Chung Ling Soo's act demonstrated, the authenticity afforded by the visual very often turned the performance into the real. Rohmer's experience working with music hall performers known for doing vaudevillian sketches of Chinamen might be seen as an apprenticeship of sorts in racial stereotyping. When he became a fiction writer, Rohmer had no qualms about appropriating "Chineseness" for his villain, and he knew exactly how to manipulate race as a signifier of the exotic and unfamiliar. Fu Manchu, with his long silk robes, mandarin cap, and opium pipe, fulfilled Euro-American expectations of what it meant to be Chinese by exploiting the kind of representational practices exposed by Robinson's death. As yellow-face performance made clear, performances of race were very often racial masquerades, farces having more to do with the desires of the performer and audience than with the desires of those being staged.

Significantly, Rohmer demonstrates a keen awareness of the ways in which his racial representations depend upon notions of a plausibly "(in)authentic" other. In *The Trail of Fu Manchu* (1934), Rohmer's depiction of the novelist Mrs. Crossland makes clear his self-consciousness concerning the orientalizing nature of much of his own work: "Mrs. Crossland's reputation and financial success rested upon her inaccurate pictures of desert life: of the loves of sheiks and their Western mistresses" (1966, 197). Focusing on the "pseudo-Orientalism" of Mrs. Crossland's work, the commentary in *Trail* reveals a self-reflexive understanding of the exploitative nature of Rohmer's own racial representations. As Rohmer acknowledged, "I made my name on Fu Manchu because I know nothing about the Chinese!" (van Ash 1972, 72). Fu Manchu's skill with disguises and his ability to reverse racial masquerade by passing as a European doctor or professor—talents that often render him invisible to those pursuing him—foreground the ways in which the white protagonists, unlike Rohmer himself, refuse to see beyond their conventions of racial representation.

The blindnesses exemplified by Rohmer's white protagonists are structurally reinforced by the Manicheanisms permeating the texts. The battles waged are mythic, "starkly contrasting white and black, good and evil, superiority and inferiority, civilization and savagery, intelligence and emotion, rationality and sensuality, self and Other, subject and object" (JanMohamed 1983, 63; see also E. Kim 1982, 8). Such conflict, although easily read as naive racism, marks a complex series of "perverse identifications" and "crucial exclusions" that both threaten and reinforce ideas of national culture and racial purity (Shohat and Stam 1994, 20, 14). The cultural hybridity that inevitably attends imperial interests constitutes one such "crucial exclusion," an integral aspect of imperial culture that is often marked by a calculated lack of scrutiny. In *The Native Races of the Empire,* part of a twelve-volume series directed at giving "a complete survey of the history, resources, and activities of the [British] Empire looked at as a whole," Sir Godfrey Lagden argues that the book's aim precludes an "account of the classes known [as] Half-castes" (1924, iii, xv). As Lagden's justification notes, "Half-castes" are "known in every possession," an undeniable reality of imperial rule.

Half-Castes in Every Possession

Perhaps the most famous "half-caste" ever to make an appearance in the Fu Manchu series was the first: Karamaneh, the Arab who captured Petrie's heart with her "predilection, characteristically Oriental," for him. Petrie paints her as an enchantress of mixed parentage: "With the skin of a perfect blonde, she had eyes and lashes as black as a Creole's which, together with her full red lips, told me that this beautiful stranger ... was not a child of our northern shores" (Rohmer 1970, *Insidious*, 13). Early descriptions focus on Oriental features that lend her "a beauty of a kind that was a key to the most extravagant rhapsodies of Eastern poets" (176). Her delicate loveliness masks the skill with which she implements Fu Manchu's daring schemes. She is the first assault on the "truth" that Smith commits himself to upholding: "East and West may not intermingle" (120). Smith, disappointed by an unspecified love affair while in the East, never loses his conviction in this "undeniable" truth. Petrie, on the other hand, revises his philosophy to accommodate his romantic interests. When Karamaneh becomes too "exquisite" to be resisted, Petrie's previous distinctions of what is East and West become meaningless, if only momentarily: "Her eyes held a challenge wholly Oriental in its appeal: her lips, even in repose, were a taunt. And, herein, East is West and West is East" (176).

Significantly, Karamaneh's active part in the adventure soon ceases. After marrying Petrie and retiring to Cairo, Kara, as she is renamed, becomes progressively more passive. Whereas she was once capable of swinging on wires, racing across moors, and perpetrating crimes in various disguises, her marriage to Petrie renders her weak, nervous, and unable (or at least not allowed) to do things by herself. Smith and his later partners make much of her happiness as Petrie's wife, but in so doing, they relegate her voice to the background. Despite the surface rhetoric of the books that juxtaposes her slavery to Fu Manchu with the freedom enjoyed by English and U.S. women, Kara's Anglicization does not make her more free; rather, she is trapped by her fear of being alone, controlled by Petrie's demand that she "conquer ... the barbaric impulses that sometimes flamed up within her" (Rohmer 1929, *Hand*, 85). By the fourth book of the series, *Daughter of Fu Manchu* (1931), the erasure of her "oriental" attributes—not to mention her name—signifies Kara's successful assimilation: "In *Mrs.* Petrie's complex character there was a marked streak of Oriental mysticism—*although from her appearance [one] should never have suspected Eastern blood*" (Rohmer 1986, 210, emphasis added). Karamaneh's incorporation into British colonial society exemplifies an attack on imperial structures of representation that has been (predictably) overcome through the subgenre of (inter)racial romance. However, Fu Manchu is not so easily reincorporated.

Fu Manchu's "fiendish armory" of "natural" weapons, both human and animal, bolsters his threatening presence. Color as an unproblematized signifier seems to indicate racial, ideological, and political alignments. By association, Fu Manchu links himself to the brown and black men he employs to help him win control of the world. Brown-skinned Burmese dacoits who signal the commencement of his crimes with their "low, wailing cry" are later joined by Indian thugs, Middle Eastern phansigars (religious stranglers), and African assassins.[9] In the overt discourse dictated by Manichean allegory, clear distinctions demarcate white from nonwhite. Consequently, Fu Manchu's alignment with the darker side of the equation reinforces his "discoloration," positioning him against the whiteness—and by extension, moral superiority—claimed by Western imperial desire.

Despite such clearly delineated positioning, a repeated emphasis on Fu Manchu's honor and integrity sets the stage for a specular affiliation with the Euro-American community against which he is ostensibly posed. At times, Rohmer constitutes him as a mirror image of Smith, perhaps inverted or distorted, a relationship of similarity which works to undercut Fu Manchu's connection with darker peoples. The repeated assertions of political, cultural, and racial opposition between Fu Manchu and Smith obscure their similarities. The "febrile glitter" of Smith's eyes mirrors the "viridescence" of the Doctor's "reptilian gaze." Petrie's description of Smith as "a great, gaunt cat" yokes two of the signature characteristics ascribed to the Doctor: his "gaunt" frame and "cat-like gait." Smith's customary "staccato" style of speech lapses, in moments of extreme stress or provocation, into the "sibilance" that marks the speech of Fu Manchu (see especially Rohmer 1929, *Return).*

While these similarities between Smith and Fu Manchu problematize clear distinctions of difference, the inversions and distortions registered between the two are revised and given wider implications in *President Fu Manchu* (1936). Professor Morgenstahl, Fu Manchu's unwilling accomplice, spends every waking hour trying to sculpt a life-sized bust of the Doctor from a tiny picture that turns out to be a "three-cent Daniel Webster stamp, dated 1932, gummed upside down upon a piece of cardboard, then framed by the paper in which a pear-shaped opening had been cut" (Rohmer 1936, 238–39). The framing of the stamp renders one surprising fact "unmistakable: inverted and framed in this way, the Daniel Webster stamp presented a caricature, but a recognizable caricature, of Dr. Fu Manchu!" (239). Rohmer's depiction of the Doctor as Webster's inverted distortion capitalizes on, as well as challenges, the science of phrenology. While the use of inversion and distortion seems to reinforce the racial and attendant moral differences between Webster and Fu Manchu, their similarly large foreheads problematize the racial distinctions made by phrenological science. According to Orson and Lorenzo Fowler, the leaders of practical phrenology in the United States during the mid–nineteenth century: "The European race (including their descendants in America) possess a much larger endowment of these organs [the frontal and coronal portions of the head], and also of their corresponding faculties [intellect and morality], than any other portion of the human species. Hence their intellectual and moral superiority over all other races of men" (qtd. in Horseman 1981, 143).

By juxtaposing Webster's prominent forehead with the Doctor's "Shakespearean" brow, Rohmer not only refigures the basic precepts of phrenology; he also calls to attention Fu Manchu as a threat figured in both internal as well as external terms. The evolution of the Si-fan into an organization boasting among its members high-level Western politicians, as well as Eastern leaders, refigures racialized fears into political concerns exceeding racial boundaries. Morgenstahl's need to invert the Daniel Webster stamp in order to see the face of the Doctor metaphorizes Fu Manchu's evolution from a clearly and easily recognizable foreign threat to imperial interests into one embedded in the very structure of what empire desires to protect. The other that is projected, rejected, and held at arm's length is also, paradoxically, the one whose incorporation nurtures imperial growth.

Physically, Fu Manchu could very well fall into Lagden's "Half-caste" classification, although his political and ideological leanings mark him as an outsider and a threat to the hegemony exercised by British and U.S. imperialism. Fu Manchu *cannot* be purely Chinese, despite Smith's conjecture that he descends from "a certain very old Kiangsu family" (Rohmer 1970, *Insidious,* 174). His height (over six feet), his eye-color (green) and his hair ("sparse and neutral colored") make it clear that Fu Manchu claims partial Caucasian ancestry. Significantly, none of the characters in the series, despite repeated and closely detailed physical descriptions, ever see him as anything other than purely Chinese. The doubled discourse of empire encourages single-minded categorization even as it introduces hybrid formulations. To extend Homi K. Bhabha's discussion on colonial discourse to include imperialism, the idea of "fixity" constitutes an important feature of the "ideological construction of otherness." Bhabha contends that "fixity as the sign of cultural/historical/racial difference . . . is a paradoxical mode of representation: it connotes rigidity and an unchanging order as well as disorder, degeneracy and daemonic repetition" (1994, 66). "Fixing" the other, making its "degeneracy" the mark of unwavering difference, becomes a way of satiating the desire to enact binaristic choices, a mentality typified by Rohmer's white protagonists despite shifting allegiances created by interracial romance and politics.[10]

A Way of Not Seeing

In creating such an interesting discrepancy between Fu Manchu's appearance and how he is seen, Rohmer makes visible one of the ways in which orientalism works. Although the characters train their dissecting gaze on Fu Manchu, their attitude reflects a carefully cultivated "way of not seeing" that works by designating cultural others in such a way that they can be easily dismissed as always already "other" (Thompson 1993, 69). Fah Lo Suee, Fu Manchu's daughter, is definitely Eurasian. However, the books postulate her destiny as racially overdetermined by her part-Chinese ancestry. This classificatory practice runs throughout the series. Smith and his cohorts immediately regard as suspicious every character who has any kind of oriental background. This practice remains uncountered until the final book, *Emperor Fu Manchu* (1959), which introduces male and female protagonists Tony McKay and Jeannie Cameron-Gordon, both one-quarter Chinese and unimpeachable allies in the fight against Fu Manchu.[11] The deliberate refusal to see any affinity between self and other comprises an important part of an entire system of classification and representation crucial to imperial definitions of self.

This "refusal to see" plays itself out in the two levels of rhetoric structuring the Fu Manchu novels. Smith, and to some extent the narrators, vocalize the surface disquisition. Smith's racist assertions, many of which are initially adopted or sporadically ventriloquized by other protagonists, laid the basis for the xenophobic attitudes that have caused critical dismissal of the series. However, a closer examination of the descriptive language of several narrative protagonists reveals that while most of the narrators *consciously* subscribe to Smith's view of Fu Manchu, their impressions of the Doctor often register deviances that can be read as opposing or subverting the controlling discourse of empire represented by Smith.

One of the key sites of subversion to imperial discourses of representation—a subversion whose potential presence rests deeply hidden within the "subconscious logic" of imperialism—involves the relation hybridity bears to purity (JanMohamed 1983, 63). Although imperial interests rendered hybridity an ineradicable part of empire, a negative view of cultural and racial mixing continued to dominate the images produced by imperial machineries of representation. Shohat and Stam acknowledge hybridity as a "power-laden and asymmetrical" relationship: "Historically, assimilation by the 'native' into a European culture was celebrated as part of the civilizing mission [while] assimilation in the opposite direction was derided as 'going native,' a reversion to savagery" (1994, 43). In the Fu Manchu books, this "asymmetrical" relationship between hybridity and empire, which either seeks to coopt hybridity through the amalgamating redemptions offered by assimilation or completely denigrate it by an alignment with the "savage," is circumvented and given new permutations in the figure of the Doctor.

Beyond the biological/physical, Fu Manchu is also a culturally hybrid character. Despite the political and ideological concerns that posit him as "other," he exists as a singular product of both Eastern and Western discourses. He simultaneously embodies Chinese cruelty—the logical product of a society that kills its girl children—and Western scientific accomplishment. His knowledge, partly cultivated while he is the most outstanding student at three or more distinguished European and U.S. universities, pushes science and medicine to unimagined levels of achievement. His ability to mold elements from both East and West into new products and new visions dismantles an understanding of cultural identity as the outcome of an overdetermined binaristic choice. Fu Manchu never feels constrained by the "either/or" option articulated by Shohat and Stam. He is a "native" who moves in Euro-American society, both as himself (he possesses the mysterious title of "Marquis") and in disguise (quite often he appears as some European professor or doctor), and he excels at its most civilized tasks.

However, Western identity never subsumes him: He resists the "assimilation" that such performances often dictate. His ability to see beyond cultural and racial borders makes him threatening to Western hegemony, since he has no compunction about harnessing whatever cultural elements, taken from both sides, he can use. This mentality is reflected in his decisions to employ half-caste servants for high-profile positions in the Si-fan; embodied in his daughter Fah Lo Suee, who has a Russian mother; and expressed in his choice of Fleurette as his empress-bride, a woman chosen for her "pedigree on both sides," chosen because "she has [both] Eastern and Western blood" (Rohmer 1933, 160).

A measure of Fu Manchu's threat to the political and social economy of empire rests in his ability to envision new coalitions between East and West. Although he begins the series as a representative intent on "paving the way" for a powerful, unnamed shadow organization and later progresses into empire building on a large scale, his eventual preoccupation with preventing war and combating Communism finds him willing to forge an alliance with Smith. Fu Manchu offers his services in their common goal of maintaining a peaceful world: "I ask you to join me now—for my enemies are your enemies" (Rohmer 1939, 33). Smith and those he represents refuse to entertain any notion of alliance, although Fu Manchu's aim "must enlist the sympathy of any sane man" (30).

Smith's denial disavows his own history as a man formed by both East and West. Although he toils tirelessly in the interests of British and U.S. imperialism and is awarded a baronetcy for "saving the Empire" from the fatal infection posed by the "insidious breath of the East," he feels more comfortable in Burma than in London. Smith informs Petrie that "although I can stand tropical heat, curiously enough the heat of London gets me down almost immediately" (Rohmer 1929, *Return,* 133). He feels out of place in Britain, a displacement underscored by his immediate departures after each case. As readers, we are never privy to his time in the East unless he is actively in pursuit of the Doctor, and his life before confronting Fu Manchu in Burma remains a mystery. These blanknesses typify his refusal to see the influence of his Eastern experience on his own character formation, even though such experience allows him the role in which he finds his truest expression: Fu Manchu's nemesis. Only the necessary construction of the East as the "insidious enemy" allows Smith to posit a self-image of the West as "clean efficiency"; paradoxically, such a construction is authorized by Smith's own exposure to the East, marked by the fact that only he can match Fu Manchu's ability to perform racial masquerade convincingly.

"Primitive" In(ter)ventions

Fu Manchu's scientific and technological endeavors manifest most fully in his negotiation of hybrid formulations. Contrary to Smith's ideological objections to his projects, cast primarily in moral terms, Fu Manchu does not view as ugly or sordid his explorations of new combinations of elements found in the natural world. For him, engineering hybridity productively harnesses the exciting potentials of nature. The Si-fan, a transnational, multiracial organization that includes members from both "East" and "West," reflects such a philosophy. As an inventor, Dr. Fu Manchu fuses "primitive" elements with "modern" advancements to create new technologies that defy penetration by Smith. In *Island of Fu Manchu* (1940), the Doctor uses one of his "inventions" to deliver a message to Bart Kerrigan, the novel's protagonist. A curious contraption, it inspires "revulsion" in Kerrigan, who views it as a "dreadful exhibit." What Kerrigan sees is a human head, "that of a bearded old man, reduced by the mysterious art of Peruvian head-hunters to a size no greater than that of an average orange, . . . mounted and set in a carved mahogany box having a perfectly fitting glass cover" (Rohmer 1971, 96). Its "repellent" appearance stems partly from the primitivism it seems to celebrate. As Marianna Torgovnick writes, primitivism is the name we assign the darker aspects of ourselves, the label we use to distance our "untamed selves" from our images of self. By its projection of "id forces—libidinous, irrational, violent, [and] dangerous" onto other peoples as a way of demarcating difference, it continually tropes "Otherness" by figuring it as exotic and degraded (1990, 8).

Kerrigan recoils from the shriveled head and the "native work" on the box encasing it because they seem emblematic of the wide gulf between him and the Doctor. Ironically, when "a low, obscene whispering" begins to emanate from the head, the differences structuring Kerrigan's world begin to blur, devouring carefully wrought distinctions between self and other:

> "So it befell—so it befell . . ." The whispering was in English! "Ica I was called—Ica . . . Chief was I of all the Quechua of Callao. But the Jibaros came: my women were taken, my house was fired, my head struck off. We were peaceful folk. But the head-hunters swept down upon us. Thought still lived in my skull, even when it was packed with burning sand . . . My brain boiled, yet I knew that I was Ica, chief of the Quechua of Callao." (Rohmer 1971, 106)

This narrative of violence and dismemberment seemingly corroborates the expectations of primitivism aroused in both Kerrigan and the reader as they gaze, frozen with fascination, at the decapitated head. Nevertheless, Ica's head, framed by its glass case, problematizes even as it foregrounds Western notions of primitivism.

While Ica's story reinforces Kerrigan's horror and disgust, it also partly negates his preconception of the primitive as completely other, and vice versa. Kerrigan's surprise at the whispering *in English* foregrounds his own horrified visual consumption of the shriveled head, a consumption highlighted by the museum display case within which the head rests. While the Jibaros who destroy Ica's home might refer to either the peasantry or to the Jivaros, a tribe of Indians known for their skill in shrinking heads, Ica's narrative invokes a sequence of colonial relationships that are no less "primitive" than the examples of native violence it explicitly articulates. Quechuans, linked to the Incan empire through a marital alliance between Viracocha Inca and the daughter of the chief of Anta, lent their language to Incan bureaucracy and government, thereby cementing the expansion of the Incan empire. Calling up the violence of both Incan and Spanish imperialism, Ica's fragmented tale ruptures the clear boundaries between self and other by accenting the violent legacy and the absent presence of Spanish colonialism on native peoples.

Yoking "primitive" and "civilized," the "undeveloped" with the futuristic, Fu Manchu's hybrid experiments—and ultimately, even Fu Manchu himself—reimage racial and cultural categories only to have imperial structures of representation reabsorb their disruptive potential through the fetishization of freakishness. In *Fu Manchu's Bride* (1933), the Doctor cultivates a "freakish" tsetse fly capable of spreading a "hybrid germ" that combines sleeping sickness and plague. At once meticulously honorable and cunningly cruel, Fu Manchu gains his power from the fact that nothing about him can be considered normal. He can claim to be the world's greatest intelligence. His green eyes are covered with a thin film that reminds Petrie of the *"membranas ninctinas"* possessed by birds. His skull is of a prodigious (and nearly unbelievable) size, a physical detail considered abnormal for a Mongoloid. As the texts illustrate, the discomfort Smith feels about the disruptive potential of Fu Manchu's hybrid formulations is one that can be assuaged by fetishizing hybridity as freakishness.

Different Performances, Performing Difference

According to historian Richard Altick, freakishness inspired a "common curiosity [that] erased social distinctions: the quality and the rabble, the cultivated and the ignorant mingled to see the latest marvel" (1978, 36). The "marvels" they paused and paid to wonder at included a variety of the visibly deviant, the more deformed or grotesque the better. At Bartholomew Fair (the biggest and longest-lived of London fairs), William Wordsworth observed that

> All moveables of wonder, from all parts,
> Are here—Albinos, painted Indians, Dwarfs,
> The Horse of knowledge, and the learned Pig,
> The Stone-eater, the man that swallows fire,
> Giants, Ventriloquists, the invisible Girl,
> The Bust that speaks and moves its goggling eyes,
> The Wax-work, Clock-work, all the marvellous craft
> Of modern Merlins, Wild Beasts, Puppet-shows,
> All out-o'-the-way, far-fetched, perverted things,
> All freaks of nature, all Promethian thoughts
> Of man; his dullness, madness, and their feats
> All jumbled up together to make up
> This parliament of Monsters.
> (Wordsworth 1971, ll. 679–91)

Clearly, what constitutes freakishness includes physical deformity, exoticism, unbelievable "skills" and "talents," a certain amount of illusion (and gullibility), and the demonstration of technology so new that it borders on the "magical." To read Wordsworth's graphic list of what fairgoers paid to gawk at is, after taking into consideration the changed sensibilities effected by the "progress" of a century, to have an idea of what kind of display Rohmer offered his readers in the Fu Manchu books. Most of the creatures used or created by the Doctor, and even the Doctor himself, possess freakish characteristics. Fu Manchu is consistently identified by the enormous size of his skull, yet the descriptions, tempered by the "dignity" and "majesty" of his expression, are nonetheless reminiscent of the hydrocephalic children popularly displayed for public viewing during late-nineteenth-century freak shows. The conception of the Doctor as "freakish" also made sense in the context created by the traveling exhibition that featured Chang and Eng, the Siamese twins whose presentation to both British and U.S. publics "further contributed to the institutionalization of Chinese racial representation as appropriate for museum or freak show display" (Moy 1993, 13).

Each of the books in the series introduces at least one new exotic or deformed specimen to the reading public. From the Zayat Kiss delivered by the giant scolopendra centipede imported from Burma to three-and-a-half-inch Negritos from West Africa; from the *Cynocephalus hamadryas,* a sacred baboon with "an unreasoning malignity towards [men]" to the shriveled but still-talking head of a Peruvian Indian chief; from Hassan the white Negro to Zazima the Panamanian Dwarf, Fu Manchu—courtesy of Rohmer's vivid imagination—provided a veritable freak show for his audiences. Altick writes that "the March of Intellect had not progressed so far as to deprive countless . . . visitors of their credulity and their appetite for human wonders, whether natural or contrived—armless artists, hydrocephalic children, fat or pigfaced ladies, spotted men and women, and so on" (1978, 253). Rohmer's immersion in the music halls had prepared him to take advantage of the visual as spectacle. In an increasingly modern and alienating world, the spectacle of otherness performed by freak shows and their later cousins forged a sense of community in the face of what could be seen as the truly alien.

Although the freak shows of the nineteenth century gradually disappeared from public view, the popular fascination they catered to did not simply evaporate. Rather, the curiosities and human differences they exploited for the purposes of show were adopted by a variety of other institutions. The latter half of the nineteenth century saw the rise of anthropology and ethnology as scientific discourses. What was previously gaped at as exotic was now closely studied in the name of science and progress. Science legitimated the public desire for spectacle and the display of difference and made it respectable. Zoos, museums, and international exhibitions provided increasingly scientific forums for the study of exotica, along with programs that educated and enlightened their patrons. A close look at the presentational structure of the novels makes Rohmer's deliberate appropriation of popular interest in a burgeoning museological culture startlingly clear.

As exhibits like Ica's mummified head demonstrate, Rohmer exploits a quasi-scientific desire to see, in one panoramic sweep, a wide range of the foreign. Thanks to the Doctor's ability to penetrate the deepest jungles of Asia, Africa, and the Middle East, Rohmer's audiences enjoyed the thrill of "seeing" exotic sights and people without leaving the comfort of their homes. While the surface rhetoric of the books condemns Fu Manchu for attempting to build a Chinese empire, the Doctor's techniques of collection and demonstration actually mirror *Western* imperial practice. Like the "human showcases" featured at international exhibitions, Fu Manchu's scientific companions are "specimens" who have been collected and processed into an imperial project; each scientist is placed in his "natural environment" and observed while "performing" in his established area of expertise. What made Fu Manchu's "human showcase" so repellent to audiences were considerations that should have been equally at play in the collection and display of native peoples. Rohmer exposes Fu Manchu as the ultimate man of empire, and such exposure horrified readers, who discovered the ability of the other to be as imperialist, as Western, as themselves. The inversion of empire presented by the Doctor not only reveals the limits of a fully articulated critique against his design, a pattern of imperial acquisition already forged by the Western nations that hypocritically condemned his project, but also emphasizes a threatening mimicry of Western imperial agency.

However, Fu Manchu is not the only one to take advantage of visual display in the interests of empire. Rohmer's books undermine many of the critiques against imperial representation that he embeds within them. While specific elements of the Fu Manchu novels critique, sometimes unconsciously, the gaze of empire as it had been trained against other peoples, the books also exploit the curiosity and fears that created that imperial gaze. Ultimately, the texts functioned as justification for British and U.S. discrimination against the Chinese.

As such, Rohmer often treats Fu Manchu himself as an exhibit. Like Afong Moy, a " 'Chinese Lady' . . . offered to the public gaze at the American Museum in New York City," Fu Manchu's performances take place in settings that conform to public expectations of "Chineseness." Moy's "performance" of ethnicity relied upon an elaborate set decorated with chinoiserie: James Moy notes that the "simple foreignness of Afong Moy was deemed sufficient novelty to warrant her display" (1993, 12). Rohmer's textual presentation of Fu Manchu borrows heavily from public displays of Chineseness exemplified by "exhibits" like Afong Moy, where much of what was considered representative of the Chinese emerged from the display of material objects. Rohmer's depiction of the Doctor emphasizes those aspects of the Doctor's setting that would provide the "authenticity" expected by his reading public. The Doctor usually dresses in a "long yellow silk robe," wears a "black mandarin cap with a coral bead," and smokes opium from a "jade pipe" in a room decorated with "lacquer furniture" and other appropriately "authentic" chinoiserie.

Rohmer carefully deploys exotic elements in the familiar framework of British and U.S. social structures. Although some of the novels take place in exotic locales, most of them maintain contact with territorial landscapes with which readers could identify; London and New York figure prominently in the series. The contrast of the familiar with the exotic provides a frame, a setting for each of the unfamiliar places—and by extension, the most recent specimens—promised in each new installment of the Fu Manchu drama. Rohmer's writing embodies the impact of the visual by articulating it within the context of an enormous exhibition. Responsible for staging as well as enacting the exhibit, Fu Manchu amazes his audience with a dizzying array of new species of men, animals, and plants. In these texts and performances, authority resides not only in the spectacular nature of the display but in its capacity to extend the visual to the visceral. The displays are ordered not so much for educational value as for their ability to produce a reaction in the reader. The horror they engender proliferates from the displacement of specimens from their perceived "natural environments." Kerrigan's horror at Ica's glass-encased head derives, in part, from its removal from a museum setting and displacement onto a landscape that foregrounds his own specular consumption of the head. Similarly, much of the terror inspired by the Doctor's "fiendish armory" of scorpions and poisonous flowers derives from its (mis)placement in the "sanitary" environment of the metropolis.

The formulaic nature of the books reinforces the image of a carefully constructed museum of wonders. As Fu Manchu is the most important exhibit in this museum, it is the "authenticity" of his performance that inspires readers' confidence in the rest of the exhibits. The framing provided by a metropolis and the careful deployment of current events lends credibility to the wonders populating Rohmer's fantasy museum. The series constructs the museum slowly, careful to take visitors through already familiar parts of the display before introducing new and stranger sights. Just as museum exhibits gradually took on thematic organization, the rooms in Rohmer's museum of wonders annexed various parts of the world and turned them into displays that both edified and frightened their patrons: Limehouse, New York's Chinatown, Haiti, Communist China, the French Riviera, Persia, Venice—all of these places became rooms in a textual edifice dedicated to the specular consumption of racial and cultural difference.

At the end of Fu Manchu movies, the Doctor's voice is always heard threatening his return. His longevity as a character and his various incarnations in popular culture suggest that he has had a lot to say about Western desire and the contexts for Asian American representation. Fu Manchu demands an investigation into the complicated ideological issues of representation that produce the anxiety and desire characteristic of stereotype as a discursive formation. Reading Fu Manchu as a stereotype reflective of a racist agency must involve more than denigrating the negative images he embodies. I do not argue against acknowledging the dangerous ramifications of stereotype, or losing sight of racism's use of stereotype to persecute otherness; rather, I suggest moving beyond denunciations of racist agency to explore the powerful ways in which that expression works to structure the representational frameworks that Asian Americans have necessarily had to engage. To that end, I have tried in this essay to look at Fu Manchu as stereotype in the most productive sense—by recognizing the complicated nature of Rohmer's deployment of the Doctor, with all its intended and unintended ambivalence, as a necessary step toward deconstructing the pervasiveness of stereotype.

Notes

1. Comments by Chan et al. concerning the depiction of Fu Manchu as a homosexual menace are based on the filmic representations of the doctor. According to Frank Chin: "Unlike the white stereotype of the evil black stud, Indian rapist, Mexican macho, the evil of the evil Dr. Fu

Manchu was not sexual but homosexual." The reasons for such an assertion are based on a generic scene drawn from the films: "Dr. Fu, a man wearing a long dress, batting his eyelashes, surrounded by muscular black servants in loin cloths, and with his bad habit of caressingly touching white men on the leg, wrist, and face with his long fingernails is not so much a threat as he is a frivolous offense to white manhood" (1991, 66). *Mask of Fu Manchu* (1932) stages him in all the ways Chin asserts (Rohmer 1970, *Mask)*. See also Kim 1998.

2. Fu Manchu has become so deeply embedded in the Euro-American cultural unconscious that he has attained quasi-mythical, quasi-historical status. Cay van Ash and Elizabeth Rohmer write that "the name of Fu Manchu had [by 1932] become a household word, to the extent that many people had a tentative belief in his physical existence" (1972, 215). A letter sent to the U.S. State Department signed "President of the Si-Fan" warranted the attention of the FBI, who wrote Rohmer for information about the organization.

3. Malibu Graphics has reprinted a series of 1930s newspaper comics that feature Fu Manchu. For a discussion of Fu Manchu's influence on creating pulp fiction's Dr. Wu-Fang and Dr. Yen Sin, see Hutchinson 1991.

4. Smith's colonial appointment to Burma is significant. As Maung Htin Aung writes in his study of Anglo-Burmese relations, "the period 1890 to 1920 could be termed the Golden Period of British rule [in Burma]" (95). After four years of fighting, for about thirty years Anglo-Burmese relations were represented as a model of imperial rule, where "the British officials did not air a sense of superiority, [and] the Burmese, in turn, did not come to acquire an inferiority complex against the new rulers" (1965, 96).

5. The hyphen was dropped from Fu Manchu's name after the first three novels.

6. The popular critical reviews treated Rohmer more kindly. The *Bookman* review of *The Insidious Dr. Fu-Manchu* found it "a very creditable specimen of its kind, . . . [which] fulfills all the requirements the most exacting reader of that type of fiction could demand" (Phillips 306). The *New York Times Book Review* of 6 July 1929 concluded in "Secret Egypt," its review of *Tales of Secret Egypt:* "If you like to dream over the fascinating Orient, with its hashish and perfumes, its veiled ladies and eunuchs, its harems and lattices, its bazaars and mosques, its tombs and its mummies, you will revel in these Eastern tales" (358).

7. Robert Briney has identified the twenty-nine episodes in the first three novels as adventures where Nayland Smith and Dr. Petrie are either "a) menaced by one of Fu-Manchu's exotic death-traps, b) captured by his agents, or c) engaged in trying to foil a murderous attempt on the life of someone who Knows Too Much" (1970, 47–48). Christopher Frayling outlines nine plot elements common to these same three books (1973, 70).

8. Elizabeth Sax Rohmer revealed that Rohmer "could not sit through the film versions of his work" and according to Frayling, "the Karloff adaptation (*The Mask of Fu Manchu*, MGM 1932) is more blatantly racist than anything Rohmer ever wrote ('Kill all the white men and take their women!')" (1973, 74).

9. Fu Manchu often laments that his position as an unrecognized minority in relation to the British and U.S. governments brands him a criminal rather than a diplomat working on behalf of an internationally recognized organization. At times, the books do expose the hypocrisy of distinguishing between Fu Manchu's projects and the political activity of national governments represented by Smith (see Rohmer 1939, 1971).

10. Miscegenation is confronted directly in the texts, although subsumed as part of an orientalizing project. The penchant oriental women have for forming sudden and mysterious attachments to Western men reinforces the feminization of the Orient, as well as bolsters the image of Western masculinity.

11. This sympathetic rendering of part-Chinese characters might have much to do with the fact that *Emperor Fu Manchu* takes place in China. In the face of "Chinese-Chinese," McKay and Cameron-Gordon, both extensively influenced by U.S. culture, are repositioned within the oppositional economy of the books.

Works Cited

Altick, Richard D. 1978. *The Shows of London*. Cambridge: Harvard University Press, Belknap Press.

Anderson, Benedict. 1991. *Imagined Communities*. Rev. ed. London: Verso.

Aung, Mating Htin. 1965. *The Stricken Peacock: Anglo-Burmese Relations, 1752–1948*. The Hague: Martinus Nijhoff.

Bhabha, Homi K. 1994. "The Other Question: Stereotype, Discrimination, and the Discourse of Colonialism." In *The Location of Culture*, 66–84. London: Routledge.

Brien, Alan. 1985. "My Enemy's Enemies." *New Statesman* 109, 2827 (24 May): 32.

Briney, Robert E. 1970. "Sax Rohmer: An Informal Survey." In *The Mystery Writer's Art*, ed. Francis H. Nevins Jr., 42–78. Bowling Green, Ohio: Bowling Green University Popular Press.

Cawelti, John G. 1976. *Adventure, Mystery, and Romance: Formula Stories as Art and Popular Culture*. Chicago: University of Chicago Press.

Chan, Jeffrey Paul, Frank Chin, Lawson Fusao Inada, and Shawn Wong, eds. 1991. *The Big Aiiieeeee! An Anthology of Chinese American and Japanese American Literature*. New York: Penguin.

Chin, Frank. 1972. "Confessions of a Chinatown Cowboy." *Bulletin of Concerned Asian Scholars* 4, 3: 58–70.

Frayling, Christopher. 1973. "Criminal Tendencies—II: Sax Rohmer and the Devil Doctor." *London Magazine* 13, 2 (June/July): 65–80.

Horseman, Reginald. 1981. *Race and Manifest Destiny: The Origins of American Racial Anglo-Saxonism*. Cambridge: Harvard University Press.

Hutchinson, Don. 1991. *It's Raining Corpses in Chinatown*. Mercer Island, Wash.: Stannont.

JanMohamed, Abdul R. 1983. *Manichean Aesthetics: The Politics of Literature in Colonial Africa*. Amherst: University of Massachusetts Press.

Kim, Daniel. 1998. "The Strange Love of Frank Chin." In *Q & A: Queer in Asian America,* ed. David Eng and Alice Y. Hom, 270–303. Philadelphia: Temple University Press.

Kim, Elaine. 1982. *Asian American Literature: An Introduction to the Writings and Their Social Context*. Philadelphia: Temple University Press.

Lagden, Sir Godfrey. 1924. *The Native Races of the Empire*. London: W. Collins.

Lee, Rachel. 1997. "Journalistic Representations of Asian Americans and Literary Responses, 1910–1920." In *An Interethnic Companion to Asian American Literature,* ed. King-kok Cheung. Cambridge: Cambridge University Press.

Mackenzie, John M. 1984. *Propaganda and Empire: The Manipulation of British Public Opinion, 1880–1960*. Studies in Imperialism. Manchester: Manchester University Press.

Moy, James S. *Marginal Sights: Staging the Chinese in America*. Studies in Theatre History and Culture. Iowa City: University of Iowa Press.

Phillips, Ralph Hobart. 1913. "Sax Rohmer's 'The Insidious Dr. Fu-Manchu'." *Bookman*, November, 305–6.

Rohmer, Sax. 1929. *The Hand of Fu Manchu.* In *The Book of Fu Manchu,* 189–308. New York: McBride.

———. 1929. *The Return of Dr. Fu Manchu.* In *The Book of Fu Manchu,* 91–187. New York: McBride.

———. 1933. *Fu Manchu's Bride.* Garden City, N.Y.: Doubleday, Doran.

———. 1936. *President Fu Manchu.* Garden City, N.Y.: Sun Dial Press.

———. 1939. *The Drums of Fu Manchu.* Garden City, N.Y.: Doubleday, Doran.

———. 1959. *Emperor Fu Manchu.* London: Herbert Jenkins.

———. 1966. *The Trail of Fu Manchu.* 1934. New York: Pyramid.

———. 1970. *The Insidious Dr. Fu Manchu.* 1913. New York: Pyramid.

———. 1970. *The Mask of Fu Manchu.* 1932. New York: Pyramid.

———. 1971. *The Island of Fu Manchu.* 1940. New York: Pyramid.

———. 1986. *The Daughter of Fu Manchu.* 1931. New York: Zebra-Kensington.

Shohat, Ella, and Robert Stam. 1994. *Unthinking Eurocentrism: Multiculturalism and the Media.* London: Routledge.

Thompson, Jon. 1993. *Fiction, Crime, and Empire: Clues to Modernity and Postmodernism.* Urbana: University of Illinois Press.

Torgovnick, Marianna. 1990. *Gone Primitive: Savage Intellects, Modern Lives.* Chicago: University of Chicago Press.

van Ash, Cay, and Elizabeth Sax Rohmer. 1972. *Master of Villainy: A Biography of Sax Rohmer.* Bowling Green, Ohio: Bowling Green University Popular Press.

Watson, Colin. 1979. *Snobbery with Violence: English Crime Stories and Their Audience.* London: Eyre Metheun.

Wordsworth, William. 1971. *The Prelude: A Parallel Text.* Edited by J. C. Maxwell. London: Harmondsworth.

Wu, William F. 1982. *The Yellow Peril: Chinese Americans in American Fiction, 1850–1940.* New York: Archon.

Meredith Wood

15   Footprints from the Past: Passing Racial Stereotypes in the Hardy Boys

In the early 1900s, Edward Stratemeyer founded a publishing empire that ultimately produced more than thirteen hundred juvenile novels in 125 different series under a variety of pseudonyms. Many of these series continued for decades and some endure today, including the landmark *Nancy Drew, Bobbsey Twins, Tom Swift,* and *Hardy Boys* series (see Watson 1991, 50), with total sales of more than two hundred million—approximately half of which belong to the Nancy Drew and Hardy Boys series. The books were written during years of economic, military, and social crises, were conceived largely by one man, and targeted readers who looked to them for both entertainment and an understanding of the world in which they were coming of age. Despite the variety of characters in these texts, including soldiers, pilots, nurses, and school children, all of Stratemeyer's books celebrate the deeds of young white people who succeed through individual effort and determination—perhaps the author's vision of his own publishing success. In short, because the texts addressed children but were written, designed, and sold by white adults, they provide an excellent opportunity to examine how ideas about race, nation, gender, and sexuality were constructed and communicated during the first half of the twentieth century.

This essay looks at a single text in the Hardy Boys series in its historical context to begin an assessment of the Stratemeyer Syndicate's significance and its impact on U.S. culture.[1] *Footprints under the Window* was issued under the pen name "Franklin W. Dixon" in 1933, at the height of virulent anti-Asian sentiment and legislation. The plot concerns the disappearance of the brothers' Chinese-American laundryman, and their subsequent attempt to foil a smuggling operation in their hometown of Bayport. The brothers' wealthy upbringing, gender expression, and race are presented as indexes of their Americanness; in contrast, the Chinese American men in the novel are represented as effeminate and as a threat to both national security and white heteromasculinity. Sex and gender stereotypes function as vehicles through which racial supremacy and nationalism are asserted. While many scholars have pointed out that stereotypes of Asian American men as either sexually threatening or sexually impotent have social, political, and historical consequences, the use of stereotypes in this novel is complicated by the specter of homo-eroticism (see Okihiro 1991; R. Lee 1999; Fung 1998, 115–134). Foregrounding the text's use of racial and sexual passing, and the links between racial and sexual stereotypes, this essay reveals the centrality of heterosexuality to the maintenance of white supremacy and to discourses of Americanness during the 1930s (see also Somerville 2000). I also suggest a difficult question facing lesbian, gay, and queer Asian American scholars today: Is it possible to combat racist stereotypes that link Asian maleness with homosexuality without reinscribing heterosexuality as both an American and an Asian norm?

Edward Stratemeyer and the Birth of the Stratemeyer Syndicate

Edward Stratemeyer, the product of an idealized American youth, was born in Eliza-beth, New Jersey, in 1862 to white, middle-class parents of German decent. The short story "Victor Horton's Great Idea," which he wrote on a sheet of brown wrapping paper while working in his uncle's tobacco store, was published in 1889 in the popular boys' magazine *Golden Days* and earned Stratemeyer seventy-five dollars. In 1893, Strate-meyer was offered an editorial position at the magazine's publisher, Street and Smith, where he wrote numerous adventure stories about young white boys of humble origins who traveled the world and achieved success through hard work and virtuous charac-ter, a theme popularized in the Horatio Alger and Oliver Optic books Stratemeyer enjoyed as a child. Stratemeyer's career accelerated in the late 1890s when he began using current events as the background for his stories of young white male achievement. Literary historian Bruce Watson claims that the idea originated with Stratemeyer's edi-tor, who asked the writer to create a story about the Spanish-American War—a mili-tary action notable for its accompanying propaganda—that would make it accessible to children (Watson 1991, 54). *Under Dewey at Manila; or, The War Fortunes of a Cast-away* was released only a few days after Commodore Dewey opened fire in Manila Bay; the text was immediately and enormously popular, with four printings in 1898 alone, and Stratemeyer used it to inaugurate his Old Glory children's series.

Under Dewey at Manila focused on the daring and patriotic endeavors of a young white boy who escaped poverty and boredom by stowing away on a navy vessel, where he was soon pressed into service by wartime casualties and performed heroically. Strate-meyer continued the theme of a young boy's coming of age through military service in later novels: The Old Glory series included stories of boys who fought in the "jungles of Luzon" and on battleships at sea. One boy even accompanied Theodore Roosevelt on his charge up San Juan Hill. In 1899, Stratemeyer released a second successful series; "The Adventures of the Rover Boys" followed a trio of brothers who were world trav-elers, thrill seekers, and moralists. Their success provided Stratemeyer with the financial stability to begin his own publishing company, the Stratemeyer Syndicate. Multiple-hero series like the Rovers emphasized leadership and teamwork, skills Stratemeyer thought young men needed to be successful in the more industrialized twentieth century.[2] In 1910, the Rovers' pal Tom Swift received his own series. Swift was a boy genius who invented a submarine, a telescope, and a giant cannon to guard the Panama Canal (Watson 1991, 56). Like the Old Glory series, Stratemeyer's Rover Boys and Tom Swift series offered their young male readers stories that featured heroes their own age, settings that seemed realistic, and plots that related to the preservation of national security. By suggesting that U.S. cultural and military supremacy was threatened by foreign countries, and that hard-working young white boys were responsible for the defense of the nation, the Old Glory series, the Adventures of the Rover Boys, and the Tom Swift, Boy Genius series prefaced a project of cultural consolidation that continued with Stratemeyer's legendary Hardy Boys series.

The Hardy Boys and the Assertion of Racial and (Hetero)Sexual Supremacy

Stratemeyer's early series succeeded because they allowed their young readers a role in contemporary world affairs. By identifying with the Rovers, Tom Swift, and the heroes of the Old Glory series, readers vicariously participated in the expansion of U.S. military and economic influence. But the popularity of these series was also facilitated by changing demographics in the United States. By 1899, nearly half of the nation's population was under twenty, and Stratemeyer's novels tapped into the anxiety and excitement Anglo-Americans believed the "closing of the frontier" and the impending twentieth century held for young people (Watson 1991, 56). Many members of Stratemeyer's target audience—young white boys between the ages of eight and thirteen—also enjoyed economic and cultural privilege. The advent of child labor laws and the establishment of compulsory schooling institutionalized adolescence as a time between childhood and adulthood when young people were encouraged to develop interests and talents outside the family. According to Watson, the burgeoning youth population, the advent of a new youth culture, prewar U.S. industrialism, and military and economic expansion fueled the desire for Stratemeyer's work:

> Stratemeyer stumbled upon a formula that would define juvenile fiction for the next 50 years. In the first decade of the new century, airplanes, cars, radios, and movies entered the public imagination. Peary reached the North Pole, miners flocked to the Alaskan frontier, and American inventors, statesmen, and athletes dominated the headlines. Suddenly, "rags-to-riches" was no longer the only dream. Adolescents trapped in a classroom, tenement, or city yearned to journey to distant lands, go to college, toy with technology, play in the major leagues. (1991, 56)

Stratemeyer's texts were part of a project of cultural consolidation. Like U.S. military and economic missions in Asia, South America, and the Caribbean, Stratemeyer's texts provided readers with access to "unknown" lands and confirmation of the superiority of whiteness, heterosexuality, maleness, and capitalism. Stratemeyer's series lauded the United States as a land of unencumbered opportunity—at least for young white men. Throughout World War I and during the chaotic 1920s, Stratemeyer's works assured readers that hard work, dedication, and determination would lead to success. By suggesting that the only impediment to good fortune was laziness, Stratemeyer camouflaged the existence of race, sex, and religious oppression and economic disparity. On the surface, his texts ignored the social and economic changes taking place in the United States at that time: African American migration from the South; the eradication of American Indian languages, religions, and cultures with the institutionalization of boarding schools; massive immigration from eastern and southern Europe; agitation for women's suffrage; and widespread agricultural failure coupled with the rise of Fordism. But why would Stratemeyer abandon the historically based children's novels that established his career? The answer, of course, is that he didn't: The social and cultural changes of the 1920s and 1930s formed the unacknowledged background, rather than the primary setting, of Stratemeyer's Hardy Boys series. That is, though the brothers did not participate in military expeditions or invent weapons for the protection of U.S. resources, the social and economic changes of the 1920s and 1930s were manifest in the novels through challenges to the Hardys' white, heterosexual privilege by characters of color.

The Hardy boys' 1927 debut, *The Tower Treasure*, was published only three years before Stratemeyer's death in 1930.[3] Frank and Joe Hardy are the teenage sons of Fenton Hardy, a renowned New York City police detective who has retired to his suburban home in Bayport to work as a private detective. Bayport's exact location is never identified, but its proximity to New York City and the brothers' frequent travel by train suggests that Bayport is in the metropolitan area—perhaps in Stratemeyer's home state of New Jersey.[4] Unlike their fictional counterpart, the "girl sleuth" Nancy Drew, the Hardy boys are identified as "amateur detectives." The distinction is significant: Unlike Drew, the brothers do not get involved in cases simply because they stumble upon them. Rather, they are asked for help by their father and often by their father's clients. In *Footprints under the Window*, for example, the brothers are approached by shipping magnate Orrin North after he learns that their father is unavailable to assist him. Initially reluctant to hire the brothers, North eventually agrees. The absence of Fenton Hardy, though, is only temporary; a typical Hardy Boys mystery involves father and sons unwittingly working on the same case. At a novel's conclusion, their investigations overlap; father and sons determine a suspect's guilt separately, then jointly apprehend him. The relationship between Frank and Joe and their father suggests the paternalistic relationship between the brothers and their friends and clients. As a paragon of white, male, heterosexual authority, the Hardys are responsible for protecting their friends and family. By identifying with the Hardy brothers and following their investigation, young white male readers respect and validate authority, both Fenton Hardy's and the state's. Stratemeyer's strategic use of the mystery formula—a literary convention predicated upon the revelation of "truth"—further encourages readers to see the world as the Hardys do. Their beliefs, values, and most importantly, their race, class, and gender privilege, are presented as normal. Feminist critic Sherrie Inness argues that texts like the Hardy Boys are a pivotal site for the maintenance of hegemony: "[They] present an adult-centric view of the world, which gains legitimacy by simply being presented as 'natural' or 'real'" (1998, 108).

Racial Passing and Sexual Crossing in
Footprints under the Window

Footprints under the Window, published in 1933, is the first of three texts issued by the Stratemeyer Syndicate during the Depression in which the Hardy boys battle villains who are explicitly identified by their racial backgrounds. In *The Mark on the Door* (1934), the brothers travel to the Southwest, where their investigation is thwarted by both Mexican Americans and American Indians. In a stunning reversal of historical fact, the Hardys are nearly lynched by an "angry Negro mob" in *The Hidden Harbor Mystery* (1935). In all three texts, the brothers' success as detectives is facilitated by their race, class, and sexual privilege. They have the time and money to abandon school while pursuing cases throughout the country; witnesses place their unwavering trust in the Hardys because their whiteness and masculinity command respect; and the brothers' father is an agent of the state. And yet, while sexuality and gender are not entirely absent from racist stereotypes in *The Mark on the Door* and *The Hidden Harbor Mystery,* they are not pivotal to the outcome of the Hardys' investigation, as they are in *Footprints under the Window.* As we will see, this suggests the inextricability of race and gender in Asian American stereotypes (see Leong 1996; Lim-hing 1994; Ratti 1993; Chin et al. 1993; Eng and Hom 1998). As David Eng and Alice Hom state in the introduction to *Q&A: Queer in Asian America:*

> The integration of sexuality into Asian American Studies has widespread implications for the historiography of both fields, bringing to bear a number of pressing issues: how race and queerness intersect at cross purposes in the articulation of historical events; how racial difference is sublimated into and masked by questions of sex and sexual difference in the narrating of history, the writing of it, and the production of subjects and cultures; how race and queerness merge—how they collide—in the fields of the psychic, the social, and the material. (1998, 4)

Footprints under the Window commences with the visit of the Hardy brothers' tyrannical aunt Gertrude while their parents are away. This compels the boys to take their dirty linen to Sam Lee, "the best Chinese laundryman in town" (F. Dixon 1933, 4).[5] Lee's excellence in the stereotypically feminine profession of domestic labor is contrasted with the teenage sleuths' budding white, upper-middle-class masculinity. The reader is asked to accept that Frank and Joe can drive automobiles, pilot airplanes, handle firearms, and decipher codes but cannot operate a washing machine. From the outset of the novel, Sam Lee is positioned as inferior to the Hardy brothers, and as the best Chinese laundryman, his race and occupation are indelibly linked in the brothers' minds. But Lee's employment also affects the brothers' interpretation of his gender, and when their clothes are dirty, they easily substitute his labor for their absent mother's.

On the way to the laundry the brothers encounter their friend Chet Morton, who upon seeing their laundry bag breaks into a chorus of "Washee? Washee? Any colla's today?" (4). In *Strangers from a Distant Shore,* historian Ronald Takaki notes that the "Chinese laundryman" was a fixture in urban areas with large Chinese American populations for a number of reasons. By the 1920s, Takaki notes, Chinese agricultural laborers had been pushed from small towns and the general labor market by racist labor and immigration laws and had begun to develop a Chinese ethnic economy based in the service industry. Laundries were hard work; in 1870 only 8 percent of all Chinese American workers were so employed. But by 1928 this number had risen to 28 percent, and in New York City the number rose to 38 percent in 1940 (Takaki 1989, 240). Laundry work provided many Chinese Americans with the opportunity to be their own employers and to work with other members of the Chinese American community without facing overt racial and economic discrimination. For many whites, this concentration of Chinese labor in one industry may have seemed unusual and perhaps threatening. Takaki concludes that for white youth like Chet Morgan, "the 'Chinese laundryman' seemed to become ubiquitous in U.S. cities, he became the object of ridicule and stereotyping. He talked 'funny' and was fond of eating a strange delicacy—dead rats" (241). In *Footprints,* Chet's mimicry of pidgin English reflects his limited understanding of Chinese American culture, his ignorance of U.S. politics and immigration law, and the belief by the majority of the Euro-American population in 1930 that all Chinese Americans spoke with "funny" accents and worked in laundries solely because they either enjoyed or excelled at the demanding labor.

Chet Morton is part of a recurring set of friends in the Hardy Boys series that also includes Tony Prito, Jerry Gilroy, and Phil Cohen. These latter three form a literal trio of the early-twentieth-century white ethnic immigrant groups: Italian Americans, Irish Americans, and Jews. Unlike the Chinese Americans, who Chet claims "stick together," these white ethnics are able to assimilate into [white] America through their association with the Hardy boys, an assimilation that is facilitated in part by the presence of Asian and African Americans, Latinos, and American Indians as the racial other against which the friends' newfound whiteness acquires value (see Rogin 1992). By continually helping the Hardys with their investigations, Tony, Jerry, and Phil both support the brothers' ideological project and validate the brothers' race and class authority; the friends "become" American by assisting the all-American Hardy boys.

Chet tells the boys that Sam Lee no longer runs the laundry, that he "sold out to another Chinaman a while back," the evil Louie Fong. Chet thinks Fong has a "wicked grin," but the brothers "don't care what he looks like. If he's in the laundry business [they] have a job for him and the sooner he gets started on it the better" (4–5). But as the rest of the mystery unfolds, it becomes increasingly obvious that the brothers care very much what Fong looks like, because it is their belief in the physical manifestation of race that distinguishes the "good guys" from the "bad guys" in Hardy Boys texts, and in so doing inscribes racial stereotypes for youthful white readers.[6]

At the laundry, Sam Lee's name is still on the sign. "Ordinarily Sam Lee would come hurrying forward to serve them, quiet, friendly, and smiling. There would be much joking and high-pitched chatter among Sam Lee's helpers beyond the partition in the back. But now no one came" (5). The brothers have to repeatedly bang on the counter for service. They then hear voices in a back room, including one that is "obviously white," which they believe explains "the fact that [the other men] speak in pidgin English" (6).

Suddenly there is "a sharp exclamation in Chinese, then a silence. A swift pattering of slippers on the floor heralded the approach from beyond the counter of the most villainous-looking Oriental the boys had ever seen. He had a long, lean face with high cheekbones. His head was pointed and almost bald, while a cruel mouth was partly concealed by a drooping wisp of mustache. His eyes were as cold and glittering as those of a snake" (6). Such a description is not far from the one Takaki offers as a popular racist stereotype:

> According to white children . . . the Chinese laundryman chased white children with a red-hot iron and did all kinds of mysterious and sinister things in the back room of the laundry. He was the kidnapper of little boys, carrying them away in bags to unknown places. He became a neighborhood's Fu Manchu—the spooky crook, the bad guy, associated with murder and the darkness of the night. (1989, 241)

Louie Fong *is* Fu Manchu to the Hardy boys—he has the same "sinister" look, the same accent, and importantly for illustrated editions of this text, the same mustache. Adolescent white readers are invited—in the same way that a mystery book, by its very structure, invites the reader to solve it—to make their own comparison between Fu Manchu and Louie Fong, and between the fictional villain and any Chinese American they may meet in their own lives. The racialized evil of the Chinese laundryman becomes the foil against which the Hardy boys' all-American [white] good looks and actions play out. Fong's defeat at the end of the novel is, for Stratemeyer, the Hardy boys, and the white child reader, the logical outcome of the struggle between good and evil embodied in white and Asian bodies.

In contrast, the missing Sam Lee represents what cultural critic Gary Okihiro has called "Charlie Chan" to Louie Fong's "Fu Manchu." The brothers recall that Lee was deferent and friendly, and that he smiled when he served the brothers. Because of Aunt Gertrude's visit and the temporary absence of their mother, the brothers are forced to undertake domestic duties that are usually done for them as affluent white men in U.S. society by an underclass of people of color and, to a lesser extent, by white women. Lee's apparent willingness to "serve" the Hardy boys feminizes him in the brothers' eyes, because he undertakes labor that the brothers associate with their mother and aunt. Okihiro notes that Charlie Chan is also "feminine. He is led by a white man, speaks with a broken tongue, and is docile and polite to a fault" (1991, 144). Film director and cultural critic Richard Fung argues that depictions of Chan and Manchu are also explicitly sexualized:

> Asian men—at least since Sessue Hayakawa, who made a Hollywood career in the 1920s representing the Asian man as sexual threat—have been consigned to one of two categories: the egghead/wimp, or—in what may be analogous to the lotus blossom-dragon lady dichotomy—the kung fu master/ninja/samurai. He is sometimes dangerous, sometimes friendly, but almost always characterized by desexualized Zen asceticism. (1998, 117)

In the text, these stereotypes govern the Hardy Boys' relationship with Chinese Americans. While they view Louie Fong as threatening and aloof, they eroticize Sam Lee, believing him to be both deferent and available. He stands in for stereotypes of "passive" Asian women; film critic Renee Tajima notes that such stereotypes are characterized by Asian women's "willingness to serve as love interests for white men" (1984, 29). The brothers' feelings for Lee are soon made evident to the reader. Upon learning that Sam Lee is gone, the Hardy boys act like jilted lovers; they feel betrayed and bemoan Lee's having "sold out his laundry to another man" (F. Dixon 1933, 4).

When the brothers arrive to meet their aunt's ship, Aunt Gertrude fails to appear. Instead, a young man named Sidney Pebbles disembarks to tell the brothers of her mishap; Aunt Gertrude had fallen down some stairs and missed the boat. In relaying this information, Pebbles misses his own ferry, and the boys offer him a spare room at their home until the morning ferry departs. Pebbles is a mysterious individual; when the boys first notice him outside the terminal, he is talking with two Chinese men. Despite the fact that there are only two Asian Americans among dozens of passengers and that the two men have done nothing suspicious, the brothers feel that they're "bound to bump into a Chinaman at every turn" (9). Such a statement echoes racist fears of an Asian "invasion" in the 1930s: Anti-Chinese sentiment was a staple of U.S. popular culture during the Depression, and newspapers and comic books encouraged fears of a Yellow Peril with cartoon heroes like Buck Rogers battling "Mongol hordes." (Historian Roger Daniels defines the Yellow Peril as "an irrational fear of Oriental conquest, with its racist and sexist fantasy overtones" [qtd. in Okihiro 1991, 119]).

Curiously, Pebbles departs from the brothers' house in the middle of the night and appears to have taken some of their father's papers with him. Outside the bedroom window they discover footprints (hence the book's title) and a small slip of paper with Chinese characters on it. Because of racial stereotyping, the Hardys initially wonder if the paper is a laundry check, and if the missing houseguest is somehow in league with Louie Fong. No mention is made of how the boys know the characters to be Chinese and not, say, Japanese. One imagines that the presence of two Asian American groups in Bayport is simply beyond the scope of the brothers' (and author's) imagination. Perhaps Stratemeyer purposely displaces Japanese and other Asian Americans; with no defined economic role in the suburb, they literally vanish. Such presumptions—that the note is written in Chinese, that it must therefore be a laundry check and thus must belong to Louie Fong, who is their laundryman—illustrates how the brothers' ability to solve a crime is dependent upon their being able identify the written characters as Chinese and the book's Chinese American figures' threatening character (distinguishing social and moral qualities). It is the Hardy boys' reliance on racist stereotypes that provides them with the knowledge to solve the ensuing crime; in their minds, Pebbles's laundry check is not a coincidence, but evidence of a racial conspiracy.[7]

Chet arrives to tell the boys that a fight broke out at the municipal pier after the brothers left the night before, involving scuffling—surprise—"Chinamen." The police have failed to arrest a suspect because no one involved will talk about the fight's cause, despite another Bayport Chinese American resident, Tom Wat, having been stabbed. Chet is not surprised: "They're a secretive crowd. . . . They like to settle their little quarrels in their own way without getting mixed up with the law. I doubt if the police will ever know just why that battle began" (49).

Chinese Americans are depicted as secretive and clannish, living outside the European-based U.S. legal system and subject to only their own laws. Throughout the novel, this fight, and others like it, are referred to as "feuds," harking back to some primitive *feudal* society. And because it is a fight between nonwhites, it is trivialized: Despite a town resident having been stabbed, the event is a "little quarrel." The implication of a "secretive crowd" in this context is deceit and trickery, not stoicism and teamwork. In other novels, when the brothers and their white friends decide against involving the police, they are lauded for settling things themselves; when Chinese Americans do it in this text, they're being secretive. That the brothers and their friends believe that they are able to solve things among themselves elides the real power of the law over Asian Americans and underscores the privilege the Hardys enjoy in the legal system: As young white men, they can be certain that the law recognizes their authority to settle disputes.

Eventually the boys' aunt Gertrude appears; she had been drugged on the ferry by Sidney Pebbles and slept through her Bayport stop, arriving the next morning on the ferry's return trip. When the brothers stop by the laundry, they find out that Louie Fong has mysteriously closed it. Annoyed, the Hardys return home, where they are soon visited by Orrin North, a local shipping magnate. North hopes to secure an audience with their father; when Frank and Joe remark that their parents are out of town, North at first declines their offer of help. But he suddenly changes his mind and asks the Hardys to investigate the scuffles outside the ferry terminal; he thinks the disagreements might be part of a smuggling ring operating out of Bayport. The brothers tell North of their experience outside the ferry terminal the previous night and are surprised when North claims to know both Sidney Pebbles and his place of employment: a Chinese roadhouse called Lantern Land.

At the roadhouse the boys meet Sidney Pebbles, who turns out not to have been the Sidney Pebbles who stayed—and subsequently vanished—from their home a few nights before: Pebbles believes that someone is masquerading as him, for unknown reasons. The Hardys are confused by Sidney Pebbles's identity, and they are not alone. An injured Tom Wat appears at Lantern Land and claims to recognize Pebbles from the fight at the ferry building the night before. Though it is clear to the Hardys that they have never seen Pebbles before, and that Pebbles was not part of the fight they witnessed at the ferry the previous evening, Wat inverts racist assumptions that "all Asians look alike" by failing to distinguish Pebbles from other white men. As Wat, Pebbles, and the Hardy boys sort out the night's events, a knife comes hurtling through the bushes and barely misses killing Wat. A brief but futile chase through the undergrowth leaves the brothers with a fleeting glimpse of the man who propelled it: Louie Fong. Despite the urgings of Pebbles and the boys, Wat refuses to go to the police.

> The little Chinaman seemed convinced that there was no hope for him. Even Louie Fong's arrest would not save him from revenge and death at the hands of the leaders, and a cruel, heartless death it would be. "I think you ought to tell the police," advised Frank seriously.

Tom Wat would not hear of this. He shook his head. "Chinaboy no tellee police," he declared. "No good. Cause plenty trouble." (104)

Wat's distrust of the police, his small physical stature, and his pidgin English are signifiers of his Asianness. Yet they also mark him as feminine. Perhaps because these traits make him seem vulnerable—Wat cannot defend himself from injustice—the Hardy boys volunteer to protect him, to apprehend Fong, and to get to the bottom of the "other" Sidney Pebbles and the disappearance of their father's papers. To accomplish these tasks, the boys need to conceal Wat at their home. Fearful that Fong or his companions are still nearby, they plan to disguise Wat—as a woman. Says Frank, "We can dress him up as a girl. He's just the type" (106).

But what "type" is this? Frank believes that Wat can pass as female. But pass to *whom*? Despite the fact that Wat needs to be secreted from Louie Fong—another Asian man—the brothers force Wat to dress as a woman. Clearly, the boys think that white people will be fooled by the disguise, because as an Asian male, Wat is portrayed as physically small, and this makes him appear feminine to the brothers. If young readers are still unsure of the difference between Asian American and white men, the narrator makes it clear. Wat is "slight of build, with a sallow, effeminate face" (93). By disguising Wat as a woman, the Hardys seemingly assert their heterosexuality, since the hallmark of much detective fiction is the male hero's quest to save a defenseless woman. Wat's disguise thus foregrounds white heterosexuality and femininity as cultural norms. But it also eroticizes the relationship between the brothers and Wat, who they know is really a man.

Cultural critic King-Kok Cheung argues (without distinguishing among "women") that "the racist treatment of Asian [men] has taken the peculiar form of sexism—in so far as the indignities suffered by men of Chinese descent are analogous to those traditionally suffered by women" (1996, 147). The Hardy boys' imposition of a female disguise upon Tom Wat underscores their perception of him as already effeminate. Because Wat is repeatedly identified as "little," the (white) reader understands that he cannot pass for a white man, and because Wat cannot possibly pass for a white man, he is instead forced by the Hardy brothers into drag. This reaffirms the brothers' belief that physical appearance determines and reveals character. Despite his joking tone, Frank Hardy is no doubt only expressing what he feels to be the truth when he tries to borrow a uniform from one of the waitresses at Lantern Land to serve as Wat's disguise: "Our friend here decided that he'd like to dress up as a girl" (108). Hardy's racism thus enables him to conflate Wat's "effeminacy" with his own desire: Frank wants to see Wat in a dress; therefore Wat must want to be a girl.

Significantly, Wat's disguise (e)races his Asianness in addition to his maleness. The brothers are spotted with Wat when they drive past Chet and some female friends. Later Chet asks:

"Who is the new girlfriend?"
"What girlfriend?" asked Frank.
"No use pretending you don't know what we're talking about.
The girls know all about it so you may as well 'fess up.
Who was the swell-looking girl you two were driving with this morning?" (115)

Clearly Chet does not recognize that Wat is a man—but he also does not recognize that Wat is *Asian American*. Since everyone in this novel is identified specifically by their race unless they are white, Chet's omission shows that he thinks that Tom Wat in drag is both female *and* white. And his ability to comment on the quality of Wat's disguise (in the 1930s, "swell" was perhaps more of a compliment than it is today) only reinforces Chet's belief in his racial and sexual privilege; he is not uncomfortable evaluating the attractiveness of the brothers' female companion. Not everyone in the novel shares Chet's appraisal of Wat's disguise. On the way to their car, the Hardy boys and Wat bump into "an elderly, near-sighted chambermaid" in the hallway of Lantern Land. After "taking one look at Tom Wat," she declares: "Mercy! It's a female tramp. Mr. Pebbles, get that woman out of here at once" (110). If Tom Wat is able to pass as a white woman up close, then it is only as a white woman of dubious virtue.[8] The suggestion that the brothers are in the company of a prostitute, though clearly played for laughs, further establishes the Hardys' heterosexuality for young male readers. Wat's disguise thus answers questions about why the brothers are so eager to help a man they barely know, and who is not a client of their father. By dressing Wat as a woman, the Hardys reveal to readers what they believe to be his true identity: a damsel in distress. In sum, Tom Wat's disguise is used both to naturalize and to bolster the Hardy boys' whiteness, maleness, and heterosexuality.

A trip back to North's address finally yields the break the Hardy boys have been waiting for: "A light shone from the garage window. Through the glass they had a momentary glimpse of the evil, yellow face of Louie Fong. Then it vanished. They saw the red, square visage of Orrin North, who came over toward the window. A shade was pulled down" (130).

Not only are Orrin North and Louie Fong in cahoots, but the two are engaged in what the narrator calls the vile practice of "smuggling Chinamen." The boys overhear North say to Fong: "You know there's a head tax on every Chinaman that comes into the country. There's good money to be made by any man who can smuggle 'em in" (138). After Fong leaves, the brothers confront North, who maintains his innocence. The brothers don't believe him and stake out Fong's laundry for further evidence. Their efforts are rewarded when Sam Lee emerges onto the street. While Frank goes inside, Joe Hardy follows and confronts Lee, who he thought had left Bayport. After Joe assures Lee that he will tell no one but his brother, Lee confesses:

> Louie Fong is indeed in league with Orrin North. They are smuggling Chinamen into the country. Louie Fong pays North to bring them here in his ships. These men think they will make their fortunes once they are in America. But when they reach here they find that they are the slaves of Louie Fong. . . .
>
> The Chinamen know that they have not entered the country according to law. They know that they will be deported if they are found out. They are afraid of that. When they are taken off the ships they are sent to Louie Fong. He finds work for them. But always he demands part of their wages. . . . They would have saved more money if they paid the head tax in the first place. (164–65)

But of course there was no head tax in 1933, because Chinese immigration was prohibited until 1948. By intentionally misrepresenting immigration policy to young readers, *Footprints under the Window* encourages white Americans' racist fear of the Yellow Peril. The book further suggests that national security depends upon vigilant private citizens like the Hardy boys to guard against the Chinese American presence on their town's shores, even as Bayport's economy depends upon the work of Chinese American men like Sam Lee and Tom Wat. Louie Fong's temporarily successful smuggling operation both undermines the white fraternity of domestic security and challenges the white heteromasculinity of the Hardy boys. To diffuse this threat, Stratemeyer uses Sam Lee, an Asian American character who defers to the brothers' economic and racial authority. This suggests that both whiteness and masculinity are constituted in relation to Asian male bodies: The brothers' recollection of Sam Lee's years of loyal service reassures the Hardys of their ability to thwart Louie Fong and to reassert the status quo.

By telling Joe about the North-Fong partnership, Lee assists the Hardy brothers' investigation. He is neither evil, like Louie Fong, nor reluctant and comical, like Tom Wat. He occupies a middle ground between the other two Chinese American characters in the novel; he is an assimilated Chinese American resident of Bayport, not unlike the brothers' friends with white ethnic immigrant backgrounds. That Lee is a "good" Chinese American is conveyed to readers this way: "Sam Lee had been in the laundry business in Bayport for years. He spoke good English with only a trace of an accent" (162). Unlike Tom Wat and Louie Fong, whose Asianness is indicated to the reader by their physical descriptions, Sam Lee's Americanness is indicated through a description absent of physical signifiers: he is defined by his long-term Bayport residency and "slight" Chinese accent. Cultural critic Gary Okihiro calls such a mediary a "white man's Chinaman." Sam Lee is *necessarily*, rather than *inherently*, good. His willingness to learn English, and to help the brothers—with their investigation now, and with their laundry in the past—represents the "natural superiority" of white American culture. He has abandoned his language, his "foolishness," his "clan-like nature"—those negative things depicted in the book as essentially Chinese.

The Hardys and Lee establish a plan to apprehend Louie Fong: Frank Hardy will infiltrate the smuggling ring—disguised as a "Chinaman." Using his father's collection of disguises, including "a coat, trousers, slippers and a queer, flat hat" and makeup, Frank "soon transformed himself into a very realistic Oriental" (201). The ease with which Frank transforms himself into an "Oriental" should not be contrasted with the difficulty Wat had in pulling off his disguise as a white woman. Rather, Frank strategically employs his disguise to spy—to "observe" rather than to "pass," to be an agent rather than pass[ive]—on Fong and North inside the laundry.

Ultimately, it is Frank's inability to shed the physical manifestations of his white male privilege that lead to his discovery: " 'Mellican boy dress up like Chinaboy,' [Fong] said scornfully. 'Mellican boy talkee Mellican talk in alley.' He laughed derisively. Frank flushed as he realized how they had been caught. Someone had been watching them as they came down the alley. . . . Frank had forgotten that he was supposed to be a Chinaman. He had spoken in his natural tone of voice. Louie's henchmen, then, had lost no time in surrounding the group and taking them prisoners" (208).

Frank Hardy can temporarily adopt an Asian identity, not because he is feminine, but because he is the son of a master of disguise employing racial drag in the service of a larger national project (stopping illegal immigration). However, he cannot conceal his manliness—the masculine *tone* of his voice—and this ultimately reveals his [white male] identity to Fong. In sum, Wat successfully passes because Chinese American men are portrayed as inherently feminine in this work; Hardy fails to pass because as a white man, he is inherently masculine.

Passing, then, operates in a number of ways in this text. Because the Hardy boys are the sons of a master detective, they are understood by their young readers to have mastery over the elements of detection, including the twin practices of concealment and revelation: The brothers must be able to employ disguises *and* recognize the truth. By forcing Tom Wat to wear a dress, the brothers believe they are both concealing his maleness and revealing his effeminacy. In this sense, Wat's disguise is contradictory. It both hides his "true" identity from outsiders and exposes it to the boys. The boys' manipulation of Wat's body and their control over how it will be seen by others demonstrate to readers not only their mastery of the art of detection but their social power as well.

The brothers also need to disguise Wat as a woman in order to contain the threat of interracial homoeroticism. Donning a dress, however, cannot alter Wat's maleness; rather than containing the text's homoeroticism, the disguise instead draws attention to it. Initially Wat's drag paradoxically accentuates the homoeroticism implied by the brothers' chivalrous actions; ultimately, however, Wat's passing allows the Hardys to reinforce their white, heteromasculine stance. Wat is perceived by the brothers' friends to be a white woman, suggesting not only that perceptions about race and gender are interconnected, but that the Hardy boys are "presumed innocent" by Bayport's white citizens: If Wat in disguise passes as a woman, it can only be as a white woman. The brothers' detection skills can be put in service only of a proper heterosexual(ized) relationship; their social standing demands it, and Wat's disguise confirms it. As a white woman, Wat ensures that the boys remain untainted by unsavory social questions that might bring the detectives themselves under suspicion.

Frank Hardy's failure to pass as Chinese American similarly reveals the complicated relationship between race, gender, and sexuality in the text, and again confirms for readers the unassailable social position accorded the brothers. Fong's discovery of Frank is presented as the natural consequence of the young Hardy's budding masculinity (his walk and deep voice), giving him away as white/male/a Hardy boy. And Frank's half-hearted regret over his failed disguise foregrounds his belief in the naturalness of white heteromasculinity: He should have known better than to try and pass as a Chinese American man, because he would "obviously" be discovered. If Wat's passing reveals contradictions and potential fissures in the complex balancing act of social perceptions, the discovery of Frank's white masculinity is meant to be unequivocal and irrefutable.

Joe Hardy and Sam Lee are also captured, and the foursome is soon joined by the "fake" Sidney Pebbles: Henry Pinkerton, a private detective. Fong misjudges the strength of the Hardy boys and the detective, who overpower Fong's guards and run for the laundry's front door at the precise moment Fenton Hardy enters with the police. Hardy had been in Bayport all along, discreetly investigating Fong and North's involvement in the smuggling operation. Unaware of his sons' involvement in the case, he is shocked to find them in the same room with the evil Louie Fong. The brothers are such skilled investigators that their own father couldn't detect them. *Footprints under the Window* ends abruptly with the Hardy family reunited and the narrator promising another mystery soon. In restoring the laundry to Sam Lee's possession and bringing Louie Fong to justice, the Hardy boys vanquish both the smuggling operation and the threat of the Yellow Peril. They return Bayport to its pre-Fong/pre-peril status quo: Tom Wat returns to a neighboring town, and Sam Lee continues in his stereotypical and minor[ity] role as the Chinese laundryman of Bayport.

Racist Stereotypes and the Erasure of Asian American Queerness

To an extent, the racist stereotypes and political agenda of *Footprints* are obvious. What is unusual about this adolescent novel is that racism is made explicit through discourses of sexism and heterosupremacy, and that the brothers' interest in Sam Lee is legitimated through the suggestion of a homosexual relationship—albeit a relationship that can be acknowledged only through the trappings of white heteronormativity. Lesbian and gay historians have recently argued that visible gay, and to a lesser extent lesbian, populations existed in major metropolitan areas like New York during the 1920s and 1930s, and that heterosexuals were well aware of these queer communities and may not have pathologized them (to the extent that lesbians and gays are imagined to have been historically persecuted, at least during the 1920 and 1930s) (see Chauncey 1996).

To the best of my knowledge, "overtly" gay characters are entirely absent from the eighty-year history of the Hardy Boys series. But it is never suggested that gay people do not exist, or that the Hardy boys do not have gay friends (or for that matter, that the Hardys are not gay themselves)—in a series in which even minor challenges to the brothers' superiority are portrayed as threats to be vanquished or overcome.[9]

This is not to say that Sam Lee is gay—or that he is not. Such a statement is important because the refuting and deconstruction of pernicious and virulent anti-Asian stereotypes is a cornerstone of Asian American studies that often obscures the existence of gay, lesbian, bisexual, queer, and transgender Asian and Asian American people. Fung explains the absence this way: "The Asian man is defined by a striking absence down there. And if Asian men have no sexuality, how can we have homosexuality?" (1998, 117). Scholar JeeYeun Lee (1996) similarly asserts that racist stereotypes of Asian women deny the existence of queer female sexuality: By defining Asian women solely through their putative sexual "role" with white men (passive/lotus blossom, aggressive/dragon lady), racist stereotypes deny the possibility that lesbian loves and identities exist. And by failing to validate Asian American lesbians and lesbianism—by refuting what are, in essence, heterosexualized stereotypes without acknowledging heterosexuality's role in imperialism, and heteronormativity's relationship with anti-Asian discrimination—some Asian American scholars condemn racism while leaving heterosupremacy unchallenged.

The Hardy Boys Today

For his part, Edward Stratemeyer succeeded in providing white U.S. youth with the same type of racist and sexist role models he enjoyed in children's books when he was growing up in the 1860s and 1870s. The simplistic mystery formula that he replicated allowed white children to "solve the puzzle" along with the Hardy boys, a process that involves the discovery and reassertion of proper race, sex, and gender roles. The mystery format also promises white male children that individuals perceived to be transgressing the boundaries of heterosexual white masculinity—as Asian men are in this novel—will be "detected" and punished. In 1933, the footprints under the window were not simply Fenton Hardy's (he quickly and silently entered the house and retrieved his own papers after Pinkerton left), but specters of thousands of Asians who were denied the opportunity to immigrate to the United States in the early part of the twentieth century because of the Chinese Exclusion Acts and other xenophobic legislation.[10]

For years after the anti-immigration laws were repealed, racist stereotypes continued to appear in the Hardy Boys and other Stratemeyer Syndicate novels. In the late 1950s Edward Stratemeyer's daughter Harriet Stratemeyer Adams, who had assumed control of the publishing venture after his death, mandated that every book be rewritten to update technological references and to remove ethnic stereotypes and dialect. Her efforts suggest that stereotypes can be "corrected"—that they are merely incidental to the text. But many of the new editions simply swapped one stereotype for another. At the height of the Cuban missile crisis in 1961, *Footprints under the Window* was re-released with an entirely different plot—one that focused on a "swarthy" and "evil" Latin American dictator in control of a small island. Ultimately, Harriet Stratemeyer's revised texts show that racist stereotypes are not incidental but fundamental to the success of the Hardy Boys series. Apparently Grosset and Dunlap, the books' publisher, agrees. In 1991 the reprint rights were sold to Applewood Books, who have begun reissuing the first-edition texts.

Notes

1. The original series—texts Stratemeyer directly helped author—was comprised of thirty-eight volumes published between 1927 and 1959. Twenty additional texts were published between 1959 and 1979. For a complete listing of all Hardy Boys texts and spin-offs, see the Unofficial Hardy Boys Homepage at <http://www.geocities.com/Athens/Atlantis/3191/hb3.htm#top> (2 July 2001).

2. Military-themed novels for boys were also tremendously popular in the years during and immediately after World War II. These series are listed on the back cover of an unidentified 1940s edition of Dixon 1933.

3. In addition to his Rover Boys, Old Glory, and Tom Swift series, Edward Stratemeyer wrote two hundred books in twenty-three other series before his death; he provided loose, formulaic outlines for eight hundred others. The outlines were given to ghostwriters, who were paid fifty dollars per book. Stratemeyer checked the final manuscript for stylistic and ideological consistency; his daughter continued this practice after his death. The names of the ghostwriters were known only to Stratemeyer. For more on the Stratemeyer Syndicate and the relationship between

the Nancy Drew and Hardy Boys series, see Billman 1986; Plunkett-Powell 1993; Johnson 1993; Dizer 1982; Murphy 1991; Watson 1991, 50–56; T. Dixon 1993.

4. It seems consistent with Stratemeyer's race and gender stereotyping to suggest that the locale is an index of the characters' whiteness and heterosexuality; the brothers' residence in suburban New Jersey suggests early "white flight" from New York.

5. Unless otherwise noted, page numbers in parentheses in the text are from F. Dixon 1933.

6. Film critic and director Richard Fung believes that such pernicious stereotypes are widespread and fail to distinguish among Asian peoples: "In North America, stereotyping has focused almost exclusively on what recent colonial language designates as 'Orientals'—that is East and Southeast Asian peoples—as opposed to the 'Orientalism' discussed by Edward Said, which concerns the Middle East. This current popular usage is based more on the perception of similar physical features—black hair, 'slanted' eyes, high cheek bones, and so on" (1998, 123).

7. Many thanks to literary critic/detective Kate Griffin for her assistance in unraveling this passage in the text.

8. Another interpretation of this scene raises a different possibility: that the chambermaid realizes that Wat is Chinese American, but not male. If this is true, then her exclamation—"tramp"—stems from the only relationship she can imagine between the esteemed brothers and Wat: sexual commerce. In both cases, the chambermaid's discomfort alerts readers to the differing ways that discourses of race and gender are being deployed by the Hardy boys. For some readers, this acknowledgment may create the possibility of oppositional readings of the text.

9. An exception is the swishy "Hardly brothers" in Mabel Maney's cleverly queer Cherrie Aimless/Nancy Clue series. Interestingly, the brother's gender is still used to denote their (homo)sexuality. See Maney 1995 and others.

10. Cultural critic Avery F. Gordon calls this significant absence "haunting": "Haunting describes how that which appears to be not there is often a seething presence. . . . The ghost is not simply a dead or missing person, but a social figure, and investigating it can lead to that dense site where history and subjectivity make social life" (1997, 8).

Works Cited

Billman, Carol. 1986. *The Secret of the Stratemeyer Syndicate: Nancy Drew, the Hardy Boys, and the Million Dollar Fiction Factory.* New York: Ungar.

Chauncey, George, Jr. 1996. *Gay New York: Gender and the Making of the Gay Male World, 1919–1949.* New York: Basic.

Cheung, King-Kok. 1996. "The *Woman Warrior* versus *The Chinaman Pacific:* Must a Chinese American Critic Choose Between Feminism and Heroism?" In *Conflicts in Feminism,* ed. Marianne Hirsch and Evelyn Foy-Kellers, 234–51. New York: Routledge 1990. Quoted in Leong 1996, 147.

Chin, Curtis, et al. 1993. "Witness Aloud: Lesbian, Gay, and Bisexual Asian American/Pacific Writings." *Asian/Pacific American Journal* 2, 1: 45–62.

Dixon, Franklin W. [Edward Stratemeyer]. 1933. *Footprints under the Window.* New York: Grosset and Dunlap.

Dixon, "Tex" W. 1993. "Ghost Story." *Texas Monthly,* September, 60–64.

Dizer, John, Jr. 1982. *Tom Swift & Company: "Boys' Books" by Stratemeyer and Others.* Jefferson, N.C.: McFarland.

Eng, David, and Alice Y. Hom, eds. 1998. *Q & A: Queer in Asian America*. Philadelphia: Temple University Press.

Fung, Richard. 1998. "Looking for My Penis: The Eroticized Asian in Queer Video Porn." In Eng and Hom 1998, 115–34.

Gordon, Avery. 1997. *Ghostly Matters: Haunting and the Sociological Imagination*. Minneapolis: University of Minnesota Press.

Inness, Sherrie. 1998. *The Lavender Menace: Ideology, Identity, and the Representation of Lesbian Life*. Amherst: University of Massachusetts Press.

Johnson, Deidre. 1993. *Edward Stratemeyer and the Stratemeyer Syndicate*. New York: Twayne.

Lee, JeeYeun. 1996. "Why Suzie Wong Is Not a Lesbian: Asian and Asian American Lesbian and Bisexual Women and Femme/Butch Gender Identities." In *Queer Studies: An Anthology*, ed. Brett Beemyn and Mickey Eliason, 115–32. New York: New York University Press.

Lee, Robert G. 1999. *Orientals: Asian Americans in Popular Culture*. Philadelphia: Temple University Press.

Leong, Russell, ed. 1996. *Asian American Sexualities: Dimensions of the Gay and Lesbian Experience*. New York: Routledge.

Lim-Hing, Sharon, ed. 1994. *The Very Inside: An Anthology of Writing by Asian and Pacific Islander Lesbian and Bisexual Women*. Toronto: Sister Vision Press.

Maney, Mabel. 1995. *The Case of the Good-for-Nothing Girlfriend*. Pittsburgh: Cleis Press.

Murphy, Cullen. 1991. "Starting Over: The Same Old Stories." *Atlantic*, June, 18–21.

Okihiro, Gary. 1991. *Margins and Mainstreams: Asians in American History and Culture*. Seattle: University of Washington Press.

Plunkett-Powell, Karen. 1993. *The Nancy Drew Scrapbook: 60 Years of America's Favorite Teenage Sleuth*. New York: St. Martin's.

Ratti, Rakesh. 1993. *A Lotus of a Different Color: An Unfolding of the South Asian Gay and Lesbian Experience*. Boston: Alyson.

Rogin, Michael. 1992. "Making America Home: Racial Masquerade and Ethnic Assimilation in the Transition to Talking Pictures." *Journal of American History* 79, 3: 1050–77.

Somerville, Siobhan. 2000. *Queering the Color Line: Race and the Invention of Homosexuality in American Culture*. Durham, N.C.: Duke University Press.

Tajima, Renee. 1984. "Lotus Blossoms Don't Bleed: Images of Asian Women." In *Anthologies of Asian American Film and Video*, 28–33. New Work: Third World Newsreel.

Takaki, Ronald. 1989. *Strangers from a Different Shore: A History of Asian Americans*. New York: Penguin.

Watson, Bruce. 1991. "Tom Swift, Nancy Drew, and Pals All Had the Same Dad." *Smithsonian*, October, 50–61.

Helena Grice

16   Face-ing/De-Face-ing Racism: Physiognomy as Ethnic Marker in Early Eurasian/Amerasian Women's Texts

The body offers potential boundaries to the self. It is a cultural text that can be rewritten to project a particular identity. Yet our bodies are constraining as well as facilitating and may signify in unwanted ways. One recurrent preoccupation in texts both by and about Eurasian/Amerasian women is the question of *visible* racial identity. It is possible to identify a concern with the way that the ethnic subject is "marked" by her physiognomy in texts about Eurasians/Amerasians, from Sui Sin Far's 1911 autobiography to Aimee Liu's recent novel *Face*. These discussions identify a correlation between the body and one's psychology; between the politics of corporeality and the dynamics of selfhood. This is represented in differing ways, but all the representations assert the primacy of the body-as-text, the body as a dominant signifier of one's racial identity. As Maibelle Chung tells her brother in Liu's *Face*: "Aren't you ignoring one fundamental factor? . . . Looks! Skin color. Hair. Eyes. Body type. Far as most whites are concerned, Chinese are Chinese—for that matter, any Oriental is Chinese—and blacks are black. No difference where they were born or what language they speak" (1995, 55).

The discussion of visible racial identity in these texts is contextually specific in that it is a dynamic of cross-cultural engagement. The move on the part of Eurasian and Amerasian women writers to interrogate the relationship between exterior and interior subjectivity relates to their position as liminal ethnic subjects in the United States. Occasionally this exploration may pertain to their position in Asian countries as well. For example, in the case of Sylvia Chen's position in Diana Chang's *The Frontiers of Love* as an Asian American woman in an Asian country places her as much as an outsider there as other Asian Americans felt themselves to be in America.

As the editors of this collection rightly observe, it is important for us to not only (re)collect, remember, but also interpret the past of Asian American culture. Read together, the corpus of texts discussed in this essay function as a record of differing psychological responses to shifting racist environments. As such, they also chart the history of interaction between Eur/Amerasians and Euro-Americans, their reactions and responses to each other, with a particular emphasis upon the first decades of the twentieth century. Thus, for example, the Eurasian sisters Edith and Winnifred Eaton's experience as new ethnic subjects in America at the turn of the century was characterized by feelings of exclusion and inferiority in the face of extreme racism, a racism supported by pseudoscientific discourses of racial hierarchies. Racism is highly durable, however, so a delineation of Eur/Amerasian women's writing up to the present day sadly continues to demonstrate both the potency of racist phenomena and the psychological effects of racism upon ethnic subjects.

In constructing links between texts written as much as eighty years apart, I do not intend to homogenize them: As textual responses to appearance-instigated racism they illustrate historical, geographical, and cultural divergences that should not be erased. It is important, for example, to recognize that the particular situation of early-twentieth-century Eurasian women, whose experience was often characterized by an acute sense of ambivalence, was partly produced by late-nineteenth- and early-twentieth-century anti-miscegenation discourses, the credibility of which had eroded by the time Amerasian writer Aimee Liu published *Face* in 1994. The commonality among these texts is not based on an assumed transhistoric racial/ethnic similarity/sensibility, but is instead predicated on a shared encounter with racism and its concomitant psychoactive effects. Furthermore, these textual rejoinders to racism actually highlight a historical shift in the way that "race" is understood. A historical survey of these texts shows the ways that they are linked to the evolution of discourses of race in the United States from a biological, pseudoscientific understanding to a far less stable interpretation. This shift may alternatively be tracked through a change in the way "race" is understood as a classificatory term, to its more prevalent later usage as a nonspecific signifier of difference. In particular, I want to link my discussion of early Amer/Eurasian women's textual responses to racism, to an understanding of race in relation to physiognomy. I intend to demonstrate that discourses of the "science" of physiognomy surface in many of these earlier works, although they continue to have a residual influence in late-twentieth-century works too, and to suggest why this might be the case.

A Brief History of Physiognomy

Physiognomy, the form of one's features, expression, and body, is also understood as the art of supposedly judging character from facial characteristics. Therefore, although physiognomy may refer simply to corporeal form, it is also used (as I will often use it) specifically in relation to the face. As Thomas F. Gossett (1975) makes clear, there has long existed a science of physiognomy that attempted to link physiognomic characteristics with racial difference. As early as 1610, Giovan Della Ponta published *On the Physiognomy of Man,* an analysis focusing in depth on facial characteristics, which read "facial features as a kind of graphism or writing which in turn is in need of the systematic decoding that physiognomy claimed to provide" (Schiesari 1994, 57). In 1684 a study was made by Francois Bernier on the relationship between the face, the body, and racial classifications. Bernier is held to have coined the term "race," so that from its genesis, "race" has been identified as a form of categorization associated with physiognomic features (Humm 1989, 182).

Indeed, racial classification was and continues to be understood—despite being widely discredited to some limited extent—in terms of shared prototypic features (Rothschild 1981, 87).

As Gossett goes on to show, theories of physiognomy and scientific racism contributed significantly to the construction of the idea of race, especially in the United States. As ideological scaffolding that supported the building of institutionalized racism like slavery, the science of physiognomy was crucial. For example, the comparative study of crania of African Americans and Caucasian Americans supposedly revealed significant intelligence differences, which in turn functioned to support notions of white racial superiority (Gossett 1975, esp. 73–74). Because the idea of "race," as Joseph Rothschild notes, "had no inherent cultural meaning . . . predating its use as a device for imposing and enforcing stratification and segmentation," "race" as a concept has always been racist, because of its role in the production of prejudice based on the belief of the superiority of races (1981, 87). This kind of essentialist racism produced a tendency to read cultural differences between groups as absolute and inextricably tied to biology.

Clearly, then, the assumption that the face and other physiognomic features may be read as clues to internal characteristics endorses biologist theories of race and, stemming from that, of racial superiority. The "supposition . . . that conduct can be deduced from physical form" is capable of producing a very invidious racism (Schiesari 1994, 60). As Juliana Schiesari notes, "a working definition of racism can be found precisely in the attempts by the 'science' of physiognomy to attribute common behavioural characteristics to shared physical features" (57). Because of their recognition that any theory of physiognomic difference works as an ideological apparatus that preserves both racial hierarchies and stereotypes, and that racism continues to work in a physiognomic currency, many Eur/Amerasian women writers have often investigated the imagined correlation between physiognomy and behavior in their work. This is partly because there is a history of using such connections to derogate Asians in popular cultural media, as Elaine Kim makes clear in her discussion of images of Asians in Anglo fiction and film (1982, esp. Chap. 1).

Asian Americans have been subject to essentialist racism since the mid-nineteenth century. Gompers and Gustadt's 1908 piece "Meat vs. Rice: American Manhood against Asiatic Coolieism: Which Shall Survive" is an example of one such text. One of the assertions of the article was that the Chinese were "without nerves and without digestion" (qtd. in Gossett 1975, 291). Another early-twentieth-century "explanation" of Chinese "inferiority," by Henry George, stated that "the Chinaman was capable of learning up to a certain point of adolescence . . . but unlike the Caucasian he had a limited point of development beyond which it was impossible for him to go" (290). A later example quoted by Elaine Kim from Wallace Irwin's *The Seed of the Sun* in 1921 notes that Asians are "ridiculously clad, superstition-ridden, dishonest, crafty, cruel . . . marginal members of the human race who lack the courage, intelligence, skill, and the will to do anything about the oppressive conditions that surround them" (1982, 6). Unfortunately, these representations are not specific to the earlier part of the century: Kim cites examples as recent as 1969, as well as this example from the 1980 Charlie Chan film, where he is described as "wise, smiling, pudgy . . . symbol of the sagacity, kindliness, and charm of the Chinese people" (18). Such racist conclusions about groups of people based on their biology have evolved and produced enduring images and stereotypes of cultural groups. As Schiesari writes: "At its worst [physiognomy] . . . proceeded to a highly suspect classification of humanity based upon the assumed behaviour imputed to derive from bodily types. Anatomical difference thus became the pretext for prejudicial moral judgements" (1994, 57).

As Kim shows, these early representations of Asian Americans, which make assumptions about behavior based on physiognomic characteristics, have continued up to the present day. Asian American women writers have inherited a tradition of representing Asian Americans encumbered by such images. Sau-ling Cynthia Wong asks: "When subject and sign have both been altered by the gaze of white society, how is a Chinese American writer to represent his/her own experiences?" (1994, 251). Although Wong's discussion relates to representing Chinatown, several aspects of her argument may be usefully transposed onto a discussion of the rehabilitative representation of the Eur/Amerasian subject.

Wong's analysis in this piece draws upon semiology to explore the process of representing (and misrepresenting) Chinatown. She uses William Boelhower's (1987) work on ethnic semiosis to suggest that the "cultural product" of Chinatown (that is, the dominant cultural image of Chinatown), is created by a process of joint semiosis, in which the gazes of the dominator and the dominated (the white and the ethnic subject respectively) engage in a "process of mutual constitution" to represent Chinatown (1994, 251). Wong notes (and this is where she differs from Boelhower) that this mutual semiosis/gaze "hardly implies equal partnership," because the gaze of the ethnic subject is economically and discursively less powerful than that of the white subject (252). Wong's analysis of this process is useful because it acknowledges first that for the ethnic subject, *self* representation is not always possible, precisely because the "gaze of white society dominates," and, as she notes, "the 'Chinaman' no longer fully owns his experiences" (252). The question then is again of how exactly to divorce ethnic self-representation from the debilitating images with which it has been saddled. Second, because of the potency of the white gaze, Wong states, the ethnic subject is "now *marked*. . . singled out, blemished" (252). And third, the ramification of the all-powerful and controlling white gaze is that ethnic self-representation becomes highly problematic and fraught with near-insurmountable difficulty: "The Orientalizing sign may become so pervasive and invasive as to monopolise all expression. When that happens, the subjectivity of the ethnic subject is in danger of being drained from any effort at self representation" (252).

In opening this discussion I suggested that there is a concern with the relationship between corporeality and selfhood. It is the politics of representation that mediate this relationship. As Wong shows, in the process of joint semiosis, the gaze of the "dominated" ethnic subject is less potent than that of the dominator. The ethnic subject therefore lacks agency to control self-representation; and as the controlling white gaze "marks" the ethnic subject as ethnic, other, the body becomes the dominant signifier. Thus, being caught in the racializing gaze of another constitutes a crisis of self and self-representation.

Spec(tac)ular Acts

Sau-ling Wong goes on to suggest that in the gaze of the white voyeur, "Chinatown means *spectacle*" (1994, 253). I would suggest that the Eur/Amerasian subject herself becomes a "spectacle" in the way that Wong posits, because she too becomes an object attracting the sight of the white cultural voyeur. Likewise, representation itself is a "spectacular act," which can, as Wong warns, all too easily reinforce the ethnic subject as a spectacle (254). Indeed, the process of mutual gazing/semiosis proposed by Boelhower and elaborated by Wong may also be labeled a spectacular act or exchange (between racialized subjects and white onlookers), as it also functions as an unequal form of representation in which the ethnicizing/racializing (Anglo) gaze produces the ethnic subject as a spectacle of otherness.

In the racializing gaze, which fails to acknowledge individual response/nuance, the subjectivity of the individual disappears. The face, the eyes, and other physiognomic features visibly signify difference from a culturally normalized ethnic or racial majority; and through the gaze as spectacular act the "minority" ethnic subject is objectified. Eurasian writers like Han Suyin, Diana Chang, and Aimee Liu depict different ways in which they (in the case of auto/biographical works) or their characters could begin to escape this objectification, and thus pave the way for a possible rehabilitative representation of the Eur/Amerasian subject.

R. D. Laing has written: "Self identity ('I' looking at 'me') is constituted not only by our looking at ourselves, but also by our looking at others looking at us and our reconstitution of and alteration of these views of others about us" (1966, 5–6). It is this consciousness of the spectacular act that surfaces repeatedly as an anxiety in Eur/Amerasian texts by women, from early autobiographical works up to recent fiction. The spectacular act here becomes a *specular interaction*, as the ethnic subject finds her self-identity produced by, and reflected back to her by, another. Eurasian Sylvia Chen constantly attracts unwanted attention: "People never ceased to be curious about her" (Chang 1994, 5). In her autobiography, Eurasian Winnifred Eaton (Onoto Watanna) writes that people gazed at her "as if I interested them or they were puzzled to know my nationality." For Eaton, such spec(tac)ular gazes are unwelcome. She continues: "I would have given anything to look less foreign, my darkness marked and crushed me" (1915, 166). Sylvia Chen tries to avoid this marking by turning away from the racializing gaze: "She averted her face as she passed them" (Chang 1994, 5). This awareness of the gaze is what W.E.B. Du Bois called "double consciousness," which is the sense of watching one's self-image being produced by another.[1] Eaton's comment that her "darkness" in the eyes of another crushes her highlights the perils of adopting, however unwittingly, such a negative self-image, and the possible consequences of this for the assertion of a positive or rehabilitative self-image.

Anti-Miscegenation Discourses and the Eurasian Subject

Although an awareness of the gaze surfaces as a preoccupation in many Asian American texts by women, it is for Eurasian women that the crisis of selfhood is most entangled with corporeal identity. The Eurasian, a mix of Caucasian and Asian, presents a visibly literalized hybridity, as her identity appears to be embodied in her appearance. The body/face again functions as text. This divided external identity produces an even more conflicting sense of selfhood, as Amy Ling writes: "Coexisting and unresolvable opposites are daily experiences for bicultural people and particularly for Eurasians.... By which race shall one be known?" (1990, 112). Ruth Frankenberg notes that " 'Chineseness,' 'Blackness,' and 'Whiteness' " are states of being in theories of racial superiority, so that "the 'half' or 'mixed' person . . . does not belong anywhere" (1993, 95).

Like the better-known figure of the "tragic mulatta," the Eurasian was often depicted in popular (Anglo) cultural fictions as out of place, stranded between two states of being. Kim notes that "the dilemma of the Eurasian in Anglo-American literature is unresolvable. He must either accept life as it is, with its injustices and inequalities, or he must die" (1982, 9). The Eurasian, like the mulatto/a, constitutes a threat to essentialist theories of racial superiority precisely because, as Nancy Bentley writes in relation to mulattos in antebellum fiction, "the person of mixed black and white parentage stood precisely at the place where nature and culture could come unbound" (1995, 198). Any theory of race predicated upon the assumption that racial differences are absolute and tied to biological belonging will be "troubled" by the miscegenated subject.[2] Nancy Bentley's work on the mulatto identifies a cultural preoccupation with how to classify the American subject who is neither black nor white and the underlying cultural anxiety this causes, which, she argues, is evident in the production of terms like "octoroon" and "quadroon" to classify the miscegenated subject (198).

Frankenberg argues that this cultural anxiety is manifested in a discourse against interracial relationships which claims that mixed race children don't—and can't—fit in (1993, 95). It is such cultural anxieties and anti-miscegenation discourses that resulted in California miscegenation laws that referred to Negroes, Mulattos, and Mongolians, in place from 1880 until they were finally declared unconstitutional in 1967 by the U.S. Supreme Court. Anti-miscegenation arguments circulating at the time of the first of these laws bear testimony to a specific turn-of-the-century cultural abhorrence and fear of miscegenation. In a letter to Kentaro Keneko in 1892, anthropologist Herbert Spencer claimed that "if you mix the constitutions of two widely divergent varieties which have severally become adapted to widely divergent modes of life, you get a constitution which is adapted to the mode of life of neither—a constitution which will not work properly, because it is not fitted for any set of conditions whatever" (qtd. in Gossett 1975, 151). This is an example of Social Darwinism, which equated "race" with "species," producing an argument implicitly suggesting that miscegenation is also mutation (151). (It is also worth noting at this point that this passage expresses the exact opposite of hybrid vigor, the positive valence of biraciality.)

Like the mulatto/a, there are many early-twentieth-century Anglo-cultural fictions written about/against the Eurasian (comparable in many ways with mid- and late-nineteenth-century texts like Mayne Reid's *The Quadroon* or H. L. Hosmer's *Adela the Octoroon*) (Bentley 1995, 215). These texts also demonstrate the abhorrence of miscegenation seen in fiction about the mulatto/a, as well as an emphasis on their positions as doubly liminal subjects. This was not just an aesthetic issue: The growing animus against miscegenation that reached a crescendo around 1907 was precisely a response to the manner in which biraciality threatened to disturb and destabilize ossified racial hierarchies. Early-twentieth-century examples include Wallace Irwin's *The Seed of the Sun,* where the Eurasian character feels that "the dragon's tail of the Orient [is] fastened to the goat's head of Europe" (1978, 51); Achmed Abdullah's "A Simple Act of Piety," in whose Eurasian protagonist's body, we are told, "the Chinese blood in her veins, shrewd, patient, scotched the violence of her passion, her American impulse to clamor loudly for right and justice and fairness" (1919, 219); and Rex Beach's *Son of the Gods* (1929), among others.

In fiction and autobiography both by and about Eurasians, there is a corresponding preoccupation with the identity of the miscegenated subject, which is linked (in different ways) to corporeality, although it does not result in death. In particular, both the fiction and the autobiographies of the Eurasian sisters Edith Maude Eaton (pseudonym Sui Sin Far) and Winnifred Eaton (pseudonym Onoto Watanna) betray such a concern. Both sisters were writing between 1899 and 1925, so they were writing at the same time as Anglo writers like Wallace Irwin and Rex Beach, and their work reflects the same preoccupation with miscegenation and its effects that can be seen in their contemporary, Herbert Spencer's, 1892 letter. As Amy Ling makes clear in her discussion of the Eaton sisters, the autobiographies of both—Winnifred's *Me: A Book of Remembrance* and Edith's "Leaves from the Mental Portfolio of an Eurasian"—engage with the bigotry they experienced as Eurasians.

By the time that *Me* was published in 1915, its author, Winnifred Eaton, had been using the Japanese-sounding pen name "Onoto Watanna" for several years. Although she was, like her sister, actually Chinese American, Winnifred chose a Japanese name in order to mask an undesirable identity. *Me* charts Eaton's dissimulations as a Eurasian woman at a particularly difficult moment in Chinese American history, when Sinophobia had reached an all-time high. Winnifred decided to publish under a Japanese pseudonym, a more ethnically compatible identity at the turn of the century, partly because her physical appearance prevented her from passing as white. Yet, a publishing identity obscures physical appearance, so Winnifred's disguise must have served other purposes. In fact, she was partly forced to continue an authorial ruse that she had started much earlier, when she had invented a Japanese ancestry for herself for her entry in *Who's Who*. But in contrast to many of her fictional works, *Me* was published anonymously, a textual disguise as effective as her physical passing as Japanese. However, Winnifred filled the text with clues as to her ethnic identity. For example, she explores in detail the desire to pass in *Me*. She describes Nora, her corresponding character, as "a native of a far distant land" (W. Eaton, *Me*, 3), yet the lack of ethnic specificity here is a form of identity evasion. Through Nora, Winnifred extensively explores the psychological anguish of being Eurasian, but in a very indirect way. Nora attempts to deflect the racializing gaze of those "interested" in her or those "puzzled" by her nationality: "People stared at me . . . but in a different sort of way, as if I interested them or they were puzzled to know my nationality" (166). *Me* also shows an awareness of the spectacular act, as Winnifred notes: "I would have given anything to look less foreign. My darkness marked and crushed me" (qtd. in Ling 1990, 166). It is interesting to note, as Ling does, that *Me* reveals a consciousness of the gendering, as well as the racializing, gaze, so that it is clear that Winnifred was conscious of both pressures upon her appearance.

Me's reviewers caught the scent of Winnifred's evasive publishing tactics. As Linda Trinh Moser has pointed out, both the *Chicago Tribune* (21 August 1915) and the *New York Times Book Review* (22 August 1915) guessed that the author was Eurasian (1997, 365). Shortly after, on 10 October, the *New York Times Book Review* declared that Onoto Watanna was *Me*'s author. None of the reviewers detected Winnifred's real identity as Chinese Eurasian, and so we must conclude that her technologies of writerly evasion were successful.

Edith Maude Eaton was much more open about her biracial identity. Her pseudonym worked quite the opposite way to Winnifred's: By adopting the name Sui Sin Far, Edith actually declared her ethnic identity far more than her given Anglo name was able to do. Edith used her ethnic identity in order to actively combat and confront racial prejudices. Her autobiography, like *Me*, discusses the connection between physiognomy and racism in detail, but she is especially concerned with Eurasian identity:

> I meet a half Chinese, half white girl. Her face is plastered with a thick white coat of paint and her eyelids and eyebrows are blackened so that the shape of her eyes and the whole expression of her face is changed. She was born in the East, and at the age of eighteen came West. . . . It is not difficult, in a land like California, for a half Chinese, half white girl to pass as one of Spanish or Mexican origin. This the poor child does, though she lives in nervous dread of being discovered. (E. Eaton 1909, 187)

Edith clearly disapproves of this girl's passing tactics and rejects technologies of racial disguise as a means of coping with biracial identity in a hostile environment, whereas she would, rather like her sister, "carry a fan in my hand, wear a pair of scarlet beaded slippers, live in New York, and come of high birth" (E. Eaton 1909, 189); despite this,

FIGURE 16.1.   Diana Chang. Courtesy of Gordon Robotham.

she empathizes with the psychological feelings that are their motivation. Edith's encounter with her racial double, when she sees another Chinese person for the first time, leads her to "recoil with a sense of shock" (qtd. in Ling 1990, 35). Amy Ling's discussion of "Leaves" demonstrates Edith's double consciousness, whereby racial taunts along physiognomic lines, " 'yellow-face, pig-tail,' " produce a negative self image and over-produces a tendency to blame miscegenation for all her bodily ills: "She attributes her life-long physical frailty to the social burden of being a Eurasian" (35).

Later fiction and autobiography by Eurasians continues to demonstrate debates over the conflicting identity produced by miscegenation, which again is often instigated by the racializing and gendering gaze. In Diana Chang's 1956 novel *The Frontiers of Love*, we are told that Sylvia Chen "was both as American as her own mother, and as Chinese as her father. She could not deny her own ambivalence" (19). Like Edith Maude Eaton, Diana Chang is quite open about her Eurasian identity, as her jacket cover on the University of Washington Press edition of *The Frontiers of Love* shows. Her photograph clearly advertises the fact, and the accompanying biography includes details of her ancestry (Fig. 16.1).

Eurasian identity, and the crisis of self that may result, is the subject of much of Chang's work, but perhaps most notably in *The Frontiers of Love*. It was published to critical acclaim, with many contemporary reviews approving of Chang's description of the "tragic" Eurasian figure of Sylvia Chen. Samantha Ramu Rau, for example, in the

New York Review of Books, described Chen as "a tragically ineffectual figure" (1956, 26). Yet Chang does not simply subscribe to and reproduce the stereotype of the miscegenated subject, but extensively explores the social and historical contingencies of Eurasian identity. Set in 1945, the context of *The Frontiers of Love* is World War II, a time of particular intensity and instability for racialized subjects in Euro/American(ized) cultural milieus. The novel also asserts its geopolitical specificity as a reason for the confusion of identity experienced by its Eurasian characters: "People were true to nothing in Shanghai; they belonged only to the surface values of both East and West and leaned heavily toward the exoticism of the West. If one did not hold carefully to one's sense of self, one might wake up one morning looking for one's face, so easily lost" (Chang 1994, 87).

Chang's novel both extensively thematizes and literalizes the problematics of biracial identity. Its setting is biracial, as Shanghai is described explicitly as a "Eurasian city." In fact, Chang has insisted upon this geographical specificity in the novel, asserting that "while it is about identity, it is not about ethnicity here," referring to the United States (1994, 39). In *The Frontiers of Love* we see Diana Chang interrogating antimiscegenation ideas as they are articulated by the novel's Eurasian characters, in the context of Western ideals of beauty, as this example shows:

> Poor Paul, Sylvia thought, and that was more accurate. My brother, she thought, seeing him as he had been at six, angelic and so beautiful (part porcelain and part flame) he had been painful to look at. At their best, half-breeds who had Chinese blood in them had fine features, thin skins and eyes that caught the light in a blaze. So much tragedy seemed to lie beneath Paul's physical perfection, his puzzling Chinese-Western looks, which seemed like an optical illusion. (144)

Sylvia's subscription to a stereotypical image of the tragic Eurasian in this passage is subtly undermined by Chang. The viewpoint is that of an observer, Sylvia, and it is this sense of the gaze in this section that highlights Sylvia's internalization of acute double consciousness. The pain here is not Paul's, but crucially it is Sylvia's, as she identifies her brother's looks with her own sense of inferiority. Sylvia's ambivalence about her identity is often reflected, and thus accentuated, by others' reaction to her when in public, as this passage shows:

> She averted her face as she passed them . . . (people never ceased to be curious about her), a slight girl of twenty, tanned to an even brown by the Shanghai sun. Her eyes were startlingly large, dilated, as her father said . . . but her hair was not all black; she walked with all the freedom and impatience of a foreigner, yet in her there was something inescapably oriental. (Chang 1994, 5)

Sylvia's contradictory identity is mirrored by her observer's *assumed* reaction to her physiognomy. Once more the viewpoint in this passage is Sylvia's own, and therefore we identify the reactions of the passers-by to be projected by Sylvia herself.

In Han Suyin's autobiographical *The Crippled Tree,* published in 1965, it is her (Caucasian) mother, rather than an anonymous passer-by, who forces Rosalie to confront the racializing gaze: "Look at yourself! You a Chinese. You will never be Chinese, and let me tell you why: the Chinese will not have you! Never, never! They won't accept you. They will call you 'yang kweitse' devil from over the ocean, as they call me. They will call you half-caste and mixed-blood, for that is what you are" (1965, 416).

Once more, the racializing gaze is linked to context, as Rosalie and her mother are both outsiders in China due to their Caucasian blood. Rosalie's mother suggests that in this Chinese context, it is Rosalie's non-Chineseness, rather than her Chineseness, that is significant. Repeatedly, the failure to signify as either Caucasian or Asian is presented in negative terms, as the Eurasian defines herself as a nonmember of either racial group, rather than a member of both. Sylvia Chen notes that she looks "not even Aryan, but just non-Chinese" (Chang 1994, 86). Physiognomy is repeatedly held responsible for a fractured sense of identity. Blood is to blame, as Edith Eaton writes: "the white blood in our veins fights valiantly for the Chinese half of us" (1909, 216).

Another way in which anti-miscegenation discourses surface in many of these early- and mid-twentieth-century texts is through images of mutation, homelessness, and tragedy. Like the mulatto/a, the Eurasian is depicted as a tragic figure: "Tragic faces of half-breeds, pawns of an undesired fate. Something of wildness, something of sadness, something of intense longing and wistfulness looked from the strange eyes of the breeds" (W. Eaton 1925, 245–6). In this example, the face and eyes again signal otherness, here a tragic and sad otherness. It is the language of mutation that surfaces in *The Frontiers of Love* as we are told that Sylvia Chen's father "could hardly bear to pronounce the word 'Eurasian'; it was as though his seed had produced mavericks, a mutation" (Chang 1994, 162). In Han Suyin's *The Crippled Tree*, too, it is Rosalie's father, like Sylvia's father, who regrets producing Eurasian children: "My children would belong nowhere. Always there would be this double load for them, no place they could call their own land, their true home. No house for them in the world. Eurasians, despised by every-one" (1965, 290).

Thus, as in Anglo portrayals, in Asian American women's texts, from the early auto-biographies of the Eatons to Chang's 1956 novel, we see that the Eurasian is represented as visibly embodying the racial split that reproduces a fractured sense of identity, and this works through the racializing gaze. This bodily split, and its relationship with the gaze, is symbolized much later in *Face*, by character Maibelle Chung's self-portrait, *Oriental I*, a "wall-sized mosaic of one hundred forty-four separate photographs of disconnected body parts" (Liu 1995, 172). This self-portrait expresses the bodily fragmentation all these women experience in the face of the racializing and gendering gaze. As Patricia Waugh observes: "As a consequence of their social alienation, women experience their body as parts, 'objects,' rather than integrated wholes" (1989, 178). This is even more the case for the Eurasian subject, who feels herself to be alienated due to both her social and racial identity.

There is a difference between Anglo and Asian American portrayals of the Eurasian's situation, however. Anglo portrayals, as Kim notes, offer no possibility for coming to terms with one's mixed racial ancestry: "Most of the stories about Eurasians end with the death of the protagonist. The only real victory possible . . . is mistaken identity" (1982, 9). This is in marked contrast to Asian American depictions, where even if the option of choosing to pass for only one racial identity is available, it is rejected. Both of the Eaton sisters chose to swap between identities as Asian and Caucasian, thus manipulating their position for their own gain. So for the Eatons, self-representation *was* possible, although it remained linked to feelings of inferiority. In *The Crippled Tree*, Rosalie finds a way to come to terms with her identity by accepting the inevitability of self-division:

> In Rosalie a fragmentation of the total self occurred. . . . Others born like her of two worlds, who chose not to accept this splitting, fragmentation of monolithic identity into several selves, found themselves later unable to face the contradictions latent in their own beings. . . . In Rosalie the necessity of knowing mutually contradictory truths without assuming any one of them to be the whole truth, became in childhood the only way to live on, to live and to remain substantial. (Han 1965, 369)

It seems, therefore, that one form of rehabilitative representation of the Eurasian subject's predicament is to posit a way of coping with the contradictions of biracial identity, which for both the Eatons and Rosalie Chou (Han Suyin) is an acceptance of those contradictions. It is not surprising that it is not Anglo representations of Eurasians, where there is a vested interest in preserving racial hierarchies and classifications, where we find such rehabilitative writing, nor that it should be the project of Eurasian women themselves to rescue Eurasian subjectivity from association with anti-miscegenation arguments.

In texts like *The Crippled Tree* and *The Frontiers of Love*, the Eurasian's awareness of the inevitability of self-division replaces her desire for racial wholeness and her yearning for unfragmented selfhood, which is denied her with each engagement with the racializing/gendering gaze. Rosalind Coward notes that "in this society, looking has become a crucial aspect of sexual relations, not because of any natural impulse, but because it is one of the ways in which domination and subordination are expressed" (1984, 76). Looking is an aspect of racial, as well as sexual, relations. Frequently, Eurasian women are seen in these texts trying to evade the gaze, precisely because it signals subordination within a racial and gender hierarchy, by turning away as Sylvia Chen does: "She averted her face" (Chang 1994, 5).

Yet it is not just the gaze of the voyeur that must be avoided, but also the reflection of one's body image in a mirror, the act of specularization. The inability to control self-image is often presented through the use of the mirror as trope in these texts. In her autobiography, Japanese American Lydia Minatoya tells us that a fellow Asian American woman told her that "sometimes I catch sight of my reflection in a store window . . . and I am shocked to see that I am oriental" (1993, 58). This woman's encounter with her self-image here constitutes as much of a shock to her as Edith Eaton's seeing another Chinese person for the first time. Negative external identity is reimposed each time, as *Face* character Maibelle Chung notes: "I see myself" (Liu 1995, 1).

Gendered Responses and the Technologies of Race

For Eur/Amerasian women in many of these texts, the double consciousness of the racializing gaze is rendered further threatening by the double bind of the awareness of gender as well as racial differences. For these women are caught not only in the racializing gaze but also in the gendering gaze. As Teresa de Lauretis writes: "Concurrent representation of the female body as the *locus* of sexuality, site of visual pleasure, or lure of the gaze is so pervasive in our culture . . . it necessarily constitutes a starting point for any understanding of . . . the construction of social subjects, its presence in all forms of subjectivity" (1984, 38).

The recognition of the hegemony of the gaze in our culture owes much to Laura Mulvey's now seminal essay "Visual Pleasure and Narrative Cinema" (1975). Sau-ling Wong's piece, "Ethnic Subject, Ethnic Sign," to which I alluded at length earlier, draws mainly upon William Boelhower's thesis on ethnic semiosis for its theoretical substructure. But is in the area of film criticism, pioneered by Mulvey in "Visual Pleasure," that we find the confluence of feminist theories of the fetishization of female sexuality and the semiotics of representation. It is useful to reiterate two assertions of Mulvey's essay here. Like Wong, Mulvey stresses the power of the gaze, but also its compulsiveness: "Curiosity and the wish to look intermingle with a fascination with likeness and recognition: the human face, the human body, the relationship between the human form and its surroundings" (1975, 9). The compulsion to look reinforces the hegemony of the gaze. But it is women who are objects of this gaze. "Women are simultaneously looked at and displayed, with their appearance coded, for strong visual and erotic impact so that they can be said to connote *to-be-looked-at-ness*" (11). Thus, the ethnic subject finds herself prey to objectification as both an ethnic and female spectacle, drawing the gaze of the white/male spectator. This process of objectification can be seen to produce the pressure to conform to dominant definitions of beauty. Many early Eur/Amerasian women's texts repeatedly articulate both a yearning for and a recognition of the failure to achieve those standards. Elsewhere, for other women, it is their eyes in particular that are the orientalizing sign. Sylvia Chen in *The Frontiers of Love* is recognized as part Chinese because "her eyes were startlingly large, dilated" (Chang 1994, 5).

In the earlier texts that I have discussed, tactics of disguise are often employed as a means of escaping the racializing gaze, notably through passing by dressing in particular ways. Winnifred Eaton/Onoto Watanna and Edith Eaton/Sui Sin Far also used textual strategies to mask their identities, by adopting pseudonyms. In contrast, texts written in the latter part of the twentieth century depict women who find themselves marked as outsiders by their physiognomy, resorting to a sliding scale of cosmetic technologies in order to align their appearance with the contextual "norm." This move illustrates a shift in the way that "race" is understood, as well as charts the development of cosmetic technologies. Earlier I noted that "race" as a term has changed in meaning, and this is demonstrated through a reading of these Eur/Amerasian women's texts, where "race" is seen to be an idea, like "gender," in flux. In *Consumer Culture*, Celia Lury describes this shift "*from* a racism tied to a biological understanding of race in which identity is fixed or naturalised *to* a racism in which race is a cultural category in which racial identity is represented as a matter of style, and is the subject of choice" (1996, 165).

The claim that racial difference may be seen as a question of aesthetics rather than as a political reality is a contentious one; but it may constitute one attempt at rehabilitative representation. If racial identity can be seen as something to choose to "wear"— or not—then this would signal a move from objectified subject devoid of agency to a position whereby self-representation was possible. Lury cites Susan Willis's argument that this move *is* possible and furthermore can be seen in the well-documented case of Michael Jackson's self-representation through physical transformation. This constitutes a technology of race. In *Technologies of Gender: Essays on Theory, Film, and Fiction,* de Lauretis notes that "gender . . . both as representation and as self-representation is the product of various technologies, . . . institutional discourses, epistemologies, and critical practices" (1987, ix). The move from regarding "gender," like "race," as a biological category to regarding it as a culturally constructed entity subject to change is echoed by de Lauretis. Certainly, this possibility is explored in one of the texts of interest here. In *Face,* Maibelle Chung bumps into one of the "Yellow Butterflies," women whose Asian features she had admired as a child, and finds that she has tried to erase her orientalizing features: "Much later, between years of college, I ran into one of the Yellow Butterflies selling panty hose at Bloomingdale's. She'd had her eyes done, had the lids lifted, folded, and cut until the almond shape was gone and with it her exotic, imperious beauty. Now she looked innocent. Cute. She could pass for American" (Liu 1995, 2).

This woman's attempts to erase the orientalizing sign of her physiognomy are the result of the double consciousness of the spectacular act defining her from the outside. For this woman, self-image seems to reside close to the surface; the pressure to attain standards of occidental attractiveness engenders an acute awareness of the *look* as well as one's *looks.* Late-twentieth-century technologies enable her to change her appearance in ways not open to women in the earlier texts that I discuss, where women's ultimate defense was evasion, to turn away. Yet, it remains that cosmetic technologies may be only provisionally welcomed as a means of escaping the racializing gaze, because the gendering gaze is still there, and the culture of othering through looking also remains undisturbed, just deflected. In fact, diminishing encounters with the racializing gaze only reinforce the hegemony of the gendering gaze; as we see in the example I have just quoted, this woman exchanges her racializing appearance for one that conforms to American stereotypes of Anglo "girl-next-door" attractiveness. Ultimately, Liu's representation of the spectacular act in *Face* is just as debilitating for the women who encounter it as for the Eaton sisters almost ninety years earlier.

Notes

1. See Amy Ling's discussion of the relation between double consciousness and the writings of the Eaton sisters (1990, 21–55).

2. I mean to evoke Judith Butler's (1990) use of "trouble" here.

Works Cited

Abdullah, Achmed. 1919. "A Simple Act of Piety." In *The Honourable Gentleman and Others.* New York: Putnam.

Beach, Rex. 1929. *Son of the Gods.* New York: Harper. Bentley, Nancy. 1995. "White Slaves: The Mulatto Hero in Antebellum Fiction." In *Subjects and Citizens: Nation, Race, and Gender from Oroonoko to Anita Hill,* ed. Michael Moon and Cathy Davidson. Durham, N.C.: Duke University Press.

Boelhower, William. 1987. *Through a Glass Darkly: Ethnic Semiosis in American Literature.* Oxford: Oxford University Press.

Butler, Judith. 1990. *Gender Trouble: Feminism and the Subversion of Identity.* New York: Routledge.

Chang, Diana. 1994. *The Frontiers of Love.* Seattle: University of Washington Press.

Coward, Rosalind. 1984. *Female Desire: Women's Sexuality Today.* London: Paladin.

de Lauretis, Teresa. 1984. *Alice Doesn't: Feminism, Semiotics, Cinema.* London: Macmillan.

———. 1987. *Technologies of Gender: Essays on Theory, Film, and Fiction.* London: Macmillan.

Eaton, Edith Maude. 1909. "Leaves from the Mental Portfolio of an Eurasian." *Independent* 21 (January): 187.

Eaton, Winnifred. 1925. *His Royal Nibs.* New York: Watt.

———. 1997. *Me: A Book of Remembrance.* 1915. Jackson: University of Mississippi Press.

Frankenberg, Ruth. 1993. *White Women, Race Matters: The Social Construction of Whiteness.* Minneapolis: University of Minnesota Press.

Gossett, Thomas F. 1975. *Race: The History of an Idea in America.* Dallas: Southern Methodist University Press.

Han, Suyin. 1965. *The Crippled Tree.* London: Lowe and Brydore.

Humm, Maggie. 1989. *The Dictionary of Feminist Theory.* Hemel Hampstead: Harvester Wheatsheaf.

Irwin, Wallace. 1978. *The Seed of the Sun.* New York: Arno.

Kim, Elaine. 1982. *Asian American Literature: An Introduction to the Writings and Their Social Context.* Philadelphia: Temple University Press.

Laing, R. D. 1966. Introduction to *Interpersonal Perception,* ed. R. D. Laing, H. Phillipson, and A. R. Lee. London: Tavistock.

Ling, Amy. 1990. *Between Worlds: Women Writers of Chinese Ancestry.* New York: Pergamon.

Liu, Aimee. 1995. *Face.* London: Headline Review Press.

Lury, Celia. 1996. *Consumer Culture.* Cambridge: Polity.

Minatoya, Lydia. 1993. *Talking to High Monks in the Snow: An Asian American Odyssey.* New York: Harper.

Moser, Linda Trinh. 1997. Afterword to *Me: A Book of Remembrance,* by Winnifred Eaton, 357–72. Jackson: University of Mississippi Press.

Mulvey, Laura. 1975. "Visual Pleasure and Narrative Cinema." *Screen* 16, 3 (Autumn): 6–18.

Rau, Samantha Ramu. 1956. "The Need to Belong." *New York Times Book Review,* 26 September.

Rothschild, Joseph. 1981. *Ethnopolitics: A Conceptual Framework.* New York: Columbia University Press.

Schiesari, Juliana. 1994. "The Face of Domestication: Physiognomy, Gender Politics, and Humanism's Others." In *Women, "Race," and Writing in the Early Modern Period,* ed. Margo Hendricks and Patricia Parker, 55–70. London: Routledge.

Waugh, Patricia. 1989. *Feminine Fictions: Revisiting the Postmodern.* New York: Routledge.

Wong, Sau-ling Cynthia. 1994. "Ethnic Subject, Ethnic Sign, and the Difficulty of Rehabilitative Representation: Chinatown in Some Works of Chinese American Fiction." *Yearbook of English Studies* 24: 251–62.

Part IV

Recollections

Amy Ling

---

17   Yan Phou Lee on the Asian American Frontier

> *Meaning resides "in some" underlying [realm of] the inexpressible, inchoate, [and] silent.*
>
> —David Porush, quoted in Krupat 1992, 79

> *It is better . . . to suffer . . . in silence.*
>
> —Yan Phou Lee

As the first person of Asian ancestry to write and publish a book in English in the United States, Yan Phou Lee and his autobiographical text, *When I Was a Boy in China,* first published in Boston by D. Lothrop in 1887, hold a unique position in Asian American literary history. However, few scholars of Asian American literature or history have paid any attention to either the man or his text.[1] Thomas E. La Fargue noted that "Lee Yenfu" was one of three students who returned to the United States at the demise of the Chinese Educational Mission and "completely divorced themselves from any service to the Chinese Government," implying that they were ingrates and renegades (1942, 140).[2] La Fargue's focus was the careers in China of the returned students as a measure of the success of the Mission, in place between 1872 and 1881, whose purpose was to bring China into the twentieth century by giving Chinese boys a Western education; the three who "forgot their obligations" could thus be interpreted only as aberrations (141).[3] Because La Fargue's book predated the creation of Asian American studies, he did not think of these three in terms of their positive choice: Asians who claimed the United States as home.

None of the early anthologies of Asian American literature mention Yan Phou Lee. Although Elaine Kim's groundbreaking critical study *Asian American Literature* does give him some space, she dismisses him as an "Ambassador of Good Will" who doubled as a tour guide. Kim acknowledged that "Lee Yan Phou" (reordering his name in the Chinese way, contrary to his own practice) was the author of one of the first texts in "a series of books by young men from various lands . . . solicited by D. Lothrop Publishing Company" whose purpose was to educate readers about other cultures (1982,

25). Kim criticizes Lee's upper-class bias, his exoticization of Asian culture (concentrating on "the charming superficialities of ceremonies and customs of food and dress, which [he] hoped would appeal to the benign curiosity of the Western reader"), and the politeness and restraint of all the "Ambassadors of Good Will" by expressing "indignation . . . at American race policies" in "tentative and apologetic" tones (25). Moreover, since Kim's discussion of Asian American literature focuses on work written by Asian Americans in English and set in the United States, Lee's book about his boyhood in China falls outside her parameters.

In Lee's defense, I think it safe to assume that the topics of his book—the Chinese calendar, domestic architecture, cooking, schooling, religion, games, and the social position of girls—were largely dictated by his editor, who undoubtedly sought a certain uniformity and coherence for the volumes in the series. For example, New Il-Han's 1928 *When I Was a Boy in Korea,* one of the last in the series, focused on similar topics: "holidays, sports, housing, food, and silkworm culture" (Kim 1982, 25). Lee wrote of what he knew, and he cannot be faulted for the class into which he was born. In fact, his choice of verb explicitly acknowledges the role of fate, for as he put it: "I *happened* to be born into the higher middle condition of life" (1887a, 20, emphasis added). Furthermore, writing in the late nineteenth century, he could hardly be expected to treat "American race policies" in terms entirely satisfying to a late-twentieth-century post-civil-rights feminist consciousness. Finally, we should consider it an unexpected bonus that a book entitled *When I Was a Boy in China* contains any impressions of the United States at all.

In revisiting Yan Phou Lee—reading between the facts of his life and between the lines of his writings—I believe he is deserving of a far more luminous title than "Ambassador of Good Will." A useful theoretical frame is Gloria Anzaldua's borderlands or the frontier, which Arnold Krupat defines as "that shifting space in which two *cultures* encounter each other" (1992, 5), as opposed to Frederick Jackson Turner's "frontier" as the boundary line between civilization and wilderness. I see Lee as an Asian American frontier man and founding father, nearly a century before the term "Asian American" was coined. Although some may consider *When I Was a Boy in China* more anthropology than literature, I find enough evidence of artistic crafting and rhetorical grace to consider it the founding text of Asian American literature. Not only is it chronologically the earliest, but it bespeaks Lee's frontier position.

For Lee, the frontier was not a geographical space or a physical place. Lee's frontier lay within, a psychological and emotional state that found external expression in his life choices and in his writings. In these external expressions, Yan Phou Lee revealed a between-worlds stance, the fluctuating double-consciousness of all racial minorities, and anticipated the themes and concerns of future generations of Asians in America. He undoubtedly wrestled with such questions as: Where is home? Where do my loyalties lie? Which forces are stronger in the shaping of my identity—biology or culture? By choosing one culture, am I betraying the other? Must I forever be a bridge between worlds, a mediator between cultures and races? Can I get out of the ethnic box and join the mainstream, or is that turning my back on my people?

Classification of people into neat defining boxes is, of course, a treacherous endeavor. Human beings are so various that no matter how carefully one has constructed the box, someone will always come along who doesn't fit—what Bakhtin called "an unrealized surplus of humanness" (1981, 37). Yet, to name, classify, and organize is basic mental housekeeping, so I shall attempt to delimit the "box" called Asian American. An Asian American is a person whose external features, biological ancestry, or both proclaim "Asia," but who by birth or choice has decided that the United States is home. To the Asian American, Robert Frost's bleak definition of home as "the place where, when you have to go there, / they have to take you in" (1953, 898) does not apply, for the United States has long excluded and rejected Asians as alien. Yet, despite this history of rejection, the United States is nevertheless the place that provides the greatest psychic, spiritual, and material comfort and ease. It is home by birth or by conscious choice. At the same time, Asian Americans cannot totally erase their connection to Asia, for how does one deny a great-grandmother or amputate "yellowish" skin? On the other hand, not to be recognized as an American but to be treated as an Asian foreigner when one's family has lived many generations in this country is a high insult. Thus, to be Asian American is to be between worlds—not entirely here or there, vacillating and fluctuating between feeling familiar and alien, comfortable and estranged. One must live, as Maxine Hong Kingston put it, with paradoxes, among the most vexing of which is one's own identity.

The very first frontier man who negotiated the encounter between China and the United States was Yung Wing (Yale, class of 1854), founder of the Chinese Educational Mission, and first ambassador from China to the United States. He married an American woman, Mary Kellogg, and bought a house in Connecticut, and yet tried to be of service to China. Although Yung Wing's 1909 autobiography, *My Life in China and America,* tells of his shuttling back and forth between his two countries, it is apparent that he wished to be of service to China *while living in the United States,* and this desire/choice seems to underlie many of his proposals and petitions to the Chinese government. Although Yan Phou Lee was a generation younger than Yung Wing, Lee's slender autobiography, commissioned while he was still an undergraduate, appeared in print twenty-two years before his mentor's. While Yung Wing continued to work abroad for the Chinese government as educator and diplomat, Yan Phou Lee completely severed his ties to China for most of his life, preferring to take his chances on making a life for himself in the United States.

As I have noted in an earlier essay (Ling 1994) that compared the autobiographies of the first two Chinese American males (Yan Phou Lee and Yung Wing) and the first two Chinese American females (Sui Sin Far and Onoto Watanna), the men omitted personal emotions and motivations from their accounts and recorded only dry facts. I attributed the male reticence to gender conditioning. Lee himself contributes to this notion. As a Chinese boy, he was taught to endure injustice in stoic silence: "It is better for an accused son, pupil, or servant to suffer punishment in silence although he may be conscious of no wrong doing" (1887a, 19). Because the late nineteenth century in the United States was a period of intense Sinophobia, Yan Phou Lee, in his many travels across the land, could hardly have avoided racial discrimination. Yet to complain was to be an unmanly whiner. Furthermore, Lee was not only addressing a predominantly white audience but dependent on it for survival; thus, a modicum of tact, diplomacy, and silence on sensitive issues was necessary. To understand how Yan Phou Lee might warrant the title of an Asian American frontier man and founding father, we must read his silences and interpolate from his actions the motivations and feelings that he found unacceptable to express or expressed only through irony and indirection.[4]

Yan Phou Lee was born in 1861 in Xiangshan (fragrant hills), seventy-five miles south of the city of Canton (Guangdong), and grew up, the middle child among three sons, in one of the wings of his grandfather's large house. Confucian order and stern discipline characterized the household, for "obedience and respect, rather than affection, are required of the Chinese child. His home-life, therefore, is constrained, sober and dull" (Lee 1887a, 18).[5] As Lee recalled, "The only one event of my infant life worthy of record" was "the death of my adopted father" (15). Lee's father's brother, age twenty-one, lay on his deathbed, unmarried and without offspring. Needing someone to make offerings at his grave, the uncle adopted Yan Phou Lee. But since Lee later made his life in the United States, he could not fulfill the obligations of a filial Chinese son and may have felt some qualms about his dereliction of duty.

When Lee was twelve, a cousin from Shanghai arrived with glowing accounts of the Chinese Educational Mission and its promise of "golden prospects" for participants. Lee's mother left the decision to her child, and Lee, who described himself as "more or less adventurous in disposition" (1887a, 95), did not hesitate. What he does not reveal is that 40 boys, one-third of the total 120 in the Chinese Educational Mission, came from Xiangshan, half in the first detachment and ten in Lee's own second detachment (see Robyn 1996, 129–30), and all three of the students who managed to return to the United States after the recall were his townsmen. Thus, in 1873, Yan Phou Lee, age thirteen, arrived in Springfield, Massachusetts, to live with Mrs. H. R. Vaille, whose name he would later give to his second son.

As a student, Lee distinguished himself and excelled in languages. He graduated from Hopkins School in New Haven, Connecticut, with the highest rank in his class and first prizes in both English and Greek composition. In 1880, he had begun studies at Yale, but the following year, he was recalled to China and subsequently sent to a Chinese naval academy. In 1885, with the help of U.S. missionaries, he "escaped" from China and returned to the United States.[6] Back at Yale, he won prizes in English composition and oration and earned honors in political science, history, law, and English. He was elected to Phi Beta Kappa and became a member of the Pundit Club. Not only did his considerable verbal skills win him academic honors but also they provided an income, for he supported himself by giving lectures and "in the disposal of . . . literary wares" (Lee 1887b, 310), rare accomplishments for any undergraduate, and even more rare for one from China.

The year 1887 may well have been the apex and turning point of Lee's life. In this one year, he graduated from Yale, published *When I Was a Boy in China* and "Why I Am Not a Heathen," and married Elizabeth Maude Jerome, a portrait painter and relative of Winston Churchill. The author's photograph in *When I Was a Boy in China* depicts a wide-eyed young Chinese man, with close-cropped hair, in a double-breasted Western suit. From the Chinese perspective, by cutting his queue, converting to Christianity, and marrying a Euro-American woman, Yan Phou Lee committed the three taboos that would make him unfit for Chinese government service. He had irrevocably turned his back on China and chosen the United States. The wedding took place on 6 July 1887, in New Haven, Connecticut, and the couple later had two children— Jennie Gilbert Jerome, born 15 May 1888 and Amos Gilbert Nelson Jerome, born 13 November 1889.[7] However, in the following year the marriage ended in what appeared to be a rancorous divorce, for the family ties were completely severed. The children reverted to their mother's last name and, reared by their mother and maternal grandmother, never knew their father.

For the next seven years, Lee's life was highly peripatetic, characterized by numerous large geographical and occupational shifts in what suggests a series of unsuccessful attempts to find a permanent place for himself in the United States. Here are the dizzying particulars in Lee's own words:

> In the past decade I have kept a country store in North Carolina; lectured through South Carolina, Georgia, Florida, Tennessee and Kentucky; studied medicine in Vanderbilt University; was connected with the World's Fair at Chicago in 1893; wrote for the press in St. Louis; interpreted in Courts for my countrymen in New York; worked at the Atlanta Exposition; had an Exhibit at the Nashville Exposition; was manager of the Chinese village at the Export Exposition at Philadelphia. (*Yale Class Records* [hereafter YCR] 1903)

The Chicago World's Fair and other expositions undoubtedly provided cosmopolitan excitement, high visibility, and an opportunity to play the role of cultural bridge, but they offered only short-term employment. Lee continued to lecture and published "articles for New York, San Francisco, St. Louis, Nashville and Delaware papers" (*Yale Class Book* [hereafter YCB] 1903) but seemed rootless.

In 1896, after an absence of twenty-three years, Lee made a visit to China. He did not specify whether this trip was occasioned by family obligations or dissatisfaction with his life in the United States. However, he seems to have made a conscious decision a second time to throw in his lot with Americans, for on 3 November 1897, he was in Nashville, Tennessee, marrying Sophie Florence Bolles. With his second wife, he had two sons: Clarence Vaille Lee, born 29 July 1898 in Minster, Ohio, and Louis Emerson Lee, born 19 June 1903 in Lincoln, Delaware, where Lee purchased a truck farm and became, as he put it, "a man with the hoe" (YCB 1903).[8] In five years, he and his wife changed residences three times before settling on the Delaware farm, where they remained for many years. Farming had the advantage of self-employment, and Lee even held some offices in local husbandry organizations.

After he sold the farm in 1909, Lee's list of occupations continued to be varied and short-term but geographically centered on the Northeast; he eventually settled full-time into newspaper editing. Lee first moved his family to Wood Ridge, New Jersey, where he was a member of the Congregational church. He was also a member of Lee and

Company at 229 Park Row in Manhattan, which he initially identified vaguely as "merchants" (*YCB* 1912) and later as "a live poultry business" (*YCB* 1924). (Was his initial vagueness perhaps motivated by shame over his source of livelihood?) Lee and Company survived for five years, 1912–1917, until "high prices and disagreement among the partners" led to its sale. "As a sideline," he was associate editor of the Hasbrouck Heights *Newsletter,* and he later worked on the *Enterprise* and the *Bergen Advertiser* of East Rutherford, all local weeklies.

In addition, as he put it: "Strange as it may seem, I was campaign manager for a man who aspired to be mayor of Wood Ridge. He was elected by a majority of thirty votes in 1912. I likewise managed his campaign in 1914, when he had a majority of one vote" (*YCB* 1924). The slender margins of victory must have amused Lee, since he took the trouble to note them. The fact that his candidate won twice testifies to Lee's being attuned to the political climate of his New Jersey town. Charles R. Ruegger, the Wood Ridge mayor, had not hired an alien Chinese, but an intelligent, educated U.S. newspaper editor, a choice not at all "strange." On the other hand, since Asians were not permitted to become naturalized citizens until 1954, Lee himself could not vote, and it might well seem "strange" for a disenfranchised person to become so involved in the U.S. electoral process.

Nevertheless, in 1917, as his part in the war effort, Lee further demonstrated his patriotism by writing a set of new verses for the song that would become the national anthem in 1931. He called it "The Star-Spangled Banner in 1917 (With Apologies to Francis Scott Key)." He moved his family to New York City and again took odd jobs— "copy-holder for several months, proof-reader for half a year"—until he landed an editorship at the *American Banker,* a commercial paper for the banking industry. He was managing editor from 1918 until 1927, the longest period of continuous salaried employment at a single establishment in his entire career. Between the lines in his later description of this position, however, I sense a tone of bitterness. The dates he offers in his 1937 account to Yale, while he was living in China at war, differ from those he provided in 1924, but compelling extenuating circumstances explain the discrepancy: "From 1922 to 1927 I worked on the *American Banker* and I did my best to make it a good financial journal. From a weekly it became a daily. When I resigned on July 15, 1927, the publisher was so glad to dispense with my services that he gave me a good watch. Very nice of him" (*YCR* 1938).[9] Given his choice of words, one suspects that Lee might have been asked to resign. Clearly, a daily requires much more work than a weekly, so that Yan Phou Lee was working harder than ever, and still he was dismissed with only a "good watch" to show for nine years' effort. The laconic four words, "Very nice of him," drip with irony, a stylistic mode Lee was fond of.

Lee's subsequent actions reveal the extent of his disappointment at the loss of his editorship: "I soon traveled more than 10,000 miles to Hong Kong where I taught school for more than a year and instructed several private pupils in the rudiments of the English language." Yan Phou Lee was now sixty-five. To leave a wife and two grown sons behind in a country where he had lived for fifty-two years to return to a land he had known for only sixteen, albeit the land of his birth, he must have been keenly disillusioned and without hope of ever being totally accepted in the United States. As a boy, he had been feted by the media, hosted and assisted by kind Americans. Famous people like Samuel Clemens and Ulysses S. Grant had championed the Chinese Educational Mission and protested its closing. But as a man visibly Chinese competing with whites for jobs, he had probably known more rejection and humiliation than he could stomach. Finally, the *Yale Class Records* regularly gave him the opportunity to compare his struggles to make a living with the undoubtedly more illustrious careers of fellow graduates. The awards and prizes he earned as a youth led to great expectations that never materialized in his later life. The gulf between the two in fact was enormous. Nonetheless, it was beneath his dignity to complain. To salvage his pride, he finally turned his back on the adopted country that he must have felt had rejected him and "returned" to China, the land he had been pleased to "escape" from half a century earlier.

But in China, too, life continued to be a struggle until another editorship opened up: "In 1931 I had an offer to become editor of the *Canton Gazette*, (*Guangdong Bao*) and I have remained as such up to two weeks ago. I was compelled to resign, because the paper could not pay my salary, as the Government had canceled its subsidy" (*YCR* 1938). After six years, he again abruptly lost a good job. Did the government cancel its subsidy because of dissatisfaction with the paper's politics? In 1937, China was besieged by Japan, but the Kuomintang under Chiang Kai-shek was more intent on fighting the Chinese Communists than the Japanese. Perhaps Yan Phou Lee questioned the wisdom of Chiang's policy, which resulted in the shutting down of his paper. This is mere speculation, but what is patently clear was that in China, also, Yan Phou Lee found no security or steady income, no nurturing "home."

In December 1937, in response to the Yale Alumni Office's request for additional details, Lee wrote with a hint of bitterness tinged with disappointment and even impatience: "I have very little to add. I have not received any honors, have no political affiliations, nor any outside activities. We Cantonese are threatened daily with death from Japanese bombs, so please excuse the curtness of the above." In a meaningful shift, he now refers to himself as "We Cantonese." On 29 March 1938, Lee wrote even more poignantly of his plight: "We are having war here, inhuman, brutal, savage war. Japanese bombing planes raid the city every day—sometimes three or four times. One has to think of saving his life. Little time can he give to such a thing as Class histories."

This was Yan Phou Lee's last communication with the Yale Alumni Office. He was seventy-seven. His daughter-in-law remembers that shortly after she and Clarence were married in 1938, they received a letter from his father asking for money, a sad acknowledgment of need that must have been extremely difficult for a father to make to a son. After a lifetime of work in the United States and ten years of work in China, Yan Phou Lee was apparently penniless. Clarence answered the letter and sent money, but a month later the letter was returned marked "Address Unknown." In 1986, Lee's grandson, Richard Lee, visited China to find Yan Phou Lee's last known address, 52 Pak Tze Road, Canton, but the road was no longer there. The family presumes that Lee was killed by Japanese bombs. However, the tie to China remains intact in the Lee family, for his great-grandson, Benjamin Lee, spent 1992 to 1994 in China teaching English.

Though Lee's body has disappeared, his writing remains. The product of a Chinese-born, U.S.-educated man, the writing reveals a fluid, dialogic quality. Lee's occupation of the frontier space between two cultures was bodily enacted in his six crossings of the ocean between his two countries. In his writings, Lee's fluctuating perspective, now Chinese, now American, may be found explicitly in declarations of preference, more subtly as shifts in pronoun reference, and generally by virtue of his role as mediator between two cultures, each ignorant and somewhat distrustful of the other, while he is knowledgeable about both.

The very first paragraph of *When I Was a Boy in China* reveals Lee's mediating between-worlds stance. One would assume that one's day of birth could be easily told in a few words, but for Yan Phou Lee it is not so simple: "On a certain day in the year 1861, I was born." Doesn't this autobiographer know the date of his own birth? Having manipulated the reader to ask this question, Lee answers it at great length.

> On a certain day in the year 1861, I was born. I cannot give you the exact date, because the Chinese year is different from the English year, and our months, being lunar, that is, reckoned by the revolution of the moon around the earth, are consequently shorter than yours. We reckon time from the accessions of Emperors, and also by cycles of sixty years each. The year of my birth, 1861, was the first year of the Emperor Tung-che. We have twelve months ordinarily; and we say, instead of "January, February," etc., "Regular Moon, Second Moon, Third Moon," etc. Each third year is a leap year, and has an extra month so as to make each of the lunar years equal to a solar year. Accordingly, taking the English calendar as a standard, our New Year's Day varies. Therefore, although I am sure that I was born on the twenty-first day of the Second Moon, in Chinese, I don't know my exact birthday in English; and consequently, living in America as I have for many years, I have been cheated of my birthday celebration. (1887a, 7–8)[10]

Caught between two incompatible systems, solar and lunar, Lee heightens the reader's consciousness of the cultural constructedness of such a taken-for-granted thing as a calendar. But the effect of his minutely thorough description of the Chinese calendar, with such bewildering complexities as accessions of emperors and leap-year catch-ups, is ludicrous. By the time he arrives at his humorous personal conclusion, the reader is at once charmed, amused, and even sympathetic over the author's loss of birthday celebrations. Lee's own attitude is somewhat difficult to ascertain. Although he uses the pronoun "we" for the Chinese way of doing things, I suspect that he may be relieved to take "the English calendar as a standard" because of its greater regularity and simplicity.

Lee is more overtly critical when he speaks of the rigid social hierarchy in Chinese society, where "every person . . . is in strict subjection to somebody" (17). Those in superior positions have absolute authority, and those in inferior positions cannot contradict their superiors or even explain what might appear to be bad conduct, lest the punishment be doubled. Here is the passage that follows the statement that it is better to suffer in silence, even when one is not conscious of having done anything wrong: "This seems very unreasonable; and in fact, it does foster sullenness and a spirit of rebellion which fear alone keeps under. But the Chinese deem this method absolutely necessary for the preservation of authority. In every household, the rattan stick is always ready to the hand of the majestic wrath of outraged family law" (19).

This may be the key to Yan Phou Lee's choice to live in the United States, for love and respect are certainly preferable to fear and sullen submission. Here, significantly, Lee does not employ the first-person-plural pronoun but the more distant "the Chinese," as though to disassociate himself from them. However, fearing he may have gone too far and alienated his reader, Lee hastens to explain: "It is not my intention to represent the Chinese as naturally cruel. They are not. They simply maintain family discipline by customs handed down from one generation to another. Fathers and teachers have undergone the same training. The customs of their ancestors enjoin it, the teachings of Confucius prescribe it, and the laws of the empire arm it with authority" (19–20).

Ironically, in a painful passage about traditional authority maintained through corporal punishment, Lee's writing is extremely graceful and disciplined. The last sentence, with its three parallel constructions—two nearly identical clauses and one a variation—has a pleasing balance and rhythm that gives evidence of both a sensitive ear and a mastery of English rhetoric.

With extraordinary empathy and reasonableness, Lee readily acknowledges that Chinese girls had to endure even greater "tortures" in the "fashion they are obliged to follow" to become marriageable young ladies. He frankly admits that the bound foot comes at the cost of a broken spirit: "It is true that the spirit is taken out of them by this species of suffering, and that they are oppressed by a sense of physical helplessness and dependence" (47–48).

On the subject of religion, Lee's perspective is decidedly American and Christian. He writes of Chinese gods as "idols" and Taoist priests as "men whose business is to impose on the people, and who make a living out of their superstitious fears" (65). He suggests, with great originality, that *The Journey to the West* was the monk Hsuan Tsang's attempt to find the "marvelous Nazarene" (66), but that he was mistakenly diverted into India by Buddha.

Although these examples reveal a perspective shift from one passage to the next, the perspective is predominantly singular within each passage. However, in the following, Lee manages to express both perspectives: "On account of the conservative spirit of the Chinese, *their* traditions, the pure morals which Confucius taught, the peculiar school system and the prejudices which *they justly* entertain against foreigners, the work of missionaries must progress slowly" (71, emphasis added). On the one hand, Lee, the Christian, uses the third-person pronoun to distance himself from the conservative Chinese in their treatment of missionaries. On the other hand, Lee, the Chinese, understands that Chinese prejudice against foreigners is grounded in experience.

From "we Chinese" in the first paragraph, Lee has traveled to "they" in the foregoing sample. However, on the subject of stories and storytellers that follows, Lee's Chinese nationalism is unequivocal:

Story-books [in China] . . . can be counted by the tens of thousands. . . . Some of the legends are really beautiful and are as interesting as a good English novel. There is one book which is the unfailing delight of all classes; I mean the *History of the Three Kingdoms*. It is an historical novel in twenty volumes, illustrated with wood-cuts. For arrangement of details, delineation of character and elegance of diction, I have found few books in English its equal. (81–82)

Again using the English as a standard, Lee finds that not only are Chinese legends "as interesting" as English novels, but one particular Chinese text is better than most English books.

Between the factual details of Lee's book lie glimmers of humor, irony, and understatement, revealing qualities of his personality that made it possible for him to marry two Caucasian women during a period when anti-miscegenation laws were prevalent. The best example of Lee's playful humor and understatement is his description of his transcontinental railroad journey, which begins: "Nothing occurred on our Eastward journey to mar the enjoyment of our first ride on the steamcars—excepting a train robbery, a consequent smash-up of the engine, and the murder of the engineer" (107). The rest of the paragraph describes an eventful, even harrowing, adventure—the very stuff of Hollywood westerns.

We were sitting quietly looking out of the windows and gazing at the seemingly interminable prairies when the train suddenly bounded backward, then rushed forward a few feet, and, then meeting some resistance, started back again. Then all was confusion and terror. Pistol-shots could be made out above the cries of frightened passengers. Women shrieked and babies cried. Our party, teachers and pupils, jumped from our seats in dismay and looked out through the windows for more light on the subject. What we saw was enough to make our hair stand on end. Two ruffianly men held a revolver in each hand and seemed to be taking aim at us from the short distance of forty feet or thereabouts. Our teachers told us to crouch down for our lives. We obeyed with trembling and fear. Doubtless many prayers were most fervently offered to the gods of China at the time. Our teachers certainly prayed as they had never done before. One of them was overheard calling upon all the gods of the Chinese Pantheon to come and save him. In half an hour the agony and suspense were over. A brakeman rushed through with a lamp in his hand. He told us that the train had been robbed of its gold bricks, by five men, three of whom, dressed like Indians, rifled the baggage car while the others held the passengers at bay; that the engine was hopelessly wrecked, the engineer killed; that the robbers had escaped on horseback with their booty; and that men had been sent to the nearest telegraph station to "wire" for another engine and a supply of workmen. One phase of American civilization was thus indelibly fixed upon our minds. (107–8)

Not only was the experience a baptism by fire, but also the narration demonstrates that after a dozen years in the United States Lee had mastered American humor, puns, irony, and understatement. His good-natured laughter encompasses both the frightened Chinese teachers and this sampling of American "civilization."

The two essays Lee published two years apart in the *North American Review* provide further evidence of his Asian Americanness. "Why I Am Not a Heathen" places him squarely into American culture as a faithful practicing Christian, in opposition to his countryman Wong Chin Foo, whose article "Why Am I a Heathen?" provoked Lee's response. However, in "The Chinese Must Stay," Lee argues for the much maligned

Chinese workers in the United States, in a passionate rejoinder to all the arguments supporting the Chinese Exclusion Act of 1882.

Wong Chin Foo's argument in "Why Am I a Heathen?" primarily centers on the wide gulf between Christian belief and behavior, in theory professing love but in practice driven by greed. Wong asserts that his sense of morality and goodness came from Confucian thought. Yan Phou Lee agrees that Confucius was a good man and that he inculcated a social order among the Chinese but argues that Confucius was not concerned with a man's relationship to God. Lee then draws a distinction between belief and behavior, arguing that the frailty of those who fall short of the tenets of their religion does not invalidate the rightness of their beliefs. Lee has found friendship and succor among Christians, and he boldly labels as non-Christian those who behave in un-Christian ways.

> When the Chinese were persecuted some years ago—when they were ruthlessly smoked out and murdered—I was intelligent enough to know that Christians had no hand in those outrages; for the only ones who exposed their lives to protect them were Christians. The California legislature that passed various measures against the Chinese was not Christian, the Sandlotters were not Christians, nor were the foreign miners. They might *call* themselves Christians, but I don't call a man a great genius simply because he *claims* to be one. Let him *do* something worthy of the name first. You shall know a man by his works. If there is any sentiment in this country in favor of the Chinese today, it is only to be found in the Christian church. (1887b, 309)

These passionate lines are a far cry from polite restraint and diplomatic tact. Lee's angry tone is readily apparent in the words he emphasizes. Hardly the ambassador of goodwill, he points an accusing finger at specific examples of outrages against the Chinese, which he—as a Chinese—feels intensely. Because their actions speak louder than their words, he boldly denies bigots the religion they profess but do not deserve.

Two years later, in "The Chinese Must Stay," Yan Phou Lee again used his pen to write/right wrongs—tackling racism and Sinophobia head-on. Like an impassioned defending attorney, he employs logic and scathing irony, marshals facts, and quotes authority to make his points. Setting up no boundaries between himself as a Yale graduate and unskilled Chinese "coolies," he rebuts eleven common charges against the Chinese. The arguments of his opening paragraph are unfortunately still current today. As he held up the ideals of Christianity in the preceding essay and found some Americans lacking, so he holds up the ideals of democracy in this essay and finds many Americans lacking.

> No nation can afford to let go its high ideals. The founders of the American Republic asserted the principle that all men are created equal, and made this fair land a refuge for the whole world. Its manifest destiny, therefore, is to be the teacher and leader of nations in liberty. . . . But now, looking at the actions of this generation of Americans in their treatment of other races, who can get rid of the idea that that Nation, which Abraham Lincoln said was conceived in liberty, waxed great through oppression, was really dedicated to the proposition that all men are created to prey on one another? (1889, 476)

Thoroughly familiar with the ideals and discourse of the U.S. founding fathers, Lee invokes them like a son. When he disrupts expectations by changing the words—from "all men are created equal" to "all men are created to prey on one another," he draws attention to the great gulf between the ideal and the real. He hopes to shame Americans into living up their professed high ideals.

To the most serious charge, that cheap Chinese labor has displaced white labor, Lee argues that by building railroads, reclaiming swamplands, and improving fruit culture, Chinese labor has created "an immense vista of employment . . . for Caucasians." Because the Chinese is willing to do the most menial work, he "enables many to turn their whole attention to something else." Furthermore, Lee argues with unassailable logic, "You may as well run down machinery as to sneer at Chinese cheap labor. Machines live on nothing at all; they have displaced millions of laborers; why not do away with machines?" (1889, 479). His loyalty to the Chinese is unequivocal, his sarcasm biting.

On the charge that the Chinese are pagans, he cites a wonderful speech by Henry Ward Beecher that employs the irony Lee himself was fond of: "We have clubbed them, stoned them, burned their houses, and murdered some of them; yet they refuse to be converted. I do not know any way, except to blow them up with nitro-glycerine, if we are ever to get them to heaven" (1889, 481).

San Francisco, where harassment of Chinese was most virulent, and where Dennis Kearney, an Irish labor leader, held anti-Chinese rallies in sandlots—making famous the slogan "The Chinese must go!"—receives the brunt of Lee's sarcasm and contempt. His essay ends with a scathing response to the charge that the "Chinese bring women of bad character to San Francisco, and that their vices are corrupting the morals of the city."

> Have you ever been to San Francisco? Unless you can endure paradise and Eden-like purity, you would better not go there. Why the Sabbath stillness in that city is simply appalling. The people all go to church. . . . There are no drunken brawls at any time (except in Chinatown). . . . Besides churches, they have numerous temples dedicated to Venus, wherein pious persons work off their surplus devotion. Why is it that these fair vestals wear so little clothing? They are afraid to clog the things of the spirit with the habiliments of sense. Californians are pure, moral, and religious, in all that they do. (1889, 483)

Clearly, Lee means the opposite of what he says. If Chinese prostitutes are making money in San Francisco, that is because others are also profiting and clients are numerous. Furthermore, they are merely joining the other prostitutes ("vestals" in the "temples dedicated to Venus") in a city that was rife with vice and lawlessness. Thus, Lee does not understand the "periodic outbreaks and outrages perpetrated against them [the Chinese] without arousing the public conscience." "The Chinese Must Stay" is Lee's effort to rouse this dormant conscience. The year was 1889; the Chinese Exclusion Act of 1882 was renewed in 1892 and again in 1902, and not repealed until 1943, several years after Lee's death. Lee's voice was an unheeded cry in the wilderness.

Nevertheless, his last known publication is a three-stanza verse, "The Star-Spangled Banner in 1917 (With Apologies to Francis Scott Key)," published in local newspapers in New Jersey. Lee reported: "As poetry they are punk, as sentiment they are bunk, but as prophecy they are all to the good. I have a letter from Secretary of War Baker, commending them for their sentiments of loyalty and patriotism" (*YCR* 1924). Again like a son, Lee seems particularly proud, not so much of his own writing, but of the letter of commendation from a high government official. Lee's assessment of his work is fairly accurate. The rhyme is predictable, even humorous (fume/gloom/doom, peoples/steeples), the rhythm in places a bit ragged, but what is striking is the patriotic passion of these verses. He writes of "our President," "our Army," "our debt," "our nation." The enemy is Germany ("God forbid that the 'Huns' shall oppress as they list"), the lady in distress is France, and the knight in shining armor, the United States. Here is the end of the second verse, from Hackensack, New Jersey's *Evening Record,* 26 April 1917:

> When our Army brings aid that our debt may be paid
> To a land that for us a great sacrifice made,
> Then its flag with our Star-Spangled Banner shall wave
> O'er a France that's set free by the deeds of the brave.

Particularly significant is that the author is identified as "Y. P. Lee, Woodridge." For the first time in print, Lee used initials instead of his full name and thus effectively hid his Chinese identity. Had he lived so long in a Sinophobic United States that he was emotionally battered and ashamed of his ancestry?[11] He held on for ten additional years after the publication of these verses, but he finally abandoned home and family and turned his back on the United States permanently. His motivation to leave had to have been extremely strong to counteract a lifelong love of the United States as the land of freedom, equality, and opportunity. But he neither explains nor complains.

Traditional Chinese believe that after death their bones must rest in Chinese soil and that they must have sons to carry on the family name and care for their spirit by placing "spirit" money and food on their graves. Otherwise, they will be doomed to wander homeless and uncared for in the spirit world and cannot intercede on behalf of their living descendants. With no known resting place, Yan Phou Lee, in death as in life, remains literally between worlds, neither here nor there.[12] No one can tend his grave, as he did not tend his adoptive father's. However, as one of the first to occupy the difficult space of the frontier where two cultures meet, it is perhaps fitting that Yan Phou Lee has no known resting place, for he seems thereby to be asserting his independence from confining traditional Chinese customs, as well as his distance from U.S. racism. He rests, therefore, in his own space, an Asian American place of distinction.

Notes

Acknowledgments: I am indebted to Anne Nahn for copies of the Yan Phou Lee entries in *Yale Class Records* [YCR] and *Yale Class Books* [YCB] and information gleaned from her letters and from telephone conversations with descendants of Yan Phou Lee: Mrs. Clarence Lee (wife of Yan Phou Lee's son) of McLean, Virginia, and Dr. Richard Lee (son of Yan Phou Lee's son

Louis Emerson) of Orchard Park, New York. Chris Robyn (1996) generously gave me a copy of his thesis. I also thank Edward Skipworth of Rutgers University Archives. The epigraph by David Porush is quoted in Krupat 1992, 79.

1. In Ling 1994, I compare the autobiographical writings of the four earliest Chinese American authors—Yan Phou Lee, Yung Wing, Sui Sin Far, and Onoto Watanna—and find divisions along gender lines.

2. Yan Phou Lee's name has been romanized and ordered differently in various texts. In China, the family name precedes the given name, and the three scholars whose texts I consulted all used this ordering (but see La Fargue 1942; Robyn 1996; Kim 1982). All Lee's published writings but one are signed Yan Phou Lee, a preference I honor in this essay.

3. La Fargue summarizes the careers of the three: Lee Kwai-pan, Jann Ting-seong, and Lee Yen-fu. Lee Kwai-pan engaged in the tea business in New York but died within a few years of the "abandonment of the Mission." Jang Ting-seong "subsequently became well known in New York as a consulting engineer, and was one of the engineers who designed and erected the Brooklyn Bridge. He invented the Jann coupling for railway cars and many other mechanical devices" (142). Lee Yen-fu was the author of "the widely read children's book, 'When I was a Boy in China,' … made his living as a journalist and for several years was the editor of a newspaper in New Jersey," in 1917 "attained some notice by writing a new version of the 'Star-Spangled Banner,' was married twice and lost a son in World War I" (142). Considering the intense Sinophobia of this period, both Jang and Lee were surprisingly successful in contributing to the major issues of their time and weaving themselves into the fabric of U.S. life.

4. As King-kok Cheung has demonstrated in her study of three Asian American women writers, "silence, too, can speak many tongues" (1993, 1).

5. Unless otherwise noted, subsequent page numbers in parentheses in the text are from Lee's *I Was a Boy in China* (1887a).

6. According to Robyn, the students reacted to the recall order with consternation and dismay. In Shanghai, they were initially imprisoned in a deserted schoolhouse under armed guard. Huang Kaijia complained in a letter to the Bartlett family: "You may have read about Turkish prisons or Andersonville horrors, but compared with this, they must have been enviable places" (Robyn 1996, 75). The Chinese had heard that all the students had cut off their queues, thereby becoming demons and traitors who should be tried for "conspiracy against the government, theft of valuable property, and change of religious views" (76). New England newspapers carried stories of returned students being beheaded for having fallen in love with American girls. The rumors revealed deep-seated distrust and xenophobia on both sides. Little wonder that Yan Phou Lee later wrote that he "escaped" and made his way back in time to join the class of 1887 at Yale.

7. Jennie "graduated from Mount Holyoke College in 1911 and later attended the Yale Art School. She has for some years been in charge of the art department of the New Haven Public Library" (YCR 1938). Anne Nahn notes that Jennie "became famous for her extensive collection of pictures, sketches, paintings and photographs on every subject imaginable. Blind in her later years, she died about 1985." Amos graduated from Yale in 1910 and become "a First Lieutenant in Aviation, serving with the French Escadrille Spah 90." Trained at MIT, he was sent to France in September 1917 and was "killed in battle on July 12, 1919, at Berdenal" (YCR 1924).

8. Clarence Vaille Lee was a midshipman on convoy duty on the U.S.S. *South Dakota* in 1918, graduated from the U.S. Naval Academy in 1919 and in 1937 was an instructor in navigation there, married in 1938, and is now deceased. Louis graduated from Yale in 1927. Although

he and his wife have died, their son, Dr. Richard Lee, lives in New York, and their daughter, Mrs. M. L. Winfield, lives in Connecticut.

9. Lee reports in *YCR* 1924 that he was assistant editor of the *American Banker* in 1918 and managing editor in 1919. A number of reasons make his 1937 account of this period suspect: He was writing ten years after the fact; he had returned to Canton, then undergoing daily aerial bombardment from Japan; and he was seventy-six and had just lost his source of income.

10. Unless otherwise noted, page numbers in parentheses in the text are from Lee 1887a.

11. A December 1997 note from Lee's grandson Richard Lee informs me that he learned that he had a Chinese grandfather only when he announced that he intended to get married. Because of strong discrimination, the family had kept its Chinese ancestry a secret.

12. My thanks to Rocio Davis of the University of Navarra for suggesting this idea.

Works Cited

Bakhtin, M. M. 1981. "Epic and Novel." In *The Dialogic Imagination,* trans. Caryl Emerson and Michael Holquist. Austin: University of Texas Press.

Cheung, King-kok. 1993. *Articulate Silences: Hisaye Yamamoto, Maxine Hong Kingston, Joy Kogawa.* Ithaca: Cornell University Press.

Frost, Robert. 1953. "The Death of the Hired Man." In *The Literature of the United States.* Vol. 2, ed. Walter Blair, Theodore Hornberger, and Randall Stewart. New York: Scott, Foresman.

Kim, Elaine. 1982. *Asian American Literature: An Introduction to the Writings and Their Social Context.* Philadelphia: Temple University Press.

Krupat, Arnold. 1992. *Ethnocriticism: Ethnography, History, Literature.* Berkeley and Los Angeles: University of California Press.

La Fargue, Thomas E. 1942. *China's First Hundred.* Pullman: State College of Washington.

Lee, Yan Phou. 1887a. *When I Was a Boy in China.* Boston: Lothrop.

———. 1887b. "Why I Am Not a Heathen." *North American Review* 145, 370 (September): 306–12.

———. 1889. "The Chinese Must Stay." *North American Review* 148, 389 (April): 476–83.

Ling, Amy. 1994. "Gender Issues in Early Chinese American Autobiography." In *A Gathering of Voices on the Asian American Experience,* ed. Annette White-Parks et al., 110–11. Fort Atkinson, Wis.: Highsmith Press.

Robyn, Chris. 1996. "Building the Bridge: The Chinese Educational Mission to the United States: A Sino-American Historico-Cultural Synthesis, 1872–1881." Master's thesis, Chinese University of Hong Kong.

Edward Marx

18   "A Different Mode of Speech": Yone Noguchi in Meiji America

Asian American literature is the literature of Asian America, not simply the literature of Asian Americans. The literature of Asian Americans—whether legally or more inclusively defined—has a special place in Asian American studies, a discipline largely founded on the premise that Asian American voices should be heard. The literature of early Asian Americans is particularly important because their works can articulate a point of origin for contemporary Asian Americans. As writers committed by birth or choice to U.S. ideals, they offer a compelling subject for a mainstream U.S. culture that continues to marginalize Asian American perspectives.

But the literature of early Asian America—which I take to be an America transformed by the impact of Asian people and culture—offers a far wider field, including many writers who would never qualify for inclusion as Asian Americans under either the policies of the immigration office or the consensus of contemporary Asian American communities. These writers include those who wrote in or about America as visitors, critics, and opponents, some of whom perhaps never set foot in the United States, but all of whom nevertheless exerted an influence in one way or another on the development of Asian America.

We may take a step further and allow that Asian America in this broader sense includes American Asianists like the writer Lafcadio Hearn or the photographer Arnold Genthe. In doing so, we will have stepped through a sort of veil, to invoke the useful theory of "double consciousness" developed by W.E.B. DuBois to explore parallel issues of African-American identity, a reminder that subject positions in a racially determined world may be fixed by boundaries permeable to theory. The people who lived in early Asian America were, by and large, Asians. That some of them became or gave birth to Asian Americans is the basis of many important and interesting stories, but they are not the only stories of Asian America, and for some groups, not even the main ones. Asian American studies should be committed to telling as many of these stories as can be recovered, with Asian American literature serving as the place where we look first to hear them told by the people who lived them.

Early Japanese America in this broader sense offers a field full of extraordinary writing by gifted and articulate writers in a variety of genres, in both English and Japanese, most of which has received little attention within contemporary Asian American studies. Among autobiographers, only the work of Etsu Sugimoto is widely known; few have even heard of, let alone read, such precursors as Joseph Heco and Tel Sono. The names of the Japanese American poets Sadakichi Hartmann and Jun Fujita are mentioned occasionally, but there are no studies of their poetry. Important Japanese fictional works set in the United States such as Tokai Sanshi's *Kajin no Kigū* (Strange encounters with beautiful women) and Kafū Nagai's *America Monogatari* (American stories) have been out of the purview of Asian American studies, although the latter, happily, has recently been made available in translation.[1] In this essay, I explore the work of one of the most versatile of these early writers engaged with the United States: Yone Noguchi.

Yone Noguchi's story did end in the production of a Japanese American—a very famous one in fact: the sculptor Isamu Noguchi—but this was, one might say, accidental. Yone Noguchi's story, like the stories of many early Japanese in the United States, did not end in his own adoption of America as his permanent home. After a little more than a decade spent mainly in California and New York, he returned to Japan, where, according to his 28 July 1947 obituary in *Time,* he "discarded his Western wife and ideas, [and] became a great booster of Japanese imperialism" (84). Evaluating Noguchi's intentions toward the United States as a potential home, one might cite only a single passage from a letter to his future wife: "I am sorry to inform that I am not American citizen. Sometime I will, I think. I made up mind concerning about this matter" (*CEL* 74). In 1902, when the letter was written, naturalization remained a real possibility for Japanese in the United States: several hundred had achieved it. But Noguchi returned to Japan in 1904, and the window of opportunity closed in 1906 when the U.S. attorney general ordered the federal courts to deny naturalized citizenship to Japanese aliens (Takaki 1989, 207).

The legal obstacles were of course only one factor in Noguchi's decision to remain Japanese, and after returning to Japan, Noguchi showed little more than an occasional symptom of nostalgia for his U.S. life and was even prepared to argue in 1913 that "the American naturalization extended to Japanese would be a damaging affair for Japan," though he upheld the Japanese claim to "equal treatment with other Western people" (Noguchi 1913b). As Japan's relationship with the United States became more troubled, Noguchi's attitude became more critical. Although he was still calling himself a "person of dual nationality" *(nikokusekisha)* in the early 1920s, his engagement with Western culture lessened in the 1930s, and from the so-called Manchurian Incident, the beginning of Japan's undeclared war in 1931, to the end of World War II he was, like most Japanese writers, a vocal supporter of the war effort, contributing two volumes of propagandistic poetry to it. Yet his last act before his death was to orchestrate a reconciliation between his Japanese family and his American son Isamu.

Noguchi's immense contribution to Japanese American literature during his eleven-year stay, and after, has resulted in only an occasional mention in Asian American literary histories as a pioneering poet. His pseudonymous authorship in 1902 of the first Japanese American novel, *The American Diary of a Japanese Girl,* is rarely noticed.

Despite the occasional efforts of scholars, mainly Japanese, to draw attention to Noguchi's case, there has been continued skepticism concerning Noguchi's claims to inclusion in the Asian American canon. As noted, there has admittedly been little enough interest in any prewar Japanese American writer. But the scope of Noguchi's literary career makes his exclusion particularly difficult to explain. The list of books Noguchi published in the United States includes several poetry collections, a novel, a collection of essays, a book on Japanese poetry, and another on Japanese art; his articles and poems appeared in many prominent U.S. magazines. The list of his British publications is nearly as long, and that of his publications in Japan, many of which form a part of his American work, is much longer.

Of his U.S. works in English, the most important are Noguchi's autobiographical writings, particularly those collected in *The Story of Yone Noguchi* (1914); his two volumes of poetry published in California, *Seen and Unseen: Or, Monologues of a Homeless Snail* (1897a) and *The Voice of the Valley* (1897b); a third, London-published volume of American poetry, *From the Eastern Sea* (1903); and his two novels written in the United States, *The American Diary of a Japanese Girl* (1902) and *The American Letters of a Japanese Parlor Maid* (1905). Noguchi's later interactions with the United States may be partially followed through his contributions to periodicals like the *Nation* and the *Bookman* as well as in the book that came out of his 1919–20 American lecture tour, *Japan and America* (1921), but beyond that must be pursued through his Japanese writings. This essay will be primarily concerned with Noguchi's life and literary production during his residence in the United States, with some preliminary consideration of the Japanese context from which Noguchi emerged onto the American scene.

Meiji Boyhood

Yonejirō Noguchi was born in Tsushima, a small town near Nagoya, in 1875.[2] His father, Denbei, about whom he wrote little, is said to have been a merchant of *geta* (wooden clogs), paper, and umbrellas; his mother, Okuwa, came from a family with strong connections to the Buddhist priesthood (Takai 1985, 23). Their four sons all left home to pursue various careers: as a railway engineer, a Buddhist priest, a Tokyo merchant, and Yonejirō, the youngest, a poet. There were apparently two sisters, one of whom died in childhood.

Yonejirō was sent at the age of thirteen to the Ōtani school in nearby Nagoya "newly opened, under the support of the main Buddhist temple of the Otani sect." There he had his first foreign teacher, evidently a common sailor: "In those days, when we had little experience with foreigners," Noguchi notes, "a white skin and red hair were a sufficient passport for a Western teacher in any Japanese school" (1915, 4). After a short time, Noguchi moved to the Nagoya Prefectural High School, but finding the work "far too easy for my mind," he soon left for Tokyo, intending to prepare for the Tokyo University entrance examination, "not waiting for father's permission ... as my boyish ambition had grown too big to be peaceful in a provincial city" (6). Once there, however, he despaired of passing the difficult mathematics section of the examination and set his sights instead on Keiō Gijuku, the private school established by Yukichi Fukuzawa (1834–1901), "the greatest educator modern Japan ever produced" (7).

Fukuzawa, in 1860 a minor figure in the first Japanese embassy to the United States, had returned to Japan full of enthusiasm for the achievements of the West and convinced of the need to rebuild Japanese institutions along Western lines. Before 1890, Keiō had been an elite secondary school, but that year it opened its first three departments as a university with the help of three newly imported American professors sent by Fukuzawa's friend, Harvard president Charles W. Eliot. Rejecting the insular scholasticism of traditional Japanese education, Fukuzawa told his students to "always be aware of the 'great school' called society outside of the classrooms." "If a student is able to study while learning from society," Fukuzawa suggested, "he will be prepared to serve in society or at home, in private enterprise or in an official capacity, in industry and in commerce" (Fukuzawa 1985, 203).

Fukuzawa was a strong advocate of Westernism in education, society, and politics. Like many of his era, he regarded establishing Japanese equality with Western countries as a major objective. To that end, he was prepared to sacrifice Japan's Asian identity, as he wrote in an 1885 editorial entitled "Escape from Asia" *(Datsu-A ron)*: Since "today China and Korea are no help at all to our country," he argued, "we should escape from them and join the company of Western civilized nations" (Pyle 1969, 149). Nevertheless, as Kenneth Pyle points out, "the Japanese who first advocated the adoption of Western culture appear, paradoxically, to have been among the first to show an interest in studying their national cultural past" (88), and Fukuzawa's *Outline of Civilization* (1876) was among these early critiques of the lack of historical interest in Japanese culture.

Fukuzawa, as Yūji Ichioka points out, not only helped to create "a popular vision of America" through books like *Seiyō jiyō* (Western conditions, 1866) and *Seiyō tabi annai* (A travel guide to the West, 1867), but also directly encouraged young men to go abroad, in *Jiji shimpō*, the newspaper he launched in 1882, and in speeches at Keiō Gijuku. Japanese society, he argued, was unable to absorb the growing number of educated Japanese youth, and the United States was a land of opportunity. He even helped to finance an agricultural colony in Calaveras County, California, in 1887 (Ichioka 1988, 9–10).

Noguchi's reminiscences of Keiō in *The Story of Yone Noguchi* are both sketchy and rather lacking in enthusiasm: "At this Keio," he writes, "I was put to learn somebody's economy and history; and you will wonder to know that I learned also Spencer's Education (why Education for a small boy to be educated?), to which I clung as if, in an old story, a blind man to a huge elephant" (1915, 7). His memory of the American English teacher is vague ("I often excused myself from the conversation class under an American teacher," he writes), but although he "grew now even to despise the spoken English language," he nevertheless developed an interest in American literature, reading Longfellow for school, and Irving's *Sketch Book*, "which made me long for England and Westminster Abbey," as well as Thomas Gray, and Oliver Goldsmith's "The Deserted Village," on his own (8).[3]

Shigetaka Shiga and the "New Generation"

Fukuzawa was by this time among the older generation of Japanese reformers and, by the time Noguchi arrived in Tokyo, had already begun to be supplanted by the "New Generation" of Meiji intellectuals, of whom Kenneth Pyle has provided a careful study.[4] In the late 1880s and early 1890s, this New Generation was polarized between, on the one side, the avid pro-Westernism of Sohō Tokutomi (1863–1957) and his group, the *Min'yūsha* (Friends of the People)—represented by the magazine *Kokumin no tomo* (Thenation's friend), which began publication in 1886—and, on the other side, the *Seikyōsha* (Society for Political Education), formed in 1888 and led by Shigetaka Shiga (1863–1927) and Setsurei Miyake (1860–1945), who offered opposition to Tokutomi's *Kokumin no tomo* with a competing, culturally nationalistic magazine, *Nihonjin* (The Japanese).

It was Shigetaka Shiga, Noguchi's "life-long mentor," who was to play the most important role in Noguchi's story. Shunsuke Kamei notes that while in Tokyo, Noguchi lived with Shiga, working as his "houseboy," and that it was at Shiga's home that Noguchi first came into contact with Den Sugawara, the exiled political activist to whom Noguchi later carried a letter of introduction (no doubt Shiga's) after arriving in San Francisco. According to Kamei,

> while he was living in Shiga's house as a houseboy, Den Sugawara . . . temporarily returned home and visited with Shiga. Overhearing Sugawara speak of the life in that "sacred land of liberty," Noguchi instantly determined to go there and see the life himself. Yukichi Fukuzawa, the founder and principal of Keio Gijuku and the most influential leader of Japan's modernization in the Meiji era, encouraged Noguchi, a practically penniless boy of eighteen years old, in his resolution to tread on the lion's tail, and the dreamy boy's friends contributed the money for the passage. (1965, 46)

On 3 November 1893, Noguchi's friends saw him off at Tokyo's Shinbashi station, where he boarded the train for the port of Yokohama. Stepping onto the boat was a painful experience for the eighteen-year-old, who later recalled, "I stood by an iron rail on the deck, a boy only eighteen years old, alone, friendless, with less than one hundred dollars in my pocket. I immediately grew conscious of the fact that I had to face unknown America, a land of angels or devils, the darkness" (1915, 25–26).

San Francisco, 1893–1900

Autobiographies, poststructuralists tell us, are always fictions, and yet we cannot help feeling that some are more fictional than others. Noguchi's autobiographical writing, with its alternative versions, casual disregard for dates and events, and occasional inclusion of events that never took place, certainly falls into this more aggressively fictional category. The problems begin with Noguchi's first day in the United States, in December 1893, which comes in two incompatible versions. Let us consider first the standard version in "Some Stories of My Western Life," included in *The Story of Yone Noguchi,* which trenchantly evokes the experience of the new Japanese arrival in America:

> The steamer duly reached San Francisco on a certain Sunday morning; we, I and a few other fellow-passengers, were taken to the Cosmopolitan Hotel, whose shabby appearance looked then palace-like and most wonderful. And within it was not less handsome. The American room was the first thing for us; even the sheets and the soft pillow, quite strange for the head acquainted only with hard wood, were a novelty. We put all the fruits we had bought (what splendid California fruits!) in a white bowl under the washing table; when we were told, to our utmost shame, that that bowl was for another purpose, we at once thought that we were, indeed, in a country alien in custom, and had a thousand things to study. We acted even more barbarously at the dinner-table; we took salt for sugar, and declared the cheese to be something rotten. We did not know which hand, left or right, had to hold a knife; we used a tablespoon for sipping the coffee, in which we did not know enough to drop a lump of sugar; we could not understand that those lumps were sugar. I stepped alone out of the hotel into a street and crowd; what attracted my immediate attention, which soon became admiration, was the American women. "What lovely complexions, what delightfully quick steps," I exclaimed. They were a perfect revelation of freedom and new beauty for my Japanese eye, having no relation whatever with any form of convention with which I was acquainted at home. (1915, 26–27)

As the story continues, however, the pleasures of exoticism, the strange manners and customs of the Americans, the edible novelties, beds instead of familiar *futon,* these evident delights to the young traveler, give way to another, darker side of the American experience:

> I again stepped out of the hotel after supper, and walked up and down, turned right, and again left, till the night was growing late. When I felt quite doubtful about my way back to the hotel, I was standing before a certain show window (I believe it was on Market Street), the beauty of which doubtless surprised me; I was suddenly struck by a hard hand from behind, and found a large, red-faced fellow, somewhat smiling in scorn, who, seeing my face, exclaimed, "hello, Jap!" I was terribly indignant to be addressed in such a fashion; my indignation increased when he ran away, after spitting on my face. I recalled my friend, who said that I should have such a determination as if I were entering among enemies; I thrilled from fear with the uncertainty and even the darkness of my future. I could not find the way to my hotel, when I felt every thing grow sad at once; in fact, nearly all the houses looked alike. Nobody seemed to understand my English, in the ability of which I trusted; many of the people coldly passed by even when I tried to speak. I almost cried, when I found one Japanese, fortunately; he, after hearing my trouble, exclaimed in laughter: "You are standing right before your hotel, my friend!" (1915, 28)

On the following day, after passing a sleepless night on the hotel's soft bed, according to this account, Noguchi took his letter of introduction from Shigetaka Shiga to the Japanese newspaper office on O'Farrell Street, which was to become his new home.

This most excellent account, however, is thrown into doubt when we compare it to an earlier version of the story where we find, simply, "One led me into a wooden house at the back of O'Farrell St., leaving the 'Belgic.'"[5] No Cosmopolitan Hotel, no chamberpot or dinner-table comedy, no red-faced racist or traveler's angst on Market Street. This earlier account, which was rejected by *Harper's Magazine* in 1903 as "almost too rambling in character" (the editor suggesting that Noguchi try "a skit in lighter vein"), while admittedly less appealing, is far more plausible. Going directly to the Japanese newspaper office (with the help of one of the many Japanese meeting a ship arriving from Yokohama) seems a far likelier course of action for an eighteen-year-old student facing "a land of angels or devils, the darkness," with little money and less English than checking into an expensive downtown hotel.

We may, however, consider the version of "Some Stories" truthful as a composite picture of the shock of arrival and the reality of California racism. In 1893, the Japanese population in California was hardly large enough to justify the sort of anti-Japanese sentiment that would erupt onto the political scene seven years later and eventually lead to the 1913 Alien Land Law that prevented "aliens ineligible to citizenship" from owning land in the state. From 1861 to 1890, the number of Japanese immigrants to the United States was only about 2,600; during the 1890s this number would grow by a factor of ten, though still representing only 0.7 percent of new immigrants (Spickard 1996, 21). Nevertheless, even the small influx of students and agricultural workers in the late nineteenth century did encounter racism and resentment, constructed at first upon anti-Chinese feeling, but soon tailored to specific Japanese-related fears in reaction to increased Japanese immigration and the emergence of Japan as a military power in the 1890s.

Noguchi used various strategies to counter the racism he undoubtedly encountered in California, including the humor and irony evident in the passages cited above. He determined not to be bothered by the term "Jap" and even came to use it frequently himself. And he rarely spoke in his English writings about the experience of racism, presumably believing along with other Japanese that it would disappear when they proved themselves worthy of equal treatment. When he treated the subject, he was generally careful to deploy the sort of balance and humor characteristic of the passages cited.

But one should not confuse Noguchi's literary nonchalance about California racism for evidence that it was not a serious problem. Indeed, Noguchi's friend, the painter Yoshio Markino, wrote far more frankly and critically about California racism in his autobiography, *A Japanese Artist in London* (1910). Markino, who may have known Noguchi as far back as Nagoya, where he studied English beginning in 1887, arrived in San Francisco just six months ahead of Noguchi, armed with a letter from none other than Shigetaka Shiga, this time to the Japanese consul in San Francisco, Sutemi Chinda. Discouraged by Chinda from a career in English literature, Markino enrolled in the Hopkins Art School. As he recalled:

> I was rather amused with my poor life, but by no means did I feel pleasant with the way those Californians treated me. It is the world-known fact that they hate Japanese. While I have been there four years I never went to the parks, for I was so frightened of those savage people, who threw stones and bricks at me. Even when I was walking on the street the showers of pebbles used to fall on me often. And I was spat on more occasionally. . . . If I got into a tram-car and sat down on an empty seat beside some ladies, they used to glare

at me with such disgusting expression, and would get up and go away to find out a seat far away from me. (1910, 5–6)

Markino found London much more congenial and remained there until forcibly repatriated during World War II. But the experience of California racism remained with him, as he noted in 1910: "Even now, after some thirteen years' stay in London, I often have nightmares of California, and wake up in midnight and wonder where I really am" (8).

The Japanese in America

Indigent students like Noguchi represented a large sector of the Japanese population in the United States in 1893. About two hundred passports a year were issued to students during this period. (Agricultural and contract workers made up most of the rest.) A few were officially studying at such places as the University of California or Stanford, while the majority looked for learning in more accessible places. "Lacking the wherewithal to travel east, the students tended to settle in San Francisco and its vicinity where they constituted the majority of local Japanese residents until the late 1890s, the total Japanese population in the city being about 2,500" (Ichioka 1988, 9).

A small group of these student laborers were political exiles who had participated in the People's Rights Movement in Japan, which had grown out of local protests against the power of the central government in the late 1870s but subsequently collapsed under severe government repression in the early 1880s. Under the weight of government restrictions, the Liberal Party was dissolved in 1884, and the journalistic wing of the radical movement was further hindered in 1887 by the revision of the National Press Law. As a result, a number of the movement's leaders went into exile in the United States (Ichioka 1988, 14–15). One of these leaders was Tsutau Sugawara, also known as Den Sugawara. On 7 January 1888, Sugawara and others "established in San Francisco a political club called the Patriotic League" (Aikoku Dōmei). As Noguchi explained, the "principal object was to reform the bureaucracy at home, to speak more directly, to put an end to the government of the Satsuma and Chōshū Clans, by demonstration with the publication of free speech" (1915, 30).[6] Elsewhere, however, he says the group's "chief aim was to bring about a new treaty with the foreign country" ("Sodachi," 211). Ichioka observes that "the aims of the League were threefold: to sponsor talks and debates, to publish a newspaper, and to maintain contacts with movement leaders in Japan" (1988, 15–16).

"The origins of the immigrant press," Ichioka writes, "can be traced to the members of the Patriotic League and the student-laborers" (1988, 19). The first publication, *Shinome* (Dawn), appeared in 1886, followed by the short-lived *Shin Nippon* (New Japan) in 1887 and 1888. Japanese government bans effectively ended the life of many of these early papers, as distribution in Japan was a primary objective. Thus the name of the weekly published by the Patriotic League from 1888 to 1893 changed six times, in response to successive bans. The group began the first daily paper in 1892, under the name *Sōkō Shimbun* (San Francisco news), and it was this paper that Noguchi was primarily involved with during his San Francisco years, although the title was changed to *Sōkō Shimpō* (San Francisco daily) in 1893 and *Sōkō Jiji* (San Francisco times) in 1895. Noguchi also had some connection with the *Shin Sekai* (New world), competitor to the *Sōkō Shimbun* and the first typeset daily, which began publication in the spring of 1894. And there was a rather troubled relationship with another group, the *Enseisha* (expedition club), who ran the *Kimmon Nippō* (Golden gate), another early daily (1893–95), and were perennially at odds with the Aikoku Dōmei (1915, 33–34; Ichioka 1988, 20).

The Aikoku Dōmei's office in a run-down house at the edge of Chinatown, to which Noguchi brought his letter of introduction, reminded him, he wrote, "of something I had read about the Russian anarchists" (1915, 30). In his account, the members of the group were at that moment discussing the fate of the Hawaiian kingdom with a Hawaiian activist, Robert Wilcox, who had come to enlist support to oppose the recent American-led coup. Noguchi had read about Wilcox, perhaps in Shiga's *Conditions in the South Seas,* and was readily drawn into the group's plan to send three members back to Japan to advocate Hawaiian independence, contributing all his spare money to the cause, though he later conceded that "it was partly from my little vanity not to be taken for a mere boy" (31). The effort was of course fruitless—Hawai'i became a U.S. territory in 1900—but it is important as an indicator of the atmosphere of imperialism which was pervasive during the period.[7]

Noguchi joined the group and was appointed to the position of delivery boy. As the paper then had a circulation of under 150, and five or six employees, "I did not enter into any talk about payment; I soon discovered it was perfectly useless when we hardly knew how to get dinner every day" (1915, 32). Ichioka notes that the paper's total monthly income in 1895 was about sixty dollars (1988, 21). Noguchi recalled that "by turns, we used to get up and build a fire and prepare big pancakes, you understand, with no egg or milk, just with water. And a cupful of coffee was all we had for our breakfast" (1915, 32). From another writer's recollections, it may be added that "the coffee had no milk and was like piss" (Ichioka 1988, 21). Sometimes, however, the staff was able to eat at a Chinese restaurant on Dupont Street in exchange for advertising. As "there was no bed in the house," Noguchi recalled, "we used to sleep upon a large table, a mass of newspapers serving as mattresses" (1915, 32).

Noguchi found the lifestyle "unbearable at the beginning; but I became soon satisfied, even glad, as I could have plenty of time for my own reading." Volumes of the *Encyclopædia Britannica,* when not being used in place of pillows, were available for Noguchi's perusal, and there he found Macaulay's essay on Lord Byron, who became his new favorite. He also began the rather lengthy task of reading *Hamlet.* As he delivered his eighty or so papers, Noguchi "always thought about some English book," and if no one was in sight he "was pleased to recite loudly the lines" from memory (1915, 11). One of the group's older members, Tokuji Watari, took a "rather fatherly" attitude toward Noguchi, who recalled that "it was one of my delights to talk with him, more often listen to him, every morning, while still in bed, on poetry and politics," though he also recalled how Watari "tired me with his Darwinism, which I little understand even to-day" (32–33).

"Schoolboy"

"When I began to reflect on what I had come to America for, to ask myself how far my English had improved, and what American life I had seen, I regretted my mistake in associating with the Aikoku Dōmei and put an advertisement as a 'schoolboy' in the *Chronicle*, following the way of many other Japanese boys." So Noguchi says in "Some Stories of My Western Life" (1915, 35), though elsewhere he cites as the primary cause "the immediate necessity of bread and butter" (8). Noguchi found a job "as a kitchen boy in a certain Jewish family," where he assisted an Irish cook who taught him the names of the unfamiliar objects in the wealthy family's kitchen, dining room, and parlor. Many Japanese "schoolboys" bitterly resented the job, which, as "maid-servant's work," affronted their class and gender sensibilities, and in which they commonly encountered depersonalizing attitudes and racism, but Noguchi had sufficient curiosity and irony to find value in the experience, which later provided ready material for his unsuccessful second novel, *The American Letters of a Japanese Parlor-Maid* (1905), and he offered a memorably humorous account of the schoolboy experience in *The Story of Yone Noguchi* as well:

> What domestic work has that "schoolboy" to do? The work is slight, since the wages are little—one dollar and a half a week. We have to leave our bed before six, and build a fire for breakfast. Don't throw in too much coal, mind you; your Mrs. Smith or Mrs. Brown will be displeased with you, surely. She can hear every noise you make in the kitchen, she can see how lazy you are as clear as can be, no matter if she be busy with her hair upstairs. "Charlie, isn't the water boiling?" she will cry down. Charlie! Your father didn't give the name to you, did he? A great pile of dirty dishes will welcome you from the sink when you return from your school about four o'clock. Immediately, a basketful of peas will be ready to be shelled. You must go without dessert, if you eat the strawberries too often while picking. Saturday was our terror-day. We had to work all day beginning with the bathroom. Your lady will let her finger go over the furniture when you finish. "See!" she will show you her finger marked with dust. Patience! What a mighty lesson for the youth! You must not forget to wash your stockings before you go to bed, and hang them on a chair. How could we afford two pair of stockings in our schoolboy days? What a farce we enacted in our first encounter with an American family! Even a stove was a mystery to us. One of my friends endeavoured to make a fire by burning the kindling in the oven. Another one was on the point of blowing out the gaslight. One fellow terrified the lady when he began to take off his shoes, and even his trousers, before scrubbing the floor. It is true, however fantastic it may sound. It was natural enough for him, since he regarded his American clothes as a huge luxury. Poor fellow! He was afraid he might spoil them. I rushed into my Madam's toilet-room without knocking. The American woman took it good-naturedly, as it happened. She pitied our ignorance, but without any touch of sarcasm. Japanese civilisation, if it was born in America, certainly was born in her household—in some well-to-do San Francisco family, rather than in Yale or Harvard. (1915, 35–36)

Noguchi's irony served him well throughout his years in the United States, allowing him to tolerate the arrogance of employers and friends without losing appreciation for kindness offered to him; he could always fall back on the stoical "determination as if I were entering among enemies" when reduced to a "Charlie" (which, Ichioka notes, "had strong condescending overtones" in contrast to "neutral" names like Frank or Joseph [26]), or when performing the morning ritual required by "the master of the house" whom Noguchi "hated with a sense of fear," who "came down to the cellar every morning calling me John, and pushed out his foot for his shoe to be cleaned." This indignity was compensated for by the generosity of the beautiful young lady of the house, "who taught me the Third California State Reader every evening in my little down-cellar room," despite his "great sensitiveness to female beauty, which was in a speedy way of development," and which "made me restless rather than learn the lesson" (1915, 10). Finally, however, he writes, "the feeling of being something like a slave made me rebel," and faced with the prospect of working a week without pay after breaking a window, he made his escape.[8]

Palo Alto and the Sino-Japanese War

Noguchi had a friend studying at Stanford, and in accordance with the Japanese proverb "The children who live by the temple learn how to read a sutra," he determined to try his luck in Palo Alto. Presenting himself at the home of the professor where his friend was then working, Noguchi was permitted to stay until he found a way to support himself and subsequently found places in a lawyer's house and at a preparatory school, Manzanita Hall, "where I was admitted to appear at the school for my service in cleaning the classrooms and waiting on table for the student-boarders" (1915, 37). Noguchi later had little recollection of these months aside from being generally impressed by Stanford's academic atmosphere. Ashamed of his heelless shoes and dirty coat, Noguchi took a job as a dishwasher at the Menlo Park Hotel, which must have brought his scholarly efforts to a quick end, as he reports, "I had to rise every morning before four o'clock, and my work was never finished till ten o'clock at night" (38).

The most memorable events of his stay in Palo Alto took place on the other side of the globe. On 1 August 1894, Japan declared war on China, an event that was to have important repercussions for Noguchi, Japan, and the world. The Sino-Japanese War was an enormously exciting event for Noguchi and for other Japanese at home and abroad. It began only sixteen days after the renegotiation of Japan's unequal treaties after decades of determined struggle and represented, for the Japanese, their country's emergence as a world power. Primarily a dispute over supremacy in Korea, it was essentially an imperialistic war, as was the Russo-Japanese war a decade later, and represented the Japanese determination to pursue an expansionist policy, in the belief that "only by doing so would they be counted among the world's great nations" (Iriye 1989, 765). Nor was the belief a mistaken one, as the two wars succeeded in raising dramatically the position of Japan in international esteem.

It was a great help for Noguchi's English, as the Japanese chef at the hotel would send him upstairs to read the paper with instructions to "come down after one hour with the news of victory" (1915, 15). "What a delight it was to read the paper with the battle news," Noguchi recalled (1915, 38). "My mind grew restless from a sudden burst of desire to see my friends at San Francisco, and talk over the war, if it were necessary, even to fight with them," and so, he "dismissed [himself] from the hotel, and hurried back again to the *San Francisco News*" (38). There, after being divested of his recent earnings, the now-seasoned translator was begged to stay on to translate stories from the U.S. papers for inclusion in the *Sōkō shimbun*. He stayed on for three months, translating "everything from the American papers, from the Japanese Emperor's Imperial Edict to a tragedy of a street girl," and for a short while, he declared, "it was I who ran Soko Shimbun" (16).

The war also changed public perception of the Japanese in the United States, and Noguchi recalled that "it was in those days of the China-Japan War that I had more chances to speak English; to anybody I came across, I tried to explain the difference between China and Japan, and above all, why we won the fight." Japanese patriotic spirit was in the air, and Noguchi felt suddenly compelled to "shout from the pit or gallery" denouncing the absurdity of Gilbert and Sullivan's *Mikado,* then in vogue, and attended the lecture of "a certain Mr. Creelman ... on the so-called Port Arthur brutality, on his way to New York from the war field at Manchuria," prepared with his protest, "which I had all ready to deliver against that lecturer on the spot, if my courage had not failed" (1915, 16).

Joaquin Miller

In March 1895, China sued for peace, bringing the war to a close, and the excitement no doubt began to fade from the office of the *Sōkō shimbun.* Noguchi began to feel restless, and he developed the peculiar idea "that books should be read slowly but thoroughly after having a good sound rest" (1915, 17).

Noguchi had heard in Palo Alto about an eccentric poet living in the Oakland hills by the name of Joaquin Miller. Miller's name was no more known to Noguchi then than it is to most literary scholars today, but he was at that time the premier poet of California, and when Noguchi stumbled upon his name half a year later, thumbing through his *Webster's Dictionary* in the *Shimbun* office, his reverence toward Miller "doubled at once" (56). Other Japanese had made the pilgrimage to Miller's home in "The Heights," as Miller called it then—today the place is well known to contemporary Bay Area residents as Joaquin Miller Park—and this, combined with his manner of living in a style reminiscent of certain legendary Japanese poets, led to his being "regarded most reverentially by Japanese as a *sennin*, or 'hermit who lived on dews.'" So when Noguchi complained to another friend of his "great despair of American life," a visit to Oakland was the prescription (39).

The sixty-year-old Miller had not always been a "hermit who lived on dews"; earlier, he had lived a varied and adventurous life that included an early trip west in a covered wagon with his family, panning for gold during the gold rush, fighting both with and against various American Indian tribes, and studying law and serving as a judge in

Oregon, where he also ran a newspaper. He had established himself as a literary figure in 1870, traveling to England to publish *Songs of the Sierras*, his first collection of poetry, and the quasi-autobiographical *Life among the Modocs*.

Noguchi found him in top-boots and bearskin, with a red crêpe sash "tied round his waist most carelessly" and "a large diamond ring on a finger of his right hand which threw an almost menacing brilliancy"; "I accepted him," he wrote, "without any question for the very symbol of romance and poetry of which my young mind often dreamed." He was warmly welcomed in turn by Miller and was pleased by "Miller's manner in calling me 'Mr. Noguchi,' as it was the first occasion to hear myself so addressed since my arrival in California; hitherto I had been a Charley or a Frank according to the employer's fancy" (1915, 58). Though Miller warned Noguchi that "he had no lesson or teaching to give me, or if he had any, it was about the full value of silence," this seems only to have confirmed his impression of Miller as a kind of "Japanese Buddha monk" (40, 68). "When I retired in the house right next to his own to sleep that night," Noguchi wrote, "I secretly decided that I would become a poet" (40–41).

Noguchi quickly discerned that he would have to "live and grow independently like a lone star in solitude; to make a Miller out of myself, I thought at once would be absurd and foolish"; moreover, he found, "it would be certainly futile to think you might study or even mention poetry when you lived here at the 'Heights'" (1915, 70). Miller advised Noguchi that "books are nothing," advising him rather to "read the history written on the brows of stars," but in his cottage, Noguchi found a few books "nailed high up near the ceiling," as if "it might have been perhaps Miller's idea to make them stand for decoration," and thus made his first acquaintance with Miller's "early poems or what-not," though he was more interested, he confessed, in "a little book of his reminiscences" in which Miller described how he had appeared in London with his poems and, after weathering the rejection of the publishing world, finally published his first London book at his own expense to great acclaim (65).

Some years later, Noguchi would himself embark on a similar mission to England in Miller's footsteps. But San Francisco in the 1890s was becoming a literary power of some significance, and it was there that Noguchi began his search for poetic success. Among the important little magazines of the day was the *Lark*, launched in May 1895 by Gelett Burgess and Bruce Porter and printed on Chinatown-bought bamboo paper by local printer and bookseller William Doxey. A kind of "joke in earnest and a protest against journalism that is merely commercial," as Burgess announced in the first issue, its editors had "no more serious intention than to be gay—to sing a song, to tell a story;—and when this is no longer to our liking—then this little house of pleasure will close its doors." The *Lark* was "surprisingly successful," as David Sloane notes, boasting a circulation of about five thousand and securing an honored place among the little magazines of the period (1987, 137). So despite its generally nonserious air, it was a respectable setting for Noguchi's first poetic productions, which appeared in the *Lark*'s fifteenth number in July 1896, accompanied by Burgess's introduction, "The Night Reveries of an Exile."

"I would have you think of him as I know him," wrote Burgess, "alone on the heights, in his cabin,—'even yellow-jackets-abandoned,'—listening to the 'tireless songs of the crickets on the lean, grey-haired hill, in the sober-faced evening.'" Noguchi, Burgess explained, was "an exile from his native land, a stranger in a new civilization,—a mystic by temperament, race, and religion," his poems an attempt "to voice the indefinable thoughts that came to him on many lonely nights; the journal of his soul,—nocturnes set to words of a half-learned, foreign tongue; in form vague as his vague dreams." Burgess acknowledged "rephrasing" Noguchi's lines and "setting his own words in a more intelligible order," but he had "retained his own words in accordance with his explanations, and with his consent,—preferring rather to excuse the liberties he has taken with the language, than to lose the vigor of his unworn metaphors, unfettered by the traditions of expression." Though Burgess clearly regarded the poems as somewhat curious—as indeed they were—they were not presented as mere exotica, nor were they intended to be amusing, as was much of the *Lark*'s material. "That these songs are sincere," he wrote, "must be evident from the lack of art (in its technical sense) in their construction" (Burgess 1896).

Of these early poems, "What about My Songs" is among the most remarkable, a definitive expression of the poet's inaugural quest for voice and audience, realized through dazzling imagery and tranquil rhythm:

> The known-unknown-bottomed gossamer waves of the field are colored by
> the travelling shadows of the lonely, orphaned meadow lark:
> At shadeless noon, sunful-eyed,—the crazy, one-inch butterfly (dethroned
> angel?) roams about, her embodied shadow on the secret-chattering
> grass-tops in the sabre-light.
> The Universe, too, has somewhere its shadow;—but what about my songs?
> An there be no shadow, no echoing to the end,—my broken-throated flute
> will never again be made whole!

Just as the shadows provide visual confirmation of the existence and flight of the meadowlark and butterfly, and the echo provides aural proof of the compass of the flute's sound, the poet requires a kind of analogous audience response: a recognition of presence and an acknowledgment of action. Like many of Noguchi's early poems, this one suffers from occasional verbal misfirings—the "known-unknown-bottomed gossamer waves of the field" is awkward at best—but other images, "the secret-chattering grass-tops," for instance, are both successful and memorable, and it is easy to see why these early productions produced enthusiasm in a literary world still dominated by the tired conventionalism of the fireside poets. The songs did find their shadow and echo, even as far as the vaunted East Coast: Noguchi records "hoeing round and watering the flowers in the plum orchard at the 'Heights'" when he received a letter from Gelett Burgess, informing Noguchi that there were several notices of his poems in the eastern papers, and that his work had been "very well received." It was confirmation that Noguchi's decision to become a poet had not ended in failure. "With his letter," Noguchi recalled, "my heart jumped high in joy ... it was the dawn of my new page of American life" (1915, 41).

Noguchi survived accusations of plagiarism in the San Francisco papers with some damage to his reputation and went on to publish two collections of poetry in 1897: *Seen and Unseen: Or, Monologues of a Homeless Snail,* containing his poems from the *Lark,* among others, and *The Voice of the Valley,* a short collection featuring poems written on a walking tour of Yosemite that spring. The former volume was favorably written up in the *Nation* and the *Dial,* while the latter caught the eye of the young Willa Cather, who reviewed it for her Nebraska paper.[9] He continued to live in California until 1900, dividing his time between Miller's Oakland estate and San Francisco, with occasional travel to places like Los Angeles, and what appears to have been a brief stint as an agricultural worker in Gilroy during the summer of 1899.

In 1900, he decided to try his literary fortunes on the East Coast, stopping in Chicago for two months, where he formed friendships with Frank Putnam, a journalist and poet, and Onoto Watanna, the half-Chinese journalist and novelist who was passing so successfully as half-Japanese that Noguchi himself seems never to have guessed the truth.[10] He also wrote a series of articles conveying his impressions of Chicago for the Chicago *Evening Post.* After Chicago, he continued east to New York, stopping briefly in Washington to visit Charles Warren Stoddard, with whom he had corresponded since 1897.

While still in California, Noguchi had, with the help of a young journalist, Blanche Partington, begun writing a novel in the form of a diary of a Japanese girl visiting America, and once in New York, he took it up again with the help of a new assistant, a young woman named Léonie Gilmour who responded to a newspaper advertisement Noguchi placed in January 1901. The novel was completed later that year and appeared serially in *Frank Leslie's Popular Monthly Magazine* before being published in book form in 1902, in both cases under the pseudonym "Miss Morning Glory."

Both Noguchi and his New York publisher, Stokes, had great hopes for *The American Diary of a Japanese Girl,* appearing as it did at the height of the *Madame Butterfly* vogue recently capitalized upon by Onoto Watanna's *A Japanese Nightingale* (1901). Among the reasons for the relative failure of *The American Diary,* one may point to the novel's complacent plotlessness and aggressive use of unexplained Japanese words as irritations for some readers, while the narrator's distracting staccato paragraph style and running critique of U.S. manners and customs no doubt exhausted others. Nevertheless, the novel is witty and full of interesting cross-cultural observations, and it is in many respects an improvement over the pseudo-Japanism of *Madame Butterfly,* which is itself critiqued in the novel. In the following scene, Miss Morning Glory applies similar treatment to English composer Sidney Jones's 1896 light opera *The Geisha,* which enjoyed a lengthy run in San Francisco during the 1890s:

> 17th—I went to the gallery of the photographer Taber, and posed in Nippon "pera pera." The photographer spread before me many pictures of the actress in the part of "Geisha." She was absurd.
>
> I cannot comprehend where 'Mericans get the conception that Jap girls are eternally smiling puppets.
>
> Are we crazy to smile without motive?

What an untidy presence!
She didn't even fasten the front of her kimono.
Charm doesn't walk together with disorder under the same Japanese parasol.
And I had the honour to be presented to an extraordinary mode in her hair.
It might be entitled "ghost style." It suggested an apparition in the "Botan Toro" played by Kikugoro.
The photographer handed me a fan.
Alas! It was a Chinese fan in a crude mixture of colour.
He urged me to carry it.
I declined, saying:
"Nobody fans in cool November!" (1902, 76–77)

Americans, we may suppose, were not prepared to see their amusing dress-up game of "Japan" spoiled in this manner. They would rather have agreed with Oscar Wilde's playful suggestion that "the whole of Japan is a pure invention. There is no such country, there are no such people" (1989, 988).

Noguchi had confidently written one sequel and planned another by the time of the *Diary*'s publication, as he prepared to set off on a much-anticipated voyage to the greater literary mecca of London in November 1902, where he planned to publish a collection of poems and to collect material for a "Morning Glory in England" sequel. The latter project was scrapped when news of the *Diary*'s lackluster performance reached him, and he turned his efforts toward his poetry. Impatient with the slowness of publisher John Lane, Noguchi, with the help of his friend Yoshio Markino, adopted Miller's strategy of publishing his own chapbook, a sixteen-page pamphlet entitled *From the Eastern Sea,* and mailed it off to the literary lights of London. Again, the bold Yankee strategy paid off, and Noguchi was soon on friendly terms with the cream of London literati: Laurence Binyon, Arthur Symons, Robert Bridges, William Michael Rossetti, and Arthur Ransome, among others. The Unicorn Press would publish an enlarged edition of *From the Eastern Sea* (1903). As he wrote happily to Frank Putnam on January 27: "Yone Noguchi at last! London found out Yone!"[11]

In the spring, Noguchi returned to New York, where in spite of his London success, he continued to have difficulty publishing his work; only with the onset of the Russo-Japanese War was he able to break through the barricades of the editorial desks, finding his articles on any Japan-related topic suddenly in demand everywhere. But for personal as well as professional reasons, he finally decided to return to Japan in the autumn of 1904.

In one sense, Noguchi's return to Japan marks the end of his career in Japanese America, but in another sense it was only a beginning. He was now an authority on the United States and England and their literatures, a fact confirmed by his appointment as professor of English literature at Keiō in 1905. He would continue to serve as an important bridge between the three countries until the eve of World War II, writing hundreds of articles for U.S. and English periodicals and English-language publications in Japan, and many more in his increasingly preferred language of Japanese. Gradually, Japanese attitudes toward the United States changed, in view of the inescapable evidence that Japan's modernization would not gain Japan and the Japanese equal treatment with other nations and people, and Noguchi's criticism of the United States became increasingly harsh. "What I fear most," he wrote in an angry letter to the *London Times* concerning the 1913 Alien Land Law, "is the moral effect on the minds of the Japanese when they become familiar with the inferior treatment in California" (1913a). In 1914 he declared World War I to be "the downfall of Western civilization" (Noguchi 1914; a phrase gleefully picked up by white supremacists in their call for white solidarity against the Asian invasion); a few years later he declared the failure of Whitmanism, by which he meant "the general failure or bankruptcy of the optimism of American literature" (1919). On his transcontinental lecture tour of 1919–20, he harangued Californians for losing sight of the ideals of democracy and "the sacredness of manual labour" (1921, 64).

Nevertheless, he retained some optimism for the future, suggesting, for example, in "Literary Co-operation Between America and Japan," that American poets might learn from the Japanese poets' contemplative approach to nature "a sense of the solidarity of the universe"; he thought this "would invigorate the minds of American poets so that they can escape from emotional sentimentalism." "If it is true to say that the opportunity of the Pacific Coast as the future centre of the commercial world hangs on how she will respond to and communicate with Asia," he reflected, "I do not see why she will, for the matter of literature, object to the Oriental influence. We dare say that we Orientals can contribute some new poetical strength to the Pacific Coast to make her a literary centre of America, when the opportunity smiles" (1921, 49–50).

Notes

1. Nagai Kafū, *American Stories,* trans. Mitsuko Iriye (New York: Columbia University Press, 2000).

2. Japanese names will be given with family name last throughout this essay.

3. Elsewhere Noguchi states that he first read Irving's *Sketch Book* in Palo Alto (1915, 38).

4. The Meiji period (1868–1912), or reign of the Meiji emperor, began with the elimination of the Shogunate and is regarded as Japan's critical period of transition under Western influence into a modern nation and international power.

5. The earlier account is found as an English chapter with a Japanese title, *"Ikaga ni shite gojin wa gojin wo sodachi suru"* [How we raise ourselves], *Eibei no Jūsan'nen,* 207214 (henceforth, "Sodachi"), undoubtedly the "little article on 'How Young Japanese Educate Themselves'" rejected by *Harper's* on 2 June 1903 (Noguchi 1975, 203).

6. In 1866, two years before the Meiji restoration, the Satsuma and Chōshū groups, which opposed the Tokugawa Shogunate, joined forces to form a military coalition, with the more moderate Satsuma group funding the purchase of Western arms for the more radical Chōshū clan. The alliance was a major factor in the eventual fall of the Shogunate, and the two groups came to dominate the new imperial government.

7. The imperialist atmosphere of the United States in the 1890s strongly calls into question the suggestion in Noguchi's *Time* obituary that in becoming "a great booster of imperialism," Noguchi was "discard[ing] his Western . . . ideas."

8. There are some discrepancies between the two autobiographical essays regarding this period. In "How I Learned English," Noguchi works as a schoolboy *upon his arrival,* leaving "under the dusk of the night," and then takes a job as a carrier boy (1915, 10); whereas in "Some Stories of My Western Life," he "slipped out of my employer's house one early morning from the window" and then went to Palo Alto (1915, 37).

9. "'Monologues of a Homeless Snail,'" *Dial* 22 (16 March 1897): 187; "Recent Poetry," *Nation* 64 (18 March 1897): 207; Willa Cather, "The Passing Show," *Courier* (Lincoln, Neb.), 8 February 1898, 2–3 (reprinted in *The World and the Parish,* ed. William M. Curtin [Lincoln: University of Nebraska Press, 1970], 579–80).

10. Noguchi wrote a scathing article on Watanna, whose real name was Winnifred Eaton, a few years after his return to Japan: "Onoto Watanna and Her Japanese Work," *Taiyō* 13, 8 (June 1907): 18–21; 13, 10 (1 July 1907): 19–21.

11. Yone Noguchi to Frank Putnam, 27 January 1903, *Yoné Noguchi Letters and Ephemera, 1899–1921,* Bancroft Library, University of California at Berkeley.

Works Cited

Burgess, Gelett. 1896. "The Night Reveries of an Exile," *Lark* 15 (July).

Daniels, Roger. 1962. *The Politics of Prejudice: The Anti-Japanese Movement in California and the Struggle for Japanese Exclusion.* Berkeley: University of California Press.

Fukuzawa, Yukichi. 1985. In *Fukuzawa Yukichi on Education: Selected Works,* ed. and trans. Eiichi Kiyooka. Tokyo: University of Tokyo Press.

Ichioka, Yūji. 1988. *The Issei.* New York: Macmillan.

Iriye, Akira. 1989. "Japan's Drive to Great-Power Status." In *Cambridge History of Japan,* 5:721–82. Cambridge: Cambridge University Press.

Kamei, Shunsuke. 1965. "Yone Noguchi, an English Poet of Japan: An Essay." In *Collected Poems,* by Yone Noguchi, ed. Usaburo Toyama. Tokyo: Yone Noguchi Society.

Markino, Yoshio. 1910. *A Japanese Artist in London.* London: Chatto and Windus.

Noguchi, Yone. 1897a. *Seen and Unseen: Or, Monologues of a Homeless Snail.* San Francisco: Burgess and Garnett.

———. 1897b. *The Voice of the Valley.* San Francisco, W. Doxey.

———. [Miss Morning Glory]. 1902. *The American Diary of a Japanese Girl.* New York: Stokes.

———. 1903. *From the Eastern Sea.* London: Unicorn Press.

———. 1905. *The American Letters of a Japanese Parlor-Maid.* Tokyo: Fuzanbō.

———. 1913a. "Charges of Unfair Treatment." *London Times,* 2 May, 5.

———. 1913b. "The Naturalization of Japanese." *Nation,* 19 June, 616–17.

———. 1914. "The Downfall of Western Civilization." *Nation,* 8 October, 432.

———. 1915. *The Story of Yone Noguchi.* 1914. Reprint, Philadelphia: Jacobs.

———. 1919. "Whitmanism and Its Failure." *Bookman* 49 (March): 95–97.

———. 1921. *Japan and America.* Tokyo: Keiō University Press; New York: Orientalia.

———. 1975. *Collected English Letters.* Edited by Ikuko Atsumi. Tokyo: Yone Noguchi Society.

Pyle, Kenneth B. 1969. *The New Generation in Meiji Japan: Problems of Cultural Identity, 1885–1895.* Stanford: Stanford University Press.

Sloane, David E. E. 1987. *American Humor Magazines and Comic Periodicals.* Westport, Conn.: Greenwood.

Spickard, Paul. 1996. *Japanese Americans: The Formation and Transformations of an Ethnic Group.* New York: Twayne.

Takai, Sōfū. 1985. *Eishijin Yone Noguchi no eikō: sono Bei-Ei ni okeru henreki kutō no hiroku* [English poet Yone Noguchi's glory: Secret memoirs of an arduous pilgrimage]. Tokyo: Kioi Shobō.

Takaki, Ronald. 1989. *Strangers from a Different Shore: A History of Asian Americans.* New York: Penguin.

Wilde, Oscar. 1989. "The Decay of Lying." In *The Complete Works of Oscar Wilde,* 970–92. New York: HarperPerennial.

Josephine Lee

19   Asian Americans in Progress: College Plays 1937–1955

> *Not because I think these short sketches have any tremendous literary value, but because I am convinced that many of them deserve a fate better than the oblivion of a student's notebook I have gathered together this cross-section of student thinking and have had the examples bound together for the library of the University of Hawaii.*
> —Willard Wilson, 2 April 1937

College Plays 1937–1955 comprises ten volumes of student plays written for the classes of English professor Willard Wilson.[1] It is not clear who, aside from Wilson and perhaps other students in the class, would have played audience to these works; the majority were class assignments by first-time playwrights, rather than scripts for professional production.[2] Relatively few were produced in student workshops or one-time amateur productions at the University of Hawai'i.[3] Some were published in Hawai'i's *Quill Magazine* and several have been republished in recent collections; others have been made more widely known through the work of scholars such as Roberta Uno.[4] Most, however, sit largely forgotten on the shelves in Hamilton Library at the University of Hawai'i at Manoa.

A significant number of these works were written by Asian American playwrights and have Asian American or Asian characters. As Uno suggests, some can be considered the first known writing for the stage by Asian Americans, although of the 127 plays included in these volumes, only 22 were written by students with obviously Asian surnames.[5] To examine these collections is to correct views of Asian American writing—particularly writing for the theater—as limited to the mainland. Although Misha Berson's 1990 *Between Worlds* is often hailed as the first collection of contemporary Asian American plays, Dennis Carroll's 1983 *Kumu Kuhua Plays* was in fact the first widely distributed published collection to include works by Asian American writers from Hawai'i, such as Edward Sakamoto and Bessie Toishigawa. Wai Chee Chun's 1936 *For You a Lei* has also been cited by some scholars as the earliest example of Hawaiian Creole English ("pidgin") writing (Chock 1989, 235; Sumida 1986, 312).[6]

But although the timing of this inquiry invites immediate comparisons between these plays and more recent works of drama by mainland Asian Americans, we should be suspicious of assuming immediate kinship. To do so might be to presume some Asian American essence—some pure racialized or ethnic difference—expressible through theatrical performance (Sumida 1997, 1991; Fujikane 1994). Constructing theater history as Asian American cannot, as Stephen Sumida argues, simply celebrate "the process of forging a new national identity through politics, economic strides, and the raising of our own voices" (1997, 278). Rather, examining these student works reminds us that in Hawai'i, as on the mainland, ethnic and racial categories are not essential states of being, but rather dynamic and relational social formations that encompass multiple differences.

During the years between World War II and statehood, the social status of Asian Americans in Hawai'i was in flux. In Hawai'i as on the mainland, Asian immigration in large part was spurred by economic hardship in Asia and the demand for cheap labor in the United States; once arrived, these immigrants were systematically exploited and victimized by racist laws and prejudice. The history and present situation of many Asian American communities and individuals in Hawai'i manifests institutional and legal discrimination, racial oppression, and inequality. The years between 1937 and 1955 might be remembered in terms of the anti-Japanese paranoia inspired by the attack on Pearl Harbor, the instatement of martial law, and the internment of Japanese Americans, as well as the racist harassment inspired by postwar anti-Communist fervor. The period immediately following World War II also saw significant economic and political gains by Asian Americans in Hawai'i. Notably, the success of the 1946 and 1949 interethnic labor strikes by pineapple and sugar plantation workers and dockworkers, organized by the International Longshoremen's and Warehousemen's Union, ended years of plantation feudalism. Interethnic solidarity, especially between Japanese American and Filipino workers, also contributed to later wins by the Democratic Party over the haole-dominated Republican Party. In the years following World War II, the status of Japanese Americans, Chinese Americans, and Korean Americans in Hawai'i changed to the extent that, "in the minds of many in the local community, Asians are more central than marginal" (Morales 1998, 116).

Although seemingly modest in its artistic claims, *College Plays* nonetheless registers these changes in interesting ways. Here, I have selected student works that reveal some of the broader lines of these cultural identities under construction. These do not serve as radical counter-narratives; any political or ideological challenge that they voice is limited. And yet their rendering of Asian American characters does illuminate the fault lines in fantasies of progress, cultural assimilation, and mobility at play during this formative time period. Central to each of these fantasies, as we shall see, is a myth of Hawai'i as a melting pot in which Asian American assimilation becomes the living proof of a more liberal and tolerant postwar America.

"A World No Longer Broken into Racial Compartments": Interracial Romances

The envisioned improvement of Hawai'i through European and U.S. modes of "progress," central to the rationalization of Hawai'i's colonization, articulates itself in familiar ways during the period in which *College Plays* was written. Following World War II, the rhetoric of progress becomes even more central, as Hawai'i's strategic location gave it military importance for the United States and made it a prime target for material redevelopment as part of a Pacific Rim strategy. This narrative of benevolent development relied on a certain reimagining of race relations in Hawai'i that stressed the viability of cultural assimilation, rather than the exclusion or segregation, of Hawai'i's Asian and native Hawaiian population. This emphasis on assimilation was supported by a more general shift in the terms of U.S. racial politics: the rise in the first half of the twentieth century of a more progressive and liberal view of race relations, championed by the Chicago school of sociology. Within this framework, a more "cultural" and "ethnic" view of difference emerged that stressed a process of immigration and inevitable assimilation and identified a set of generational differences that would pass away with succeeding generations (see Omi and Winant 1986). This larger shift in the attitudes toward race enables the imagination of the multiracial population of Hawai'i to be considered Americans as well (or at least as Americans-in-progress). Significantly, as Henry Yu pointed out in the 1920s, Hawai'i became one of the prime sites of study for the Chicago sociologists, "the ultimate racial laboratory, a place where the formation of the cultural melting pot they had predicted for the West Coast was already taking place" (2001, 81).

This interest in Hawai'i as the racial frontier renewed the island fantasy already put in place by the white planter class of "a Hawaii supposedly dominated by the old native Hawaiian aloha mentality of hospitality and tolerance" (Yu 2001, 82). The vision of Hawai'i as melting pot has served, as Elizabeth Buck suggests, to support a version of Hawaiian history as essentially "comedic" in nature, embodying the "reconciliation of conflict through the harmony of *aloha,* economic progress, and cultural assimilation" (1993, 15). This picture must downplay racial tensions in Hawai'i through contrast with racial tensions elsewhere. Hawai'i epitomizes the future of U.S. race relations, untouched by the history of mainland slavery, segregation, and violence.

Such an image was particularly important during and after World War II, when the United States sought to distinguish itself as a land of liberty and racial tolerance, in contrast to its fascist and openly racist enemies. As Ronald Takaki notes, "The war against Nazism generated a greater awareness of racism at home, and notions of white superiority became less popular and less plausible" (1989, 406). Of course, sustaining the vision of Hawai'i as (embodying America's) melting pot required the suppression of active U.S. participation in colonialism, forced annexation, the genocide of indigenous people, slavery, anti-immigration laws and restrictions, and segregation. Such a denial might be effected, at least in part, through a new kind of attention paid to Asian Americans. According to Robert Lee, in the postwar period the prevailing stereotype of Asian

Americans became refigured as the "model minority"—"a *racial* minority whose apparently successful *ethnic* assimilation was a result of stoic patience, political obedience, and self-improvement" (1999, 145)—that helped distinguish them from other, less obliging minority groups such as African Americans. "The representation of Asian-American communities as self-contained, safe, and politically acquiescent became a powerful example of the success of the American creed in resolving the problems of race" (160). (This new designation, of course, ignored the history of exclusion laws, unfair and oppressive labor conditions, and violent prejudice that affected the lives of Asian Americans, or appropriated this history as part of its own Asian American success story.)

This change in how Asian Americans figured in the public imagination was consistent with U.S. economic interests in the Pacific Rim; the emphasis was on an Asian-friendly climate that would eventually be ideal for attracting multinational corporate investment and tourism from the willing consumers of Japan, as well as the United States. Most importantly, such a view of Asian Americans fit the model of assimilation based on white European immigrant groups, thus affirming the ability of the melting pot to absorb even radically different newcomers in its all-encompassing democratic values.

A closer look at *College Plays* offers some interesting responses to the rhetoric of the melting pot and to the narratives of Asian American assimilation that accompany it. Willard Wilson's volume introductions, for instance, register these sentiments openly. Wilson urges the student to "present life as it has impinged upon him and as he sees it" rather than in "imitation of Broadway or Hollywood technique" (Vol. 2). His insistence on students writing from "local experience" has mixed success, which Wilson attributes to the rapid cultural changes associated with modernization. "This inability to seize local material and turn it into grist for the dramatic mill may be unfortunate from a historical point of view, but it seems to me a somewhat inevitable result of the cosmopolitan and almost international way in which the society of Hawaii has been going for many years" (Vol. 5). But Wilson notes that one aspect of regional flavor was in fact compatible with the changing times:

> Our "folk" material in Hawaii today lies all around us and consists more of a spiritual climate of tolerance than it does of calabashes, hulas, feather capes and kahunas. There will be occasionally the charming historical play or story with the romantic accoutrements of "old Hawaii," but we ought to get over the idea that in such nostalgic (and often badly documented) excursions into traditional "folk" material lies our best chance to exploit the essence of this fair fleet of islands.
>
> That essence of Hawaii, as many of us hope and a few of us actually believe goes very deep and is intimated by the external marks of tolerance and cooperation and amalgamation we see all around us: three *races* obviously wedded in the names above a law firm's door; religious tolerance exemplified by a Jewish congregation celebrating their Passover (by invitation) in the parish house of a Congregational Church; a senior class in sociology made up of Chinese, Japanese, Portuguese, Negroes, Filipinoes, Porto-Ricans, Hawaiians, Englishmen, Europeans and Texans, all discussing with interest and comparative objectivity the problems of men in a world no longer broken into racial compartments; a casual and unremarked dinner starting with an Indian mango salad and Chinese clear soup, followed

by good English roast beef with Japanese rice, Polynesian baked bananas, Portuguese sweet bread and New Zealand butter on the side, and American apple pie and ice cream for dessert. (Vol. 3)

What Wilson highlights as a spirit of "tolerance and cooperation and amalgamation" is consistent with the fantasy of the postwar United States as a tolerant and pluralistic society in which individual freedoms are extended to all, regardless of race or religion. This fantasy of multiculturalism is crucial to sustaining the rhetoric of U.S. superiority over, first, Nazi Germany and Japan, and then cold-war Russia. The United States is destined to become the leader of the postwar new world, a "world no longer broken into racial compartments." The true "essence" of Hawai'i is imagined as residing not in native Hawaiian culture—the "calabashes, hulas, feather capes and kahunas" that not only testify to native histories but also bear the glaring evidence of U.S. colonialism—but rather in Hawai'i as the preeminent melting pot of the United States.

Two student plays, Louis Hurwitz's *Escape* and Edward Sakai's *C'est le Guerre*, also comment on Hawai'i as a melting pot. Their contrasting presentations might illustrate a subtle wartime change in the rhetoric describing Hawai'i's multiracialism, with Hurwitz writing in 1937 and Sakai after the war. (The war interrupted the production of the *College Plays*, which resumed with the second volume in 1947–48.) Hurwitz presents a dormitory full of students who discuss the anxieties of university life (perhaps taking to heart Wilson's advice "to present life as it has impinged upon him and as he sees it"). Chief among them is Hugo, a young working-class haole whose anger about his limited career choices and his dissolute younger brother makes him eager to do "anything to get off this rock." When his roommate Bob praises Hawai'i for its racial mixing, Hugo is quick with his sarcasm.

> BOB. You know, that's one good thing about this place. Everybody mixed together. Japs, Haoles, Kanakas—everybody seems to get along somehow. I sort of like that.
> HUGO. Why. Isn't it really that way on the mainland?
> BOB. Hell no. I'll say it isn't. You're white—or you aren't! A Jap there is an *Oriental,* and that's all there is to it, and never the twain shall meet.
> HUGO. *(Sarcastically)* Sounds familiar. Hawaii, the melting pot of the world. East is East and West is West, and here the twain kiss each other! (Hurwitz 1937)

Edward Sakai's *C'est la Guerre,* however, gives a more idealistic view of Hawai'i as a melting pot, consistent with the patriotic representation of the U.S. military in the drama. The play depicts two U.S. soldiers (race and ethnicity unspecified) who visit an Italian brothel. Tom and Joe are presented more as benefactors than clients, bringing food, cigarettes, amusement, and comfort to the starving and war-weary prostitutes. The discussion of Hawai'i's racial mixing is central to this demonstration of U.S. largesse. As Joe, one of the soldiers, describes it to Maria, an Italian woman forced into prostitution, Hawai'i is not only "very beautiful" but "the Melting Pot of all different races; and the people work and live harmoniously together." Maria exclaims, "Hawaii must be a Paradise." Just as Joe's gentlemanly behavior suggests a model of American responsibility (unlike Tom, he does not have sex with any of the prostitutes, thus refusing to take advantage of the destitute Maria), so does Hawai'i, his home, become the emblem of America's pluralistic tolerance. Maria affirms that the German soldiers, in contrast, were "mean and arrogant" and treated Italians "as inferiors"; Joe attributes this behavior to German notions of racial superiority—"they believed they were the super-race" (Sakai 1947–48).

The image of a Hawaiian racial paradise, a cliché in the earlier play, takes on new meaning after the war. *C'est la Guerre*'s idealism suggests a new place for Hawai'i in a United States whose victory over racist and imperialist enemies manifests moral as well as military superiority. The visible presence of many races in Hawai'i is transformed from a liability into a kind of vindication. Hawai'i is redefined as a bastion of racial tolerance, the emblem of the new world order in which the United States plays a leading role.

Such a shift also seems to occur in a number of the presentations of interracial romance in *College Plays*. Comparing one such romance from 1937, Wai Chee Chun's *Marginal Woman*, with its postwar counterparts also shows a change in attitudes toward Asian assimilation into U.S. culture. Chun's play at first seems to insist upon the fusion of culture as commonplace, both in its setting ("A spacious living room furnished comfortably. . . . The colors and decorations are harmoniously blended, with a smattering of the West and East") and characterization. In the opening scene, daughter Mei-Mei, "simply dressed in a sports outfit," plays Sibelius's *Finlandia* on the piano while her brother Sammy, "in baggy gray flannels and a dirty tennis shirt," comes in from his tennis game; they speak to each other in colloquial English. Yet the play reveals, through Mei-Mei's crises of identity, that this is no harmonious fusion but rather cultural incompatibility. Mei-Mei experiences this dissonance both on a trip to Shanghai ("In China and at home I'm too haolified to be a Chinese. And to the Westerners I am not really an American. Oh, God, what am I?") and through her mother's opposition to her involvement with Dwight, a haole.

Marginal Woman depicts parental opposition to interracial union as the most obvious manifestation of a larger problem: an assumption that the "hybrid" protagonist inevitably falls between two worlds separated by essential cultural differences. Even before her mother finds out about the romance, Mei-Mei has already despaired of finding a resolution: "We've dragged through the mess trying to find a ray of light, but, oh . . . the whole trouble lies in the center. Dwight would be an American without a country, and I would be a Chinese without a country." *Marginal Woman*, even while offering the possibility of interracial romance, depicts it as inherently impossible.

Significantly, the interracial romances that follow in later volumes of *College Plays* offer a somewhat different picture. In three of them, James K. Irikura's *Broadminded*, Edward Sakai's *And Never the Twain Shall Meet?* and Bessie Toishigawa's *Nisei*, interracial romance become associated with a characteristically "American" hybridity, where the absorption of Asians—particularly the unassimilable "enemy" Japanese—into the U.S. body politic is seen as part of America's new postwar identity. Opposition to interracial union, while still strong, is imagined less as some "universal" incompatibility of East and West, and more as located in the unreasonable prejudice of "traditional"

Asian parents. In each of these cases, racial prejudice is presented primarily as a trait of traditional Japanese characters, in marked contrast to a more progressive and liberal American love.

In Irikura's *Broadminded,* the gossipy Mrs. Nakamura tells Mother and Father that their daughter Jane is seeing a haole. At first, Mother and Father are not alarmed; Mother declares that Bill is a "nice fellow" and that "we try to be broadminded." But upon learning that Jane and Bill are engaged, Father rails against Jane's romantic choice: "Haole's [*sic*] are no good, they just get all the breaks, so they think they're better than anybody else! We're better than them anyday!" Although he hints that Jane's choice may be prompted by her desire to assimilate into haole culture ("Maybe you think you're too good to marry a Japanese!"), it is in fact he who holds on to unreasonable notions of Japanese racial superiority ("A haole! A Pake's [Chinese] bad enough!"). Jane's brother Bob joins in to reinforce this vision of Japanese racism:

> BOB. I bet he's a damn Jew too! How you like that! A Jap an' a Jew! The kids would look good with a Jew nose and Jap bowlegs!
> JANE. *(Defiantly)* Bill's not Jewish! And it wouldn't make any difference if he were, I love him!
> BOB. Aww the hell, you might as well marry a nigger! (Irikura 1947–48)

Driven to despair, Jane declares: "Oh . . . you're all hopeless. . . . You're nothing but a bunch of Japs!" Her own racial epithet is met with violence, as her father slaps her, "knocking her on to the sofa," and Bob threatens, "I oughta kick your damn brains out!" after which the play ends, unresolved (Irikura 1947–48).

Jane's use of the racial slur "Japs" suggests the rampant anti-Japanese racism, which in fact could help explain some of the vehemence with which her father and brother cling to notions of Japanese racial superiority. That Bob's angry and ugly possessiveness might stem from his own feelings of ethnic marginalization is suggested by his comments: "When us guys was overseas, we used to hear about wahines like you. They used to call you wahines, 'Kamikazes.' I see why now. What's so damn good about white meat?" (Irikura 1947–48). *Broadminded,* however, does little to rationalize or even contextualize the father and brother's rampant hatred of other races; this is staged more as an inherently Japanese (or, as more broadly referred to in the stage directions, "Oriental") characteristic. That Jane's declaration that they are "Japs" is met with brutal violence only reinforces how much her father and brother deserve this name. The family's virulent "Oriental" prejudice ultimately overshadows any version of white racial supremacy.

Although *Broadminded* registers some of the larger anxiety around what to do with racism at home, it banishes these fears through projecting them onto the figures of "aliens" who are associated with already vanquished enemies abroad. The parents' initial attempts to seem broadminded only temporarily disguise their real feelings of racial animosity; Mother complains: "They say we should be broadminded about inter-racial marriages. It's alright, but why does it have to be our own daughter?" The mask of liberalism slips to reveal the true self of racism, a self figured as "Japanese." In the character descriptions, racial prejudice becomes the defining attribute of what is truly

"Oriental"; Bob is "the son, a university student with narrow-minded race prejudice"; the Father is "an alien Japanese with the Oriental ideals of racial purity"; and Mrs. Nakamura is someone who "also carries the 'Oriental stigma'" (Irikura 1947–48).

Edward Sakai's *And Never the Twain Shall Meet?* uses many of the same devices and patterns of action as *Broadminded*. It is again the father and eldest son, Yoshio, who, according to their character descriptions, harbor "racial prejudices." The play begins with their criticism of interracial dating, particularly between Japanese women and haole men.

> FATHER. But this Japanese girl going around with a haole man.... What'sa matter with this kind Japanese girl?
> YOSHIO. Japanese girls of today going to the dogs.
> FATHER. They not like good Japanese girls. Before ... Japanese girls quiet and good ... now they run around like damn fools.
> YOSHIO. All they want is good time now ... just like the other nationalities. And they think they big-shot when they go out with a haole guy.
> FATHER. Haole no good. *(He returns to his newspaper.)* (Sakai 1947–48a)

Although the father has been lenient with Kimiko, he comes down hard on her when he finds that she is in love with Tom, a haole veteran. Unlike her unfortunate counterpart Jane, however, Kimiko finds some sympathy from another brother, Mitsuo, who tries to defend her choice of partner. Mitsuo's father and brother offer more concrete arguments for their pointed dislike of haoles, but at every turn his rejoinders point out that their observations are unreasonable. The father states that he dislikes haoles because they are "not honest" and "no pay the bills on time," and Yoshio says: "They don't care about anything. They get drunk, they fight, they chase girls ... they worse than dogs." Mitsuo replies, "Yeah ... but what you say is true of every nationality, even the Japanese." When Yoshio calls Tom "more white trash," Mitsuo responds, "We have some yellow rubbish too." Mitsuo even offers his optimistic take on mixed-race children ("Everybody says that those kids are really good looking. Maybe I'll marry a haole girl and get some cute kids"), to which his father answers: "Mitsuo ... if you marry haole girl, she not welcome in my house. To me, she not your wife. Haole no good" (Sakai 1947–48a).

In contrast to *Broadminded*, Sakai's *And Never the Twain Shall Meet?* offers a more complicated presentation of racial tension. Sakai places more emphasis on the rationale for the fear of interracial marriage. Sakai's father and brother are not just worried that Kimiko has become a fast "kamikaze" in her desire for a haole; they have genuine concerns that Tom, a soldier, will play fast and loose with her. Father warns her: "Haole soldiers no good. You know what happened during the war. Plenty of haole soldiers came here. Now they all go back to America." Yoshio chimes in: "Yes; and look around. You'll see a lot of bastard kids running about. Lots of Japanese girls were taken in by the smooth lines ... and now they're left holding the bag ... an empty bag" (Sakai 1949–50a).

These mixed-race children of Japanese girls and haole soldiers, Yoshio insists, may be "cute" but are nonetheless illegitimate: "Those kids cute? Maybe ... maybe ... but where's the daddy? On the mainland married to his kind of girl." These arguments reveal that their worries about interracial marriage have to do with not only "Japanese" racial taboos, but also their awareness of U.S. racism. Father is worried that if Kimiko marries Tom and moves to the mainland with him, she will be ostracized: "You think his people going to like you? You get [*sic*] slant eyes . . . you Japanese." Yoshio puts it more crudely: "Even if you change your name to Mrs. Bellows or some other haole name, you still have slant eyes and a yellow belly." Even the loyal Mitsuo, in the final dialogue with his sister, urges her to think "realistically" about her future: "You must remember that a caucasian has a different cultural background from you. He thinks differently from us who have some oriental background" (Sakai 1947–48a).

Although the ending of the play affirms Kimiko's decision to leave her family and marry for love, it does not present racial prejudice as the characteristic of Orientals alone; rather, it parallels Japanese racism with anti-Asian prejudice on the mainland and comments on the fallacy of the idealized melting-pot version of Hawai'i. "In Hawaii, we talk about racial harmony . . . how different nationalities get along with each other; but it's not true," Mitsuo sagely comments. "The idea is . . . if you don't bother me, we'll get along; but if you ever cross the social or racial lines; then you're in for trouble" (Sakai 1947–48a).

Sakai's play offers some corrections to the prevailing myth of Hawai'i as an untroubled racial paradise. Its uncertainties speak directly to what must be suppressed to believe in such a myth. Yet Sakai's play too is guided by a particular understanding of the postwar United States as a progressive melting pot in which interracial romance is but one of the ways in which Asian characters demonstrate their inevitable acculturation. Opposition to interracial union again lies not in the dictates of rigid biological determinism (in which intermarriage is "against nature"), but in the old-fashioned reservations of parents. Moreover, their resistance is eroded by the "inevitable" force of U.S. assimilation, a force that validates the intermarriage of Asian and haole. *Broadminded* and *And Never the Twain Shall Meet?* suggest that their heroines' love affairs with haoles are not just individual romantic encounters but part of a larger pattern of racial mixing inspired by the inevitable effects of American leniency. Believing that they are more broadminded than they really are, Jane mistakes the ferocity of her family's opposition. In *And Never the Twain Shall Meet?* Yoshio fears that his sister Kimiko has been "spoiled" by their father's laxity: "Since mother died you are not so strict. You do not ask where they go or who they go with." Indeed, the father can only confess to this cultural lapse that has allowed his daughter to stray down the path of interracial romance: "I try to be good father. I want my children to be good Americans." To be a "good American" is to set the conditions by which a young Japanese woman is inevitably drawn away from her family into a relationship that exemplifies a quintessentially American dream. When her father insists: "Love come from respect. American love silly. Japanese love better," Kimiko replies, "But we're in America, not in Japan" (Sakai 1947–48a).

And yet the unhappy disaffiliation of parents from children that most commonly ends so many of these plays (not only *Broadminded* and *And Never the Twain Shall Meet?*

but a host of others as well) indicates a kind of inherent tension in the vision of a broadminded America.[5] This is resolved differently in Bessie Toishigawa's *Nisei*, one of the few interracial romances that ends happily; the play does so by presenting a thoroughly comedic presentation of Hawai'i's racial mixing. Here it is a Japanese mother, Mrs. Takaki, who in the first scene seems the epitome of Japanese parental control, forcing her son Saburo to practice the piano and reacting strongly when she hears of her daughter Ayako's romance with a haole. But in subsequent scenes, her character exemplifies not so much an inherently race-prejudiced Japanese but rather a first-generation immigrant in the United States, highlighting the stages of the "natural" progress toward American identity. Significantly, Mrs. Takaki's strictness and prohibitions against interracial dating are exacerbated by her grief over her elder son Ichiro, killed in action. Thus the play pictures not just the rebellious Ayako and Saburo as exemplars of inevitable cultural assimilation; Mrs. Takaki, grieving over a son who is a U.S. soldier, is also presented as the raw material of the melting pot, the living demonstration of the older generation whose resistance to change is but a temporary barrier.

The characterization of Ayako's fiancé Dave is crucial to this reading of *Nisei*. Dave, as it turns out, is not just any haole, but in fact is more specifically a second-generation German American who can refute Ayako's claim that haoles are "more broadminded, more liberal" by pointing out that his own mother was equally dismayed when he wanted to go out with "an Italian girl." Dave waxes philosophical about the inevitability of cultural assimilation, in light of which first-generation behavior becomes a clinging to obsolete values and practices: "I don't think your mother and mine are much different, Ayako. Both of them cling to their native customs and want to see them carried on in their children." He advises Ayako on the importance of carrying on some of these "native customs," less to maintain a viable culture than to appease the sorrow of first-generation immigrant parents: "Don't try so hard to discard all that your parents have taught you, Ayako. Your rebellion only aggravates the nostalgia they feel for a past life which will soon disappear. They know that life must go inevitably but they feel sad anyway." Dave draws a parallel between his situation and Ayako's: "Just our tough luck to be born 'Niseis.' Maybe our kids will have an easier time" (Toishigawa 1946–47).

That Dave calls himself a Nisei foreshadows the final scene of the play, in which Mrs. Takaki readily accepts Dave into their home, impressed by his ability to speak "nice Japanese" and his experience as a veteran. Dave wins a dinner invitation by looking through Ichiro's album with her mother, and reminiscing about his military service in Japan. His interest in Japanese Buddhism, his facility with conversational Japanese, and his near-instant acceptance by Mrs. Takaki suggest that because of his cultural fluency he can become a surrogate son and brother as well as husband. The family is preserved and, in fact, reinforced by these cross-cultural liaisons, because they are all headed in the same direction.

Like *Broadminded* and *And Never the Twain Shall Meet?* Toishigawa's *Nisei* affects a displacement of racial prejudice onto parent countries (Germany, Japan), thus presenting the United States in contrast as a place of racial tolerance, and the "American" Hawai'i as an arena ripe for interracial romance. And yet in the final scene the expected confrontation between haole lover and angry parent does not occur. What takes place is a dialogue that smoothes over potential political conflict. Although Mrs. Takaki has felt the effects of the war firsthand, there is no mention of wartime politics. Dave's service in Japan is presented more as a kind of cultural exchange than as a military occupation.

> MRS. T. Tokyo nice place before war.
> DAVE. Oh, you've been there?
> MRS. T. Yes, I go back to Japan twice from Hawaii.
> DAVE. Oh, I see. Has Ayako been there too?
> MRS. T. Yes, but she small girl.
> DAVE. I guess she wouldn't remember much about the city.
> MRS. T. Only very little. You stay only Tokyo?
> DAVE. No, I was in Fukuoka for awhile, about a month.
> MRS. T. Oh—you been Fukuoka too . . .
> DAVE. Yes, do you have any relatives there? *(Dave lights a cigarette.)*
> MRS. T. *(Passes an ash tray to him)* Yes, my mister brother in Fukuoka.
> DAVE. Oh, and what does he do?
> MRS. T. Oh him school teacher.
> DAVE. I see. *(At this moment Ayako comes in the front door.)*
> AYAKO. Ta da ima! *(She looks with great surprise at Dave.)* Well, aren't you two chummy!
> (Toishigawa 1946–47)

The young lovers are of Japanese and German descent, and Dave's former love interest is Italian, yet there is no mention of Japan, Germany, or Italy as wartime enemies. Ethnic difference is both strategically evoked and erased, testifying to the success of American ethnic assimilation.

In 1932, in response to the racially polarizing and highly publicized 1931 Massie case, the U.S. Department of the Interior published the tract *Hawaii and Its Race Problem.*[7] Its author, William Atherton Du Puy, was eager to reassure his readers that "in Hawaii oriental races are passing through the melting pot just as occidental races have been doing in New Jersey and Illinois": "All of these wear American clothes (there is not a pigtail in Honolulu) and disport themselves much as do natives of Vermont or Virginia, but their skins are yellow" (1932, 127, 20). Postwar, the rhetoric of Hawai'i as a melting pot—and the demonstration of Asian Americans as testimony to the successful process of U.S. assimilation—took on greater urgency as the United States assumed its new role as liberal overseer of world affairs, reorganizing national boundaries and infrastructures and protecting liberty from the threat of its cold-war opponents. If the war became the crucible in which a new world order was formed, Hawai'i, with its multiracial and largely Asian population, became its ultimate measure of success.

"Civic Models": The Nisei Veteran

The plays' depictions of Nisei World War II veterans (serving in the U.S. 100th Battalion and 442nd Regiment) similarly present a kind of anxiety about the prospect of Asian assimilation into Asian American; here, it is tied not to the consideration of interracial romance (what needs to be melted together), but rather to a narrative of necessary loss (what needs to be excised in order for this melting to occur). Certain of the plays question as well as foreground this process of upward mobility by which Nisei supposedly gained their legitimacy as Americans.

Through their service in these all–Japanese American units, Nisei altered their social status in a number of ways. They were offered opportunities for education through the G.I. Bill and given a new view of their racial inequality by their experiences in the military (see Duus 1987; Tanaka 1987). Later political and labor solidarity was fueled by the intense bonds within these military units and the important connections these men made with working-class labor organizations on the mainland through wartime service. The tight-knit groups formed a force that helped change the course of Hawai'i's politics, aiding the Democratic Party's landmark defeat of the Big Five–dominated Republican Party that had run Hawaiian politics for half a century.

The war not only provided material opportunities for upward mobility, including the opportunity to travel abroad and military benefits, but also enabled a highly symbolic change in the perception of Americans of Japanese descent that was crucial to the political mechanism of statehood and citizenship. The considerable accomplishments of the 100th Battalion (composed of Hawaiian Nisei and nicknamed the Purple Heart Battalion) and later the 442nd Regiment (Nisei from Hawai'i and mainland internment camps) in northern Africa, Italy, and France, "probably the most decorated unit in United States military history," helped legitimate their insistence on an American identity (Takaki 1989, 402). Ronald Takaki relates that "after the war, on July 15, 1946, on the lawn of the White House, President Harry Truman welcomed home the Nisei soldiers of the 442nd: 'You fought for the free nations of the world . . . you fought not only the enemy, you fought prejudice—and you won'" (403). Notably, the accomplishments of the 100th and 442nd, as well as later military service by Japanese Americans, may have indeed influenced arguments for Hawaiian statehood. After visiting Hawai'i to judge its qualifications for statehood, the Senate Interior and Insular Affairs Committee concluded: "It is submitted that if the ultimate test of loyalty and patriotism is willingness to fight and die for one's country, then Hawaii has nobly met this test . . . on the battlefields of Europe and, more recently, in Korea" (Tabrah 1984, 191).

Kathy Ferguson and Phyllis Turnbull suggest that we read the figure of the Nisei veteran as it seems to re-articulate a particular paradigm suggested by Mark Kann: that of the "evolving triangle of patriarchal fathers, soldier sons, and domesticity" that configured civic virtue in the United States:

> Older men are envisioned as sober breadwinners, as heads of families, as owners of property. They are entitled to their rights because their individualism rests on, and is tamed by, women's moral policing and young men's death in battle. They are, in Locke's phrase, "'nursing fathers' who are 'tender and careful of the public weal.'" Women, in this symbolic economy, represent domesticity, bourgeois sobriety, control over men's desires. Proper Spartan mothers maintain the home front, agree to be protected, uplift the morale of the

troops, honor heroes, mourn the dead, and defer to male authority upon men's return from battle. Young men are the circulating currency in this domestic/civic economy: boys raised by republican parents into appropriate manly fortitude become youth who long for military adventure and are disciplined by military virtues toward a future of productive and trustworthy citizenship. (Ferguson and Turnbull 1999, 158)

In particular, Ferguson and Turnbull's astute analysis focuses on Senator Daniel Inouye, whose service in the 442nd, reflected by the sacrifice of his right arm in battle, became the "key to membership in the national political elite, transforming his racial and class alienness into masculine belonging" (1999, 161). Inouye and other Nisei veteran heroes translate the roles of both the "nursing father" and the youth whose masculinity is confirmed by "the desire, skill, and duty to bear arms for the state" (Kann 1991, 17). Likewise, women of Japanese ancestry in Hawai'i marked "the boundaries of domestic life that the young Japanese American males needed to leave behind in order to enter the manly world of soldiering" (Ferguson and Turnbull 1999, 167).

This compelling reading helps explain why the historical example of the Japanese American veterans in the 100th and 442nd carries so much weight—in terms of both Asian American and U.S. history in general. Seen in one light, their service can affirm the power and inevitability of an American way of life: "From the beginning, the Army followed a policy of wide publicity of the units, with a view to building up their morale and presenting them to the world as examples of America's assimilative capacity" (Allen 1950, 271). These young men are positioned as U.S. heroes within an immediately recognizable framework of values; their demonstration of "civic virtue" puts to rest fears of disloyal "ethnic" Americans who must otherwise be interned or interrogated.

On the surface, the plots and characterizations of plays such as Bessie Toishigawa's *Reunion* and *Nisei* and Robert Suyeoka's *The Last Refrain* seem to celebrate the Nisei veterans' new access to identities both American and masculine, as they prove their loyalty and mettle through military service and bodily sacrifice. But significant elements of these plays not only draw attention to but also undercut the iconography of civic virtue that dictates the portrayal of these veterans.

To begin with, these plays are populated almost exclusively by mothers and sisters. Compared with those plays depicting interracial and interethnic relationships, where the Japanese or Chinese father plays a crucial role, here the father is conspicuously absent, presumed dead. It seems plausible that given these terms, the head of the family cannot be pictured as Japanese, since the Issei father remains an eternal alien. Instead, the state itself becomes the "nursing father," instilling manly virtue through the son's enlistment. Yet a constant disjunction is maintained between the state as father surrogate and the absence of the real father. Killing off the father points to a real-life disjunction, especially given the possibility that the state is itself responsible for this absence. The father's marked erasure points to the arrest and internment of prominent Japanese American community leaders under martial law during World War II, some of whom were sent to mainland camps, and to the systematic measures designed to eradicate Japanese culture, such as the campaigns to remove Japanese signs and the closing of Japanese-language newspapers and schools.[8]

In the same way, the portrayal of the Issei mother seems to place her solidly within the domestic space, promoting discipline and virtue in her children and mourning her dead son, the very portrait of the "Spartan mother."[9] In *The Last Refrain* and *Nisei*, both grieving mothers and dead sons seem to be part of the iconography of "civic virtue," where Japanese alienness becomes incorporated into the U.S. body politic through a pattern of heroic loss.

Robert Suyeoka's *The Last Refrain* places at its center a mourning mother who, much to the chagrin of her daughters, at first refuses altogether to acknowledge the death of her son Takeo. She finally comes to her senses when his body is brought home and she recognizes his personal effects. The play suggests that this Japanese American family has won American status for themselves through Takeo's sacrifice. Takeo's body is brought home for a special service; it is made clear that this special privilege honors this dead Japanese American soldier without regard to his race. Moreover, his status as American is demonstrated by the objects, such as his prized harmonica, that he leaves behind.

At the same time, *The Last Refrain* sounds less patriotic notes on Nisei incorporation. The play emphasizes the mother's grief rather than her pride in her son's accomplishments. The dialogue between the sisters, Jane and Elaine, who view their mother's mourning as unreasonable, undercuts the patriotic tableau of sacrifice, the "reassuring image of the loving mother and her virtuous sons" (Ferguson and Turnbull 1999, 127). When Takeo's body is brought home, it is by military personnel whose priority is informing the family of regulations and processing bureaucratic forms, not declaiming the dead son's patriotism or valor. Moreover, the soldiers who bring in the coffin are painfully unaware of traditional mourning practices; one of them even sneaks an apple from the offerings that Mrs. Tanaka has placed in front of her son's picture. These breaches of etiquette stress not the valor of the Nisei who wins his family American legitimacy, but rather the frustration of the growing distance between those who ostensibly proved the inevitability of U.S. assimilation and the members of their families, who were still considered by law and practice "unassimilable." As Eileen Tamura suggests, many of the Issei and Kibei experienced "increasing tension, disorientation, and frustration during the course of the war, as they witnessed the destruction of Japanese artifacts, the rejection of long-held practices, and the collapse of familiar cultural institutions" (1994, 236).

By interweaving its interracial romance with this background of Nisei loss and Issei grief, Toishigawa's *Nisei* also complicates as well as sustains a portrayal of American legitimation through military heroism and sacrifice. On the one hand, the death of Ichiro, presumably killed in action, can be read as another means by which the Nisei children earn their American status; if Ayako's desire for the haole Dave is presented as a "natural" extension of her progressive assimilation, the service of Ichiro also demonstrates the family's Americanness. After looking at Ichiro's pictures, Dave comments to Ayako, "Your brother was quite a man." She replies, admiringly, "You're quite a man yourself" (Toishigawa 1946–47). Both the dead Ichiro and Dave, who takes Ichiro's place in the family, win their status as real American men through their military experience, a patriotism that wins out over "blood" ties to now-enemy countries such as Japan and Germany. Mrs. Takaki's grief over Ichiro also translates her into the domestic center of the triangle of "civic virtue"; moreover, it provides a way by which she can come to accept the Japanese-speaking haole Dave as a surrogate son.

Within the paradigm of "civic virtue," these plays can be thought of as affirming the dead soldier's and the mourning mother's identities as American, again affirming the potential for Japanese Americans to be "model Americans." But one aspect of the play—the younger son, Saburo, who refuses to practice piano, insists on speaking pidgin, and spends his time at the pier with his friends—undercuts this reading of Japanese American heroism, not so much by suggesting the "unassimilability" of Nisei children, but rather by suggesting their incorporation into a very different melting pot indeed. Although Saburo is presumably reintegrated into respectable adolescent behavior in the end (he is properly abashed on seeing his sister and Dave together, and Dave might in fact provide the missing authority needed to put him back in his place), his desire to "go out," presumably to join a local gang, introduces an alternative vision—undisciplined, unvirtuous—of an interracial masculine community.[10]

Since the 1890s debates over annexation, the question of Asian assimilability into the U.S. body politic has remained an issue of U.S. policy in Hawai'i. The postwar drive toward statehood renewed this question. Proponents of statehood needed to counter strong opposition raised by southern states (sensitive to the growing pressures of civil rights programs) to granting legislative power to a population with so many "Orientals," particularly Japanese (Bell 1984, Chap. 5). They eagerly sought evidence of "acculturation," using the example of the Nisei soldier in World War II and the Korean War to argue that Hawai'i had "made its Americanism work" and "met the test of two world wars with unquestionable loyalty to the flag she served" (Hawaii Statehood Commission, qtd. in Bell 1984, 87). Like the interracial romances, however, these plays about Nisei veterans help us read into and against the overstatement of these tropes of civic virtue and sacrifice and hard-won assimilation. They render a much more complex staging of Hawai'i's racial dynamics and the place of Asian Americans within them.

In *Reunion*, Bessie Toishigawa contrasts the idealized picture of military heroism with more immediate concerns of this transitional time, casting some doubt on whether these young veterans are necessarily "disciplined by military virtues toward a future of productive and trustworthy citizenship." *Reunion* depicts a gathering of young veterans of the 442nd combat team one year after the war. Although their banter is light-hearted, it suggests how the war has profoundly affected these young men. For some, upward mobility seems newly possible; they have affirmed their own worthiness for citizenship and statehood. The possibilities allowed by the G.I. Bill permit Masa and Taka to make plans to attend the University of Michigan to become doctors.

Yet the effects of military service on them are far from universally uplifting. For Duke and Shig, education is not a possibility, a problem aggravated by the economic limitations of the islands and their own growing discontent and wanderlust. Shig finds "Honolulu one dead town, boy. No more nutting to do. Mo betta when I stay in New York"; the heroic "silver star man" Masa makes the bitter observation that even after his military service he returns to a job earning only "$1.50 an hour pounding nails! Some fun. Give me a few years and mebbe I'll be foreman" (Toishigawa 1946–47).

The young men have clearly sacrificed much for the United States; Shig, recently released from the hospital, walks slowly with a cane, and Duke recalls: "Dat mortar shell shua wen hit, man! Tanaka lose one eye, Shig almost lose his leg, Yamamoto lose one piece scalp." This dismemberment is not framed as virtuous sacrifice but laughed off rather irreverently. Shig brushes off the others' concern ("Only when cold time, eh, inside sore. Da doc said going be sore while. No can walk fas, do'. . . . Humbug. Mo betta cut om off") and reminisces fondly about his hospital stay ("Boy, I had good fun in da hospital. Da nurses, oh boy . . . some meats") (Toishigawa 1946–47).

Moreover, wartime trauma can be used for personal gain. The young men joke about Jits's war wounds and subsequent infection that release him from active duty. As Shig says: "Jits, da son-of-a-gun, he gets one million-dollar wound. Tree months combat, eh, shrapnel scratch his feet, he no can walk, stretcher come take om. When he pass he yell, 'Hey paisanos, I got million-dollar wound.' He no come back, da baga, he get jaundice afta dat. I tink maybe he swallow yellow shoe polish, no?" (Toishigawa 1946–47). Taka urges Masa to cash in on disability compensation for his malaria to finance his college education. The rewards earned by military service have less to do with pride and honor for individual and community than with knowing how to work the bureaucratic system. Toishigawa's *Reunion* is concerned less with idealizing these young Japanese Americans who have served "their country" than with illustrating their uneasy changes in status afterward. The play ends with Masa and Taka finally making their decision to leave for the mainland. Their exuberance disguises the extent to which their decision marks the end of this close-knit group of friends and family; however, it is clear that the new mobility of the Nisei veteran will change this local community for good.

During World War II, the new Pacific Rim era, and the drive toward statehood, "Asian American" identity in Hawai'i was necessarily determined both by the everyday interactions of Hawai'i's multiracial population and a set of elaborate fantasies that responded to Hawai'i's perceived importance as racial "showcase" (Kent 1983, 122).[11] These fantasies have been both wholeheartedly celebrated and, more recently, energetically critiqued. Noel Kent reads the rise of Japanese, Chinese, and Korean Americans to economic success and political power in Hawai'i during the 1950s not as a victory for racial equality so much as the perpetuation of exploitative capitalist hierarchies. In Kent's view, the opportunities offered to these Asian Americans were conditioned by a particular ideological perspective, one that "no matter how liberal, infused the young Asians with an individualistically oriented competitive world view exalting middle-class materialistic goals and equating success with wealth, status, and power—an education for selfishness and self-aggrandizement in the traditional sense" (130).

These selections from *College Plays* present us with a somewhat different view of how Asian American student playwrights encountered both the ideology and the experience of "progress" and upward mobility. In their own limited ways, these plays can remind us that the dynamics of change for Asian Americans cannot be assessed simplistically as testimony to some triumph of the "model minority" or the idealized vision of some melting pot of a multicultural American future; nor can they necessarily be seen as selling out, the unmitigated perpetuation of exploitative hierarchies by the once oppressed. At times openly celebratory, at other times much more tentative, these plays illustrate their authors' active engagement with significant changes in the nature of Asian American culture, affiliation, community, and identity in Hawai'i.

Notes

1. *College Plays* is one of three collections in this set. There is some overlap between the plays in this collection and those in the other two collections. Volumes 1–9 of *University of Hawaii Plays 1958–1969* includes plays from the playwriting classes taught by Edward A. Langhans of the Department of Drama. *Theatre Group Plays 1946–1969* includes fourteen volumes of plays from the annual University of Hawai'i Theatre Group (HTG) Playwriting Contest, edited by Edward A. Langhans. See Langhans 1973.

2. Wilson notes in his introduction to Volume 2 (1946–47): "Very few students are encouraged ever to hope to do anything with playwriting professionally. If some of them do, it would not greatly surprise their teacher, because there is indicated in the work a remarkable amount of talent and flare for expression."

3. Indexed in *Theatre Group Plays 1946–1969* are plays that the HTG awarded or produced locally, among them Bessie Toishigawa's *Reunion* (7–10 May 1947) and Robert Suyeoka's *The Return* (13–14 and 18–21 May 1949).

4. Charlotte Lum's *These Unsaid Things* and Wai Chee Chun (Yee)'s *For You a Lei* appear in Chock 1989. *Reunion,* by Bessie Inouye (née Toishigawa), is in Carroll 1983. Uno 1993 has a bibliography that includes some earlier works by Asian American women in Hawai'i.

5. These include Margaret C. Kwon's *Mama's Boy* (Vol. 1), Mary Akimoto's *Strangers* (Vol. 5), and Henry Chun's *The Man They Left Behind* (Vol. 8) in Wilson n.d.

6. *For You a Lei* received its first reading by the Rainbow Interpretation Organization at a workshop of "Literary Pioneers . . ." at the "Lucky Come Hawaii: The Chinese in Hawaii" conference at the East West Center on 20 July 1988.

7. In *Massie,* an upper-class white woman, Thalia Forescu Massie, accused five local men, Benny Ahakuelo, Henry Chang, Horace Ida, Joseph Kahahawai, and David Takai, of rape and assault. After a deadlocked jury found insufficient evidence to convict, Ida was seized on the street and severely beaten, and Kahahawai was killed by Massie's husband, mother, and friend. The subsequent trial of the three murderers resulted in conviction, but they were released after serving just one hour of their sentences in the judge's chambers.

8. "Some 540 were interned in small camps on O'ahu, and 930 were transferred to mainland camps. . . . In October 1944, when military rule was rescinded by the president, the military maintained martial law. Some 413 internees were allowed to go home, but 50 aliens remained in internment camps; and 67 Japanese Americans were shipped to the mainland" (Haas 1992, 19–20; also see Allen 1950 (134, 139); and Odo and Sinoto 1985 (216). On the humiliation and pain suffered by these Issei men, see Okihiro 1991 (Chaps. 9–11); on Japanese-language schools, see Tamura 1994 (Chap. 7, 145–64).

9. This mother figure was the frequent subject of photographs; see Allen 1950 (132) and Tanaka 1987 (166).

10. Two plays that deal more directly with youth gangs are Miyoshi Ikeda's *Lest We Forget* and Henry Chun's *Kindness to Cobras (A Modern Hawaiian Melodrama)* in Wilson n.d., vol. 7.

11. Fujikane points out that many of those of Asian descent in Hawai'i "strategically refuse the name 'Asian American,' a continental term that fails to recognize the anomalous status of Local Asians who are a part of a non-Native Hawaiian, multiracial Local Movement asserting its own cultural identity. At the same time, this 'Local identity' . . . can come to perform its own exclusions of more recent Asian and Pacific Islander immigrants, while it also covers over race and class divisions between locals, since Local Chinese, Japanese and Koreans have, in post–World War II years, come to constitute the middle classes in Hawai'i" (1994 24, 27).

Works Cited

Allen, Gwenfread. 1950. *Hawaii's War Years, 1941–1945*. Honolulu: University of Hawai'i Press.

Bell, Roger J. 1984. *Last among Equals: Hawaiian Statehood and American Politics*. Honolulu: University of Hawai'i Press.

Buck, Elizabeth Bentzel. 1993. *Paradise Remade: The Politics of Culture and History in Hawai'i*. Philadelphia: Temple University Press.

Carroll, Dennis, ed. 1983. *Kumu Kahua Plays*. Honolulu: University of Hawai'i Press.

Chock, Eric, ed. 1989. *Paké: Writings by Chinese in Hawaii*. Honolulu: Bamboo Ridge Press.

Chun, Wai Chee. 1937. *Marginal Woman*. In Wilson, n.d., Vol. 1.

Du Puy, William Atherton. 1932. *Hawaii and Its Race Problem*. Washington, D.C.: GPO.

Duus, Masayo. 1987. *Unlikely Liberators: The Men of the 100th and 442nd*. Honolulu: University of Hawai'i Press.

Ferguson, Kathy E., and Phyllis Turnbull. 1999. *Oh, Say, Can You See? The Semiotics of the Military in Hawai'i*. Minneapolis: University of Minnesota Press.

Fujikane, Candace. 1994. "Between Nationalisms: Hawaii's Local Nation and Its Troubled Racial Paradise." *Critical Mass* 1, 2 (Spring/Summer): 23–57.

Haas, Michael. 1992. *Institutional Racism: The Case of Hawai'i*. Westport, Conn.: Praeger.

Hurwitz, Louis. 1937. *Escape*. In Wilson n.d., Vol. 1.

Irikura, James K. 1947–48. *Broadminded*. In Wilson n.d., Vol. 3.

Kann, Mark. 1991. *On the Man Question: Gender and Civic Virtue in America*. Philadelphia: Temple University Press.

Kent, Noel J. 1983. *Hawaii: Islands under the Influence*. New York: Monthly Review Press.

Langhans, Edward A., with Fay Hendricks, comp. 1973. *An Index to Original Plays in Sinclair Library, 1937–1969*. Typescript. University of Hawai'i, Manoa.

Lee, Robert G. 1999. *Orientals: Asian Americans in Popular Culture*. Philadelphia: Temple University Press.

Morales, Rodney. 1998. "Literature." In *Multicultural Hawai'i: The Fabric of a Multiethnic Society,* ed. Michael Haas, 107–29. New York: Garland.

Odo, Franklin, and Kazuko Sinoto. 1985. *A Pictorial History of the Japanese in Hawai'i, 1885–1924*. Honolulu: Bishop Museum Press.

Okihiro, Gary. 1991. *Cane Fires: The Anti-Japanese Movement in Hawaii, 1865–1945*. Philadelphia: Temple University Press.

Omi, Michael, and Howard Winant. 1994. *Racial Formation in the United States: From the 1960s to the 1980s*. 1986. London: Routledge.

Sakai, Edward. 1947–48a. *And Never the Twain Shall Meet?* In Wilson n.d., Vol. 3.

———. 1947–48b. *C'est le Guerre.* In Wilson n.d., Vol. 3.

Sumida, Stephen. 1986. "Waiting for the Big Fish: Recent Research in the Asian American Literature of Hawai'i." In *The Best of Bamboo Ridge,* ed. Eric Chock and Darrell H. Y. Lum, 302–21. Honolulu: Bamboo Ridge Press.

———. 1991. *And the View from the Shore: Literary Traditions of Hawai'i.* Seattle: University of Washington Press.

———. 1997. "Postcolonialism, Nationalism, and the Emergence of Asian/Pacific American Literatures." In *An Interethnic Companion to Asian American Literature,* ed. King-kok Cheung, 274–88. Cambridge: Cambridge University Press.

Suyeoka, Robert. 1948–49. *The Last Refrain.* In Wilson n.d., Vol. 4.

Tabrah, Ruth M. 1984. *Hawaii: A History.* New York: Norton.

Takaki, Ronald. 1989. *Strangers from a Different Shore: A History of Asian Americans.* New York: Penguin.

Tamura, Eileen H. 1994. *Americanization, Acculturation, and Ethnic Identity: The Nisei Generation in Hawaii.* Urbana: University of Illinois,

Tanaka, Chester. 1987. *Go for Broke: A Pictorial History of the Japanese American 100th Infantry Battalion and the 442nd Regimental Combat Team.* San Francisco: Go for Broke.

Toishigawa, Bessie. 1946–47. *Reunion.* In Wilson n.d., Vol. 2. (Also published under Bessie Toishigawa Inouye in Carroll 1983).

———. 1946–47. *Nisei.* In Wilson n.d., Vol. 3.

Uno, Roberta. 1993. *Unbroken Thread: An Anthology of Plays by Asian American Women.* Amherst: University of Massachusetts Press.

Wilson, Willard, ed. N.d. *College Plays 1937–1955.* Vols. 1–10. Typescript. University of Hawai'i, Manoa.

Yu, Henry. 2001. *Thinking Orientals: Migration, Contact, and Exoticism in Modern America.* Oxford: Oxford University Press.

Robert Cooperman

20   The Americanization of Americans: The Phenomenon of Nisei Internment Camp Theater

In the many scholarly attempts to reconstruct internment camp life, cultural events such as dances, talent shows, sporting events, and holiday celebrations seem to have been given short shrift. That these events were plentiful and often the only source of socialization afforded the mostly young Nisei internees simply adds to a body of scholarship left thus far unattended. But even these "lifeboats in the daily boredom of exile" (James 1987, 65) are well documented when compared with the information we know of another significant cultural event: internment camp theater. Theatrical productions, primarily the staging of Western plays, played a significant role at every camp, providing for the incarcerated masses a means to combat the tedium of the internment camp experience, and often serving more compelling cultural imperatives as well. Internment camp theater was a widespread phenomenon, although one that ironically has enjoyed no connection to Asian American scholarship or Asian American literature.

It is very difficult indeed to reconstruct the performances of the Nisei theater groups for a number of possible reasons. First, few living internees remember theater at their camp, even when theater groups flourished. Second, those who recall theater do so fifty years after the fact, and such recollections are often hazy at best. Third, while camp newspapers often publicized theater, with few exceptions (the Tule Lake and Poston camps) theatrical endeavors were relegated to a minimal number of lines deep within the newspapers and usually included only the performance dates and times. Fourth, the plays were not original dramas, except for a script by an Anglo-American at Tule Lake and some comic sketches written by internees at Poston.[1] In addition, at this point there is no information about how the plays were interpreted as texts, so the issue of internment camp drama remains purely speculative. However, the plays chosen provide some insights into Nisei response to the internments in this highly political landscape. What little we can reconstruct challenges the representations of the internments we have become familiar with through historical and, particularly, literary perspectives.

Although it is risky to generalize about Nisei response to internment, it is fairly safe to say that the conflict between those who supported the Anglo-American agenda and those who openly and bitterly questioned democracy in the United States was common within the Nisei population and continues to be a familiar trope in internment literature. However, the debate tends to be lopsided in favor of those who shared the latter point of view. Much attention has been paid to writers such as Toyo Suyemoto, Mitsuye Yamada, and other Nisei war poets who used poetry as "a significant means of resistance" through what Susan Schweik labels a "coded narrative of Nikkei experience on American land" (1991, 188). Postinternment literary scholarship has similarly focused on artists who share what the editors of *The Big Aiiieeeee!* term a "real" and "historically silenced" perspective of internment, among them poet Lawson Fusao Inada (author of a 1993 collection entitled *Legends from Camp*), novelist John Okada (*The No-No Boy*), historian Michi Weglyn (*Years of Infamy*), and playwrights Wakako Yamauchi (*12-1-A*) and Hiroshi Kashawagi (*Laughter and False Teeth*) (Chan et al. 1991). By contrast, Nisei performers, when singled out as a group within the interned Nisei population (even in the political hotbed of Tule Lake), showed a definite preference for what Stan Yogi labels an "optimistic" (1997, 133), and *The Big Aiiieeeee!* calls "fake," perspective (Chan et al. 1991, xiv–xv): "In the best-known . . . Japanese American literature, the non-Christian, the non-JACL, and Nisei camp resistance simply do not exist. In Asian-American writing and in American letters . . . Japanese American writers who write from the real . . . are pariahs" (xv).

In the attempt to replace the "fake" perspective with the "real" one, cultural events such as internment theater may become the new "pariah," but not without unfortunate results. On the one hand, we have a group of performers expressing a desire to accommodate—to "play" along with—the forces that oppressed them, and on the other hand we are led to believe their response was illegitimate or suppressing a "real" response hidden under layers of pseudo-accommodation and acceptance. In either case, internment camp theater becomes a casualty in the battle between what some would like to have been the case and what research and reconstruction says it was. The accommodating response of Nisei internment camp theater groups to the injustice of the internments may therefore be deemed of limited use by those weaned on the vibrancy of avant-garde and radical people's literature, as well as by those whose research has shown such a response to be "fake."

It also appears that the relationship between internment camp politics and camp theater is not yet clearly understood by mainstream sources. While we may wish that camp theater politics promoted rebellion either subtly or overtly, no evidence has yet been found to support this enticing scenario. By contrast, Anglo-American researchers such as Allen H. Eaton and Page Smith fail to connect camp theater (or the arts in general) to the politics of the internments in any fashion—an equally erroneous position. Eaton's *Beauty behind Barbed Wire*, a compilation of photos with explanatory text, demonstrates well the ingenuity of internee artists and artisans and their determination to beautify the often drab landscapes of the camps via, for example, floral arrangements, wood sculptures, and rock gardens. Inexplicably though, Eaton dismisses the Nisei involvement in the arts by omitting their contribution outright. The all-too-brief section on theater exemplifies Eaton's emphasis on traditional Issei offerings without a word of the equally prolific Nisei theatrical enterprises. Noting the "active dramatic groups in several of the War Relocation Centers," Eaton allows that "only the briefest reference can be made to them here," and although he speculates as to the raison d'être for camp art in general, he seems to look upon theater solely as a source for gorgeous stage costumes, props, and settings—a beautifully transcendent but apolitical phenomenon: "What the Japanese theater people cannot do with paper and paint in the way of stage requisites and properties no one can do. Paper in some form—often sculptured papier-mache—provided most of the needs of the camps for their dramatic productions; . . . most of [the materials used] would ordinarily be consigned to the trash pile" (1952, 78).[2]

Page Smith similarly stresses Issei artistic endeavors and places camp culture in a category separate from the "day-to-day material aspects of life" (food, clothing, and shelter) and "the political or ideological aspects." In a discussion of committees formed at the camps to arbitrate evacuee/administrative disputes, Smith curiously laments that "they soon became as politicized as most other aspects of center life (*the arts and education being perhaps the most notable exceptions*)" (1995, 355, emphasis added). Research into Nisei camp theater suggests quite a different conclusion: theater and education were indeed linked, and their linkage was the result of an uneasy merger between the ideology of a well-meaning administration and the politically motivated choices made by evacuees who sought cooperation rather than confrontation with the government. Camp theater generally was produced under the auspices of the camp administration's education policies, which dictated that the schools be part of a planned-community type of arrangement designed to "speed up the assimilation of Japanese Americans into the dominant pattern of American life" (James 1987, 38). As Thomas James explains, the school system devised for the internees purported to "reflect the experiences available in the community, thus giving traditional book learning a social context and meaning" (39). However, the concept of "community" was left for the administration to define, and "the curriculum had been designed to mirror not the normal world outside, but the bureaucratic divisions of responsibility that the government had set up for managing the incarceration" (39). Ultimately, "community schooling incorporated the structure of authority that characterized the operation of the camps" (57). This structure of authority—in no way apolitical—may be clearly seen in what I have termed the high school theater paradigm.

Theater at the High Schools: Unquestioned Accommodation

High school theater was the most common of the two broad categories of internment camp theater I have identified. As a theatrical genre it clearly resembles the amateur theater one might find in the high schools of today. High school theater was at its inception one of the many aforementioned extracurricular activities offered to Nisei students, and although such activities were generally not a part of Nisei life before the internments, theater was considered a particularly impractical vocation, as Misha Berson notes: "Many immigrant parents (Asian and non-Asian) actively discouraged their first-generation children from having anything to do with 'show business,' viewing it as a financially precarious, morally dubious career at best" (1990, x). Camp life seemed to change all that, however, and the Nisei found themselves heavily engaged in extracurricular activities such as theater. Jofu Mishima, a Heart Mountain internee/performer, in a letter (undated) to me, remembers that "drama was not an ordinary activity that the large majority of Nisei males would have participated in if we had not been segregated into camps." As internee/actor Frank Mouri of Heart Mountain recalls in a letter to me (1 May 1995): "I had no interest in acting or anything connected with the stage. I believe the others were very serious about it and they wanted to do their best. It was something for them to do in order to get their minds off of camp life at Heart Mountain."

High school theater was based at the camp high school, often the camp's cultural center, and presented in the auditorium, which served as both performance space and gymnasium. Such a venue tended to be cavernous, to seat hundreds, and to present a number of acoustic challenges. Plays were chosen and directed by Anglo-American teachers, were produced as senior- or sometimes junior-class presentations, were full-length, involved large casts, and were usually chosen based on their appeal to high school–aged spectators (which made up the majority of internees). Costumes, props, and makeup were provided by other high school extracurricular groups, therefore giving many more students something to do. Performances usually ran for no more than two nights, at ticket prices ranging from ten to twenty-five cents (with discounts for members of student organizations).

The plays themselves—farces, light comedies, murder mysteries, and teenage-angst plays—generally offered no greater conflict than the need to borrow the car for a hot date on a Saturday night or to solve a murder in an old mansion. This nonthreatening content offered the participants—and the audience—a temporary escape from the indignity of internment, as well as a glimpse of what "normal" American life might be like once internment was over (provided the Anglo-American teenage way of life was emulated). For the administration, the plays were similarly "safe" and addressed three major concerns: keeping the high schoolers busy with extracurricular activities (thus focusing on something other than their predicament), taking credit for furthering their education (and even bettering it by introducing them to theater), and assimilating them into U.S. society so that the need to mistrust this segment of the population would not again surface. Operating under a policy that endeavored to make theater education both pragmatic (for example, how to apply makeup for the stage) and politically idealistic (how participation in theater leads one to a greater participation in U.S. community life), Nisei theater centered at the high schools was administered by Anglo-Americans with a government-supported agenda and Japanese American assistants, a pattern that echoed the political structure of the camp itself. Despite what may be seen as good intentions, camp administrations essentially conducted an indoctrination program with test subjects willing to cooperate. Theater as an art form was not the concern of the administrations; its use as a means to a greater cultural end was.

As may be expected, the level of theatrical experience among the evacuees was quite limited, with apparently only a handful having any familiarity with Western theater. It was up to Anglo-American speech and English teachers to choose plays, audition actors, and direct productions, as well as teach script interpretation, acting, makeup, lighting, and costume design. On occasion, the burden placed on these teachers created a rather awkward introduction to theater for both teachers and students. In a letter to me (5 January 1996), Katsumi Kunisugu provides a cynical perspective on her experience at Heart Mountain High involving an atypical high school production: "I remember 'A Night at An Inn,' a one-act play involving a stolen gem from an idol or some such nonsense. Ms. [Lois] Runden [an English teacher] simply appointed me to be the director, and I had no understanding whatsoever what it was that a director was supposed to do."

For the most part, teachers put in charge of the theater programs did indeed have some theatrical experience, usually in the study of drama, and they often relied on their ingenuity and resourcefulness to overcome such obstacles as an inexperienced cast and crew and inadequate facilities. Robert Dierlam, an English teacher at Amache (Granada) High School, produced a particularly eclectic repertory from 1942 through 1944, including such plays as Christopher Morley's *Rehearsal,* a satire on Irish plays; Louis N. Parker's *A Minuet,* a play in verse; and E. P. Conkle's *Sparkin',* which features an Appalachian dialect often difficult to read, let alone pronounce.[3] To compensate for the camp's lack of resources, Dierlam used central staging, described by evacuee/spectator Lili Yuri Sasaki in an interview (with author, 10 September 1994) in terms similar to theater-in-the-round: "You're not supposed to put scenery or anything on the stage on the side of everyone, but put it in the center and all the people sit around it. Like a boxing ring!" With rare exceptions—a production of *Ladies of the Jury,* for example—Dierlam's repertory was quite atypical of the usual high school fare such as *Who Gets the Car Tonight?* at Gila River, *Mumbo-Jumbo* at Heart Mountain, and *Growing Pains* and *Spring Fever* at Poston.

Another Anglo-American teacher, Topaz speech teacher George Lewis, also attempted to challenge the prevailing wisdom about choosing worthy plays for camp theatrics. Lewis's April 1943 production of *Our Town* had all the elements of a typical camp high school production: a large cast, a lengthy play for an evening's entertainment, and no set requirements to strain the camp's limited resources. In addition, the play's nostalgic demonstration of the simple all-American life would surely have earned the approval of the administration, which in theory attempted to present camp life as both simple and (in particular) all-American. However, Michi Kobi's recollection of her performance as Emily Webb, in a letter to me (20 October 1994), suggests a more antagonistic relationship between Lewis and the camp government: "My knowledge of theater within Topaz . . . was limited to the high school I attended. Despite its rudimentary curriculum, there were individual teachers who were resourceful in their efforts to provide an American education in the incongruous concentration camp. Among them was George Lewis . . . who dared to defy Administration and Japanese inhibitions as well, by starting a drama group."

Kobi's implication that Lewis defied the administration by presenting plays warranted further study, and when I asked for more information, Kobi responded apologetically in a letter (5 November 1994): "I may have described Mr. Lewis as defiant because among staffers compliant to regulations, he seemed singly determined to lift us young Japanese Americans from our lowered self-esteem by involving us through the healing power of theater." Kobi's revision both clarifies and confuses her previous position. There is no evidence to support the assertion that starting a drama group at Topaz would defy the Anglo-American administration (indeed, administrations at all camps seemed to endorse Nisei high school theater for reasons mentioned earlier), although Kobi suggests quite rightly that the administration, by and large, was somewhat paranoid and on constant alert for rebellion. Still, she implies that Lewis was not "compliant to regulations" by using theater to heal, suggesting that his definition of "heal" was at odds with the administration's definition outlined earlier. For the administration, the isolation of the Japanese community needed healing; for George Lewis, the Nisei under his wing were in the greatest need of the healing power of theater.[4]

For the most part, Nisei high school theater was a benign extracurricular activity, providing little in the way of community skills (at least based on what has at present been demonstrated), but much in the battle against boredom and inactivity. Its ideological outlook was essentially that of the Anglo-American administration, well-meaning but ultimately of little value in solving the cultural dilemma of the Japanese American. With rare exceptions (Robert Dierlam's, for example), the plays produced were unambitious both from a performance- and text-based perspective. Few camps broke from this general model to create truly ambitious theater aimed at a heterogeneous audience (as opposed to an audience mostly of high school students).

Barrack Theater: The Wrong Kind of Resistance

Barrack theater, by contrast, was always ambitious in that it strove to reach wider audiences than the high school offered, it produced challenging plays, and its identifying characteristics were often in contrast to those of the high school. It was certainly a much more autonomous entity than was high school theater, as Anglo-Americans played a limited role in the artistic decisions of the group. Plays were chosen and directed by Nisei, who established the group and administered its day-to-day operation. Performances took place in a barrack fashioned to resemble a theater and could seat no more than 150 per performance. The plays chosen were almost exclusively one-act plays, many by master playwrights of note (O'Neill, Chekhov, Tarkington, etc.). Rather than various extracurricular committees to take care of props and other backstage necessities, barrack theater operated as a self-sufficient group, the goals of which went beyond (but always included) entertainment, striving instead for aesthetic awareness. The education of the participants in stagecraft seems to have been a less important goal.

Because the Nisei were the controlling force of Barrack theater, it is tempting to imagine that the performers enacted their resistance to the internments through choice of play, gesture, staging, and whatever means were available to them to make their point on stage. However, my research has shown that the performers responded to their internment from the "fake" perspective, using Western theater to express their Americanism by the seamless transition into Anglo-American roles by people with a very different appearance, and steering clear of anything considered too Japanese. Starting with the premise that the Nisei were in general unacculturated to the U.S. way of life (a premise shared by Nisei high school theater), barrack theater hoped to use dramatics as a means toward achieving the goal of assimilation, in anticipation of the day the Japanese would be released from the camps. Evacuee/performer Jiro Shimoda exemplifies the position of like-minded Nisei participants of barrack theater in a letter to me (17 October 1994): "I felt there was no way I could make it in Japan and my loyalty was to this country despite the bigots and hysteria that put us in camp."

Shimoda resided at the camp that housed barrack theater's greatest flowering: the Tule Lake Relocation Center. At Tule Lake, the call for theatrical talent was issued in the camp newspaper, the *Tulean Dispatch,* on 28 July 1942, barely two months after the opening of the camp. As the announcement "Registration for Drama" discloses, "Not only will there be acting to do, but those interested in stage setting, voice & diction, lighting, costuming, make-up or others on that line are asked to sign up." Internees Perry Saito and Sada Murayama took charge and proceeded to form what was to become the Tule Lake Little Theatre, with its first productions scheduled for Barrack 408, nothing more than a one-hundred- by twenty-foot wood and tar-paper structure.[5] A platform approximately twelve feet across and twelve feet wide placed against the short end of the barrack and raised approximately a foot served as the stage, which at first was level but later was raked. A small dressing room with mirrors was set up behind the stage for the performers to put on makeup. The stage apparently had curtains both in front of it and behind it, masking the backstage area. The long audience area could hold approximately 150 spectators, seated on, according to actor Jiro Shimoda in a letter to me (23 September 1994), "home-made benches [or] borrowed benches from the [camp] church." According to actor Hiroshi Kashiwagi in an interview (with author, 9 September 1994), the theater had no amplification, a crude lighting system, and curtains covering the barracks many windows, although these were a later addition "to make it look more like a theater."

On 13 August under the headline "Drama Club Organized," the Little Theatre published in the *Dispatch* what I have labeled its manifesto, the only such declaration of goals and purposes offered by a theater group at any camp:

1. To acquire cultural refinement through appreciation and participation of dramas;
2. To give entertainment through our efforts;
3. To develop talent in various phases of dramatics;
4. To serve as an escape from reality.

These four together provide clues toward an understanding of how theater was used as a *response to* internment, in addition to being a *result of* internment, and how it was meant for asserting, rather than resisting, the American birthright of the performers.

The desire for the acquisition of cultural refinement strongly suggests a refinement sensed to be lacking, a conclusion not difficult to draw based on the general lack of participation in theater by the Nisei generation. Therefore, I believe the participants hoped to use theater to make up for this perceived shortcoming for the express purpose of enhancing the assimilation process. It appears that Perry Saito and, particularly, Sada Murayama recognized the lack of Nisei involvement in the arts and chose to use their Little Theatre as the venue for correcting this oversight, both for the members of the Little Theatre and for their audiences (although these two entities were often at odds). As a group, they apparently tried to gear their productions around, as evacuee/performer Morse Saito (Perry's younger brother) explains, "the heavier stuff like Eugene O'Neil1," although this attempt did not always meet with audience approval. The placement of this purpose as the first on the list suggests that it was of paramount importance to the Little Theatre.

However, the fourth-listed purpose, "an escape from reality," seems to conflict with the "assimilationist" goal "the acquisition of cultural refinement" implies. The phrasing of this goal suggests, of course, that both spectators and performers needed such an escape. What remains unclear is whether theater as an activity was meant to facilitate this escape or whether the plays themselves were to serve as the vehicle of escapism. In either case, and both are certainly plausible, the Little Theatre organizers recognized that theater could become a diversion of social and psychic proportions for the internees, just as a number of Nisei similarly reflected upon the purpose of high school theater.

The implied conflict between "escapism" and the "acquisition of cultural refinement" makes it ultimately unclear to what extent assimilation ever was a realistic goal for the Little Theatre. Actor/internee Hiroshi Kashiwagi details what may have been an ongoing debate among its members: "The Little Theatre was very Americanized and we were having this bit about whether to be assimilated or not. Anyway, because I didn't register, of course, we could not discuss this, the different views. . . . You know, there'd be a conflict." No doubt conflicts regarding assimilation arose within the Little Theatre, but Kashiwagi's remarks may more accurately refer to the camp population as a whole than to his fellow performers. When asked for a rough percentage of "disloyal" fellow performers, Kashiwagi replied with a laugh, "Not many. . . . In the theater group I was [in the minority] because those who were in the theater were pretty assimilated." Sada Murayama was particularly demonstrative in her support for the United States, a position that, as recalled by Kashiwagi, led to a number of violent acts against her.

The forces that gave Murayama so much grief were generally to be found outside of her Americanized theater group. Morse Saito recalls in a letter to me (4 April 1995) that although his brother was labeled a "disloyal," it was "the pro-Japan Kibeis [who] tried to stop all such 'frivolous' activities of the rec[reation] dept and even threatened to break up the Little Theatre performances. It took courage to carry on and the [Little Theatre] group carried on even after some Christian ministers had been severely beaten up." Thus, the Little Theatre, existing within a rather volatile political atmosphere, set out to find in theater a refuge from the reality from which it proposed to escape, yet at the same time recognized that "escape" might not further the cause of assimilation. This discord additionally may reflect conflicting visions of identity felt by the Nisei (as well as by members of any immigrant group): "the self that is assimilated and the self that remains unassimilatable" (Lim 1992, 19). The assimilable Japanese self, as described by Harry H. L. Kitano, relies on a consistent strategy of adaptation: "The Japanese themselves like to compare it to a small stream; like the stream they have followed the contours of the land, followed the lines of least resistance, avoided direct confrontation, and developed at their own pace, always shaped by the external realities of the larger society. It is basically a strategy of accommodation" (1976, 2–3).

If Kitano's description indeed speaks for the majority of members of the Little Theatre, it may not be entirely representative of its audience. The level at which the general internee population followed Kitano's "small stream" analogy is of course the basis for the editorial slant of *The Big Aiiieeeee!* (Chan et al. 1991) Similarly, as Lane Ryo Hirabayashi suggests, "popular resistance by Japanese Americans in WRA camps during World War II has been underreported and often misinterpreted" (1995, xiii). Perhaps recognizing that the desire for escape was stronger among spectators than among the group members, and that spectator politics concerning assimilation generally did not match those of the group, the "assimilationist" Little Theatre astutely chose a variety of plays from various genres to appeal to diverse tastes, even though the group itself, as Morse Saito remembers in his letter (4 April 1995), "preferred the serious plays which they felt [were] real dramatics and fine literature." The decision was made to produce a comedy, a tragedy, and a fantasy on every bill, the first of which ran (ironically) 7–21 December 1942 and was performed nightly for one of the seven wards at Tule Lake. The bill featured three one-act plays: Eugene O'Neill's *Ile* (the tragedy), George Kelly's *The Flattering Word* (the comedy), and Oliphant Down's *Maker of Dreams* (the fantasy).[6]

It is believed the three plays followed a particular order of performance. The first play was always the comedy. As Morse Saito explains in his 1995 letter: "Something light for the kiddies and after they fell asleep then into a heavier play.... Taking time out for stage settings between one act plays may seem a good way to lose any audience but instead it gave people a chance to go home and put some little one to bed." Saito's recollection also implies that individual sets were "designed" to suit the plays; the three plays did not share a single set nor did they use an empty space and some symbolic props to suggest a set. Sound effects and lighting, however crude, were employed to heighten the sense of realism on the stage.[7] Sada Murayama introduced each play before it commenced. As Hiroshi Kashiwagi remembers: "We would need a little time to change the set and she'd go out there and say something. She was very charming."

Plans to present monthly plays went according to schedule through January and February 1943. The six plays produced were Edith Delano and David Carb's *Grandma Pulls the String,* Chekhov's *The Boor,* and Booth Tarkington's *Beauty and the Jacobin* in January, and Rachel Crothers's *Peggy,* A. A. Milne's *The Boy Comes Home,* and—the only original—Garrett Starmer's *Angelpuss,* a light-hearted comedy about teenage love, in February.[8] By this time the Little Theatre was getting direct feedback from its spectators through the *Tulean Dispatch,* whose reviews came to serve as the voice of the audience. Commentary in the *Dispatch,* whether favorable or unfavorable toward the performers, almost always agreed that some of the plays chosen by the Little Theatre were inappropriate given the realities of being interned. Reviews and, later, audience response sheets, showed that "escapist" comedies were greatly preferred over any other genre. *Dispatch* writer Ken Hayashi offers such a perspective in a 20 January 1943 review entitled "The Other Side" (meant as a counterpoint to the usual flattering reviews in the *Dispatch*), perhaps expressing the feelings of many of the internees who made up the Little Theatre's audience: "Living here as we are this corner feels that from a psychological and emotional standpoint, we do not go so strongly for these long, drawn out Mid-Victorian plays. Something short, snappy or at least a little lighter in vein should go over more in this project."

Further proof of audience desire for escapist entertainment may be extracted from existing audience response sheets pertaining to the final Little Theatre offerings in mid-July 1943: Theresa Helburns's *Enter the Hero,* Harry Kemp's *Boccaccio's Untold Tale,* and Beatrice McNeil's *Elmer and the Lovebug* (a comedy typical of camp high school presentations). The sheets allowed spectators to pencil in their ranking of the plays presented, as well as to offer comments. Five of the six sheets I am in possession of place *Elmer and the Lovebug* first; the one ballot that places *Elmer* third does so with the comment "I would like to see more of Elmer's play put on." Every respondent offering a comment asked for more plays like *Elmer,* an unsurprising result given Hayashi's review.

It is, of course, possible that *Elmer and the Lovebug* sported the most polished production, which added to its overall enjoyment by the audience, but it is unmistakable that audiences craved comedies. If such responses are to be taken as representative of the Little Theatre's audiences, then Perry Saito and Sada Murayama's goal of "the acquisition of cultural refinement" seems unobtainable on a large scale. For spectators seeking entertainment and escape from the boredom and injustice of internment, loftier plays meant to familiarize audiences with a range of Western genres may truly have been unsuitable choices; the message that the Little Theatre was given was that only the genre of comedy would be tolerated. Nisei audiences, while generally unacculturated in the arts, still possessed taste in art and contextualized their political situation in ways the Little Theatre may have idealistically thought it could overcome.

Compounding this situation was the registration fiasco of 1943, which forced the cancellation of the Little Theatre's monthly plays for approximately ten days that February. Tensions over loyalty questionnaires and the draft, and the resulting violence that made Tule Lake stand out as a particularly volatile camp, continued to take its toll on the Little Theatre, and the plays themselves were suspended until May, when Robert Middlemass and Holworthy Hall's *The Valiant,* Beatrice McNeil's *Elmer,* and excerpts from *Our Town* with a cast of Anglo-American staff members were produced. It is not known why Anglo-Americans were invited to perform or what Sada Murayama hoped to convey by their inclusion. Given what is known of Murayama's feelings of cooperation with the Anglo-American power base, it is possible that a demonstration of solidarity between the Japanese and the Anglo-Americans, particularly at a time of heightened political tension, was her goal. Hiroshi Kashiwagi believes it was not Murayama who invited the Anglo-Americans to perform but the administration itself that took a sudden interest in theater, perhaps sharing Murayama's desire for onstage pluralism, particularly in the aftermath of the registration debacle.

Also at this time, a number of internees (Perry Saito, for example) took advantage of the administration's offer to leave camp, which left Tule Lake stigmatized with "disloyals" from all camps who either refused to register, registered in the negative, or simply chose not to leave camp to face the uncertainties of a racist America. The Tule Lake Relocation Center was renamed the Tule Lake Segregation Center, complete with a formation of tanks in full view of the residents. These changes had an immediate effect on the Little Theatre. Knowing that potential audiences would be made up more and more of angry "disloyals" fed up with their treatment by the government and unappreciative of a theater that promoted assimilation (however subtly, although run by a known assimilationist), the Little Theatre ended its run. In April 1944 a new Nisei theater group attempted to form, under the direction of internee Wilfred Horiuchi, who had directed plays and taught speech and drama at Poston and had contributed to the unproduced *Postonese*.

Not surprisingly, this nascent group, which also called itself the Little Theatre, failed to generate any interest, and no productions are known to have been staged by it. Instead, Issei theater (usually kabuki presentations), present at all camps, rose to the forefront, as did many other forms of traditional Japanese culture. In an article detailing the folk practices of the Japanese at Tule Lake, Marvin K. Opler contends that Japanese folklore was "part of a total nativistic reaction from 1944 to 1946" (1950, 385), a reaction shared by Issei and Nisei "when it was deemed important to strike back at administrative pressures, programs, and policies with the dignified weapons of Japanese culture" (387). Thus, with the rejection of what Opler calls "the American scene," Tule Lake became more "Japanese," even among the Nisei. Western theater really had no place in the nativistic Segregation Center. As Page Smith points out, "the ironic fact [is] that the longer the evacuees remained in the centers the more Japanese most of them became" (1995, 286).

Similarly ironic was that what brought spectators like Mas Yamasaki to the theatre, the novelty of seeing Asians in "nontraditional" roles, was precisely what led to theater's downfall within its own community. Yamasaki describes in a letter to me (4 December 1994) why he attended most plays of the Little Theatre: "I went to see the plays mostly to see the Niseis performing a variety of roles (rather than only the subservient ones we so often see in the movies)—especially to see Nisei actors performing in roles that I had never seen before done by Niseis. It was something I never even dreamed or imagined possible." The demise of the Little Theatre therefore pulled the plug on the visualization of Asians acting in roles generally reserved for Anglo-Americans. Japanese forces against assimilation were successful in putting an end to the "American" Little Theatre.

This is not to say, though, that the Tule Lake Little Theatre (or its high school counterpart) was an exercise in futility. Although assimilationist goals proved to be the wrong kind of resistance at Tule Lake, they had an impact years later in the lives of the internees. I have observed that the participants of camp theater seem to have mitigated their sense of outrage by placing theater in a context apart from the injustice served by their internment. For example, to my question suggesting that camp life was "horrifying," Tule Lake actor George Katagiri responded in a letter (19 January 1995): "In the area of social activities, camp was not a 'horrible' place. The Nisei developed many friendships and have many pleasant memories of their internment." Like many other Nisei performers, Katagiri distinguishes between the injustice of the internments as government policy and the benefits of this experience on a personal level.

Ironically, were it not for the internments, this generation of Nisei would probably not have experienced theater, either as performers or spectators. In fact, a number of evacuees went on to pursue careers on the stage and in film. Jofu Mishima (Heart Mountain), in a letter to me (14 May 1995), writes, "It must have had some effect upon me for I joined the local community theaters and participated in both the Richland Light Opera Company and Richland Players for 25 years as a lead/supporting cast/chorus member, dancer, lights/sound, stagehand, and various areas of production (drama director, producer, technical director)." Hiroshi Kashawagi (Tule Lake) continues to perform as well as write for the stage; Michi Kobi (Topaz) is a working actress in New York; the late Yukio Shimoda (Tule Lake) was a featured player on Broadway; and, of course, George Takei of *Star Trek* fame and actor Pat Morita were interned, although both were very young at the time. Although the percentage of evacuees who entered the performing arts is quite low, it is not an understatement to say that within the internee population itself the percentage may have indeed doubled or tripled.[9]

"Virtually every form of injustice in U.S. history has served to stimulate socially conscious artists," argues Paul Von Blum in *The Critical Vision* (1982, 3), and the internment of U.S. citizens under the guise of military security certainly qualifies as an injustice. While we are familiar with the work of marginalized artists seeking change to ensure that oppressed groups are no longer servants of the state, internee theatrical art, existing within a similar world of oppression, seeks change so that the artist (and the spectator) indeed becomes an operative of the state. And while such a stance is not difficult to imagine at the high school level, where an enthusiastic administration set the ground rules for theatrical presentations, barrack theater tempts us to expect it to have been a theater of protest, which it really was not—unless protest is how we classify the defiant message "See, I am an American!"

Still, barrack theater remains a compelling form of internment camp theater, despite its emphasis on accommodation rather than resistance. Nisei general acquiescence to the ideological superstructure of the time was merely an example of one response to the internments and one political agenda being enacted. That the internee artists politicized their work in this generally non-confrontational manner does not make them ineffective social artists. The similarity between internee performers and, say, the Bread and Puppet Theater lies in the fact that both groups responded to injustice, and it is the *response* that is the determinant for social consciousness in art, not the nature or political ideology of that response. Although contemporary artists may approach conditions of oppression in a very different manner and may be somewhat disappointed by the Little Theatre's self-imposed positioning vis-à-vis the internments, that does not diminish what it attempted to accomplish in its brief moment behind makeshift footlights in a tarpaper barrack.

Notes

Most of the information presented here has been taken from my doctoral dissertation, "Nisei Theater: History, Context, and Perspective" (Ohio State University, 1996). In addition, portions of this essay have been taken from "Barrack 408: Theater at the Tule Lake Relocation Center," presented at the 1995 Modern Language Association conference, 28 December 1995, Chicago.

1. The Poston sketches were *Postonese* and *Sandstorm and Stars;* the script was Garrett Starmer's *Angelpuss.* No copies have surfaced.

2. Eaton concludes that art at the camps served to mitigate oppressive conditions while providing ample evidence of the arts as "an inseparable part of Japanese life" (1952, 116).

3. Robert Dierlam retired from teaching drama and theatre at Queens College, CUNY, in the 1980s. I knew him as an undergraduate, but I had no idea he had any connection to the internment camps. I tracked him down with the gracious help of his daughter, Katy, and spoke with him on Thanksgiving Day 1994.

4. The playbill for the production of *Our Town* provides more insights into Lewis's decisions—both artistic and practical. For example, he set the third act in 1940 (Wilder calls for 1913). His director's statement in the playbill reminds us "that happiness cannot be found in reliving the past, but only in living today, tomorrow and tomorrow."

5. Now deceased, Perry Saito remained at Tule Lake only until May 1943. However, in that short time he helped create the internments' most prolific theater group. He went on to a career as a minister after his release. This information has been kindly provided to me by Perry's younger brother, Morse, a member of the Little Theatre. Very little is known about Sada Murayama, but based on the comments of those who worked with her, I suspect that she was one of the rare persons of Japanese descent with a background in Western theater.

6. Of the three plays presented on the first bill, *Ile* contains the most telling metaphors for internment camp existence. The play takes place on an isolated whaling ship in the middle of the ocean; the crew is there against its will, the captain refuses to turn the ship back to civilization (he seeks whale oil, or "ile"), and his wife unsuccessfully battles insanity. The play emphasizes isolation, alienation, and ensuing madness, and these themes must have reverberated with the evacuees.

7. Hiroshi Kashiwagi believes the sound effects were phonograph recordings, perhaps borrowed from the camp record collection. Jiro Shimoda has given me such a record, a thin cardboard disk with two sound effects: "Car stopping" and "Car horn."

8. *The Boor* is commonly known as *The Bear,* but the Little Theatre probably used the title found in Shay and Loving (1925, 227–35). Since four of the fifteen plays produced by the Little Theatre appear in this anthology, it is probable that someone in the group owned a copy. The Little Theatre also used the collection's spelling, "Tchekoff." Garrett Starmer, a speech therapist in Chico, California, was hired by the WRA soon after obtaining his California state teaching credentials. Invited to join the Little Theatre by Sada Murayama, he does not recall being involved in any productions other than his own *Angelpuss.* He was, however, often credited in Little Theatre playbills.

9. At the time of the evacuation, adult Japanese were given a questionnaire that asked for their occupation. Twenty-two respondents said their occupations involved the performing arts, and all of these were listed as dancers and chorus girls (Smith 1995, 63).

Works Cited

Berson, Misha, ed. 1990. Introduction to *Between Worlds: Contemporary Asian-American Plays,* ix–xiv. New York: Theatre Communications Group.

Chan, Jeffery Paul, Frank Chin, Lawson Fusao Inada, and Shawn Wong, eds. 1991. Introduction to *The Big Aiiieeeee! An Anthology of Chinese American and Japanese American Literature,* xi–xvi. New York: Meridian Press.

Eaton, Allen H. 1952. *Beauty Behind Barbed Wire: The Arts of the Japanese in Our War Relocation Camps.* New York: Harper.

Hirabayashi, Lane Ryo, ed. 1995. Preface to *Inside an American Concentration Camp: Japanese Resistance at Poston, Arizona,* xi–xv. Tucson: University of Arizona Press.

James, Thomas. 1987. *Exile Within: The Schooling of Japanese Americans, 1942–1945.* Cambridge: Harvard University Press.

Kitano, Harry H. L. 1976. *Japanese Americans: The Evolution of a Subculture.* Englewood Cliffs, N.J.: Prentice-Hall.

Lim, Shirley Geok-lin. 1992. "The Ambivalent American: Asian-American Literature on the Cusp." In *Reading the Literature of Asian America,* ed. Shirley Geok-lin Lim and Amy Ling, 13–32. Philadelphia: Temple University Press.

Opler, Marvin K. 1950. "Japanese Folk Beliefs and Practices, Tule Lake, California." *Journal of American Folklore* 63 (October–December): 385.

Schweik, Susan. 1991. *A Gulf So Deeply Cut: American Women Poets and the Second World War.* Madison: University of Wisconsin Press.

Shay, Frank, and Pierre Loving, eds. 1925. *Fifty Contemporary One-Act Plays.* New York: Appleton.

Smith, Page. 1995. *Democracy on Trial: The Japanese American Evacuation and Relocation in World War II.* New York: Simon.

Von Blum, Paul. 1982. *The Critical Vision: A History of Social and Political Art in the U.S.* Boston: South End Press.

Yogi, Stan. 1997. "Japanese American Literature." In *An Interethnic Companion to Asian American Literature,* ed. King-Kok Cheung, 125–55. New York: Cambridge University Press.

Guy Beauregard

21   Reclaiming Sui Sin Far

The most striking issues raised by reading the work of Sui Sin Far and the flurry of criticism surrounding it involve the process of uncovering and discussing her writings; they involve, in short, what I call the politics of reclamation. This essay addresses the assumptions informing the critical reclamation of Sui Sin Far's writings and the terms on which Sui Sin Far has become, in the words of Shirley Lim, "the object of Asian American recuperative efforts" (1996, 149). A prominent mention in the introduction to the *Aiiieeeee!* anthology (Chin et al. 1974, xxi–xxii) and a conference paper by S. E. Solberg in 1976 (see Solberg 1981) began the contemporary project of reclaiming Sui Sin Far that culminated with the publication of two new editions of *Mrs. Spring Fragrance* in 1994 and 1995 and the appearance of a book-length literary biography in 1995.[1] Meanwhile, critical interest in Sui Sin Far continued to grow in the 1990s as critics brought a widening range of critical approaches and theoretical commitments to her writings.

This essay shifts the focus from the ongoing interest in analyzing Sui Sin Far's stories toward the critical practices that value and position them. My primary thesis is that the tensions in multicultural criticism identified by David Palumbo-Liu find their own particular expression in Sui Sin Far criticism. Palumbo-Liu writes that "it remains the task of critical multiculturalism to be alert both to the ways that multicultural criticism can fall in line with hegemonic assumptions and, indeed, serve to reinforce them, *and* to ways that a truly critical multicultural criticism might theorize points of opposition and resistance" (1995, 15). Sui Sin Far criticism functions as a useful example of multicultural criticism in process. At times it has been informed by liberal humanist assumptions that downplay processes of racialization and racist exclusion, and at times it has attempted to challenge the historical constitution and effects of "race." The unevenness of this critical record makes the ongoing process of reclaiming Sui Sin Far an important part of "recollecting early Asian America," especially regarding the varied ways literary and cultural critics are conceptualizing and discussing "the past" of Asian American culture.

A basic understanding of Sui Sin Far's multiple locations is crucial for any reading of her work (see White-Parks 1995b, esp. Chap. 1; also see Ling 1990, 26–32; Ling and White-Parks 1995, 1–3). Edith Eaton, later known as Sui Sin Far, was born in Macclesfield, England, in 1865. Her father was an English merchant and her mother was a Chinese woman who had received an English education. When Eaton was seven, her family moved to North America, spending time in Hudson, New York, before settling in Montreal, Quebec. As an adult, Eaton supported herself as a stenographer, a journalist, and a fiction writer. Various jobs took her briefly to Jamaica and then to the United States, where she lived from 1898 until 1912 (Ling and White-Parks 1995, 3). Under the name Sui Seen Far, she published in 1896 her first story that focuses on Chinese North Americans (White-Parks 1995b, 30); the date has become significant as a possible starting point for Asian American literature. The emergence of her political voice coincided with a shift in her subject matter from "humorous articles" in U.S. papers and stories "emphasizing the love adventures of European Canadian women" (26, 27) to an explicit focus on the lives of Chinese North Americans. In 1896, Eaton published in the *Montreal Daily Star* the brilliantly polemical "A Plea for the Chinaman: A Correspondent's Argument in His Favor," which argued vehemently against government plans to increase the racist "head tax" levied on Chinese immigrants to Canada.

Eaton's adoption of the pseudonym Sui Sin Far was a brave decision in what Amy Ling and Annette White-Parks call "a period of rampant sinophobia" (1995, 3). Many critics have found Eaton's choice of names significant. Xiao-Huang Yin, for example, writes that "Sui's consciousness of her Chinese ethnicity is . . . underscored by her selection of the Chinese pseudonym Sui Sin Far (meaning 'Narcissus') and her insistence on using the name in publication as well as in everyday life. . . . The full implications of her pseudonym become clear when one finds that 'Narcissus' in Chinese culture symbolizes dignity and indestructible love for family and homeland" (1991, 54). By naming herself Sui Sin Far, Eaton chose to identify herself as Chinese, in marked contrast to one of her sisters, Winnifred, who adopted the Japanese-sounding name "Onoto Watanna," appropriated Japanese subject matter, and became a best-selling novelist (Ling 1990, 27). Contrasting the career choices of the Eaton sisters has become a staple in Sui Sin Far criticism, but here I merely want to emphasize Ling's point that "the Eaton sisters' pseudonyms were chosen not so much to cloak their English patronym but to assert and expose their Asian ethnicity" (21). And using this pseudonym, Sui Sin Far produced her only book, a collection of stories called *Mrs. Spring Fragrance* that was published in Chicago by A. C. McClurg in 1912, two years before the author's death.

The Politics of Reclamation

The most obvious context within which to situate the reclamation of Sui Sin Far's work is the impact of multiculturalism on recent changes in the canon of U.S. literature. In their introduction to the 1995 edition of *Mrs. Spring Fragrance and Other Writings*, Ling and White-Parks write: "The recognition of the multicultural quality of American life has led to an expansion of the body of prose and poetry we recognize as representing

'American literature' and to a diversity and richness of literature in today's college curricula that was unknown before the civil rights and women's liberation movements of the 1960s and 1970s." Ling and White-Parks explain that interest in contemporary Asian American and African American literatures has led scholars to search for "our roots, ancestors, and foundations," and to recover writers such as Harriet Wilson, Harriet Jacobs, and Sui Sin Far (1995, 5). Certainly the reconstruction of Asian American and African American literary histories is a crucial part of splintering what White-Parks calls "the monologic to which European-colonized North America was so prone" (1995a, 31).

What is at stake, however, are the theoretical assumptions informing the reclamation of neglected writers, and I believe there are at least two potential problems we need to address. The first is whether enthusiasm over the "diversity" and "richness" of the literatures now taught can move beyond a form of multicultural pluralism that may obscure the continued presence of structural inequalities. Palumbo-Liu presents this first problem as follows: "As well-intentioned as it may appear, 'pluralism' is perhaps best regarded as a point of departure for a critical multiculturalism that would be likened in spirit to the antimonoculturalist trajectory of pluralism, but be unwilling to bypass an engagement with the historical and material effects of monoculturalist discourse" (1995, 5). And the second potential problem, raised by King-Kok Cheung, involves reclaiming works by excluded writers while at the same time "placing these works in cognitive grids that bracket differences as deviations" (1993, 168). But while Cheung identifies one danger—"bracket[ing] differences as deviations"—it seems to me that many (but, as I later discuss, certainly not all) critical discussions of Sui Sin Far's work have done precisely the opposite: They have presented and attempted to bracket differences as *sameness*.

Of particular importance in this respect is the body of Sui Sin Far criticism one might call early recuperative scholarship, dating from the early 1980s to the early 1990s. In its broad contours, this body of criticism is committed to a liberal humanist understanding of identity and culture. This particular theoretical commitment finds its expression in four closely related assumptions: Sui Sin Far worked toward "greater human understanding"; she demonstrated the "humanness" of the Chinese; she presented a more "objective" picture of Chinese North American life than did her racist contemporaries; and she freely chose her identity. Ling, for example, concludes an early essay on Sui Sin Far with the statement that "by her courage, her strength, her honesty, her unrelenting personal efforts, and her deeply-felt writing, [Sui Sin Far] contributed to American literature and to greater human understanding" (1983, 298). At this early critical moment, Ling attempts to argue for the importance of Sui Sin Far's work. What remains unstated in this argument, however, is the assumption that "greater human understanding" has ameliorative effects, and, by extension, that forms of social exclusion such as racism and sexism are products of a lack of understanding. Such faith in the ameliorative potential of "greater human understanding," however, may be implicated in a liberal politics that—despite Ling's careful historical work—allows certain structural forms of racism to escape scrutiny.[2]

Significantly, Ling repeatedly locates Sui Sin Far's resistance in her appeals to the "humanness" of Chinese Americans (1983, 292; 1990, 39, 44, 46). At this point, it is important to note that Sui Sin Far herself explicitly made this appeal in some of her strongest nonfiction pieces. In "A Plea for the Chinaman" (1896), for instance, she writes: "Human nature is the same the world over, and the Chinaman is as much a human being as those who now presume to judge him" (1995, 196); and, in "The Chinese in America" (1909), she writes: "The Chinese may be custom-bound—no doubt they are—but they are human beings, nevertheless" (1995, 234). A historically grounded investigation of Sui Sin Far's work has to account for the material conditions of racist exclusion within which Sui Sin Far wrote, and the discursive forms (Yellow Peril literature and its attendant stereotypes) that supported these conditions of exclusion. Specifically, it has to recognize that Sui Sin Far tried to contest the stereotype that Elaine Kim identifies as "the inhuman Asian" (1982, 8). As White-Parks points out, "skin color (being 'white' or of 'European descent') has set the standard for humanness in North America since the European invasion" (1995a, 27); consequently, " 'humanity' did not apply to people with skins darker than [that of the ruling Anglo majority]" (19). What seems problematic, however, is arguing that Sui Sin Far's emphasis on the "humanness" of the Chinese constituted her fundamental or even singular purpose. The work Sui Sin Far's texts perform is neither singular nor straightforward, and, as I argue in the next section of this essay, her literary writing performs a sophisticated subversion of desires to "fix" racialized others in a "knowable" space; such a subversion, in turn, may lead us to question the basis of her appeals to the "humanness" of the Chinese.

The third critical assumption I would like to draw attention to involves appealing to Sui Sin Far's "objectivity." Yin argues that Sui Sin Far is an important writer because she attempted "to create a more objective image of Chinese Americans" (1991, 50), and that "her portrayal of Chinatown ... has a realism that does not exist in the popular American fiction of her time" (58).[3] Although some feminist scholarship attempts to reconfigure and reclaim "objectivity" in order to avoid the political paralysis of relativism, Yin's appeal to Sui Sin Far's greater "objectivity" posits an understanding of representation in which it is possible to correct mistaken images with a "truthful depiction" of things "as they actually existed" (72). An understanding of representation as "objective" portrayal, however, seems to curtail discussion of the potentially more radical narrative strategies in Sui Sin Far's work, through which she manipulates limited points of view to comment pointedly on the uneven effects of the gaze. Again, I will return to the implications of such strategies in the next section of this essay.

The fourth and final critical assumption that deserves scrutiny is the claim that people of "mixed race," and specifically people with Asian and European backgrounds, are somehow "free" to choose their own identities. Ling begins a 1992 essay with quotations from Joan Scott, Teresa de Lauretis, and Dorinne Kondo, and puts forth the standard post-structuralist claim that "the self is not a fixed entity but a fluid, changing construct or creation determined by context or historical conditions and particularly by power relationships" (1992, 306). In the subsequent paragraph, however, Ling asserts that the identities of "mixed-race people" are open to "free" choice:

"Unhampered by physical features which may declare a particular exterior identity at odds with interior realities, mixed-race people, particularly those combining Caucasian and Asian races, are free to choose the identity or identities that suit a particular historical moment" (306). This faith in individual self-determination risks recirculating both an unproblematized notion of "race" and a notion that "mixed-race people" are somehow outside the processes and effects of racialization ("unhampered by physical features") and therefore able to freely choose their identities.

By contrast, I wish to suggest that invoking a post-structuralist model of subjectivity while relying on a notion of "free" choice outside the processes of racialization leads to what Shan He has scathingly called an act of "recuperating the humanist subject in spite of dabbling in theoretical polemics" (1995, 168). While such a position may be fueled by a desire to name a form of historical agency—that is, to refuse a model of absolute contextual and historical determinism—this presentation of historical agency as an individual *choice* may again discount the roles of "race" and gender as shifting and manipulable yet (at this historical moment) inescapable axes of identity. I agree with Larry Hajime Shinagawa and Gin Yong Pang when they argue that people "belong [to a race] because others *perceive* and *evaluate* them to be part of a race" (1996, 128); such racialized perceptions and evaluations can be challenged and resisted, but they cannot be willed away.

The fact that Ling considers the category of "race" to consist of "the insignificancies of skin color and eye shape" (1992, 316) locates her foundational assumptions in a form of liberal nonracialism. Two important studies that address the political and philosophical limitations of liberal nonracialism are Ruth Frankenberg's *White Women, Race Matters* and David Theo Goldberg's *Racist Culture,* which together provide clear and compelling arguments to rethink its usefulness in engaging with "race" as a socially meaningful marker of difference.

In the theoretical sections of her book, Frankenberg critiques what she refers to as "color evasiveness," which she calls "the dominant language of race in the United States" (1993, 145) and "the 'polite' language of race" (142). She seeks to examine "both the ways in which it [color evasiveness] has been deployed against essentialist racism and the ways it leads white women [the subjects she interviews] back into complicity with structural and institutional dimensions of inequality." Moreover, "it has in its various guises been taken to be antiracist, but color evasion, with its corollary of power evasion, ultimately has had reactionary results through most of the twentieth century" (143). While "color evasiveness" by white women may not be interchangeable with that by Chinese American critics, both forms are implicated in "liberal humanism as a philosophical discourse" (147), with its emphasis on "an essential human sameness to which 'race' is added as a secondary characteristic" (147–48). The problem with such a position, according to Frankenberg, is "the disinclination to think in terms of social or political aggregates" (148) and, consequently, the difficulty of mobilizing a form of social critique.

Goldberg's analysis pushes the implications of Frankenberg's observations further into a wholesale critique of liberal modernity's investment in what he calls "racist culture."

In a far-reaching argument, Goldberg insists on locating "race" in liberal modernity's "common sense" (1993, 1)—that which structures our most basic assumptions about identity, selfhood, and otherness. To the extent that philosophical liberalism is committed to individualism and an essential "human nature," it comes to argue that "race" is "a morally irrelevant category" (5–6). (This is precisely the philosophical tradition Ling falls within when she refers to "the insignificancies of skin color and eye shape.") Accordingly, Goldberg argues that liberal modernity fails "to take race seriously" and consequently "denies its racialized history and the attendant histories of racist exclusions, hiding them behind some idealized, self-promoting, yet practically ineffectual, dismissal of *race* as a morally irrelevant category" (7). Goldberg argues for the need to make a shift from what he calls liberal "nonracialism" to a form of neopragmatic "antiracism" (216). "While the liberal nonracialist is committed for the most part to little more than ignoring race," writes Goldberg, "the pragmatic antiracist is concerned with opposing racisms and protecting social subjects against delimitation of their gains in the name of an incorporative politics" (223). While the early recuperative Sui Sin Far criticism I have discussed sometimes shifts from nonracialism to unproblematized references to different "races," what makes it susceptible to Goldberg's critique is its collective inability to address the processes of racialization and forms of racist exclusion that structured Sui Sin Far's life and the lives of the characters she narrates.

Significant shifts have occurred in Sui Sin Far criticism since the early recuperative scholarship of the 1980s and early 1990s. From the mid-1990s onward, it has generally attempted to distance itself, overtly or implicitly, from the earlier phase—as Dominika Ferens succinctly puts it, "The celebratory story of Sui Sin Far has already been told" (1999, 118)—and has instead focused upon what Ferens calls Sui Sin Far's "literary interventions into the essentialist discourses of race" (121). Kyo Maclear, for instance, reads the work of Sui Sin Far to locate herself in relation to racial formations in Canada, and she suggests that "what is perhaps most interesting about her writing, and what has often been elided by 'Asian American' scholars and critics, is her conscious effort to explore the production of her (resisting) identity within an historical context that was wholly racialized" (1995, 14). Carol Roh-Spaulding, in a more extended discussion of Sui Sin Far's writings, argues against "a multiculturalist perspective that regards Sui Sin Far as a turn-of-the-century hero for the Chinese" (1997, 173) and instead insists on a critical perspective that accounts for "Sui Sin Far's evasiveness regarding Chinese-American identity and for the complexities of her own racial self-definition" (156). White-Parks shares Roh-Spaulding's desire to unsettle critical categories yet arrives at different conclusions. White-Parks draws on what Mary Dearborn calls "the concept of mediation"—stressing "samenesses rather than differences" (1995a, 17)—to argue that "Sui Sin Far's primary writing task . . . is not to mediate—stressing the 'samenesses'— but to create a visibility, a voice, and, ultimately, an hegemony for Chinese North Americans in her art that they were denied in their lives" (18).

This second phase of Sui Sin Far criticism, while hardly singular in its reading strategies or its theoretical commitments, can nevertheless enable us to rethink the assumptions that inform early attempts to reclaim Sui Sin Far. What is at stake here is not only reclaiming a turn-of-the-century foundational figure for an Asian American literary tradition, but also reconsidering the uneven process through which such claims are made. We might reconsider in more detail one specific critical claim—Yin's discussion of Sui Sin Far's usage of "objectivity" in her narratives—by addressing the complex narrative dynamics of Sui Sin Far's writing: Who is showing what to whom? "Her stories," writes Yin, "present a panoramic view and a realistic picture of the Chinese-American community at the end of the century" (1991, 50). What is the significance of Sui Sin Far's presentation of this "panoramic view" to those who were likely to be and still often are non-Chinese North American readers?[4] Who sees, who is seen, and what are the effects?

Sui Sin Far's Guided Chinatown Tour?

Certainly Sui Sin Far is aware of the powerful impact that "being seen" has on what she calls "Eurasian" children. In the nonfiction article "Half-Chinese Children" (1895), she writes of a girl who refuses to visit a neighbor's home because "they examine me from head to toe as if I was a wild animal—and just because father is a Chinese" (1995, 189). The issue becomes more personal still in the superb autobiographical essay "Leaves from the Mental Portfolio of an Eurasian" (1909), in which she narrates multiple experiences of being scanned and surveyed. At a children's party, she recalls being examined by an old man: "He adjusts his eyeglasses and surveys me critically. 'Ah indeed!' he exclaims. 'Who would have thought it at first glance. Yet now I see the difference between her and other children. What a peculiar coloring! Her mother's eyes and hair and her father's features, I presume. Very interesting little creature!'" (218). In this passage and others, Sui Sin Far is the object of the gaze, the one being othered and demeaned. The process of *being seen,* however, raises the possibility of *showing,* and, through the trope of the "guided tour," Sui Sin Far tries to manipulate the gaze in an urgent act of self-preservation. As White-Parks writes regarding tricksterism, "what is revealed to a given audience makes the difference in whether or not one survives" (1994, 1).

Two guided Chinatown tours that appear in *Mrs. Spring Fragrance*—in "The Wisdom of the New," and "'Its Wavering Image'"—help us address the complex effects of "showing" a culture. My point of departure is Sau-ling Wong's discussion of Maxine Hong Kingston's *The Woman Warrior* in "Autobiography as Guided Chinatown Tour?" where she writes: "Removed from Chinese culture in China by their ancestors' emigration, American-born autobiographers may still capitalize on white curiosity by conducting the literary equivalent of a guided Chinatown tour: by providing explanations on the manners and mores of the Chinese-American community from the vantage point of a 'native'" (1992, 262). The guided Chinatown tour becomes a site of ambivalence, in the sense that it can simultaneously play to the exoticizing desires of non-Chinese North American readers and subvert those desires by being untrustworthy. Wong reads *The Woman Warrior* as a subversive text in which "the protagonist has eschewed the facile authority which self-appointment as a guide and spokesperson could confer on her," and she convincingly argues that "only a careless reader . . . would be able to conclude that Kingston's stance in *The Woman Warrior* is that of the trustworthy cultural guide" (266, 267).

Wong is discussing autobiography and the particular generic problems it poses to readers of Chinese American writing. Sui Sin Far's stories are not clearly autobiographical and are therefore not likely to be read as a way of understanding her life.[5] They have, however, been read by critics such as Yin as "objective" or realistic portraits of West Coast Chinatowns at the beginning of the twentieth century. I suggest that the process of othering those racialized as "Chinese" relies on not only "misrepresentation" but also a scopic desire to see and "know" the other. The guided Chinatown tour is a classic example of how Sui Sin Far engages with and perhaps undermines scopic desire. I am not prepared to argue that Sui Sin Far presents the kind of wholesale epistemological subversion that so many critics have identified in *The Woman Warrior*. While Kingston's book can be read as articulating the impossibility of trying to "know" a culture, Sui Sin Far's stories are engaged in the more modest process of hinting about the problems with trying to "know"—problems that surface in her own guided Chinatown tours.

"The Wisdom of the New" is notable for engaging with a variety of issues, including silencing and female voicelessness (see Ammons 1991, 113–15), but here I want to address the potential subversiveness of its guided tours. Mrs. Dean, a white character, leads Adah Charlton through Chinatown: "Mrs. Dean, familiar with the Chinese people and the mazes of Chinatown, led her around fearlessly, pointing out this and that object of interest and explaining to her its meaning" (Sui Sin Far 1995, 54). They eventually run into a Chinese friend whom they ask to explain the religious chanting they hear; the Chinese man, the anonymous guide, explains that "it is a sort of apotheosis of the moon," and he goes on to provide a ludicrously overwrought translation, including lines such as "Thou art so sweet, so serious, so serene, that thou causest me to forget the stormy emotions which crash like jarring discords across the harmony of life" (55). The key moment, however, is when Adah asks the man, "Is that really Chinese?" He replies, "No doubt about it—in the main. Of course, I cannot swear to it word for word" (55–56). The man's reply begins with utter certainty ("No doubt about it"), which gets qualified ("in the main") and finally undercut by his inability to vouch for the precise meaning of the translation. What we read is less a guided tour through Chinatown, less a clear translation of culture, than an articulation of uncertainty, and, while the process of translation does not break down, its transparency is at least questioned. The certainty of being able to locate and explain "Chinese culture" is further eroded with the subsequent introduction of a character named Lee Tong Hay, a vaudeville performer who can "turn himself into a German, a Scotchman, an Irishman, or an American, with the greatest ease," and who is "as natural in each character as he is as a Chinaman" (56). Lee's cultural transitivity is never performed in the narrative, but it remains as a hint of the problems with trying to "fix" a culture in a "knowable" space.

A second story—"'Its Wavering Image'"—does not undercut the certainty of knowing but instead presents the brutal social consequences of putting a culture on display. The narrative involves Pan, a Eurasian girl living with her Chinese father in Chinatown, and Mark Carson, a ruthless white journalist who "would sell his soul for a story" (Sui Sin Far 1995, 62). Carson befriends Pan and receives the privilege of a guided Chinatown tour:

in full trust and confidence, she led him about Chinatown, initiating him into the simple mystery and history of many things for which she, being of her father's race, had a tender regard and pride. . . . The Water Lily Club opened its doors to him when she knocked, and the Sublimely Pure Brothers' organization admitted him as one of its honorary members, thereby enabling him not only to see but to take part in a ceremony in which no American had ever before participated. (62)

With knowledge he acquires from the tour, Carson publishes a "special-feature article" that scandalizes the Chinese community. Pan responds that she "would rather that her own naked body and soul had been exposed, than that things, sacred and secret to those who loved her, should be cruelly unveiled and ruthlessly spread before the ridiculing and uncomprehending foreigner" (64–65). Here, exposure of the Chinese community parallels exposure of a woman's body; race and gender intersect in the exploitive practices of the white male character, through which Sui Sin Far depicts the potentially devastating consequences of giving guided tours.[6]

After first seeing Pan, Carson asks his editor, "What was she? Chinese or white?" (Sui Sin Far 1995, 61); he feels an apparent need to locate her in one category or the other. He later forces the issue on Pan herself: "Pan, don't you see that you have got to decide what you will be—Chinese or white? You cannot be both" (63). And the final time the two characters meet, following the publication of Carson's "Chinatown" story, Pan has decided on her identity, but in a way that Carson did not anticipate:

> Mark Carson felt strangely chilled. Pan was not herself tonight. She did not even look herself. He had been accustomed to seeing her in American dress. Tonight she wore the Chinese costume. But for her clear-cut features she might have been a Chinese girl. He shivered.
> "Pan," he asked, "why do you wear that dress?"
> Within her sleeves Pan's small hands struggled together, but her face and voice were calm.
> "Because I am a Chinese woman," she answered. (66)

Pan's act of resistance—unequivocally identifying as "a Chinese woman"—marks an empowering shift in her identity from a "girl" to a "woman." Moreover, Pan subverts Carson's expectations by clearly articulating her cultural allegiances. The choice to identify as "a Chinese woman" is complex and multifaceted. Does it function as a temporary performance, an (unreliable) extension of the guided tour? Or does it announce a decision to assume a Chinese identity and thereby accept the binary "choices" laid out by Carson, and, by implication, by the dominant culture? In favor of decisive self-identification, does Pan abandon the possibility of a "Eurasian" identity or a deconstruction of the white/ Chinese binary? If so, does Sui Sin Far allow for any space outside the categories dictated by Carson? Can borders separating the putative "choices" be crossed?

Crossing Borders

Sui Sin Far's national locations—and those narrated thematically in her stories—function as important sites where borders are established, negotiated, and crossed. Early recuperative Sui Sin Far criticism tends to gloss over the potential significance of her multiple national locations—her birth in England, her brief time in New York, her adolescence and writing career in Montreal, her short stay in Jamaica, and her fifteen adult years in the United States. Ling, for instance, establishes Sui Sin Far's identity as a "Chinamerican" by syntactically discounting her other "homes": "Though Edith Eaton was born in England in 1867 [later established to be 1865 (Ling 1990, 183n1)] and died in Montreal Canada, on April 7, 1914, most of her adult life was spent in the United States in the mid-west and far west, some time in San Francisco and approximately ten years in Seattle" (1983, 287). Yin similarly finds it unproblematic to call Sui Sin Far "the first Chinese-American woman writer" (1991, 49) and to elide any mention of Sui Sin Far's experience elsewhere. James Doyle responds to Ling's and Yin's elisions by subtitling his 1994 article on Sui Sin Far and her sister Onoto Watanna "Two Early Chinese-Canadian Authors" (50). Doyle's intervention is motivated by the fact that "in most American studies of [Sui Sin Far's] life and work her Canadian background is glossed over in favour of emphasis on the sixteen years she spent in the United States, and on the relation of her work to U.S. writing" (50–51; White-Parks claims that Sui Sin Far spent fifteen, not sixteen, years in the United States [1995b, 9]). Reading Sui Sin Far as a Chinese *Canadian* writer is Doyle's attempt to "correct" a misemphasis; his move, however, risks repositioning her into a different yet once again putatively stable national category. Of all the critics working on Sui Sin Far, White-Parks has gone the furthest in engaging with the complex imbrications of her national locations. White-Parks's research on Sui Sin Far's life emphasizes the need to read her stories and their thematic concern with borders in light of the legal restrictions on Chinese immigration to and movement within North America at the turn of the century. Head taxes in Canada and legal exclusion in the United States made turn-of-the-century border crossings perilous for those racialized as "Chinese" (White-Parks 1995b, 4) and likely forced Sui Sin Far to disavow her "invisible Chinese status . . . whenever she crossed national borders" (101).

With these legal restrictions and imperatives in place, Sui Sin Far's thematic concern with the perils of border crossing acquires tremendous urgency. "The Smuggling of Tie Co" and "Tian Shan's Kindred Spirit" are two very short stories that narrate the difficulties of crossing national and gendered borders. The first story presents a relationship between Tie Co and Jack Fabian, a macho white man whom the narrator introduces as the boldest of "the daring men who engage in contrabanding Chinese from Canada into the United States" (Sui Sin Far 1995, 104). Tie Co convinces Fabian to take him across the border, where they have the following conversation:

> "Why, Tie Co, think how nice it would be to have a little woman cook your rice and to love you."
> "I not have wife," repeated Tie Co seriously. "I not like woman, I like man."
> "You confirmed old bachelor!" ejaculated Fabian.
> "I like you," said Tie Co, his boyish voice sounding clear and sweet in the wet woods.
> (107)

The queer possibilities of the story—Fabian's "ejaculation," Tie Co's expressed desire for men in general and Fabian in particular—occur while the characters are illegally crossing the border that separates Canada and the United States. The multiple transgressions are nevertheless quickly contained: When faced with the prospect of being arrested by U.S. government officials, Tie Co jumps into a river and drowns; and when Tie Co's body is recovered, we discover that he was "really" a woman. National border crossings are prevented and queer transgressions are normalized into socially acceptable heterosexual desire. Sui Sin Far's narrative, however, refuses to shy away from representing the deadly consequences of a legal system in which those gendered and racialized as white males are self-sufficient border crossers, and those gendered and racialized as Chinese females need white male guides to "cross"—and risk their lives doing so.[7]

In "Tian Shan's Kindred Spirit," border crossing again involves cross-dressing and the reassertion of a heteronormative relationship between a male character, Tian Shan, and a female one, Fin Fan. And again, the male character actively crosses national borders and returns home to tell stories to the female character: "Every time he crossed the border, he was obliged to devise some new scheme by which to accomplish his object, and as he usually succeeded, there was always a new story to tell whenever he returned to Canada" (Sui Sin Far 1995, 120–21). But although border crossing becomes a source of storytelling and pleasure, Fin Fan tells Tian Shan that "it is very foolish of you to keep running backwards and forwards from one country to another, wasting your time and accomplishing nothing" (121). The narrator notes that "as she thought it was foolish, he was going to relinquish the pleasure of running backwards and forwards across the border, for some time at least" (122). The pleasures of border crossing, however, are too great to resist, and, after twelve months of earning money in the United States, Tian Shan returns to Canada to see Fin Fan. Tian Shan has a violent altercation with a potential suitor of Fin Fan's, flees back to the United States, and is captured while trying to cross the border. Fin Fan learns about her lover's fate—he is imprisoned and will soon be deported back to China—and devises a plan: She cross-dresses and purposefully allows herself to be arrested at the border in order to be detained and deported with Tian Shan. Thus, as in "The Smuggling of Tie Co," desire is heteronormalized; the potential gender-bending effects of cross-dressing are contained in resolutions that emphasize the "real" gender behind the disguises; and women are unable to cross national borders—they either drown in order to save the man from being implicated in illegal activity ("The Smuggling of Tie Co") or (however purposefully) get arrested to be reunited with the man ("Tian Shan's Kindred Spirit").

Reclaiming Sui Sin Far

The striking contrast between Sui Sin Far's personal ability to "pass" and cross national borders, and her female characters' consistent inability to cross, suggests that Sui Sin Far was acutely aware of the legal restrictions on the mobility of those racialized as "Chinese" and gendered as "female." In Sui Sin Far's writing, borders profoundly affect the bodies of the characters within them. It is in recognition of the effects of such borders on those racialized as "Asian" that Lisa Lowe develops what she calls a "materialist concept of hybridity":

> Hybridization is not the "free" oscillation between or among chosen identities. It is the uneven process through which immigrant communities encounter the violences of the U.S. state, and the capital imperatives served by the United States and by the Asian states from which they come, and the process through which they survive those violences by living, inventing, and reproducing different cultural alternatives. (1996, 82)

Lowe's discussion of hybridity in particular, and Asian American cultural politics in general, serves as a crucial model for combining historical specificity with political engagement. Lowe reminds us that we must continue to search for a form of historical agency that neither discounts violent forms of oppression nor resorts to "chosen identities" as an assumed basis for social change. As such, her work provides a way to discuss resistance in relation to the various forms of racialization that structure modern subjectivities. Sui Sin Far's writings are significant for the multiple ways they produce the "different cultural alternatives" so evocatively theorized by Lowe: Her guided Chinatown tours challenge hegemonic attempts to "know" the other, and her border-crossing stories narrate the often violent containment of difference in sexual, gendered, and racialized contexts. At their best, Sui Sin Far's writings engage with categories and the borders between them.

Yet, the greatest contemporary significance of Sui Sin Far's work may reside in the ongoing process of reclaiming it. The unevenness of the critical record surrounding her work is emblematic of the contradictory imperatives of contemporary multicultural criticism, which, as Palumbo-Liu suggests, is characteristically implicated in hegemonic conceptions of culture and identity *and* attentive to points of opposition and resistance (1995, 15). In the case of Sui Sin Far criticism, hegemonic conceptions of culture and identity have taken the form of liberal nonracialism, while critical positions attentive to questions of opposition have focused on the historical constitution of "race" and its effects on bodies racialized as "Asian." The issue here, however, is not merely a matter of replacing "inaccurate" older readings with more "accurate" contemporary ones. It is instead an invitation to rethink the place of Sui Sin Far in "the past" of Asian American culture. In doing so, literary and cultural critics can do more than assert a "beginning" to Asian American literary history; they can also rethink and reformulate the theoretical commitments of the present moment's recuperative urges.

Notes

Acknowledgments: Russ Chace, Mary Chapman, Ruth Dyck Fehderau, and Heather Smyth provided specific and generous responses to earlier drafts of this essay. I would also like to thank the editors and the anonymous reader of my essay for their enabling comments—and Jodi Kim for the comments in the hall. The Social Sciences and Humanities Research Council of Canada provided funding during the time in which this essay was revised and is gratefully acknowledged.

1. See *Mrs. Spring Fragrance*, ed. E. Catherine Falvey, published by NCUP (formerly New College and University Press) in 1994, and Sui Sin Far 1995. The original *Mrs. Spring Fragrance* was published by A. C. McClurg in 1912. The literary biography is White-Park 1995b.

2. One example is Ling's reference to "the painful experience of growing up Eurasian in prejudiced nineteenth-century England and America" (1983, 288). But David Theo Goldberg has pointed out that to focus on "prejudice" is to commit oneself to a focus on individual expressions that are often considered irrational aberrations (1993, 7).

3. On the Anglo-American literary context in which Sui Sin Far wrote, see especially Wu 1982; Kim 1982 (3–22); White-Parks 1995a (20–22); and White-Parks 1995b (112–15).

4. On the complex subject of Sui Sin Far's readership, see Ferens 1999.

5. Elizabeth Ammons, however, argues that "although well disguised, the beginning of *Mrs. Spring Fragrance* is autobiographical" in the sense that it offers "a collection of lives, not an intensive anatomy of one life" (1991, 110, 116).

6. The "tour," of course, is not limited to the action in the narrative; it also occurs in the publishing, distribution, reading, teaching, and discussion of Sui Sin Far's work. "'Its Wavering Image'" asks readers to examine their potential complicity in the process of "seeing" a culture in order to avoid replicating the debilitating terms set out by the character Mark Carson.

7. On the queer implications of "The Smuggling of Tie Co," see Min Song, who argues that the story "literally and figuratively explores the borders that make an identity culturally legible" (1998, 304). Of particular importance here is Song's focus on class and sexuality in a border-crossing narrative. Wong and Santa Ana suggest that "the motif of cross-dressing in a cross-cultural setting . . . provides an especially effective device for expressing [Sui Sin Far's] understanding of race and gender as inextricably linked" (1999, 186).

Works Cited

Ammons, Elizabeth. 1991. "Audacious Words: Sui Sin Far's *Mrs. Spring Fragrance*." In *Conflicting Stories: American Women Writers at the Turn of the Twentieth Century*, 105–20. New York: Oxford University Press.

Cheung, King-Kok. 1993. *Articulate Silences: Hisaye Yamamoto, Maxine Hong Kingston, Joy Kogawa*. Reading Women Writing. Ithaca, N.Y.: Cornell University Press.

Chin, Frank, Jeffery Chan, Lawson Inada, and Shawn Wong. 1974. "An Introduction to Chinese- and Japanese-American Literature." In *Aiiieeeee! An Anthology of Asian-American Writers*, ed. Frank Chin, Jeffery Chan, Lawson Inada, and Shawn Wong, xxi–xlviii. Washington, D.C.: Howard University Press.

Doyle, James. 1994. "Sui Sin Far and Onoto Watanna: Two Early Chinese-Canadian Authors." *Canadian Literature* 140: 50–58.

Ferens, Dominika. 1999. "Tangled Kites: Sui Sin Far's Negotiations with Race and Readership." *Amerasia Journal* 25, 2: 116–44.

Frankenberg, Ruth. 1993. *White Women, Race Matters: The Social Construction of Whiteness*. Minneapolis: University of Minnesota Press.

Goldberg, David Theo. 1993. *Racist Culture: Philosophy and the Politics of Meaning*. Oxford: Blackwell.

He, Shan. 1995. "Between Ethnicity and High Theory." Review of *Reading Asian American Literature: From Necessity to Extravagance*, by Sau-ling Cynthia Wong, and *Articulate Silences:*

Hisaye Yamamoto, Maxine Hong Kingston, Joy Kogawa, by King-Kok Cheung. *West Coast Line* 29, 2: 165–69.

Kim, Elaine H. 1982. *Asian American Literature: An Introduction to the Writings and Their Social Context.* Philadelphia: Temple University Press.

Lim, Shirley Geok-lin. 1996. Review of *Sui Sin Far/Edith Maude Eaton: A Literary Biography,* by Annette White-Parks, and *Mrs. Spring Fragrance and Other Writings,* by Sui Sin Far. *Amerasia Journal* 22, 3: 149–55.

Ling, Amy. 1983. "Edith Eaton: Pioneer Chinamerican Writer and Feminist." *American Literary Realism* 16, 2: 287–98.

———. 1990. "Pioneers and Paradigms: The Eaton Sisters." In *Between Worlds: Women Writers of Chinese Ancestry,* 21–55. New York: Pergamon.

———. 1992. "Creating One's Self: The Eaton Sisters." In *Reading the Literatures of Asian America,* ed. Shirley Geok-lin Lim and Amy Ling, 305–18. Asian American History and Culture. Philadelphia: Temple University Press.

Ling, Amy, and Annette White-Parks. 1995. Introduction to *Mrs. Spring Fragrance and Other Writings,* by Sui Sin Far, 1–8. The Asian American Experience. Urbana: University of Illinois Press.

Lowe, Lisa. 1996. *Immigrant Acts: On Asian American Cultural Politics.* Durham, N.C.: Duke University Press.

Maclear, Kyo. 1995. "Race to the Page: Positioning as a Writer of 'Mixed Race.'" *Resources for Feminist Research* 24, 1–2: 14–22.

Palumbo-Liu, David. 1995. Introduction to *The Ethnic Canon: Histories, Institutions, and Interventions,* ed. Palumbo-Liu, 1–27. Minneapolis: University of Minnesota Press.

Roh-Spaulding, Carol. 1997. "'Wavering' Images: Mixed-Race Identity in the Stories of Edith Eaton/Sui Sin Far." In *Ethnicity and the American Short Story,* ed. Julie Brown, 155–76. Wellesley Studies in Critical Theory, Literary History, and Culture. New York: Garland.

Shinagawa, Larry Hajime, and Gin Yong Pang. 1996. "Asian American Panethnicity and Intermarriage." *Amerasia Journal* 22, 2: 127–52.

Solberg, S. E. 1981. "Sui Sin Far/Edith Eaton: First Chinese-American Fictionist." *MELUS* 8, 1: 27–39.

Song, Min. 1998. "The Unknowable and Sui Sin Far: The Epistemological Limits of 'Oriental' Sexuality." In *Q & A: Queer in Asian America,* ed. David L. Eng and Alice Y. Hom, 304–32. Asian American History and Culture. Philadelphia: Temple University Press.

Sui Sin Far. 1995. *Mrs. Spring Fragrance and Other Writings.* Edited by Amy Ling and Annette White-Parks. The Asian American Experience. Urbana: University of Illinois Press.

White-Parks, Annette. 1994. "'We Wear the Mask': Sui Sin Far As One Example of Trickster Authorship." In *Tricksterism in Turn-of-the-Century American Literature: A Multicultural Perspective,* ed. Elizabeth Ammons and White-Parks, 1–20. Hanover, N.H.: University Press of New England.

———. 1995a. "A Reversal of American Concepts of 'Other-ness' in the Fiction of Sui Sin Far." *MELUS* 20, 1: 17–34.

———. 1995b. *Sui Sin Far/Edith Maude Eaton: A Literary Biography.* The Asian American Experience. Urbana: University of Illinois Press.

Wong, Sau-ling Cynthia. 1992. "Autobiography as Guided Chinatown Tour? Maxine Hong Kingston's *The Woman Warrior* and the Chinese-American Autobiographical Controversy." In *Multicultural Autobiography: American Lives,* ed. James Payne, 248–75. Knoxville: University of Tennessee Press.

Wong, Sau-ling Cynthia, and Jeffrey J. Santa Ana. 1999. "Gender and Sexuality in Asian American Literature." *Signs* 25, 1: 171–226.

Wu, William F. 1982. *The Yellow Peril: Chinese Americans in American Fiction, 1850–1940.* Hamden, Conn.: Archon.

Yin, Xiao-Huang. 1991. "Between the East and West: Sui Sin Far—the First Chinese-American Woman Writer." *Arizona Quarterly* 47, 4: 49–84.

About the Contributors

GUY BEAUREGARD is a postdoctoral fellow in the Department of English at the University of British Columbia, where he teaches and conducts research in Asian Canadian studies and Canadian literary studies.

TINA CHEN is assistant professor of English at Vanderbilt University. Her current book project examines acts of impersonation in contemporary Asian American literature.

FABIANA CHIU-RINALDI is a program officer at the New York State Council on the Arts Museum Program and the former deputy director of the Museum of Chinese in the Americas in New York City.

CATHERINE CENIZA CHOY is assistant professor of American Studies at the University of Minnesota. Her book on nursing and immigration in Filipino American history is forthcoming.

ROBERT COOPERMAN received his Ph.D. in 1996 from the Ohio State University, where he was a modern drama specialist.

HELENA GRICE is Lecturer in American Studies at the University of Wales–Aberystwyth. She is coauthor of *Beginning Ethnic American Literatures* and author of *Negotiating Identities: An Introduction to Asian American Women's Writing.*

LANE RYO HIRABAYASHI is a professor in the Department of Ethnic Studies at the University of Colorado–Boulder and the lead editor for *New Worlds/New Lives: People of Japanese Descent in the America and From Latin America in Japan.*

JOSEPHINE LEE is associate professor of English at the University of Minnesota and the author of *Performing Asian America: Race and Ethnicity on the Contemporary Stage* (Temple University Press). She is currently completing a book on racial politics and contemporary American theater.

IMOGENE L. LIM teaches anthropology at Malaspina University–College (Nanaimo, British Columbia). Most recently, she coordinated a celebration of Chinese Canadian history in Nanaimo, which launched the city's Chinatowns Project website.

AMY LING was professor of English and director of the Asian American Studies Program at the University of Wisconsin–Madison until her death in 1999. Her publications include *Between Worlds: Women of Chinese Ancestry, Reading the Literatures of Asian America* (coedited with Shirley Geok-lin Lim, Temple University Press), and *Yellow Light: The Flowering of Asian American Art* (Temple University Press).

EDWARD MARX has taught at the City College of New York, the University of Minnesota, and Kyoto University. He is at work on a biography of Yone Noguchi.

YUKO MATSUKAWA has taught at Brown University, Rhode Island College, Tufts University, and the State University of New York College at Brockport. She currently lives in Tokyo, where she is working on a book project that examines late-nineteenth-century American culture and the gendered production of orientalism.

ADAM MCKEOWN is assistant professor of history at Columbia University and author of *Chinese Migrant Networks and Cultural Change: Peru, Chicago, Hawaii, 1900–1936.* He is currently working on a comparative global study of Chinese migration since 1840, and on a manuscript about the enforcement of Chinese exclusion laws in the American empire.

MAE M. NGAI is assistant professor of history at the University of Chicago. Her book *Illegal Aliens and Alien Citizens: Immigration Restriction, Race, and Nation, 1924–1965* is forthcoming.

JEANETTE ROAN is currently assistant professor of English and of film and media studies at George Mason University.

RANDALL ROHE is professor of geography at the University of Wisconsin–Wakesha. He has written more than twenty publications on mining in the American West and is currently working on a book-length study of the Chinese in the mining West.

RAJINI SRIKANTH is assistant professor of English at the University of Massachusetts–Boston. She is coeditor of *Contours of the Heart: South Asians Map North America;* of the multidisciplinary collection *A Part, Yet Apart: South Asians in Asian America* (Temple University Press); and of *Bold Words: A Century of Asian American Writing.*

EMMA J. TENG is assistant professor of Chinese studies at MIT. Her publications include articles in *Signs; The International History Review; Race, Gender and Class;* and the *Asian Pacific American Journal.*

GUANHUA WANG is associate professor of history at the University of Connecticut and the author of *In Search of Justice: The 1905–1906 Chinese Anti-American Boycott.*

MEREDITH WOOD is currently a development officer at the International Gay and Lesbian Human Rights Commission. Her book on politics and sexuality in lesbian detective novels is under contract with Temple University Press.

Index

Italic page numbers indicate figures.